SAGE has been part of the global academic community since 1965, supporting high quality research and learning that transforms society and our understanding of individuals, groups, and cultures. SAGE is the independent, innovative, natural home for authors, editors and societies who share our commitment and passion for the social sciences.

Find out more at: **www.sagepublications.com**

THE CULTURE OF DESIGN
GUY JULIER
3RD EDITION

Los Angeles | London | New Delhi
Singapore | Washington DC

Los Angeles | London | New Delhi
Singapore | Washington DC

SAGE Publications Ltd
1 Oliver's Yard
55 City Road
London EC1Y 1SP

SAGE Publications Inc.
2455 Teller Road
Thousand Oaks, California 91320

SAGE Publications India Pvt Ltd
B 1/I 1 Mohan Cooperative Industrial Area
Mathura Road
New Delhi 110 044

SAGE Publications Asia-Pacific Pte Ltd
3 Church Street
#10-04 Samsung Hub
Singapore 049483

Editor: Mila Steele
Editorial assistant: James Piper
Production editor: Imogen Roome
Copyeditor: Solveig Gardner Servian
Proofreader: Audrey Scriven
Marketing manager: Michael Ainsley
Cover design: Jen Crisp
Typeset by: C&M Digitals (P) Ltd, Chennai, India
Printed and bound in Great Britain by Ashford
Colour Press Ltd

Library of Congress Control Number: 2013940299

British Library Cataloguing in Publication data

A catalogue record for this book is available from the British Library

MIX
Paper from
responsible sources
FSC® C011748

ISBN 978-1-4462-7358-6
ISBN 978-1-4462-7359-3 (pbk)

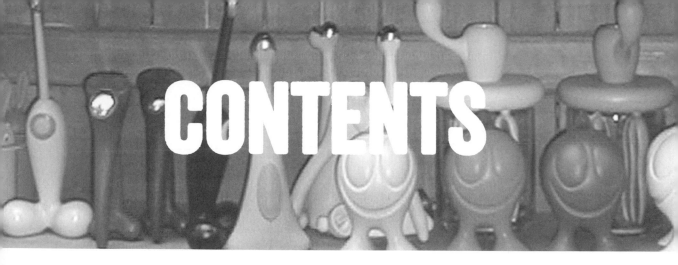

CONTENTS

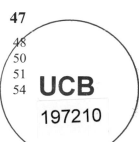

LIST OF FIGURES AND TABLES

FIGURES

TABLES

LIST OF ILLUSTRATIONS

INTRODUCTION

In developing the first edition of this book, I was excited by the links to be made between the astonishing ascendancy of design to current developments in Cultural Studies, Sociology, Political Economy and Geography. These disciplines seemed to be providing interesting perspectives on the deep shifts in cultural production and consumption taking place in this era of 'disorganized capitalism'. But the patina, nuances and detail of the artefacts that made up that cultural part needed filling in. Something had to be done.

Design history has always concerned itself, as one would expect, with the object and its relationship to processes of change. So it should also take a design historian to undertake this task with respect to the contemporary world. But the discipline seemed to have reached two methodological predicaments.

What I would call 'popular design history', the kind that fills the pages of more colourful and probably more sellable commodities of bookshops, continued to present design as the output of individuals, emphasizing design style over process or social impact. Having worked in this format myself, I was acutely aware of both the predictabilty and randomness by which particular designers, and their designs, would be foregrounded over others. This genre repetitiously favoured particular forms of design. New furniture design and highly authorial graphics that fitted with wider art and architectural historical patterns dominated, while the more ordinary, everyday stuff of design – leisure spaces, educational computer software or urban public spaces – went largely overlooked and underestimated. I knew that designers were partly reliant on this bias towards the spectacular if they wanted to be anything other than anonymous. Meanwhile, the question of why some designers may be included in this history over others is a vexing one. Clearly gender, age and socioeconomic background (often male, youngish and Western) narrowed its scope. Beyond this, inclusion would rest on such random features as the availability of photographic images, a journalist's chance meeting with a designer or the work of a designer's promotional agent.

By contrast, many academic design historians had aligned themselves with Material Culture studies during the 1990s to develop detailed and, often, charming accounts of the significance of objects in the everyday lives of people. In Material Culture studies, the work of designers or other cultural producers receives less attention in favour of researching how consumers read and understand products, through the analysis of their mediation in advertising and magazines or in their quotidian use. This is important in foregrounding this 'other side' of the life of objects. It proposes an approach that considers the adjustments that consumers make to design and the creative ways that they appropriate objects once they have left their point-of-sale. However, the focus of such studies has tended to fall mostly on private, domestic forms of design and consumption. The individuated consumer at home appears to have been privileged over other scenarios. The orchestration of leisure centres, specific urban agglomerations or online computer games, the configuration of corporate training programmes and networking events or the design of retail experiences represent significant sectors of design production and take up equally significant portions of the world of consumption. They often remain strangely absent from the scope of Material Culture studies, however.

Nonetheless, *The Culture of Design* owes a considerable debt to these strands of design history. From the 'popular' end of the discipline, the notion that design inculcates various degrees of value into objects – aesthetic, exchange, symbolic or otherwise – is significant. This resonates with Judy Attfield's idea of design as being something beyond the ordinary to being 'things with attitude' (Attfield 2000). From the 'Material Culture studies' approach to design history, the influence was perhaps more attitudinal – keeping the approach grounded in the realities of the ordinary and in viewing design promotional hyperbole for what it is. *The Culture of Design* then became a project in tracing the interactions and tensions between these two worlds. How do design objects, their producers and designers, conspire to script experience? What tensions and discontinuities exist between this aspiration and how these 'experiences' are actually encountered? How do cultural producers develop and use an understanding of consumer behaviour as data for further action? And if we are to talk about design in its fullest sense, beyond domestic objects, what analytical tools might we use in order to interrogate such relationships?

These questions strike at the heart of what is termed 'design culture'. A concept of design culture embraces the networks and interactions that configure the production and consumption of the artificial world, both material and immaterial. It lies at the interface between object and individual user, but also extends into more complex systems of exchange. It describes the normative actions, values, resources and languages available to designers, design managers and policymakers as well as the wider publics that engage with design.

Similar sensibilities to this concept of design culture have emerged *implicitly* in some important publications since the first edition of *The Culture of Design* came out. It is discernible in Scott Lash's study *Critique of Information* (2002) through his 'architectonic' conception of information. Celia Lury's *Brands: The Logos of the Global Economy* (2004) considers that the objectivity of brands emerges from the relations of its parts. Harvey Molotch, in *Where Stuff Comes From* (2003), traces the networks of producers, intermediaries and users that exist around objects or, more interestingly, the social, cultural and economic projects that they engage. Lash and Lury came together in *Global Culture Industry* (2007), a text that exemplifies a prose that, in its occasional poetic intensity, opens the imagination to the dynamics and textures that the movement of cultural goods takes along with it.

This notion of a 'culture of design' has also been used explicitly. For example, in developing an analysis of design-led urban regeneration, Bell and Jayne (2003) refer to a 'culture of design', suggesting that a nurtured, dense coexistence of producers, consumers and designers in a coherent circuit of culture can in turn generate economic, social and cultural value for a location. Chatterton and Holland

(2003) make use of the idea in the context of night-time leisure practices of city-centre bars and clubs, where a pervasive designer ambience courses through these environments. In more promotional settings, it has been increasingly common for curators and journalists to talk of the design culture of a nation or city rather than its design. This, at least, recognizes that it is perhaps more enriching to think about the way design is done, discussed, created, circulated, seen, used and thought about than in terms of the deadhand of describing the mere appearance of its objects.

The first edition of *The Culture of Design* was written in the late 1990s, and the earlier chapters of this version perhaps betrayed a somewhat giddy adherence to championing the rise of British design within a discourse of the creative industries. This was, after all, the early years of the New Labour government in the UK where policymakers were busy carving out a righteous space for creative and cultural industries, both as a way of re-branding Britain and in order to herald certain priorities of a knowledge economy. Academia followed in the early 2000s as texts, stemming mostly from business studies and the social sciences, such as Caves's *Creative Industries: Contracts between Art and Commerce* (2000) and Hesmondalgh's *The Cultural Industries* (2002) began to appear. These have proven useful in beginning to understand the broader structures and motivations of creative work.

Nonetheless, the idea of creative industries has often been a rather blunt instrument; it is a wide concept that can lack empirical specificity and focus. Even the design sector, as this book argues, shows enormous variation in its practices, business arrangements and locations to make it inadvisable to make overarching observations of it. Indeed, one of the few such views I take is that design is consistent in its fragmentation and deliberate differentiation amongst its actors. Another difficulty in many of the broader texts that analyse creative industries is the absence of the actual objects of its production. Much is often made of the clustering of creative workers and the benefits that they derive from close, flexible collaborations between them. Little is said of their focus on cultural goods. Of course creative practitioners work together; but they their work is looped through objects that appear in various forms – drawings, models, digital prototypes – and through the material culture of their workplace. This book doesn't centre itself exclusively on the design process and business environment (but see Julier and Moor 2009). Nevertheless, my interest is in bringing more precision to the discussion of design as a creative industry and also placing a bigger role for materiality therein.

In developing this third edition, it rapidly became apparent that while the basic categories and approach that I had outlined for the study of design culture were still viable, a number of fundamental developments had taken place in the 21st century. The first of these has been in the straightforward growth of design industries throughout much of the world. While design remains a potent creative industry sector in the UK where it continues to innovate approaches, its global importance to economies has risen exponentially. What's more, design has become embedded into governmental policies and regarded for its symbolic and its instrumental characteristics with mounting enthusiasm. It would be over-ambitious to attempt a worldwide, comparative survey of design cultures in this text. It has been incumbent on me in this edition to provide a more international set of examples and statistical data that demonstrate this, particularly in Chapter 2.

If the culture of design has become increasingly more widespread, then it has also continued to seep at its edges in terms of its professional reach. Hence, in Chapter 3, I give a new account of the way that design has moved beyond the brand ethos into the perhaps more structured approaches to be found in service design. Equally, in the same chapter, I demonstrate how the rise of so-called 'design thinking' demonstrates a sharper attention being paid to the material components of product and service strategy. The process of iteratively prototyping and testing of solutions, itself derived from design practice itself, finds its way into broader approaches to management. In Chapter 5 on high design, I extend the argument beyond mass-production arte-facts that, nonetheless, engage a certain connoisseurship to design that pushes commentary and critique back onto consumer culture in my discussion of 'critical design'. I continue this into a consideration of 'design art'. In both these cases, the emphasis continues the idea of design's ability to destabilize categories.

Readers may be surprised, even aghast, to see that I have kept Chapter 9, which focuses on 'on-screen interactivity', largely as intact as in earlier editions of this book. My description of a 1998 CD-ROM product may seem outdated or quaint, even. However, looking at my desktop today and the screen-grabs I made over ten years ago suggests that at least on the glowing screen of my personal computer, the fundamentals haven't changed. While download speeds have mul-tiplied and the content available has expanded enormously, the basic issues of multi-level reader-ship, cybernetic loss, the continual hyperbole and uptalking that exists amongst its mediators, the weaving of cultural products in and out of digital space and many others, remain.

Revisions for the second edition of this book were made in 2007, a year before the US and European debt crisis sent much of the global economy into a downward spiral. Even then the grey clouds of recession were visible on the horizon and this made the case for models of design prac-tice that were not dominated by an economic growth model more pressing. The case for a more equitable economic order, greater social inclusion in processes of change and, not least, a sharper response to possible environmental catastrophe has gathered even more momentum. Out of this 'design activism' has emerged more coherently (Fuad-Luke 2009; DiSalvo 2012; Thorpe 2012) as a practice and field of enquiry. The final section of Chapter 10 is therefore revised to place the issues of participation in design more firmly against discussions of design activism.

Broadband, wi-fi and smartphones were unavailable in 1998 when I began the first edition of this book. When revising it for the second edition, iPhones were only available in the USA. Mobile or distributed computing existed but was unresolved in terms of where it would find com-monplace usage. Smartphones and tablets are now the standard accompaniment of the railway commuter. A new Chapter 11, entitled 'Networks and Mobile Technologies', provides a discus-sion of the networks that make up the corporate control of their content design as well as the implications of mobile technologies on everyday life. Here I take the opportunity to develop on actor-network theory (ANT). The work of Latour (1987, 2005) and colleagues has been lurking in the background of this book since its instigation. After all, the idea of design cul-ture that comes into being through the mutually interdependent action of people and things appears in ANT thinking, albeit often with a different focus of qualities. The jargon and detail of ANT are challenging and I have taken the course of introducing these backwards – lightly reversing in, if you will, through a discussion of key terms of *agencement*, assemblage and articulation, rather than by starting with a full-blown exposition of ANT. This is done in relation to design very satisfactorily by Fallan (2010), in any case.

The primary aim of giving a critical and theorized discussion of contemporary design in soci-ety still dominates this third edition. In the second edition, I opened up a new aim which was to explore in more detail what this design culture concept meant and implied, both in its general usage and more specifically as a field of study. In so doing, my intention was to give a more reflexive account that positioned Design Culture as academic enquiry distinct from Material Culture, Visual Culture and Design History. While that initial salvo still stands, in this third edition I have developed a recapitulating final Chapter 12 that is entitled 'Studying Design Culture'. This is not presented as a route-map to 'how to do' design culture. As I had already intimated in Chapter 1, I fear methodological orthodoxy not least because the variations by which design cultures are constituted and performed demand flexibility and inventiveness in their study. Instead, I present in this chapter a series of notes that expand on 'things to look out for'.

The gestation of *The Culture of Design*, and its reincarnation in the second and third revised editions, have involved the pre-exposure of some of its parts in the form of conference papers, articles and essays, too numerous to list here. These have provided useful grounds for testing material out. The initial publication of this book led to further contact with numerous academics who are listed in the foreword to the second edition. Since then, I have had the instructive pleasure of working and interchanging thoughts with colleagues at the University of Brighton, the Victoria & Albert Museum and the University of Southern Denmark. Individual scholars such as Hilde Bouchez, Lucy Kimbell, Liz Moor and Cameron Tonkinwise have provided further inspiration. Staff and students on visiting forays to the University of Otago in New Zealand, the Vrije Universiteit Amsterdam, the Universidad de Caldas in Colombia, the Universidad de Buenos Aires and the Universidad Nacional Autónoma de México have helped me understand a little bit better the globalizing challenges and questions of design culture.

My children, Joe Julier and Becca Julier, have both grown up alongside this book and its iterations. They have figured in early 'design encounter' expeditions or in late-night discussions about what it all means and a lot more besides. For her wonderful support at all levels, ultra-girlfriend and fellow wordsmith Diane Setterfield merits special mention and heartfelt thanks.

Consonant with the notion that the objects of design culture these days are played through various media and platforms, I have authored a support website for this book where further teaching material, spin-off blogs, bibliographies and related writings can be accessed. The web address is: www.designculture.info.

CHAPTER 1
DESIGN CULTURE

What is 'design culture'? How might an academic approach to design culture be undertaken? How might this differ from other, related disciplines such as Visual Culture? Does the study of design culture require a particular scholarly sensibility? Chapter 1 provides an introduction to thinking about Design Culture as an academic field of enquiry and also the notion of design culture as a phenomenon. It reviews different usages of the term 'design culture'. It then goes on to identify design culture as involving networks of interaction between design, production and consumption and beyond this, the relationships of value, circulation and creation and practice. There follows an explanation of the structure of this book

Design is a highly entrepreneurial profession. It is also a maturing academic discipline. As a focus of leisure and consumption, it has become a source of public entertainment. It is and has been a vehicle of political coercion and symbolism, appropriated and employed by the darkest or most benign of power structures. It serves as an informal indicator of economic performance, cultural regeneration and social well-being. Spectacular displays of youth subcultures, the accumulation of wealth, mid-life crises and retirement plans all produce design. Few practices of intellectual and commercial human activity reach into so many areas of everyday private and public life. Few professions in the industrialized world have grown in terms of economic presence and cultural import as much as design has in the past three decades.

Design has become a global phenomenon. Thus to take Central and Eastern Europe alone, following the collapse of their state socialist systems in the late 1980s and early 1990s, some 350 million citizens have been drawn into liberal democracy and market capitalism. The economic rise of the BRIC countries (Brazil, Russia, India and China) in the 21st century has added exponential impetus to this turn. A new global generation of consumers of design within a capitalistic context has emerged. The remit of design practice itself has extended during the same period. It is no longer a 'value-added' extra applied to a restricted range of domestic objects; rather it extends, for example, to the planning and shaping of digital interfaces in computer games and websites, to large-scale leisure and retail spaces and even to the creation of a country's public image.

Design is represented and talked about at a range of levels. A more conservative notion of it as a commodity that signifies modernity and desirability resides in the pages of lifestyle magazines. On the television, the plethora of home-improvement shows which emerged in the late 1990s, while drawing something from this notion, also began to represent design as a process of expert decision-making and implementation. Since the early 1980s a range of professional journals has become firmly established with the growth of the industry. They have presented design variously as business news (e.g. *Design Week*) or an avant-garde cultural activity (e.g. *Blueprint*) and all points between. Design history and design studies have taken their place as discrete academic disciplines in universities with their own scholastic journals, conference circuits and key figures.

At the same time, academics from other disciplines in the humanities and social sciences have, though often tentatively, stepped into design territory. The emergence of 'science and technology studies' that investigates the interrelationships of society, culture, politics and technological innovation similarly has incorporated design into its accounts (e.g. Latour 1987; Shove et al. 2012; Marres 2012). This has also stemmed from discussions of consumption in Cultural Studies, Anthropology and Geography (e.g. Miller 1987; Jackson and Thrift 1995; du Gay et al. 2013). Some sociologists and economists have recognized the importance of design in a wider global economic growth in the first world of 'cultural goods' and creative industries within this (e.g. Lash and Urry 1994; Molotch 1996; Lash and Lury 2007). In either case, they have provided a wealth of theoretical frameworks for the investigation of design. Generally speaking, however, many of them do not approach specific design examples against which these formal perspectives may be contextualized and deconstructed.

It is hoped, then, that an academic focus on design culture will have a two-way use. For those with a specialist knowledge of design it should broaden the field of their enquiry by relating it to a wide set of theoretical discourses. For those with an interest in Cultural Studies, Sociology,

Anthropology, Ethnography and Geography, it should introduce them to the more focused activities and issues of design and the way that it brokers the material and visual relationships of production and consumption.

The interdisciplinarity of this project is in parallel with a similar trend in design practice itself. This precarious, creative activity has in recent years undergone perhaps its most fundamental revolution yet. It has shifted from being a problem-solving activity to a problem-processing one, and thus from a multidisciplinary to an interdisciplinary activity. A typical larger design consultancy may bring 'together materials, manufacturing, software and "futures" specialists, with the big ideas flowing from that chemistry' (Hollington 1998: 63). Designers also work closely with product managers and researchers, marketing specialists, advertising agents, public relations consultants and many others involved in the generation, mediation and control of the flows of images, objects and information around a product or service. Technological change, the globalization of economies and the growth of the importance of the brand (all three of which are in themselves related) have played vital roles in this process. Many design consultancies have also moved from the consideration of objects, images and spaces to the investigation and provision of relationships and structures. The traditional demarcations between disciplines such as graphic, product and interior design have receded. Designers increasingly market themselves not by the visual style they create, but by their business approach or, more loosely speaking, by the way they structure and manage the design process. Meanwhile, studies in design history and criticism have struggled to keep up with these changes. The richness of contemporary design must be met in its discussion by a strident and robust spectrum of academic disciplines.

Much work in Media and Cultural Studies takes an overly reductionist approach to the discussion of the strategies of producing and selling things. Often the study is narrowed down to skilful, but limiting, image analysis. In particular, the dominance of advertising analysis, stemming from literary criticism, has served to divert attention from the fact that these days it only represents just one of many strategies employed by corporations and institutions to colonize the consumer's world. So, for example, despite their insightful and worthy exploration of the production and meanings of Nike's advertising campaigns, Goldman and Papson are forced to admit that this approach 'nonetheless risks leaving other aspects of the story in the background. Matters central to the operation of Nike, such as sports marketing and shoe design [both of which are highly interrelated], remain out of sight' (1998: v). As I argue in the final chapter of this book, the centring of production, the designer's labour and, indeed, consumption around brand values in the 1990s drastically reconfigure the role and status of advertising.

In view of these shortfalls, my interest in writing this book is in the instigation of a concept of design culture – both as an object of study and as an academic discipline. In the first instance this is animated by the ever more pervasive role of design in contemporary society. It takes design as a culturally specific practice which is driven almost entirely by strategies of differentiation. This process appropriates and employs a wide range of discursive features: not just ones of modernity, but also risk, heritage, subculture, public space, consumer empowerment and many others. Design culture is not fixed, homogeneous or homogenizing; rather it embraces a complex matrix of human activities, perceptions and articulations. Careful analysis of its visual, material, spatial and textual manifestations provides routes into this complexity.

DESIGN CULTURE AS AN OBJECT OF STUDY

Daniel Koh is a Singapore-based art director. He maintains a personal website (www.amateurprovokateur.com) that profiles his own design work and that of others. He divides his own into two categories: 'commercial' and 'non-commercial' work. A page is devoted to what he calls 'design culture'. Here, Koh curated over 120 links to the work of designers to 'showcase their sensibilities … and to stimulate the creativity within the design community'. Profiles of practitioners in Caracas, Montreal, New York, London, Amsterdam, Rome, Krakow, Tokyo and Singapore are included in this gallery. I asked him what he meant by the words 'design culture'. He replied that it was 'a term I define as [the way] designers think and work through different mediums. Different thought processes/approach but one common objective: to communicate. Design is a way of life; it's all around us. We should all make things better' (Koh 2004).

Koh's brief exposition of 'design culture' provides a neat synthesis of many of the positions that have been taken up in relation to this term. According to Koh, design culture is located in communication. It is both something designers do but is also something that is 'all around'. Design culture, then, is part of the flows of global culture. It is located within network society and is also an instrument of it. It also expresses an attitude, a value and a desire to improve things.

The word 'design' denotes the activities of planning and devising as well as the outcome of these processes, such as a drawing, plan or manufactured object. It is both a verb and a noun. However, the term 'design culture' also gets close to being adjectival. It suggests the qualities by which design is practised – and I use the word 'practised' very deliberately to infer not only the ways that it is undertaken, but also the ways that it is lived, perceived, understood and enacted in everyday life. As such, design culture exists at a very local level. It may be embedded in the working systems, knowledges and relationships of designers or in the quotidian actions of design users. But it may also work more widely and publicly, fostered within discursive systems of power, economic structures and dynamics or social relations. A brief review of some of the ways by which the term 'design culture' has been treated may help to explain its multi-levelled existence and map out some of its qualities as an object of study. These are taken from the most particular to the more general contexts.

DESIGN CULTURE AS PROCESS

Design culture as a process is perhaps the most established usage and stems from architectural and design criticism. In particular, it describes the immediate contextual influences and contextually informed actions within the development of a design. A close term that throws light on this is the Italian usage of *la cultura di progetto* (in English, 'project culture'). The word *progetto* implies something broader than simply the form-giving within design, but extends to the totality of carrying out design: for example, from conceiving and negotiating artefacts with clients, to studio organization, to the output of the design and to its realization. Within all these there is an implied interest in the systems of negotiation – often verbal – that conspire to define and frame design artefacts. This understanding may be broadened by placing the idea of studio activity into a framework of immediate influences. Thus the project process is understood to be produced within and by a network of everyday knowledge and practices that surround the designer (Calvera 2000).

DESIGN CULTURE AS CONTEXT-INFORMED PRACTICE

The use of design culture as context-informed practice is concerned with a wider notion of 'design culture as process', to imply collectively held norms of practice shared within or across contexts. More specifically, this usually refers to the way that geographical context may influence the practice and results of design. This can fall in two ways. One is how the everyday specific features of a location – availability of materials and technologies, cultural factors that affect business activities, climate, local modes of exchange and so on – produce particularized actions. This might be contrasted with perceived globalized, dominant, mainstream forms of practice. The second may equally engage a consciousness of difference or peripherization but views design culture as a platform for communication. Design culture thus becomes a forum (often supported by the Web but also by other channels such as magazines and conferences) by which globally diasporic actors connect, communicate and legitimate their activities.

DESIGN CULTURE AS ORGANIZATIONAL OR ATTITUDINAL

When design culture is organizational or attitudinal the focus remains tightly within the scope of the producer-agents of design, though it is not exclusive to designers per se. It stems from management studies and sociological texts that have sought to analyse and provide models for human resources within innovative industries. Thus, flexible, horizontally networked, transaction-rich activities that, in particular, deal in symbolically charged products become dominant in this discourse. Within this, creative industries have begun to serve as paradigms for wider shifts in business organization, both internal and external. Team-working, creative empowerment and innovation become key words in this situation. Furthermore, in seeking coherence between the internal ethos of a company and its interactions with its public, the role of brand stewardship becomes increasingly important. Within this mode, then, the idea of a 'design culture' as an attitudinal and organizational spine within a company that concerns itself with both innovation and formal coherence has been used (Cawood 1997). Leading on from this, it may also be used to signify the 'cultural capital' of a company – its facility to qualify, critique and thus deliver distinction and differentiation.

DESIGN CULTURE AS AGENCY

If the term 'design culture' can be used as an attitudinal marker of an organization to maximize its market position, this may also be appropriated into attempts to reform the aims, practices and effects of design towards greater and more direct social and environmental benefit. Here, the emphasis is also on design culture as a 'way of doing things' but looks to be active in changing the practices of those outside its main actors. It therefore takes context as circumstance but not as a given. In this account, the world can be changed through a new kind of design culture (e.g. Mau 2004). The term is certainly not used to signify design that strives purely for commercial advantage. It implies design practice that is 'encultured' in the sense that it strives towards a higher moral ground.

DESIGN CULTURE AS PERVASIVE BUT DIFFERENTIATED VALUE

Leading on from this last observation, one might detect a spirit of openness, or almost random connection in the same way that magazine-thumbing, web-browsing and conference-networking produce chance 'pick-ups'. It involves practice within a particularized environment. Design culture engages a conceptual breadth that goes beyond traditionally used notions of 'excellence', 'innovation' or 'best-practice'. Thus singular instances of design value, as for instance exemplified through individual works of design, are subordinated in favour of a generalized setting for design culture. The locations, artefacts or practices that harbour design value become ever wider and more various as they become swept up to constitute this situation. Their connectivity implies the possibility of immersion in a specific and distinctive designerly ambience (e.g. Lacroix 2005).

A recapitulation on some of the above themes, giving examples of related discourses and actions, might help explain and account for the ascendance of design culture.

Design culture as a form of agency, as *encultured* design, may emerge in various guises. It may be viewed as a way of garnering a more general sense of innovation within a commercial firm and thus a form of management through design. An employee's everyday enthusiasm for design – as much as a consumer as a producer – in turn provides a disposition towards newness (Cawood 1997). Bruce Mau has directed a sense of design culture towards future global change, attempting to expose the ways by which the intersections of new information, bio- and materials technologies with attitudinal changes can be directed at combating climate change, social alienation or poverty. In early 2004, his website (www.massivechange.com) acted as a focus for debate towards 'The Future of Design Culture' (see also Mau 2004). In such ways, design culture is therefore a generator of *value*.

The mobilization of design culture exists within a wider framework that relates to both a quantative ascendance of the creative industries as a sector of employment and national revenue generation within developed countries, and to their qualitative development in terms of their symbolic role in signalling advanced economic development. For example, in the UK the number of first-year design students rose by 35 per cent, from 14,948 to 20,225, between 1994 and 2001. According to a 1998 European Commission report, 'cultural employment' – that is, work in advertising, design, broadcast, film, internet, music, publishing and computer games – grew by 24 per cent in Spain (1987–94) while employment in Germany of 'producers and artists' grew by 23 per cent (1980–94). Into the 21st century, statistics from beyond Europe underpin an even more global view of this ascendance. For example, by 2011, Brazil's creative industries represented 2.7 per cent of its Gross Domestic Product – higher than Italy (2.3 per cent) and Germany (2.5 per cent) and most other European countries – with design making up 12.7 per cent of the sector's employment (FIRJAN 2011). By the same year, China was producing a reported 300,000 industrial design graduates annually (UK Trade and Investment 2011).

Arguably, the creative industries indicate, or even herald, wider changes in the meanings and processes of work. In her study of London-based fashion designers, for example, sociologist Angela McRobbie (1998) shows how their working patterns were typified by the requirement to network, to be visible and available virtually on a 24-hour basis – patterns of labour that resonate with the emergent entrepreneurialism of the New Economy. Meanwhile business studies academics Scase and Davis take this notion further to claim that the creative economy is at the 'leading edge of the movement towards the information age [as] their outputs are performances, expressive work, ideas and symbols rather than consumer goods or services' (2000: 23). They are paradigmatic of broader changes in economic life. Such authors may well be accused of uncritically deriving an ideal model of creative industries and accepting the coming dominance of an information age (Nixon 2003). Nevertheless, both the growth figures and the emergent debates suggest a shifting emphasis in the modern economy to a specific mode of *creation*.

Design culture also emerges through strong changes in its contexts and localities. For example, design curatorship has, it seems, moved from a differentiated dominance to a de-differentiated model. The history of contemporary design curatorship reveals a tendency towards the exhibition of objects as paradigmatic examples of 'good design'. By contrast, exhibitions such as New York's Cooper-Hewitt Museum's show, 'Design Culture Now', are conceived to represent contemporary design activities without recourse to didactic commentary (Lupton and Albrecht 2000; Lupton 2005). Design culture was conceived here to represent a ubiquitous presence rather than a point of aspiration. Equally, there have been attempts to establish urban agglomerations such as Montreal, Glasgow and St Etienne as 'design cities' (Lacroix 2005). These are characterized not solely by a high concentration of designers or design production systems but are places where design becomes a more prominent and commonplace feature of everyday life. A more localized version of this phenomenom, for example, may be found in the corporatization of urban night life in cities, where an intensity of designer bars and clubs stakes out a particular city zone (Chatterton and Holland 2003). These locations may be differentiated from each other, but within their locale the overall effect of a pervasive design culture is implied. Design culture, then, becomes a form of *practice*.

Design culture as an object of study therefore includes both the material and immaterial aspects of everyday life. On one level it is articulated through images, words, forms and spaces. But at another it engages discourses, actions, beliefs, structures and relationships. The above concepts of *value*, *creation* and *practice* that motivate design culture as an object of study are processes that relate, respectively, to designers, production and consumption, and we shall return to these later in this chapter.

In the meantime, having established that the term 'design culture' has come into frequent, commonplace usage, the question arises as to how it might be studied. How can its object of study (lower-case 'design culture') be turned towards the development of an academic discipline (upper-case 'Design Culture')? In the first instance, it is important to try to establish how the objects of study within design culture are viewed. I do this through an assessment of a related field of study: Visual Culture. A critique of approaches within Visual Culture – and a particular *way of looking* that is found within the discipline Visual Culture – offers disciplinary starting points for developing the study of Design Culture. Subsequently, this chapter offers a structured approach to dealing with the complexities of design culture that forms the conceptual basis of the rest of this book.

BEYOND VISUAL CULTURE: DESIGN CULTURE AS AN ACADEMIC DISCIPLINE

Visual Culture is now firmly established as an academic discipline in universities across Europe and the Americas. It sports two refereed journals (*Journal of Visual Culture* and *Visual Culture in Britain*) and at least five student introductory texts (Walker and Chaplin 1997; Mirzoeff

1999; Barnard 2001; Howells 2001; Sturken and Cartwright 2001) and three substantial readers (Mirzoeff 1998; Evans and Hall 1999; Jones 2003). Undergraduate and postgraduate courses have been established. While differing in their approaches, Visual Culture authors generally include design alongside fine art, photography, film, television and advertising within their scope. Visual Culture therefore challenges and widens the field of investigation previously occupied by Art History. This project was instigated in the 1970s within the then-called 'New Art History'. Its proponents turned away from traditional interests in the formal analysis, provenance and patronage of art to embrace a more anthropological attitude to the visual in society. Thenceforth, all visual forms were admissible for academic enquiry – a notion spurred on by the rise of Cultural Studies, Popular Culture Studies and Media Studies, and indeed Design History.

The periodization of visual culture – when and for how long does it exist as a recognizable object of study – is understood in two ways. One is that the visual has come to be the dominant cognitive and representational form of modernity. This is certainly the position that was taken by Mitchell (1994) and Mirzoeff (1998). In this account, the emergence of a 'visual turn' in Western society is the result of the creation of mass consumer markets and urbanization during the industrial revolution. Indeed, the proliferation of images became a key characteristic of modern social organization (Evans and Hall 1999). From a design point of view, commodities and services needed to be made more self-consciously visual in order to advertise and market them to a wide, anonymous audience. In Europe and North America, the 19th century saw the growth of the department store, catalogue shopping, mass tourism and entertainment as spectacle – all of which hinge on the mediation of visual experience. And, of course, this was also the period of new visual technologies such as film, animation and photography.

Alternatively, we might view the issue of visual culture as a hermeneutic one. It is a question of how we interpret visuality itself. This is not to say that there is a clear historical break between, say, a literary era and the visual era. Vision is neither hegemonic nor non-hegemonic (Mitchell 2002). In the first instance, all media are hybrid or, as Bal (2002) claims, 'impure'. They do not merely engage one expression – visual, textual, aural, material – but are dissolved within the contexts through which they are mediated. Hence, for example, one cannot talk of the Internet in terms of either visual or textual culture but, perhaps, as screen culture. It therefore does not follow that the advent of a new visual technology – from oil painting to the Internet – means the strict dominance of one cognitive form over another in any era. Forms of visual presentation emerge and indeed occupy, however, some prominence at various historical junctures.

From this, it follows that an era of visual culture, Mitchell argues, is where the perception of the visual becomes commonplace, something that is mentioned casually (Mitchell 2002). In doing so, assumptions are automatically made about the ubiquity and role of the visual in society. Through this more nuanced notion of visual culture, we slip from an essentialist view (the visual is *the* medium of our times) to a complex view (we regard the visual as an intrinsic and important social and cultural expression of our times).

While proponents of the latter position may indeed acknowledge the visual as part and parcel of a complex, interlocking web of cultural production, the visual still plays a lead role in cultural formation and representation. These proponents are concerned with images, pictures, visual things and what they are doing. The focus of interest is on them as representations and in the relation of viewers and practices of vision. The dominant transaction of interest is between singularized object and individual viewer, between produced object and consuming subject. Issues of 'scopic regimes', vision, ways of looking, the gaze and semiosis crowd the literature. The 'reading' of the image is a central skill in this discipline.

This ocularcentricism in Visual Culture studies therefore renders the viewer almost inanimate in relation to the viewed. A sensibility is embedded in its practices whereby things external to the subject are seen, analysed and contemplated. This rigid process of looking is underpinned and promoted by the habit of disembodying images from their primary contexts of encounter (Armstrong 1996). Adverts or photos are quite literally cut out of newspapers and magazines for analysis, a process that is not dissimilar to those undertaken with traditional art history that Visual Culture studies critiques. Mass media images are abstracted away from their usual contexts for study in the same way that historical works of art are presented in books or in galleries, regardless of their original framing or locations. How one looks and how looking is represented may be a multifarious performance. Indeed, Martin Jay identified three common historical forms. The first is embedded in the perspectivalist Cartesian relationship between viewer and viewed that relates to Renaissance painting. Here a single, static position for the viewer is expected. Second, observational empiricism that was embedded in Dutch 17th-century art does not make the assumption of three-dimensional space external to the viewer, but revels in the particularity of surface detail. Third, the multiple and open-picturing of visual phenomena prevalent in Baroque art demands the viewer to piece together visual objects into a coherent narrative (Jay 1988). These are useful starting points for exploring visual encounters and may be transferred into the exploration of designed objects and environments. After all, we shall see in Chapter 8 on branded leisure that museums, shops or leisure centres are often designed as a series of episodes that add up to a narrative experience. This argument, it seems, still foregrounds the practice of viewing as the prior function that such objects fulfil, however. Furthermore, his interest is in whatever is, quite literally, within the frame rather than around or behind it. The notion that such artefacts also function as things in space or circulation, or in individual or collective reproduction, memory or aspiration is absent.

As visual information has become more ephemeral and immediate, so the ground on which culture is played out has shifted up a gear. The growing ubiquity of design as a self-consciously distinguishing feature in everyday life expands the grounds on which visual values lie. As Lash notes, 'Culture is now three-dimensional, as much tactile as visual or textual, all around us and inhabited, lived in rather than encountered in a separate realm as a representation' (2002: 149). He describes an architectonic, spatially-based society where information is reworked in these planes. Culture is no longer one of pure representation or narrative where the visual conveys messages. Instead, culture formulates, formats, channels, circulates, contains and retrieves information. Design, therefore, is more than just the creation of visual artefacts to be used or 'read'. It is also about the structuring of systems of encounter within the visual and material world.

Academics at the core of Visual Culture studies are not oblivious to this development. Hal Foster's writings on design, in particular, resonate with Lash's 'architectonic' conception of culture, albeit that they are attitudinally distinct. Foster places himself at the end of discursive tradition that recognizes the remaking of space in the image of the commodity, itself a prime story of capitalist modernity. In the same way that the commodity and sign appear as one (through, for example, branding), so, he contends, does the commodity and space. This is nowhere more evident than in the use of design to define the cultural value of locations – place branding, in other words. Thus for Foster, Frank O. Gehry's design for the Guggenheim Museum in Bilbao creates a spectacle that is 'an image accumulated to the point where it becomes capital' (Foster

2002a: 41). This observation closes the loop instigated by Debord where it was argued that the spectacle was 'capital accumulated to the point where it becomes an image' (1967: 23). Here design is used to establish symbolic-value over a location; or, as Foster would have it, image and space are 'deterritorialized' (2002b).

Equally, Camiel van Winkel speaks of a 'regime of visibility … that permeates all levels of culture and society [so that] increasingly works of art and other cultural artefacts are no longer simply made but designed … a productive model dominates that is all about styling, coding, and effective communication with an audience' (van Winkel, cited in Bryson 2002: 230). This pervasiveness of design is, in such accounts, however, matched by its authority. In agreement with van Winkel, Bryson argues that as they proliferate, 'a primary experience in everyday life is that of being engulfed or overwhelmed by images' (2002: 230). Alongside Foster, such Visual Culture writers express a profound and enervated anxiety as to what to do about design in contemporary culture.

At the heart of these narratives concerning the instrumentalization of design in the commodification, corporatization and formatting of culture is a telling diffidence and anxiety as to how to deal with this. The imperative of modern capitalism to make things visual in order to commodify them implies a flip-side: that more and more things are passed from a non- or pre-visual state into this aestheticized state. There is an implied 'before' and 'after' here, and equally there is an implied 'them' and 'us'. 'They' are the forces and objects of modern capitalism and design therein, and 'we' are viewers and subjects of them. Visual Culture then becomes a project in how to deal with this asymmetry.

The commentaries of van Winkel and Foster seem to assume an alienated position on the part of the subject, therefore. In this account, modernity has entailed a shift from a bodily, practical relationship with the world to a more abstract and intellectual one, and the 'disembedding of aspects of life from the social relationships and activities with which they have previously been implicated' (Carrier 2003: 10). This process began, according to Marx, with the passivization and routinization of labour and the process of objectification whereby human values are invested into alien processes of capital, exchange and the commodity (Marx 1964). This discourse emerges in Weber's account (1978 [1922]) of the spread of legal-rational thought and the resultant processes of disenchantment that form the basis of Ritzer's 'McDonaldization thesis' (Ritzer 1996). Systems are orchestrated and routinized for maximum perceived efficiency, leaving the consumer as a passive participant. Equally, it has influenced studies of alienation, from the urban milieu discussed by Sennett (1976) to those that subsequently have influenced Urry (1990) in his conception of 'the tourist gaze'. Here the conceptual emphasis is on tourism as a form of spectacular consumption in which sights are arranged for visual pleasure. Tourist spaces are produced and viewed as an alien 'other'.

The insistence on the singularization of the objects of analysis within Visual Culture accounts for the discipline's inability to make substantial contributions to the study and understanding of design. The presumption is that visual objects are intrinsically alienating. To follow a parallel Material Culture studies argument, their singularization through consumption is what interrupts and reverses this process of alienation. Its quest for meaning is in the investigation of the transactional relationship between seeing and the thing seen.

But this leaves out the possibility, even more probable in design culture, that the object can be encountered through a range of media or even that its multiple reproduction itself produces meaning. By extension, it does not necessarily follow that the primary experience of design is that of being overwhelmed or engulfed by it. Indeed, the multiplication of its artefacts may even be what makes it meaningful. They may be orchestrated into an architectonic structure, serially reproduced through a range of media.

A range of visual technologies that emerged during the 1990s has perhaps broken this relationship between viewer and viewed. Among these, the idea of virtual reality in its raw state (before it was sublimated into applications such as computer games) indicated a direction for an alternative conception of how we might handle visual culture. The discourse of 'immersion' (discussed further in Chapter 9) – whereby the subject 'steps into' the object – signifies a paradigmatic shift of the ground on which visual culture might be played out. Thinking about virtual reality shifts us away from an ocularcentricism into an account that takes on board the embodied nature of engagement (Chan 2006). Furthermore, virtual reality becomes an, albeit extreme, metaphor for change in the rules of engagement between subject and object. The emergence of mobile technologies in the 21st century, such as smartphones and tablets (discussed further in Chapter 11), adds further complexity and problematics to any assumptions of looking as a static, disembodied practice. These devices encourage a range of gestures and movements that interact with the visual experience. Furthermore, through, for example, such things as their mapping facilities or QR (quick response) codes, they present visual information that is related to spatial elements.

In the new conditions of design culture, cognition becomes as much spatial and temporal as visual. Information is presented within architectonic planes rather than in the bounded, two-dimensional space of representation. The processes of encounter go further and are more complex than the analytical tools of Visual Culture can fully aid. The last decade has seen the ascendance of a range of overlapping and interdependent visual technologies. These promise not so much convergent media, but rather simultaneous and concurrent experiential moments. The same visual information may be generated and encountered via a range of platforms: picture phones, DVD cameras, webcams, video screens, smartphones, tablets and so on. Thus imagery and information are 'played through' varying sites. Each one provides its specific form while also relating to other moments and points in a network.

So how do the ways that the term 'design culture' is articulated signal an alternative approach to Visual Culture? How might we construct a model of analysis that respects the specificities as well as the more general effects of design culture?

MODELS FOR STUDYING DESIGN CULTURE

Qualitative change in what drives the design profession and the meaning of design in society adds weight to the contemporaneity of a design culture concept that takes us beyond Visual Culture studies. The rise of branding as the key focus and driver of much design practice signals two clear challenges. One is that design culture requires its observers to move beyond visual and material attributes to consider the multifarious and multilocational networks of its creation and manifestation. Brand management rhetoric tells us that producer agents – be they corporations, institutions or individuals – are responsible for controlling a coherent brand message throughout its circuit of culture, from production through mediation to consumption to consumer feedback. If a brand is typified into a clear, simple message, which is often crystallized as a slogan, then this should be reflected in all its manifestations. This might include the way corporate workers dress, talk and act with customers and clients. Branding obviously extends into more traditional designed elements such as promotional literature graphics or the design of retail spaces, reception areas, websites or other points of corporation and consumer interface. In this way, the systems of branding inhabit much of the space of design culture, turning information into an 'all around us' architectonic form.

The rise of branding may partially account for the growing interdisciplinarity of design within the profession as designers seek, and clients demand, a greater integration of product, graphic and interior design in order to create more coherent and filled-out design solutions. It also explains the design profession's increased integration with marketing, management and public relations, mentioned earlier. Branding is by no means the only driver and expression of contemporary design culture, but it is indicative of design culture's multidimensional qualities.

I use branding for illustrative purposes, and its domination may not be permanent. Ultimately, the creation of value through design hinges on articulating 'the cultural reconstruction of the meaning of what is consumed' (Fine and Leopold 1993: 4) by various means. Designers engage in a series of repeated adjustments of the material, visual and spatial world. They reconstruct it. But they also work for clients, be they private companies, public institutions or civic groups. They source materials and processes, commission or delegate making. They enter into systems of distribution and exchange. Value is continually adjusted in response to changing everyday and global practices and systems of product and information circulation. Thus it is unstable and relational. Value is dependant on so many constantly changing factors within the culture of design – which themselves are in constant flux– that it varies continually.

No design object is an island. Rather, its meaning, function and value are dependant on a complex patchwork of other artefacts and people. The interpretation of design artefacts within a concept of design culture that goes beyond a mere visual 'reading' first requires one to both undertake close analysis of that object while also keeping another eye on its relationship to other visual, spatial and material expressions that contribute to the constitution of its meaning. Margolin expressed this contextualized thinking in terms of a *product milieu* by defining it as 'the aggregate of objects, activities, services, and environments that fills the lifeworld' (1995a: 122). Second, then, in order to develop an understanding of the conditions that form designed artefacts as well as how these artefacts themselves come to bear on these activities, their relationship with a triangulation of the activities of designers, production and consumption requires investigation (see Figure 1.1). The chapters of this book are therefore structured into two sections. The first section further develops on key issues relating to designers, production and consumption.

The *designer* is clearly bound up in this process but is given a separate nexus in this triangle. This honours the designer's role in shaping the form and content of the visual and material artefacts which are produced and consumed. However, it also allows us to pay special attention to the less conscious features which inform and structure this process. Thus heed to the peculiarities of the professional status of design and the discourses which influence and mediate among designers and between them and their public must be paid. Chapter 3 largely focuses on these aspects through a discussion of the professional, historiographical and discursive questions that are articulated by design historians and critics and which provide a set of reference points for designers. Thus while the rise of design is bound up in recent economic change, related factors such as its struggle for professional recognition and a sense of its own history provide interesting and productive inroads to design culture analysis.

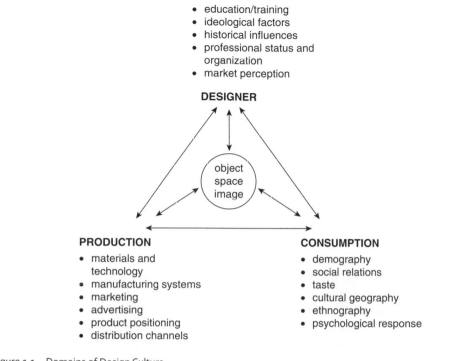

- education/training
- ideological factors
- historical influences
- professional status and organization
- market perception

DESIGNER

object
space
image

PRODUCTION

- materials and technology
- manufacturing systems
- marketing
- advertising
- product positioning
- distribution channels

CONSUMPTION

- demography
- social relations
- taste
- cultural geography
- ethnography
- psychological response

Figure 1.1   Domains of Design Culture

Production not only includes manufacture but also all forms of conscious intervention in the origination, execution, distribution and circulation of goods and services. Thus it would incorporate the influence of materials, technologies and manufacturing systems as well as the effects of marketing, advertising and distribution channels. The design industry is structured within this both to reproduce it and to modify it. Chapter 2 concentrates mostly on the interaction of design practice with wider changes in commerce and industry. In particular, it traces how design has grown as a sector in response to post-Fordist manufacture and distribution and the related processes of globalization.

Consumption completes this triumvirate. This would not only include quantitative data regarding, say, the degree of acquisition or use of particular designs in relation to demographic trends, it also involves the discussion of qualitative questions concerning the reasons and meanings of consumption. Why are certain goods which do not perform a utilitarian function accorded a special status over others? Does consuming involve an active or even a subversive practice? How are places consumed? These are some of the many questions that have interested academics in the humanities and social sciences in the past two decades. Chapter 4 outlines some of the key thinkers in this area and considers them alongside the practice of design. In particular, then, it argues for design consumption not to be analysed on its own, but to be seen as a dynamic process, to be understood in its interactions with the forces of production and the work of designers.

None of these three nexi of designers, production and consumption exists in isolation, therefore. They constantly inform each other in an endless cycle of exchange. Equally, they all have some influence to play on the form of objects, spaces and images. But these in turn are not neutral: they play an active part in influencing or making sense of the systems of their provision. Furthermore, contemporary conditions of design, production and consumption bring the three domains ever closer so that at times aspects of them may even overlap. It is the interaction and intersection of these domains and their interactions with designed artefacts that are of prime interest to the study of design culture.

To embrace Design Culture as an academic discipline requires, therefore, a different sensibility from that of Visual Culture. In the first instance, it forces one to move beyond the enervated position of the detached or alienated observer overwhelmed by images. Instead, a Design Culture enquiry traces a cartography that exposes and analyses the linkages of artefacts that constitute information flows and the spaces between them. Second, while one might dwell on individual artefacts, this process requires these to be seen relationally to other artefacts, processes and systems. Third, it may be mobilized not merely as analysis but as a generative mode that produces new sensibilities, attitudes, approaches and intellectual processes within design.

Each domain of design culture – designers, production and consumption – can be broken down into the analysis of its possible sub-elements. Thus, for example, one might look at the professional status of designers to ask how they legitimate their role in a competitive marketplace. This in turn may be analysed in relation to the way that they shape artefacts or carry out processes, bringing into view the possibility that designs are formed specifically in such a way as to underwrite that bid for professional status. Equally, domains and their sub-elements may be regarded in relation to each other. In the realm of consumption, for instance, the way that the cultural geography of a location and how this shapes taste patterns may be discussed in relation to the way that the aspirational outlooks of designers or others more involved in production activities are structured. Thus the complexity of design culture may be broken down and viewed through the various lenses of its sub-elements. Much of this book takes this approach.

However, the bigger picture of design culture, in which its totality is appreciated in terms of the active processes that bind the field together, may be understood as the relationship between the processes of value, of creation and circulation and of practice. As already indicated, these respectively map on to designers, production and consumption and are expanded on in the following three paragraphs.

The designer's role is in the generation of *value*. This most obvious value is commercial, but the concept may also include social, cultural, environmental, political and symbolic-value. This is not restricted to notions of 'good design' as value: as we shall see in Chapter 5, I argue that 'good design' itself is an unstable and contextually achieved process. Value generation involves the origination of new products and product forms, as well as their value augmentation. This occurs in an expanded field of activity that orchestrates and coordinates material and non-material processes results. A key feature of this value creation is the reproduction of 'product nodes', whereby cultural information is filtered through a range of platforms and moments. These might include, for example, retail outlets, museums, design magazines and catalogues, websites or even through the promotion of the designers themselves. Creative action may indeed originate, position and differentiate product forms and 'product nodes' to increase value.

With regard to *creation and circulation*, a range of straightforward elements underpins and shapes the productive processes of design culture, including available technologies, environmental and human factors. But non-material elements, such as existing knowledge networks, legislation, political pressures, economic fluctuations and fiscal policies, are also contextual factors on which these draw. Beyond design manufacture or production issues – whether we are talking about material or information products – 'downstream' flows of product information and distribution are channelled, formatted, interrupted or facilitated to influence their movement and/or reception through the system of provision. Within this, the specificities that produce a 'fit' or disjuncture of global/local nexi invariably play crucial roles – how comfortably a design or its production and distribution system sits in a location will impede or promote its circulation.

By understanding consumption in terms of *practice*, its contingent and dynamic characteristics may be appreciated. The engagement of design products, processes and systems in everyday life is not merely a function of consumer culture in its traditional sense. Beyond individual, privately orientated activities of use, ownership and maintenance, focused on the domestic sphere, are layers of socially constituted activities where individuals are carriers of collectively held practices and may comprise sets of conventions and procedures. Practice may be conceived as specific types and ranges of activities, which Bourdieu (1992) termed 'fields'. Here, the distinction between the two is debatable (Warde 2004), but the notion of 'field' at least implies that different practices are governed by their specific, respective rules. Practice involves routinized behaviour that is both individually enacted and socially observable (Shove et al. 2007). Consumption is therefore a part of practice.

As will be argued in more detail in Chapter 4, traditional surveys of consumption largely focus on the social role of goods in private, everyday life. Even where the relationships of consumed goods are synthesized into an exploration of concepts of lifestyle, discussion invariably falls into matters of personal choice. However, design is mobilized and encountered at both material and non-material expressions distributed across a range of platforms. Service orientations in private and public sectors, for example in corporate consumption, health provision or leisure practices, provide structures of engagement that are acted on at different bodily and mental levels. In effect, design culture contributes to the structuring of practice and the formation of the rules of engagement through the provision of interrelated elements that give meaning to these. The competition between brands, for example, reflects and contributes to their distinctions through providing differentiated rules of engagement. Brands articulate fields of their respective practices.

The model and key terms presented above offer a theoretical framework for the study of Design Culture. Beyond this, it must be stressed that this possible academic discipline demands of the researcher an open-ended sensibility in the face of the increasing complexity of design environments (Pizzocaro 2000). In Chapter 12, I come back to questions and challenges in the study of design culture.

DESIGN CULTURE BEYOND DISCIPLINE?

In this chapter I have critiqued a more conservative version of Visual Culture as a springboard to defining a sensibility that is sympathetic with the varying conditions of design culture as an object of study and that underlines the complexities inherent in Design Culture as a possible academic discipline. Visual Culture needn't be so fixed in its thinking by adopting a more flexible approach to visual phenomena. More radical views within Visual Culture studies, however, suggest that the creation of disciplines within the bureaucratic structures of universities encourages their 'ossification' (Smith 2005). Upon the development of an academic discipline, so standards and norms of teaching delivery are established and 'canonical' texts are developed that provide a 'tick-box' level of legitimation for study in order to meet targets and provide performance indicators. In its turn, this then restricts the field of study, tying it down to a specific modus operandi that ignores the very flexibility and instability of its own object of study.

Equally, as design rapidly evolves, reorganizing its professional make-up, entering into new contexts of application, innovating relations with its clients and users, being positioned into new ideological structures, or in changing its overall aims to go beyond mere commercial aims and prioritise social or environmental values, so a fixity of analytical approach becomes less and less appropriate. Thus Design Culture, as presented in this book, adopts a flexible reasoning. It moves across traditional design disciplines, plunders other academic traditions (particularly in the humanities and social sciences) and is promiscuous in its coupling with their related theoretical perspectives.

Having examined the key overarching issues and debates to design culture in the first section, this book devotes its subsequent chapters to a thematic exploration of design culture. The following chapters dispense with traditional disciplinary boundaries of product, interior or graphic design. Instead, different theatres of design culture are identified and discussed. The demarcation here is not so much on what specific design things are discussed; rather, the emphasis is on what they are doing – how are they functioning? Naturally, some of these lend themselves to privileging one form of design expression over others; for example, consumer goods involve higher degrees of product design concentration than, say, branded places. On to each of these the interactions and intersections of designer, production and consumption are mapped, although one or other of these is perhaps given more focus in each case. The chapters are arranged, more or less, in terms of the chronological order of their emergence as themes that have driven developments in design. Hence 'High design' – with all its pedigree in the decorative arts – appears first while 'Communications, management and participation' and 'Networks and mobile technologies' are historically more recent themes to consider in design culture.

Chapter 5 discusses the more conservative conception of design in what has been termed 'high design' and the manoeuvres of the avant-garde in design to mediate that meaning. In particular it challenges notions of 'high design' or 'design classics' as being intrinsic to the object by tracing the ways that these are constructed; sometimes, through the actions and reputations of their designers, their mediation by producers and other representational platforms such as magazines and museums and how their functioning (or non-functioning) in consumption works to underline this construction. It concludes by looking both at how risk and the avant-garde become a promotional device and how, conversely, the speculative in design can be used to critique design culture.

Chapter 6 considers developments in the design of consumer goods. It reveals the design processes by which material artefacts are shaped within the framework of achieving coherence between the use of contemporary materials, manufacturing systems and marketing practices. In particular it shows how quantitative and qualitative consumer information is reconciled with brand identities of clients by designers. In a final section, the discussion sets this against the more experiential world of using products.

Chapter 7 continues to investigate the role of designers and design managers in orchestrating coherence between different manifestations, but this time in the context of the shaping and selling of geographical locations. Initially it considers the city as design product, arguing against architecture as the primary expression of urban identity; instead, a web of features including the material and visual design hardware of cities and their emotional and experiential software interlock and vie with each other. This is further problematized in the context of shifting regional, national and global power structures.

Chapter 8 investigates branded leisure spaces and the challenges of designing and consuming place and placelessness in locations which are largely disembedded from traditional spatial geography. It considers the problems of differentiating leisure experiences when they are dislocated from place identities and consumed by a progressively critical and knowing audience.

Chapter 9 looks into the design of interactive digital environments, including computer games, educational packages and websites. It begins by discussing the effect that this area is having on the structural organization of design practice itself. It then contrasts some of the exaggerated expectations of these media with the pragmatic realities of its limitations. Much of this chapter hinges on the relationships this digital world has with the material world.

Chapter 10 discusses case studies where design is used to communicate and consolidate the internal identity of corporations or neighbourhoods. This is something that the public does not see, but it indirectly influences the external corporate image. Furthermore, this strategy reconfigures employees of organizations as both its workers and consumers. As such it adds further credence to the notion of design conspiring to blur the distinction between producer and consumer. A critical discussion of creative quarters, where both design production and consumption are purportedly nurtured follows. It leads on to discuss how the engagement of the end-users of design in its formulation helps to open up the imagination of how it can function.

Chapter 11 returns to questions of digitization that were instigated in Chapter 9. This time, though, it extends the discussion into mobile technologies such as smartphones and tablets. This is done by an exploration of the notion of networks. The analysis is directed both at the way that these are governed in terms of the design of software and the way that these impact on the everyday lives of users.

Chapter 12 provides a concluding recapitulation and discussion of some of the key themes that have been introduced and expanded within this concept of design culture. In particular it focuses on questions of scale and dynamics. How do we define a design culture? Does it have different registers of intensity? How do we deal with a design culture's own dynamics of change? Leading on from this, I return to a consideration of historical periodization and whether, indeed, we can identify a 'design culture turn' just as a 'visual culture turn' has been argued for elsewhere.

Each chapter in the second part of this book features a key case study. At times my authorial voice of the text shifts towards a more literary style, acknowledging the subjectivity of experiencing these design artefacts. I also discuss subsidiary case studies. This acknowledges that the key examples cannot provide an exhaustive platform to explore all the issues that are part of the chapter's theme. I hope that the debates which relate to the specific examples discussed may subsequently be carried to others outside the scope of this book. I have chosen particular examples for the richness of data they bring to their respective theme. They are also all relatively well-known ones. I hope that the reader may have some personal experience of them to compare with, or of closely related examples. Nearly all of them were experienced by myself as a consumer before being considered for this book. This is not to declare any experiential neutrality. Clearly, as a specialist in the design field my response to goods and services may be coloured by my own academic baggage: I am a 'knowing consumer' whether or not I like the feelings this brings up.

Nonetheless, the examples are not presented as paradigms of either good or bad design. Much publishing has been devoted to establishing expert canons of good design taste and criticism (e.g. Bayley 1979; Sudjic 1985). Conversely, some critics have drawn up vehement attacks on this canon and offered alternative approaches to the practice and appreciation of design framed by environmental concerns (e.g. Papanek 1972; Whitely 1993). Some important discussions of the role of gender in both design production and its consumption have emerged (e.g. Attfield 1989; Sparke 1995; Buckley 1998). While questions around gender emerge lightly within the text of this book, I am concerned not to separate it out as an issue and thereby restrict it. In choosing case studies, then, my primary interest is that objects, spaces and images exist in the mainstream of design production and consumption, and because they exist we are required to build a measure of objective understanding of their purpose. After all, only by understanding the current state of design culture can we then begin to look at routes towards its ethical and practical amelioration.

CHAPTER 2
DESIGN AND PRODUCTION

The ways by which design is produced and how it is practised have changed enormously since the 1980s. Through a discussion of the shifting commercial, economic and technological contexts in which it is produced, Chapter 2 shows how design has moved from an artisanal, problem-solving activity towards a more complex model which integrates hardware and software thinking 'beyond the object'. As such, it explains the growing sophistication of design practice and how this relates to changing production models. This is a reflection of the greater variety of technical processes available to the designer and the broadening range of 'objects' to which design can be applied. The economic frameworks of design have altered as well. In particular, this chapter places the ascendance of design in the context of a move from Fordist to post-Fordist production, or what is otherwise called 'disorganized capitalism'. Beyond this, design can also be seen to be an important factor within the so-called 'New Economy'.

If the design profession is concerned with innovation, change and invention, then during its relatively short lifespan it has consistently reinvented itself. This has happened in both haphazard and systematic ways: its ability to dodge-and-weave, wheel-and-deal in the face of economic ups and downs is matched, in some quarters, by an ambition to systemize its practice. In this context, it is difficult to generalize about its various phases: tendencies in its organization and aims are often multi-layered. The exponential growth of the design profession from 1980, alongside that of other creative industries, has produced a point of 'critical mass' whereby it now takes a prominent public and commercial role.

At the same time, this expansion is matched by ever increasing diversification of its practices. The breadth and heterogeneity of design markets, coupled with the need for design consultancies and designers to differentiate themselves from each other, mean that it is impossible to ascertain a singular model of design consultancy.

However, there have been broad structural trends in the practice of design brought about, not least, by global economic changes. In short, these have involved a convergence between design and other commercial practices such as advertising, management consultancy and public relations. Second, we have witnessed a trend within the profession to 'move up a gear' by specializing in the development of approaches, structures and relationships within which the object, image and space consequently play a role (Mitchell 1993). Rather than centre the design process just on solving specific individualized visual, spatial and material problems, then, there has been a move towards the integration of various levels with the 'systems of provision' (Fine and Leopold 1993) of goods and services. Thus many designers enter into a more sophisticated dialogue with clients in which product and service development is assessed in a broader context of corporate and brand ambitions.

THE RISE OF DESIGN

Since the mid-1980s there has been an increasing interest in measuring the size, structure and impact of the design profession in particular and the creative professions in general on the wider economy of nations and regions. This has mostly been undertaken by state government institutions or independent organizations acting on their behalf.

Table 2.1 demonstrates the growing view that design and the creative industries are important to regional or national policy making. To such examples, one must also add surveys which are directed at policy, but also at the design industry itself. These are particularly prevalent in the UK and might include the *Design Week* annual survey since 1987, Business Ratio Plus from 1987, Key Note from 1995, the Design Council surveys from 1998 and the British Design Innovation surveys, 2002–8.

Two pointers emerge from this. First, it is significant that the design profession has recently been deemed large enough to be measured and some idea of its structure determined. Attempts to quantify the design industry had historically been dogged by its fragmentation and small-scale practice. In the mid-1990s it was estimated that fewer than 200 design firms in Europe employed more than 25 designers (NDI 1994: 8). By the close of the 20th century, however, it seems that the design industry had reached a point of 'critical mass', making it, for those undertaking such surveys, more readily accessible through its representative associations and identifiable in employment statistics.

Table 2.1   Examples of national and regional design or creative industries' mapping and measurement documents

Year	Country/Region	Document
1987	United Kingdom	McAlhone, Beryl (1987) *British Design Consultancy*. London: Design Council.
1994	Europe	Netherlands Design Institute (NDI) (1994) *Design Across Europe: Patterns of Supply and Demand in the European Design Market*. Amsterdam: Vormgevingsinstitut.
1995	Canada – Ontario	Design Exchange (1995) *Design for a Strong Ontario: A Strategy for Ontario's Design Sector*. Toronto: Design Exchange.
1998	United Kingdom	CITF – Creative Industries Task Force (1998) *Creative Industries Mapping Document*. London: Department of Culture, Media and Sport.
2001	United Kingdom	CITF – Creative Industries Task Force (2001) *Creative Industries Mapping Document*. London: Department of Culture, Media and Sport.
2001	Spain	Buesa, M., Hidalgo, A., Conrado Llorens, C. and Zahera. M. (2001) 'El Diseño en España: Estudio Estratégico'. Madrid: Federación Española de Entidades de Promoción de Diseño Available at: www.idepa.es.
2002	France	Agence pour la Promotion de la Création Industrielle (2002) 'L'offre de design en France' (report). Paris: Ministère de l'Économie des Finances et de l'Industrie.
2002	New Zealand	Walton, Mark and Duncan, Ian (2002) *Creative Industries in New Zealand*. Thorndon: NZ Institute Of Economic Research. Available at: http://nzier.org.nz.
2004	Nordic Countries	Nordic Innovation Centre (2004) 'The Future in Design: The Competitiveness and Industrial Dynamics of the Nordic Design Industry'. Available at: www.nordicdesign.org.
2006	Italy - Milan	DESIGN|focus (2006) 'Milano Made in Design' (report).
2008	South Africa	Joffe, Avril and Newton, Monica (2008) 'The Creative Industries in South Africa'. Available at: www.labour.gov.za.
2009	Canada – Ontario	Vinodrai, Tara (2009) 'The Place of Design: Exploring Ontario's Design Economy'. Available at: http://martinprosperity.org.
2009	New Zealand	Andrews, Grant, Yeabsley, John and Higgs, Peter L. (2009) *The Creative Sector in New Zealand: Mapping and Economic Role: Report to New Zealand Trade and Enterprise*. Thorndon: New Zealand Institute of Economic Research.
2009	Australia	Centre for International Economics (2009) 'Creative Industries Economic Analysis'. Available at: www.enterpriseconnect.gov.au.
2009	Thailand	Kenan Institute Asia (2009) 'Economic Contributions Of Thailand's Creative Industries'. Available at: www.kiasia.org.
2010	United Kingdom	Design Council (2010) 'Design Industry Research'. Available at: www.designcouncil.org.uk.
2010	Global	United Nations (2010) 'Creative Economy Report'. Available at: http://unctad.org.

Second, these reports were produced by institutions dedicated to the promotion of the public and commercial profile of design, and yet their findings stressed the current, actual importance of design in the wider economy, rather than their potential impact. The British journal *Design Week* in its 1998 design consultancy survey went as far as to state that 'Design is finally coming of age' (*Design Week* 1998: 62).

It is widely acknowledged that accurate figures for the total value of design activity are difficult to calculate (NDI 1994; CITF 1998; Bruce and Daly 2006: 7). This is because many design consultancies are engaged in non-design activities; significant design decisions are sometimes undertaken by non-designers (Walsh et al. 1992); much of their value is hidden within the activities of other industries; the design function cannot be consistently bounded – different sectors use different definitions of design; and therefore definitive statistics are often not collected. In the early days of this process of design surveys in the UK, Mike Jones put it that 'Despite the hugely sophisticated network of rumour and gossip, nobody is entirely sure just how many small consultancies there are, or how many people are employed, let alone unemployed' (Jones 1991: 13). However, the 1980s and 1990s certainly registered exponential growth in design incomes. Annual fees earned by UK consultancies doubled from £175 million to £350 million between 1985 and 1995 (CITF 1998). Put more prosaically, when the *Yellow Pages* were launched in 1966, there were just three design consultants listed in Central London; in 1999 there were 536. Likewise, the European design market grew at an estimated 25 per cent between 1982 and 1989 (NDI 1994: 10).

Within the European market, the UK has maintained the highest expenditure on design services with $2.4 billion spent in 1994, followed by Germany with $2.2 billion and then both France and Spain with $0.9 billion. In the first decade of the 21st century, the growth of design became more internationalized. Thus, for example, employment in design in Australia grew from 59,336 in 2006 to 71,220 in 2011 (Australian Bureau of Statistics 2011).

During these decades much of the British growth had been in graphic communication and environmental design whereas the German market relied more on product development and civic or institutional design projects. The economic importance of design in the UK was matched by an infrastructural dominance. For instance, of the 30,000 annual graduates of design in Europe during the 1990s, 30 per cent were trained in the UK. Similarly, the growth of DesignUK was matched by educational growth. The years 1993–98 saw a 12 per cent rise in design degree applications and in 1998 a 63 per cent rise in students sitting the GCSE examination in Design and Technology (Design Council 1998: 24). There was a rise of 108 per cent in the number of postgraduate design qualifications available between 1994 and 2001, indicating substantial growth at the more advanced end of design education (Design Council 2003). By the end of the 1990s, there were 62,000 students specializing in design in higher education where over 900 courses were available (CITF 1998). Into the 21st century, growth in design education has also been a more global affair, though. China, for example, saw a 23 per cent increase of enrolment on art and design degree courses between 2003 and 2004. Enrolment on design degrees in Sweden grew from 2,000 to over 7,000 over the ten years up to 2003 (Nordic Innovation Centre 2004).

The European design industry is highly internationalized. Some 75 per cent of British consultancies were active in overseas markets, their main market being the USA and Northern Europe. Exports by British design consultancies rose from £175 million in 1987 to £385 million in 1997; in one survey, 45 per cent of consultancies reported that exporting their services was more profitable than UK projects (Design Council 1998: 14). The Danish design services export market grew by 46 per cent between 1999 and 2001 as against a 21 per cent growth of the export economy of the nation as a whole (Nordic Innovation Centre 2004).

Furthermore, the design industry is highly responsive to economic fluctuations in the way that it rapidly restructures to survive downturns. By 2001, UK employment in design consultancies was recalculated at 73,000 (CITF 2001). However, within this growth the tendency was towards the creation of small-sized design firms – those employing between one and five moved from 34 per cent to 54 per cent of the total design firms between 2000/1 and 2002/3 (Design Council 2003). The economic slowdown during these years – marked by the NASDAQ share index fall and the dot.com crash of 2001 and invigorated by the uncertainty following 9/11 – impacted on design and advertising to atomize the industry into leaner and less capital-intensive firms. Equally, the long-term recession from 2008 saw in the UK a reported increase in staff turnover in design agencies (Design Industry Voices 2009, 2010 and 2011), with the numbers working in consultancies having decreased by 13 per cent between 2005 and 2010 (Design Council 2010). While in this period there had been a 29 per cent growth in the overall number of designers in the UK to an estimated total of 232,000, this was predominantly in the freelance sector which experienced an increase of 35 per cent (Design Council 2010).

The various reports cited in Table 2.1. all show that the majority of design practice is in graphics and related fields, embracing corporate identity, corporate literature, packaging and/or branding, consumer literature, exhibitions, multimedia, advertising, retail and information design. Only 19 per cent of UK consultancies offer product design and only 6 per cent offer furniture design (CITF 1998). (We shall see in Chapter 3 how a hierarchy of design in its public presentation, through exhibitions, books and journals, is skewed in exactly the opposite direction in favour of product and furniture.) This in part reflects a general trend in the UK economy away from manufacturing towards the service sector in the late 20th century. But it also confirms the fact that design is bound up not just in the origination of products, but also in their marketing, promotion, packaging, distribution or dissemination (see Figure 2.1).

The high concentration of design practices in Britain is explained by a number of historical factors. These would include: the earlier industrial revolution and, subsequently, the establishment of a design schools' system in the 19th century; the fact that Britain resisted invasion in the two world wars, ensuring greater cultural continuity or, indeed, a consolidation of design practice; and the geographical and commercial position of Britain between America and Europe, thus acting as a strategic, mediating bridge between the two markets. The last of these becomes of vital importance as we begin to consider the emergence of design consultancy.

The growth of the design industry may also be read alongside a general economic and political shift in favour of the 'cultural goods' sector in the developed countries. Thus design is mapped alongside other 'creative industries' identified by the UK government's Creative Industries Task Force (CITF) as advertising, architecture, the art and antiques market, crafts, designer fashion, film, interactive leisure software, music, the performing arts, publishing, software and television and radio. These categories were largely reproduced in subsequent mappings of national and regional creative economies. Collectively, in the UK the creative industries' revenue grew at twice the rate of the economy as a whole and represented 5 per cent of the employed workforce by the late 1990s (CITF 1998).

This upward trend continued into the 21st century. A United Nations' report showed startling rises in global exportation figures for 'design goods' (UNCTAD 2010). This is a difficult category, since all goods could be termed 'design goods' in one way or another. However, it is interesting that the report claimed to define this as products 'with a presumably high design input' (2010: 156). In calculating its figures, it showed a global doubling of growth in exports between 2002 and 2008 (from $53.4 billion to $122.4 billion, reflecting mainly the growth in China) in

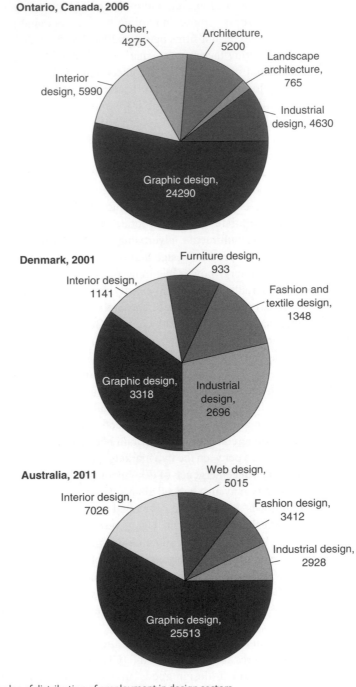

Figure 2.1   Samples of distribution of employment in design sectors
Source: Vinodrai (2009)
Source: Nordic Innovation Centre (2004)
Source: Australian Bureau of Statistics (2011)

Table 2.2   Design: exports, by economic group and region, 2002 and 2008 (UNCTAD 2010)

Economic group and region	Value (in millions of $)		Change (%)
	2002	2008	2002–2008
World	114,692	241,972	111
Developed economies	60,967	117,816	93
Europe	49,221	98,164	99
USA	6,280	12,150	93
Japan	1,521	3,783	149
Canada	3,104	2,773	−11
Developing economies	53,362	122,439	129
Eastern and South-Eastern Asia	47,534	98,851	108
China	23,529	58,848	150
Western Asia	1,916	8,452	341
Latin America and Caribbean	3,292	5,007	52
Africa	422	1,140	170
Least Developed Countries	222	467	
Small Island Developing State	47	96	102
Transition economies	362	1,716	374

developed and developing countries, with a threefold growth in 'transition countries' (developed countries moving to a market economy). Table 2.2 gives export numbers by group and region.

FREELANCE, IN-HOUSE AND CONSULTANCY DESIGN

Closer analysis of the design industries of most countries shows that employment is spread across freelance, consultancy or agency and in-house models. It is useful to be aware of the different models of commercial design practice as this demonstrates the very wide range that is available. A close analysis of how design is produced should include an understanding of the different ways by which designers work with or in companies. Equally, design cultures are intrinsically effected by the various working patterns of designers, both in the management of design projects and in the social world that they create.

Freelancers are self-employed. However, in design they frequently work in teams with other freelancers and increasingly as sub-contractees to design consultancies. They are usually valued for the individuality of their design thinking or style. However, for clients they can be very cost-effective in that they don't entail additional employment costs such as equipment or pensions contributions and do not cause expenditure when not needed. Occasionally, freelancers are retained by clients by paying them a fixed, ongoing fee. This secures their expert knowledge against competitors and helps strengthen collaborative relationships.

In-house designers are permanent employees of companies who specialize in bringing their skills to an in-depth knowledge of that company's product or service. The distribution of employment between freelancing, in-house and consultancies in various locations responds to various economic structures and commercial traditions. Within Europe it has been more common for German and Nordic companies to employ in-house designers. However, this sector also grew in the UK from 2000 as companies developed a more mature understanding of design's value to them. The advantages to a company of maintaining in-house designers may include:

- company operating costs can be more predictable with designers always appearing on its payroll;
- the company has closer control over design work rather than it being outsourced to less known designers;
- design can have a more visible role in the company structure rather than being viewed as an outsourced 'add-on';
- in-house designers can have a closer understanding of the company's brand, operating style, market, clients and production processes;
- in-house designers have a stake in the implementation and success of its services or products; and
- designers may have secondary skills that may also be an asset to the company.

The distribution of employment in the design industries is heavily weighted toward freelance work. In Denmark 'one-man-bands' constituted 92 per cent of design businesses in 2007 (Danish Government 2007). In many countries this trend continued, particularly as the economic recession from 2008 increased the pressure to cut employment costs. In the UK in 2009 there were 65,900 freelance design businesses (an increase of 39 per cent since 2005), 10,800 design consultancies (a decrease of 13 per cent compared to 2005) and 6,500 in-house design teams (an increase of 10 per cent since 2005) (Design Council 2010). The rise of in-house design teams is also notable as companies increasingly put design and brand at the centre of their operations.

Each type of design employment has its advantages and its downsides. The ability to employ an in-house designer or design team is obviously dependant on a company's scale and turnover. Apart from the financial issues, external designers are able to provide an external view on their clients, bringing their specific expertise and view of the marketplace to bear. Meanwhile, freelancers may be employed for specific design skills, but external design teams may offer greater capacity in their ability to combine design disciplines or a greater range of technical and business expertise. This is why design consultancies continue to hold a significant influence in the design industry. While the term 'agency' is frequently applied here, my preference is for the term 'consultancy'. This is in order to separate it from understandings of advertising agencies, albeit that the two are linked, as we shall see.

While they share some similarities in their structure and organization, in terms of how advertising agencies and design consultancies make their money, there is a clear delineation between the two. Broadly speaking, the majority of design consultancies work on a fee basis whereby payment is made by the client, which is agreed prior to or in the early stages of a project. On the part of the consultancy, this is calculated on the basis of such variables as time spent on the project, the expertises required, specialist subcontracting needed and other project expenses, such as travel. Alternatively, a few designers work on a royalty percentage of value of units sold. This form of working saw considerable growth by the late 1990s and was estimated to occupy as much as 30 per cent of design business (Sanders 2006; British Design Innovation 2007). By comparison, however, ad agencies mostly derive their income from a percentage commission of the media space bought for a specific campaign. Even while from the mid-1980s the level of this commission became more frequently negotiable, the impetus for the ad agency is to achieve high acquisition of media space and go for high expenditure forms of diffusion in order to maximize profit (Leiss et al. 1990: 161).

Historically, however, advertising agencies and design consultancies have a long relationship. The history of design consultancy also reflects the traffic of ideas about how design should be practised between the USA and Europe, principally the UK. A detailed discussion of this history helps to establish a specific understanding of the work of design consultancies and the culture of design production more generally. Understanding this history in the UK is useful, for while this has local characteristics – as it responds to changing economic contexts through time – many of the overall principles are applicable elsewhere. These include a tendency to organize design consultancies on the basis of advertising agencies, a 'take-off' in the number and size of consultancies in periods of market liberalization and economic growth and a reconfiguration of the services they offer in subsequent periods of economic recession.

THE ESTABLISHMENT OF DESIGN CONSULTANCY

Throughout its history, design consultancy has echoed – with some years' time lapse – the business approach and organization found in advertising. Advertising agencies first appeared in the second half of the 19th century when their mandate was to provide everything from posters to the frames in which to hang them. Thus from the outset their activities brought together an array of specialist activities. By the 1920s, their ranks included copywriters, art directors, account executives and media space buyers. The modern advertising agency, which was expected to coordinate aspects of a campaign across a range of advertising media, came into being with the medium of television. In the case of America, this was consolidated in the 1930s, while this model did not take shape in Europe until the early 1960s.

A clear model for the structure and actions of advertising was therefore forged in the USA and transplanted, primarily by the establishment of subsidiary offices of American agencies, to Western Europe. In 1937 only four American advertising agencies had branches outside the USA. By 1960, 36 had foreign branches with a total of 281 offices (Nevett 1987: 195).

In design consultancy, similar models of interdisciplinarity were developed in America. Most well-known among these was Raymond Loewy Associates, founded in 1929. By 1938 it employed 18 designers, in 1941 there were 56, and between 1947 and the mid-1960s it expanded from 150 to 180 employees (Julier 1993: 120). Loewy himself combined a background in engineering with illustration, and he sought to coordinate all aspects of design provision from product origination to its styling and brand identity. His no-nonsense book *Never Leave Well Enough Alone* (1951) positioned the role of design at the service of the corporation and consumerism. A client's market position could thus be matched with consumer trends to competitively position products through both their visual appearance and promotional strategy.

Compatriots Walter Dorwin Teague and Norman Bel Geddes also ran sizeable, complex studios which, during the 1930s, employed up to 30 individuals in design, drafting, modelling and technical activities respectively. They also drafted in specialists as required. Woodham (1997: 70) notes that undue emphasis on the individuals who headed the studios is thus misleading.

In bringing product, graphic and interior designers alongside advertising, marketing and management specialists, Raymond Loewy Associates was an important forerunner of much later European developments in design consultancy. Certainly his texts, and also Harold Van Doren's *Industrial Design: A Practical Guide* (1940), which also stressed the need for vertical and horizontal integration in design practice, were read in Europe. Nevertheless, design critics denigrated

Loewy's activities as the mere styling and packaging of products for maximum sales with little social benefit (e.g. Mañà 1983). This may partially account for the relatively slow take-up of this American approach in Europe, though we must also take into consideration the economic disruption of the Second World War and the fact that markets in Europe continued to be more segmented than in the USA until the 1960s. After all, Loewy, Teague and Bel Geddes had been servicing a more stable, homogenized and affluent market with a wider distribution base than Europe since the 1930s.

By contrast, then, early design consultancy in Europe, and in particular in Britain, was a more 'gentlemanly' affair. The Design Research Unit, set up in 1943 by the Ministry of Information, sought to bring designers and engineers together in order to provide practical advice for industry, equipping it for competition in post-war markets. The bulk of its activities, however, lay in exhibition design such as projects for the 1951 Festival of Britain.

It was not until the early 1960s that consultancies approaching the American model began to be established in Europe. In London, notable among this first wave were Allied International Designers and Fletcher Forbes Gill, both founded in 1959, Cambridge Consultants begun in 1960, Minale-Tattersfield founded in 1964, Wolff Olins which began work in 1965, and in the same year Unimark was founded in Milan.

Of these, James Pilditch's Allied International Designers set the pace for other consultancies. It began as a packaging consultancy but within 18 months was undertaking corporate identity projects; a year later it was joined by Douglas Scott, designer of London's Routemaster bus. Pilditch is also important for the books he published on product development and corporate identity (1970; Pilditch et al. 1965). Mixing anecdote and analysis, these publications helped give a voice to the emergent multidisciplinary design industry in the UK, which according to one of its key participants, Wally Olins, was 'learning as it went along' (Olins 1982: 221).

While the general buoyancy of European economies during the 1960s provided a subsequent basis for the growth of the design sector, the structural changes in commerce which took place were of more direct importance. During this decade many of the corporate giants emerged, forcing either the takeover, liquidation or repositioning of many smaller businesses. Thus Wolff Olins's first major corporate identity scheme in the early 1960s was for the paint manufacturer Hadfields. With the emergence of ICI's Dulux brand and Hoechsts's Berger, both with high-quality product, blanket distribution and massive advertising, a corporate identity for Hadfields had to be developed that made the company equally visible but also emphasized its stealth and flexibility. Hence a fox motif was adopted for its corporate logo (Olins 1982).

Peter York viewed this trend during the 1960s more satirically:

This business of designing corporate identity was all rather abstract and high-flown. When knighted artists who knew the chairman's wife had done out the head-office hall in 1935 … there'd been none of this. But these sixties designers were completely different. They'd ask you what your company really did, what its philosophy was and how people related to it, and ask to see the company archives and talk to the senior management. And they sent memos about it all. You'd think they were management consultants from the way they carried on, not sign-painters. (1984: 34)

THE 1980S DESIGN CONSULTANCY BOOM

The 1980s saw immense structural shifts in the economies of the developed world with the deregulation in developed countries of their banking and exchange systems, markets, information technologies, planning laws, labour, welfare services, energy, shipping and transportation. Out of this came a design boom that swept across the USA and Europe, fuelled by massive growths in consumer spending, the offshoring of manufacture to countries where labour and raw materials were cheaper, and technological change. At its leading edge, industrial design was rapidly replaced by retail, leisure and communication design.

Despite the economic recession brought on by the 1973 international oil crisis, several other large-scale consultancies became established during that decade. In the UK these would include Michael Peters & Partners (founded 1970), Enterprise IG (founded 1976), Fitch (founded 1972) and Addison (founded 1978). But it was in the 1980s that design practice got on to a solid corporate footing in terms of its size, structure and distribution. The most significant and debatable feature of this decade was the flotation of some design consultancies on the stock market. The first of these was Allied International Designers: when Pilditch took the consultancy to the market in 1980 it had a turnover of £23 million, with 16 companies and a staff of 600. The move was strategic in that it encouraged clients to view the design consultancy 'as a proper business' (Jones 1991: 17). When Addison took over Allied International Designers in 1984, it expanded to a group of 1,600 employees offering market research, public relations and recruitment specialisms alongside design.

The tendency of some design consultancies' outward growth was matched by marketing services groups that also began to acquire design companies. These would include the WPP Group, Euro RSCG, Havas, Aegis, Gruner & Jahr and Saatchi & Saatchi. In 1983 when it began buying design businesses, the WPP Group encompassed 54 companies employing 22,500 staff (Jones 1991: 18). Its portfolio ranged across advertising agencies, public relations and public affairs consultancies to media planning and research groups. The publicly quoted core group remained relatively small, with around 60 employees. It wholly or part owned companies, their payoff being increased capitalization and the sharing of clients across the group according to required specializations. These companies continue to be allowed managerial independence; their sole remit to WPP is profitability. Thus during the 1980s many larger design consultancies were driven by the imperative for high profits, either coming from the stock market or from their parent group.

This clearly matches a general ideological condition of that decade. In 1982 the British Prime Minister and leader of the Conservative Party, Margaret Thatcher, hosted a seminar at 10 Downing Street for designers and their advocates. She subsequently 'wrote' an article for *Design* in which she stated: 'The profit potential of product design and development is considerable. Designers themselves should be more aggressive in selling themselves to industry as wealth creators' (Thatcher, quoted in Whitely 1991: 196). In 1983, the UK's Design Council launched its 'Design for Profit' slogan. Its 1986 *Profit by Design* pamphlet echoed Thatcher's views, starkly pointing out that, 'the design process is a planning exercise to maximize sales and profits' (Design Council, quoted in Whitely 1991: 196).

Thatcher's, and the Design Council's, emphasis on the development of innovatory products for manufacture was somewhat out of kilter with the prevailing growth in design opportunities of the 1980s, however. After all, Britain, and indeed most of the developed world, with the exception of Germany and Japan, had seen a steady decline in the *presence* of manufacturing since the mid-1960s. Employment in manufacturing dropped in the UK from 38.4 per cent in 1960 to 22.5 per cent in 1990 and in the USA from 26.4 per cent to 18 per cent over the same period; Britain's share of world manufacturing exports dropped from 14.2 per cent in 1964 to 7.6 per cent in 1986 (Barberis and May 1993: 31–2). This trend has been referred to as 'de-industrialization', although in effect we are talking about the decline of just one particular sector of industry – manufacturing. Furthermore, during the 1980s many activities formerly carried out by manufacturers were subcontracted out, so that what had traditionally been included as part of manufacturing was being seen as service sector commerce. Nonetheless, during the 'Thatcher decade' of 1979–89, employment in the service sector grew by 2 million, roughly the same figure as the decline in manufacturing employment. Output in the services sector grew by 28.8 per cent as against nearly 10 per cent in manufacturing (Wells 1989: 25–6).

The chief growth area for design practice during the 1980s, then, was not in design for manufacture – though this discipline did not decline – but in design for the service sector in general and the mediation and distribution of goods and services in particular. Retail design, packaging and corporate identity, annual report design, events and exhibition design were the real boom areas.

Retail design expanded with the rapid growth of multiples in Britain during the early 1980s. This was an acceleration of a process which had been underway from the 1960s, whereby the independently owned shops in the high street were gradually replaced by the larger retail chains. In 1980, a study of the principal shopping street in Newcastle showed that 28 per cent of the shops were independent; by 1986 only 6 per cent were independent. Meanwhile the percentage of multiples in the same street rose from 26 per cent to 41 per cent (Howard and Davies 1988: 10). This was coupled with an exponential rise in retail expenditure, facilitated by a credit boom and a rise of consumer mobility through greater affluence and car ownership, which meant that shopping habits changed. Retail design was accordingly expansive and lucrative in the 1980s.

As capital investment in manufacture in the Far East was consolidated, so cheaper durable goods of more reliable production standards were attainable. In turn this enabled multiples to become mass merchandisers (Walters 1983). Food-based multiples such as ASDA and Tesco therefore moved into non-food product markets and specialist mass-merchandisers such as Currys, Rumbelow, Dixon and Comet were also consolidated (Walters 1981). In fashion, new retail patterns also emerged as a result. Wardrobes extended from a 'best suit' and a 'working suit' to two or three 'general purpose suits' and an extensive range of leisure clothing. Thus, high street brands such as Topman (part of the Burton group) catering to younger consumers were established in the late 1970s.

Packaging design was fuelled by this 'massification' of shopping. To take a focused example of this trend: in 1972, the supermarket chain Tesco had 800 stores in the UK with an average floorspace of 4,500 square feet; in 1992 it had just 400 stores, but with an average floorspace of 27,000 square feet (Sparks 1994: 323). Fewer but larger shops in turn means that there is less brand loyalty among consumers and more competition between brands. A large shop is capable of stocking a wider range of competing products, thus there is a need for packaging redesign in order to help maintain market share on the pure basis of visual attractiveness.

Corporate identity opportunities grew due to two basic phenomena. The first was the growth of mergers. During four years of the 1980s, the number of annual mergers and acquisitions in the UK exceeded the total for the whole of the 1970s (Napier 1994: 89). As the structure, size and nature of corporations changed, then so would their identity, often with the help of design consultancies. Second, the privatization programmes of state industries and services required the repositioning of these entities in a competitive market. This meant that they would be responsible to their shareholders rather than the state and that their public became their consumers. Those who remained as employees of newly privatized companies would have to relate to them as commercial, corporatized concerns rather than as state industries. Even if state services were not privatized, a clear shift in the relationship between them and their public took place. The wholesale change of public service, be it health, education, the Civil Service, the police force or social services, was based upon the application of market principles. Thus performance measurement and ratings, responsiveness to public demand and contracting out to competitive tendering gradually became features which brought the culture of public services closer to the private sector. Ultimately this led to the establishment of the Citizen's Charter in 1991, establishing levels of expectation of public services and thus repositioning their users as consumers. As such, the *presentation* of public services to either national or local government as their paymasters and to taxpayers as their consumers has gained greater importance. This has been taken to the extent that London's Metropolitan Police commissioned an audit of its 'corporate identity' from Wolff Olins. Following the design consultancy's report entitled *A Force for Change* (Olins 1988), there was little modification of the Met's visual identity. However, subsequently attention was paid to projecting greater cohesion, courtesy and sensitivity. Heward (1994) goes as far as to argue that the subsequent small-scale design changes, such as the use of calling cards by officers on the beat, repositioned the force within a retail-like 'service ethos'.

The design of annual reports perhaps did not require the complexity of project management that corporate identity demanded. Nonetheless it became a significant and highly visible source of design employment during the 1980s. The removal of foreign exchange controls in 1979, the establishment of the Unlisted Securities Market in 1980, which allowed smaller and less well-established companies to issue shares, and the progressive ending of demarcations between financial institutions, which freed up the movement of investment, all contributed to the stock market boom of the 1980s. Employment associated with corporate finance grew by 45 per cent between 1979 and 1986 (Toporowski 1989: 243). There was thus a burgeoning design market for corporate finance literature. The freedom of capital during this decade also led to more mergers and takeovers, in turn requiring more communications design. To this we must add the deregulation of banks and building societies in the mid-1980s, which allowed each to provide mortgage and banking facilities respectively, again all requiring newly designed literature.

Finally, an indirect cause of the changing cultural and economic landscape of Britain in the 1980s was the growth in events and exhibition design. As regional centres lost their manufacturing base, they then invented new forms of representing themselves. One result of this was the growth of the 'heritage industry' whereby localities were repackaged for tourist and leisure consumption. By the late 1980s, a new museum was opened, on average, in the UK every two weeks (Woodham 1997: 217).

NEO-FORDIST DESIGN

The opportunities for the expansion of design businesses during the 1980s did not, on the whole, impact on the strategic approach they took; it just meant more, much more of the same. The sheer volume of commissions implied that a publicly quoted consultancy could acquire larger premises and add more drawing boards to their studios. At the larger consultancy end (studios of over 50 employees), design businesses exhibited some of the classic features of Fordist production to deal with the explosive market. Employees undertook specialized tasks, output was relatively standardized, and they reached a mass clientele. Furthermore, clients were relatively inexperienced and thus uncritical employers of design consultancies. While there was high street competition, for many clients it was their first experience of commissioning design. As Mark Landini, who worked for retail specialists Fitch during much of the 1980s, remarked:

> One would say: well, we'll design a cash desk, but that was the end of the discussion. The cash desk would be presented to the people who had commissioned the design and then it would be built and then you'd find out that it didn't work. One just assumed that one could design a cash desk and the client assumed that you could because there was this great sense of euphoria. (Landini, quoted in Jones 1991: 18)

Again, this tendency towards Fordist structural organization and economies of scale in design consultancy was prefigured on a grander scale in advertising. Dominant in this mode was Saatchi & Saatchi, who developed a particular 'philosophy' of advertising, promoted an ethos of 'business principles' and underwent a series of acquisitions of other firms in order to operate a full range of marketing services – including design consultancy, public relations, market research, direct marketing – as part of what they called a 'commercial communications' package (Lash and Urry 1994: 140). Nonetheless, unlike WPP, Saatchi stitched its various companies together under a tight 'brand' identity.

This identity was part of what has been described as the 'second wave' of advertising which developed from the late 1960s. In terms of product, this involved a more creative, humorous approach to advertising communications on the part of British agencies in comparison with the more 'hard-sell' approach of their American counterparts. In terms of process, this approach was systematized through the development of what is known as 'account planning'. The 'planner' originated in the efforts of Boase Massimmi Pollit and J. Walter Thompson and was predicated on the assumption that the client was too close to the brand being advertised to have an objective view of the consumer's experience. Thus the planner commissioned and analysed market research, undertook qualitative surveys by testing ads out on small samples of consumers and developed tracking studies to measure the impact of ad and promotion campaigns. From this the planner developed a 'creative brief' which gives specific guidelines for the creative team as to the target audience and the message of the ad (Davidson 1992; Lash and Urry 1994). However, this approach did not only focus on the creation of specific advertisements but was used to develop a longer-term strategic view of the creative direction of a product. It was also used to prove the effectiveness of campaigns. In this way the planner played a crucial role in reconciling the creative and market research approaches to advertising and, latterly, design. Ad-agency style planning was introduced in the Michael Peters Group in 1986 in the design of packaging (Southgate 1994: 87) and was used more frequently among design consultancies during the 1990s.

POST-FORDIST DESIGN

This euphoria was broken by the 1990–93 economic recession. The European design market contracted from a total client expenditure of $10.5 billion in 1990 to $8.5 billion in 1992 (Netherlands Design Institute 1994: 9). A handful of UK design consultancies, such as Fitch, Addison and Wolff Olins, sought a buffer zone from the effects of recession by seeking markets abroad. So, for instance, Spain became a favourite destination with its Barcelona Olympic Games and Seville World Expo year of 1992, suspending the effects of European-wide recession. However, this was only a delaying tactic. The larger consultancies drastically reduced their staffing or the size of their operations. Both Crighton and the Michael Peters Group went into receivership while Conran axed 43 staff in 1990. Fitch drastically reduced from a 1987 peak of 300 staff to less than 50 by 1991. Stories of this period abound: for instance, of staff subsequently making themselves unavailable ('out at lunch') in order to avoid random sacking. If this sounds like a desperate situation, then it illustrates the design industry's high responsiveness to economic fluctuations and dips in commercial confidence. Design business is not highly capitalized: apart from premises, which are rarely of high value, there are few assets on to which risk can be spread. Its self-proclaimed flexibility and stealth could also be its weakness. Clearly, for larger consultancies there was a conflict between their business position and the needs of running a creative studio. Share prices in design consultancies dropped dramatically in 1989: it is an industry which is too small to be of interest to the City (Jones 1991: 18).

As consultancies scaled down during the recession, many of their representatives spoke of a return to 'creative work'. However, at the same time, the recession actually provided an opportunity for smaller studios to move into the gap. Clients who had been round the first time with large-scale consultancies during the mid-1980s, and had both the experience of commissioning and had at least established a design identity for themselves, could now more confidently contract individuals and small studios to carry out design consultancy work at a much reduced cost.

So far, this chapter has focused on the development of large-scale design consultancy. However, it is important to note that the sector has historically been interdependent with a halo of smaller-scale activity undertaken by individuals and small groups. Many of them work on smaller-scale design projects for smaller clients. But they may also provide specialist subcontracted services to larger design consultancies and advertising agencies. These may include specialist strategic advice, technical skills and/or creative styles. Equally, they may be employed simply to help out larger consultancies with the high volumes of work in times of buoyant business.

The structural relationship of the consultancy to freelancer might be viewed in a similar way to the core–periphery model of industry developed in the 1980s by economists (Berger and Piore 1980; Sabel 1982; Best 1990). Their interest was in the break-up of Fordist manufacture and product development. They identified the emergence of a dualistic economy, most spectacularly evident in Italy, whereby core mass-manufacturing entities were dependent on a periphery of workshop-based industries. While the core corporation controlled product origination, assembly and distribution, the peripheral smaller workshops produced components under subcontracted conditions. This putting-out arrangement meant that specialist areas of manufacture could be drawn on according to fluctuations in demand, both in terms of volume and design: hence the term 'flexible specialization' was appended to this practice.

A step on from this was realized in the so-called Third Italy (being neither the poor agricultural south nor the heavily industrialized north), where the subcontractee workshops began to forge their own networks, undertaking their own product development and manufacture, independent of the core heavy industries. Thus a highly innovative, entrepreneurial, creative, profitable and commercially flexible cottage industry was developed from the late 1970s in Italy. Indeed, much of the avant-garde design in Italy, as represented by groups such as Memphis or Solid, drew from this manufacturing culture during the 1980s. A similar dualistic model may be discerned in the design industry. Larger design consultancies are invariably dependent on the flexible support of subcontracted freelance individuals. They provide a critical, creative edge.

Furthermore, the ever diminishing price of computer equipment (Moore's law, which has held for 40 years, suggests that the near-annual doubling of density of transistors on a microchip is accompanied by a halving of its cost; see Wollen 1998) allowed individual designers increasing access to the production tools capable of dealing with complex visual problem-solving. The mid-1990s thus saw the growth of small-scale but well-known design groups such as Anti-Rom or Tomato operating within flexible networks working for a multinationalized corporate infrastructure. Thus while they operated out of cramped studios, their clients may have been Nike, Coca-Cola or Warner Brothers.

To briefly return to advertising, once again we find developments in this sector prefiguring the design industry, broadly speaking. Towards the end of the 1980s, the Fordist scale of agencies began to be supplanted by a proliferation of much smaller ad agencies. Additionally, there was a disintegration of the production side of advertising, so that there was an increased outsourcing of media buying, design and video production business (Key Note 1990). This has been called the 'third wave' in the advertising industry.

This disintegration, then, may be read as part and parcel of a wider shift in the culture industries to a post-Fordist mode. Lash and Urry (1994: 113–16) argue that in itself, Fordism arrived particularly late in the culture industries, with the exception of cinema. So while classic Fordism is ascribed in manufacture to the 1920s onwards in the USA and in Britain from around the Second World War, the record industry did not take on such characteristics until the 1960s, publishing and advertising until the 1970s, and, as we have seen, design until the 1980s. In each of these cases, a system of vertical integration was sought according to divisions of labour. Thus in this model a large design consultancy might incorporate account managers who liaise with the client, account planners who refine the brief for the design teams, and an artwork production team who are responsible for refining the design work for presentation to the client (Southgate 1994: 90). Within each of these teams, one would find subspecialisms, so that the design team might have to bring together product, interior or graphic design, and the artwork production department may include specialist model-makers or computer-graphics experts.

In design, the early 1990s recession initiated a partial disintegration of this Fordist system in design. In order to maintain clients in lean times, design consultants would offer an increasing range of services: this meant, for instance, that graphics specialists would offer more three-dimensional orientated facilities such as exhibition stand design, while product designers would diversify to graphic design. Furthermore, some consultancies began to offer other strategic services, carrying out, for instance, design audits of companies, assessing their product and market. Indeed, many of the more prominent design consultancies dropped the word 'design' from their name altogether or added the word 'strategy' (Relph-Knight 1998: 33). Nonetheless, for the smaller consultancies there was an emergent polarization between the growing sophistication of client demand in terms of the services required and the design industry's capabilities. One design industry analyst noted that 'as clients demand more strategic input, greater use of technology, more multidisciplinary skills and increased international capability, design consultants will of necessity become larger. However, a significant proportion of consultants will choose to remain small' (Key Note 1996: 37). Indeed, while a few of the larger consultancies, such as Fitch with 305 employees in 1997, returned to their 1980s size, the majority remained as small concerns without significant expansion in the 1990s (Business Ratio Plus 1998: 287, 366). After all, clients may have demanded more sophisticated services from designers but they expected to pay fees at pre-recessionary rates, thus tightening profit margins and pressurizing them to work longer hours instead of expanding their businesses (Key Note 1996: 3). This diversification required individuals to work within a more complex system than the specialized demands of the (1980s) Fordist design era and to locate their practice within the frameworks of business and commercial culture more rigorously.

TOWARDS A BRAND ETHOS

Implicit here is a convergence between advertising and design in the 1990s. In the first instance, this came about as result of the growing dominance of the 'brand' as the driving value in the creation and mediation of goods and services. If the 1980s were dominated by an increased market in and sophistication of corporate identity design, then the 1990s saw the growth of design for a brand identity. In its most general and perhaps over-simplified sense, one might argue that once new corporate identities had been established in the 1980s, then companies could move on to the more focused characteristics of the product.

At its most basic, corporate identity is concerned with the development of a system which packages the visual style of a company and gives it a distinct and unified identity by means of design. Classically, corporate identity design has centred on the logo of a company, but its application, from its use in letterheads to advertising, is important. Leading advocates of corporate identity, such as Wally Olins, are concerned that the system of corporate identity, in large companies, extends to all its visual features to the point that it becomes the embodiment of its personality (Olins 1978). Thus the 'softer' notions of values or corporate image – the more intangible impression given by a company – are paramount. Olins promoted the notion that corporate identity was not about window-dressing a company, but a tool to modify its own behaviour, bringing cohesion to its self-image. Corporate identity, in essence, is manifestly productivist: in the first instance it is concerned with identifying the originators and distributors of goods and services.

Many similar strategies and concepts of corporate identity design are employed in branding. Its specialists equally talk of the need for in-depth research, identifying the longevity of the design, the importance of values and personality. However, the crucial difference is that in branding the designer is concerned with the actual products and services *to be consumed*, rather than the producing corporation that originates and distributes them. Sometimes these might be the same, most famously in the case of Richard Branson's Virgin Group, whose corporate identity and brand identity coincide across a range of goods and services, from a cola drink, to air and rail travel, to financial services and internet provision. Conversely, a corporation might own and distribute a range of goods: thus the multinational Procter & Gamble produces a range of soap brands, some of which may even 'compete' with each other.

The burgeoning literature on branding in the 1990s uniformly proclaimed the primacy of the consumer. Nicholas Kochan of leading brand specialists Interbrand wrote: 'The brand will not attach to the group of products but to the buyers, to the consumers themselves' (1996: xiv). Paul Southgate of Wickens Tutt Southgate puts this attachment into a process when 'there comes a point in a brand's life when ownership is subtly transferred to the consumer. Beyond this point, perception is reality. The brand's values are no more and no less than what the consumer *believes* them to be' (Southgate 1994: 19). It seems, then, that the job of the branding expert is to manage the closing of the perceived separation between the producer and the consumer. This requires a vigorous understanding of the brand's audience. Indeed, while design management in the 1980s centred on the systematizing of the design innovation process, in the 1990s it progressively veered towards the discussion of the problems of managing the interrelationship between the brand and the market.

Within this move there is a marked shift towards valuing the intangible aspects of design production. Brand identity incorporates many features: the names that products are given, the abstract sound that name invokes, the typeface employed to communicate it, the 'trade dress' in terms of colours, forms and textures employed, unique design details which identify a particular brand, the patina of copywriting … a complex mesh of visual, material and/or textual factors. These may be the tangible expression of immaterial concepts that revolve around the brand's personality. Since the mid-1980s, intangible assets of corporations, which very much include the brand, have been incorporated with increasing frequency into the company accounts (Napier 1994). How these assets are actually evidenced through design has sometimes led to complex legal battles where the extent to which these values are actually expressed in design terms has come under close scrutiny (see Schmitt and Simonson 1997: Ch. 8).

SPEEDING UP DESIGN AND PRODUCTION

If the rise of branding in design draws attention further to packaging or mediation, then it is important to recognize that a fully-fledged brand-led design approach brings together a wide range of design and marketing skills. With regard to the actual products, it is useful to take note of the growth of 'concurrent design' in facilitating this process. This approach to design and manufacture effectively does away with a linear system of development whereby, in a corporation, departments worked in a chain of command. Instead, teams from different departments work simultaneously on the development of products, continuously interchanging information and the results of development. Of crucial importance in this process was the use of computer-aided design (CAD) packages to speed the exchange of complex design information between individuals and groups within the development team (see Nevins and Whitney 1989). Equally, information technologies have allowed for a more iterative relationship between designer and client, so that design proposals can be moved backwards and forwards between them with greater ease.

In culture and manufacturing industries, a distinction between 'above' and 'below the line' elements of creative production is made. The 'above the line' parts are those that the product's audience directly experiences while the 'below the line' activities are those in the development of the product which are not encountered. In design terms, above the line would include packaging, branding, advertising and the product itself; the below the line work would be in the engineering of an object, the design of tooling for its manufacture, the market research and interpretation. Concurrent design effectively brings the above and below the line aspects together. It means that data on market trends can be incorporated into the design process at various levels, not merely in the external styling of the object. Changes in functional needs, be they aesthetic or utilitarian, can be responded to more cheaply, quickly and effectively. In this way, the producer/consumer gap was drawn together by yet another route. The growth of rapid prototyping – where computer-generated, virtual product models can be relatively quickly transformed into physical artefacts – has again speeded up this process with respect to product design.

The development of 'just-in-time' methods – pioneered by Toyota in Japan from the 1950s onwards – further closed this producer/consumer gap. Under this system, goods are manufactured and distributed according to demand rather than being held in stock. Thus market fluctuations in volume and taste can be responded to more cheaply while capital is not tied up in holding components and finished products in stock. This requires a sophisticated production control system and a more flexible tooling able to change output rapidly.

DESIGN WITHIN DISORGANIZED CAPITALISM

The introduction of concurrent design, just-in-time methods and flexible specialization, either in large-scale manufacture such as the car industry or in the case of high-technology cottage industries of a Third Italy model, form part of the productive chain of what Offe (1985) called 'disorganized capitalism'. Offe, and subsequently Lash and Urry (1987), reflected on a broad condition of late-20th-century society in the developed world wherein shifts from regulation, order and concentration to independence, disorder and fragmentation in economic, political and cultural life are experienced. While these writers differ in their approach, they share several conceptual shifts which are useful for understanding the growth and character of design production in recent years (see Figure 2.3).

Lash and Urry later note (1994: 123) the importance of the culture industries, which would include design, in activating this shift from organized to disorganized capitalism. From the point of view of production, apart from the brief Fordist interlude of the 1980s already noted, the design business's propensity to constant flexibility and fragmentation, its increasing client and consumer responsiveness and its championing of visual, semantic, intuitive and creative values represent important steps in this development (see Figure 2.2).

The closing of the distance between designer, client and, indeed, end-user fosters the use of intuitive skills. In the former case, design work gets as close to the finished article as one might get, with the possible exception of traditional craft practice. In other words, there are few or no intermediary elements of production involved. In terms of design for digital applications, what the designer sees on screen is what the end-user will see. Equally, on-screen renderings of products in CAD are converted into tooling data for production. In such cases, 'what the culture

Fordist production (organized capitalism)	Just-in-time production (disorganized capitalism)
PRODUCTION PROCESS	
Mass production of homogeneous goods	Small-batch production
Uniformity and standardization	Flexible and small-batch production of a variety of product types
Resource-driven	Demand-driven
Vertical and (in some cases) horizontal integration	(quasi-) vertical integration subcontracting
LABOUR	
Single task performance by worker	Multiple tasks
High degree of job specialization	Elimination of job demarcation
Vertical labour organization	More horizontal labour organization
SPACE	
Functional spatial specialization	Spatial clustering and agglomeration
Spatial division of labour	Spatial integration
Homogenization of regional labour markets	Labour market diversification
STATE	
Regulation	Deregulation
Rigidity	Flexibility
Sociolization of welfare centralization	Privatization of collective needs decentralization and sharpened interregional/intercity competition
'subsidy' state/city	'entrepreneurial' state/city
National regional polices	'territorial' regional policies
IDEOLOGY	
Mass consumption of consumer durales: the consumption society	Individualized consumption: 'yuppie'-culture
Modernism	Postmodernism
Socialization	Individualization the 'spectacle society'

Figure 2.2   Fordist and flexible production: transitions in economic, political and ideological realms (adapted from Moulaert and Swyngedouw 1989)

sector entails is not cognitive knowledge but a hermeneutic sensibility ... or [an ability] to intuit the semantic needs of their public' (Lash and Urry 1994: 123). Thus the designer is involved in the interpretation of popular culture, fuelling it with further inflexions and innovations. The designer's understanding of the software-product's audience is filtered and synthesized with his or her creativity, itself a synthesis of influences.

However, at the same time, the idea of 'disorganized capitalism' perhaps belies its highly systemized processes of accounting, routine and measurement. Information technologies certainly facilitate the crafting of design in quicker, more direct ways. But they also provide the apparatus for the management of the tracking of design projects. As consultancies take on multiple projects so they have to ensure that they run to time and budget. They have to apportion tasks to team members and account for the hours spent on them. Software packages such as Harvest or Oracle Workflow provide accounting, management and monitoring systems to aid in this. They also facilitate a much more detailed analysis than was previously possible of the profitability of particular clients and projects. They also allow a similar logic to be applied to the contributions of individual staff members.

This systemization provides a structure through which creative decisions are regulated. But it also helps in the speeding up of through flow of design projects as the sequencing of its stages can be more tightly timetabled and designers' time more sharply allocated. This echoes wider changes in the economy instigated in the 1980s and further developed throughout the 1990s.

THE NEW ECONOMY

The switch from Fordist to just-in-time production in the 1980s marks the instigation of the so-called 'New Economy'. Originating in the USA, this term was first used in an article in the magazine *Newsweek* in 1995. Conceptions of the New Economy incorporated many of the facets of the economy that feature within the 'disorganized capitalism' notion: flexible production, demand-driven manufacture and distribution, subcontracting. These were precursors to the development of a 'knowledge economy'. This is where businesses concentrated on the areas critical to their success and where they had competitive advantage. This means that all other routine aspects, such as transportation, manufacture and customer services, could be outsourced so that their chief concerns lay in brands, product design and technical features. The development of information technology networks and systems was crucial to the growth of outsourcing. Needless to say, the growth of e-commerce contributed to the ensuing optimism surrounding the New Economy. Internet transaction systems such as Amazon.com and eBay.com (both launched in 1995) stood out as beacons as to how new business may be undertaken.

At the heart of New Economy practices was the idea of 'faster, better, cheaper'. This slogan has its origins in the defence spending policy of America's Reagan era of the 1980s and was adopted into the NASA space programme from 1989 through the 1990s (McCurdy 2001). In terms of 'faster', this ideology was highlighted by computer hardware entrepreneur Michael Dell's declaration that 'Velocity, the compression of time and distance backward into the supply chain, and then forward to the customer, is the ultimate source of competitive advantage' (Dell, cited in Thackara 2005a: 29). Dell Computers are notable for their 'mass specialization' system, whereby all computers are built to order rather than warehoused, thus facilitating a sharper responsiveness to consumer demand and more efficient stock control. The core idea of 'better' is perhaps under-lined by the turn towards foregrounding creative strategies within business management. Thus books such as Howkins's *The Creative Economy: How People Make Money from Ideas* (2001) or Ray's *The Cultural Creatives* (2001) have become the standard fodder of business manage-ment schools for this line of thinking. The notion of 'cheaper' has been underlined, not least, by the opening-up of the many new manufacturing and service bases of Eastern Europe, the Indian sub-continent and the Far East where labour costs have, so far, been dramatically lower. Thus, for example, the average cost of a television and DVD player has dropped by 45 per cent over the last ten years (Beckett 2006). Meanwhile, the diversity of goods has widened. A new product was reportedly launched every three-and-a-half minutes in the world during 2005. This incorporated 87,000 products in the food and drink sector and 68,000 non-food products (Balmond 2006).

The organization of the design industry may be viewed as paradigmatic of the kinds of labour arrangements and sensibilities that lie at the heart of the functioning of the New Economy. McRobbie (2002) notes how the same entrepreneurial practices of club culture in the 1980s, which already had close ties with some sectors of design practice, were transferred into design. Among these she lists their multi-skilling and despecialization, how creative work follows the neo-liberal model of employment with its stress on entrepreneurialism and individualism and the importance of what she calls 'network sociality' to their kind of work. Arch supporter of New Economy thinking, the American magazine *Fast Company* supported the claim that busi-ness leaders should not only understand design but also work creatively as if they were designers (Breen 2005).

If the 1980s saw the steady progress towards the foundation of the New Economy in a way that foregrounded production issues, so the 1990s was the decade of its development towards the ascendance of financialization. Having finely tuned their value-chain to maximize production efficiency, the latter is where companies and institutions give greater emphasis to their financial management in order to maintain share value or straightforward survival (Froud et al. 2000). Here greater emphasis is laid on strategies that maintain the value of shares, brands, real estate or capital flows – in other words, on the relationships of tangible and intangible assets. The manage-ment priorities of corporations, and increasingly public institutions such as universities or civic authorities, are given to manoeuvring in almost militaristic style campaigns within a competitive field. Within this prioritization, for example, financial services systems are able to liquefy the value of real estate, thus facilitating investment and an even greater flow of capital (Sassen 2003). Equally, the Ford Motor Company made more money from financial services than from the sale of cars and trucks (Lury 2004: 3). In these circumstances, design becomes a promotional tool to maintain share value or attract borrowers and lenders as much as in the shaping of the hardware that underpins them.

CONCLUSION

The 1980s and 1990s were fundamental decades for design practice. As a growth sector it enjoyed the freedom to test its own limits: initially, consultancies developed to an unprecedented and sub-sequently unsurpassed size. Alongside this growth, graphics and interior-related design emerged dominant as against product design, reflecting the structural changes in the economy and commerce at large. Simultaneously, they began to develop systems for processing commissions, some of which were adopted from models employed by advertising agencies. Such systematizing placed many design practices into a neo-Fordist mode, which ultimately would not allow them the flexibility required in a changing market. Maintaining a balance between creative and strategic practices has been, perhaps, the central concern of design in the late-20th century.

The subsequent fragmentation of the design industry as the result of the economic recession of the early 1990s in turn led to a disembedding of its actors so that new alliances between design, advertising and other creative industries were formed. This further encouraged the diversity of design practices: the parameters of what a design consultancy might actually do widened to over-lap with other sectors, such as public relations, management consultancy and advertising. Thus a combination of designers increasingly working alongside marketing-related sectors within the growing dominance of branding and the globalization of markets meant that the culture of design was drawn ever closer to the culture of consumption. By the late 1990s, design was increasingly imbricated into the pressures of the New Economy, becoming instrumental in delivering 'faster, better, cheaper'. This created demands for high speed of turnover, facilitated by digital inform-ation and manufacturing technology developments, more creative and strategic thinking and the exploitation of global distribution and manufacture. These provided further challenges to raise the professional status of designers.

The first decade of the 21st century brought a fresh wave of design growth, particularly outside the USA and Europe. While different regions and nations have their distinct industrial, commer-cial, institutional and governmental structures and relationships to each other, the processes of globalization also reveal commonalities in the organization and conception of design, not least in the discourses and debates that course through it and which are the subject of the next chapter.

CHAPTER 3

DESIGNERS AND DESIGN DISCOURSE

How are different definitions of design and images of the designer used by different people? Chapter 3 is devoted to exploring the professional and cultural construction of the designer and, subsequently, the difference between these and the representation, self-representation and actual practice of designers. The discourses of professionalization, marginality and authorship need to be addressed in order to understand the relationships between designers, their clients and their public. The chapter concludes by looking at some attempts to update this discussion in the face of new contexts and practices of design. In particular, it reviews the ways by which design has found its way into and been used by management discourses. This does not mean that all design has moved in that direction. The profession constantly accumulates new areas of practice, adding to its diversity and fragmentation.

In the previous chapter the recent changes in the organization and commercial context of design practice were explained. It concluded by arguing that on the one hand these conditions of production meant that designers were involved in a constant positioning and repositioning of themselves in response to these changing conditions, and that on the other hand their practice increasingly pushed them towards a more complex relationship with the culture of consumption. In both these cases an amalgamation of creative and strategic skills was at play.

This complexity leads us to the possibility that a solely production-based account of design is insufficient and the objects of its production must be interpreted through the interaction of information and values between the realms of production, consumption and the designers themselves. Thus under each of these headings we can identify the different causative elements we might take into consideration in creating an account of design objects, images and spaces. Scholarship and journalism in fields that relate to design have predominantly tended to isolate one approach from another, concentrating either on the business practices of design, the authorship of the designer or the reception of design goods and services by consumers. Chapter 2 began to suggest, however, that the conditions of disorganized capitalism imply that the culture of design integrates these categories so that their interaction becomes increasingly vibrant.

DEFINITIONS OF DESIGN

The meaning of the word 'design' is much contested. The debate concerning its origins is unlikely to be resolved given the breadth of interpretations that the word takes. John Walker reminds us that:

> it can refer to a process (the act or practice of designing); or to the result of that process (a design, sketch, plan or model); or to the products manufactured with the aid of a design (design goods); or to the look or overall pattern of a product ('I like the design of that dress'). (1989: 23)

It has therefore accumulated several different uses. Meanings of design are many and shift according to the context in which the word is used.

Some critics seek a consciously open definition of design. In his cult book *Design for the Real World* (1972), Victor Papanek began with the words:

> All men [sic] are designers. All that we do, almost all the time, is design, for design is basic to all human activity. The planning and patterning of any act toward a desired, foreseeable end constitutes the design process. Any attempt to separate design to make it a thing by itself, works counter to the fact that design is the primary underlying matrix of life. (1972: 3)

Papanek takes an agitational standpoint, attempting therefore to denude design of any separateness. 'All men are designers', he tells us. By contrast with Papanek's proclamation, much of the history of design may be read as the history of individuals and groups who have striven to separate design from other commercial and cultural practices. In doing so they have attempted to identify themselves and their practice as something that bestows things, pictures, words and places with 'added value'. Within this paradigm, design becomes the range of goods, spaces and services that are shaped by the intervention of professional designers. It no longer refers to the countless objects that are formed and consumed within everyday life and which do not, of themselves, carry that level of cultural capital.

The connection with Bourdieu's notion of cultural capital (1984: 12) here is important. Put most briefly (Bourdieu's theories will be explored in more detail in subsequent chapters), 'cultural capital' refers to one's ability to make distinctions between cultivated and vulgar taste. This notion effectively pushes design into a reflexive mode whereby its value becomes self-consciously recognized. Design thus links the economic to the cultural. Indeed, design emanates from the discourses of a culturally dynamic sector of society, an avant-garde metropolitan bourgeoisie. In his discussion of Veblen and Bourdieu, Hayward (1998) articulates the role of the avant-garde in a 'symbolic struggle' to 'step ahead' as cultural goods slip from left to right, from the 'cutting edge' into the mainstream. As such, varying degrees of 'designeriness' are inscribed into its practice.

The study of design history is embedded into institutions that largely support the reproduction of this meaning. It is mostly taught in art and design colleges as a support to practice-based courses. Unusually, it may be mobilized to challenge dominant practices of design through, for instance, feminist or ecologically inspired critiques. More often, however, it acts to reinforce very specific, and indeed restrictive, understandings of what design is and how it should be carried out. Much of the history and criticism of design therefore falls within a specific formal canon, thereby giving it a refined language to legitimate itself and a self-perpetuating logic that identifies 'good design' as against 'bad design' or 'kitsch'. It therefore conspires to maintain the highly reflexive, self-conscious nature of design. Chaney puts this forcefully:

> Designers' use of a language of style to ironically evoke or play with other contexts of use makes style a reflexive medium: a way of talking about itself and a way of talking about modernity. The logic of a process in which the self-consciousness or reflexivity of design grows more important is that the goods of economic exchange begin to lose any foundation in intrinsic value or function. ... It seems that an inevitable consequence of a reflexivity of production is that style comes to supersede substance. (1996: 150)

Perhaps there is a creeping pessimism in his words here. The suggestion is that the manoeuvrings of contemporary design require it to abandon all hope and purpose in addressing real human needs; that it becomes an end in itself, the mere producer of 'desires', possibly losing all relevance to its public. A view of design culture, following Chaney's reasoning, is that its world of design production and consumption is self-serving – that design culture produces its own way of justifying itself, regardless of real societal need.

In this line of thinking, the object and its mediation become one. The way by which an object is communicated to its public – as a *design* object – in turn becomes its primary value and subsequently the object itself becomes part of that communication. Equally, this is how a designed product works within a brand ethos. The object carries an emblematic status as an image. This may be part of the late-20th-century shift in design whereby the product has increasingly aspired to the graphic, or, as Lash and Urry put it, 'What is increasingly produced are not material objects, but *signs*' (1994: 4).

It is true that all man-made things, images and spaces are designed in some way. Or to put it another way, design is anything that doesn't happen by accident. They have all been subject to some level of planning and thought no matter how conscious or unconscious this might be. However, within the argument I am advancing in this book, we have to consider that definitions of design can also be discursive. In other words, how, when, where and why something is termed as being 'design' indicates something about its position or status that is generated by and for it. In respect, Judy Attfield (2000) draws a distinction of 'objects with attitude' as compared with everyday things. However this distinction may be described or the processes that produce it are analysed, a key issue is that of the delineation of the professional from the amateur designer and the historical debates that have formed this.

THE WORD 'DESIGN' IN HISTORY

In the same way that we have seen the practice of design under continual revision, so the definition of design is constantly and self-consciously not only being constructed, but also decentred, dispersed and disorganized. An historical overview of the development of the word 'design' as a practice is useful in exploring the tension between the establishment of design as a 'value added' activity and its intrinsic disembedding mechanisms.

Walker (1989: 23) draws our attention to the Renaissance use of the *disegno*, which literally meant 'drawing'. During this period drawing was the tool employed in the planning, conceptualizing phase that preceded the making of paintings, sculptures and so forth. Thus the practice of *disegno* involved intellectual thought and effectively separated conception and execution. A division of labour in the studios of artists did exist: apprentices would execute some of the more menial tasks, such as the preparation of the canvas and even the painting of backgrounds, leaving, for instance, the 'master' to paint faces and details. While, then, this division of labour did not go so far as to completely separate mental and manual tasks, it nonetheless inferred that a hierarchy existed between the planning and the making aspects of cultural production. This notion of *disegno* coincides with what Balcioglu (1994) terms the 'first phase' of design of the Renaissance and Enlightenment. During these periods, he argues, design had a more open, widely used definition connected to purposes, aims and intentions.

It is clear that the word has stood at the fulcrum of a struggle for professional recognition. In discussing the origins of typography – a subset of design in general – Robin Kinross (1992) argues that it comes into being as it is brought into consciousness through language. He locates its origins in the Enlightenment via an early treatise on typography: Joseph Moxon's *Mechanick Exercises* (1683–84). Kinross cites the following words:

> By a typographer, I do not mean a printer, as he is vulgarly accounted, any more than Dr Dee means a carpenter or mason to be an architect: but by a typographer, I mean such a one, who by his own judgement, from solid reasoning within himself, can either perform, or direct others to perform from the beginning to the end, all the handy-works and physical operations relating to typographie. (Moxon, cited in Kinross 1992: 15)

This fascinating passage indicates a struggle to position the typographer against the more 'vulgar' practice of the printer. It marks a step in the profession of design to delineate itself from that of a trade. Notably, in order to fix an identity, Moxon begins by describing what typography is *not*.

During the 'second phase' of the 19th century, this discussion of word usage becomes further refined and effectively causes the term 'design' to lose some of its potential power. The debate in Britain revolved around an awareness of the misleading parallel between the English word 'design' and the French word *dessin*. While the French 'Ecoles de Dessin' were exclusively directed towards the teaching of drawing – using the word *dessin* in its literal sense – from the mid-19th century the British 'Schools of Design' were dedicated to a broader curriculum to promote visual innovation for manufactured articles. It is not surprising that henceforward, mid-19th century reformers such as Henry Cole replaced the word 'design' with 'industrial art', 'decorative art' or 'applied art' to avoid its reductionist connotations and express greater practical and professional complexity. It also allowed the 'designers' to momentarily hijack the word 'art' to lend further status to their activities.

There was a serious disadvantage to this linguistic manoeuvring. 'Applied art' suggested that the profession was involved in the superficial addition of aesthetic measures to objects, rather than in the creation of the article itself. The 'third phase' of the early 20th century saw the retrieval of the word 'design' in order to separate it out again from art. Thus some individuals, in particular W.R. Lethaby, who was founder of the Design and Industries Association in 1915, struggled to keep the word 'art' at bay. Meanwhile, the Americans Walter Dorwin Teague, Raymond Loewy, Norman Bel Geddes and Henry Dreyfuss were calling themselves 'industrial designers' from the late 1920s, and it was mostly their influence that helped to re-establish the use of the word 'design' in Britain (Balcioglu 1994).

THE PROFESSIONAL STATUS OF DESIGN

The word 'design', then, is intimately bound up in an historical process of the professionalization of its practice. It was important that it was recognized as a pursuit that required specific education and training and could thus meet certain expected standards of knowledge, intellect and skill. As we have seen, it did this by aligning itself with other intellectualized disciplines such as fine art and differentiating itself from other trades such as printing.

This professionalizing process has involved the proliferation of institutions dedicated to the promotion of various aspects of design and the systematizing or safeguarding of its practice. These have been state or regionally funded organizations, usually instigated by designers yet highly responsive to the greater demands of government policy. They have proliferated and by 2012, across Europe, for example, there were some 78 of these; among the European member states, only Bulgaria, Cyprus, Malta and Romania were without national representation for design (European Design Innovation Initiative 2012). These various design centres have therefore frequently altered in their aims and organization as state and regional policies have changed (Whitely 1991; Julier 1995), but they are also active in debating and shaping common understandings of what the professional status and requirements of designers might be.

Professional organizations to support and validate the work of designers that are funded mostly through member subscriptions have also proliferated. A calculation put the number of these across Europe at 50 (European Design Innovations Initiative 2012), although the actual number is probably much higher. National and regional design centres may provoke a regional, national or even international homogenizing of understandings of design, while professional organizations may splinter and fragment these. As design has developed further specializations, so new professional design organizations have come about. Thus, for instance, with the rise of exhibition and museum design in the 1980s came a series of calls in the UK to establish an association for designers specializing in that field. This in turn would consolidate that discipline as a profession and help to identify its particularities, distinguishing it not merely as an extension of graphic or interior design.

The effectiveness of both national or regional institutions or independent organizations in securing and safeguarding the professional status for designers has been variable. From 1992 to 1994, for example, the UK Design Council facilitated the award of the British Standards Institution's 5750 mark to design consultancies. This awarded an 'objective' recognition of their qualities in management, client service and efficiency. Thus the institution of the Design Council was acting to establish professional standards in design. Take-up of this procedure among design consultancies was mixed, with some seeing the British Standards system as far too simplistic for application in the design industry (see, for example, Letters to *Design Week*, 23 October 1992).

Equally, the issue of 'free pitching', which arose in the late 1980s, showed that design practice in a market economy could also evade professional regulation. Free pitching involves a situation where a prospective client invites several consultancies to put forward design proposals for a scheme; out of this just one consultancy would be invited to complete the design project and collect a fee. In this system, consultancies risked spending time and resources for no financial return if they did not win the pitch. If the design industry had had a single institutional representative, then a blanket agreement among designers regarding the acceptability of this approach may have been arrived at. But with a proliferation of representative bodies, a consensus could not be achieved. Furthermore, free pitching might be resisted in buoyant times, but when there is a struggle to find clients, consultancies may not be so choosy. In whichever case, regulation, as design commentator Jeremy Myerson noted, 'points up the folly of trying to engrave regulation on tablets of stone for a business as fluid and fast-changing as this one is' (1990).

Fluctuating client demand and the design industry's own lack of institutional cohesion have meant that it has been largely unable to establish its own professional norms. This has been met by a pressure from below in terms of 'design entryism'. Briefly put, while other professions, such as law, architecture or accountancy, have norms and systems of conduct that are established by both the state and their own institutional arrangements – educational and professional bodies, in other words – design has no such normative systems. There is no minimum standard of attainment of training required for individuals to call themselves designers and practise commercially. This pressure from below has been exacerbated in recent years by the development of digital technologies. For instance, desk top publishing programmes provide easy-to-use templates for designing to different formats, thus obviating the need for a specialist to do the layout. New technologies have allowed a partial 'democratization' of design through allowing access to its tools: tasks which were once the preserve of trained specialists now become almost menial. Neither is there an agreed fee system for design services. The only known instance of such a situation was generated under Martial Law in Poland in the mid-1980s as a way of regulating entrepreneurial designers, and was short-lived and ineffective (Crowley et al. 1992: 87). This means that a rife system of fee undercutting is possible. In a climate lacking any professional and educational norms, the 'outer edges' of design practice – either the highly conceptual ends of design consultancy bordering on other professions or the low end of print design and production – are vulnerable to 'entryism' by non-design specialists. In these circumstances there is even greater demand for the designer to identify his or her services as both professional and specialist.

The problems of professionalization are not restricted to the design industry. American sociologist Nathan Glazer (discussed in Schön 1991: Ch. 2) identified an historical split between what he called 'major' and 'minor' professions that are held in tension. Major professions have 'normative curricula' in their training in that there are agreed national standards in their content and assessment. They are also professionally regulated with standard agreed working procedures and norms of commercial conduct. They also often have an agreed, but not fixed, structure of pay. For example, in the USA, Canada, New Zealand, Australia and the UK, as in many other countries, the architecture profession is standardized by registration or licensing requirements from a recognized institution. In the UK this is the Royal Institute of British Architects, and in the USA it is the American Institute of Architects. Norms of content and quality assurance in architectural education are under approval from its respective registering body. More rigorous codes of professional practice and conduct are enforced than those we have seen in design.

Meanwhile, the 'minor' professions, such as design, exhibit diverse curricula, are not professionally regulated, and their pay structures are largely market-driven. In many cases the minor profession historically has referred to a major profession for its research paradigms and its norms and procedures. At the same time the minor occupation has been engaged in a struggle to build its own discursive structures, to free itself of dominance and develop its own professional culture.

Wherever design is practised, professional organizations are established to promote and safeguard the activities of designers. For example, the UK sports the Chartered Society of Designers and the Design Business Association, as well as numerous regional groups such as the South Coast Design Forum, the Cornwall Design Forum, the West of England Design Forum and so on. But their chief focus is on the general promotion of design, rather than in the generation of self-regulatory norms or 'best practice' models. They do not lead to their establishment as normative bodies overseeing and validating professional and educational processes. The American Institute of Graphic Arts publishes 'Standards of Professional Practice' that its members sign up to. This covers broad business ethics issues such as responsibility to clients and to other designers. But it doesn't lay down any minimum expectation of educational achievement to practice or stipulate the levels of continuing professional development required. The Society of Graphic Designers of Canada publishes a broadly similar 'Code of Ethics and Professional Conduct for Graphic Designers', as does the UK-based Chartered Society of Designers. However, membership of such organisations is not a prerequisite to professional practice, although it may accord some status and recognition with clients.

Design has historically been held as a minor profession to architecture. Certainly this was the case in the late-19th and early-20th centuries. However, in more recent years, its points of professional reference have been more diverse. We have seen in Chapter 2 how the design industry has taken many cues in its management from advertising, marketing and management consultancy. Furthermore, while in the modern age some other 'minor' professions, such as nursing, are essential to social well-being, design's necessity has been a harder case to argue.

DESIGNERS AS 'CULTURAL INTERMEDIARIES'

Beside the questions of professional recognition through education systems and its own supporting institutions, it may well be that designers occupy a sociologically determined position. This means that this is not a permanent state, of course, and we must be cautiously aware that this is not going to be identical in all geographical contexts. If the self-image and status of designers are 'sociologically determined' in part, then the process of this determination will change according the different cultural and social factors. However, Pierre Bourdieu provides a useful starting point for thinking about this.

As a social class, designers may belong to what Bourdieu calls the 'new petite bourgeoisie' (1984). For Bourdieu this class includes 'all the occupations involving presentation and representation' (1984: 359) that are involved in the 'symbolic work of producing needs' (1984: 365). Jobs in advertising and sales would fit this description, but so would some public sector or non-governmental organization (NGO) occupations in social and health care, such as marriage guidance, sex therapists, dieticians and vocational guidance, where the need for these services has to be argued in order to *create* their jobs. They are involved in 'needs production'. Bourdieu also notes that certain sectors of this new petite bourgeoisie, such as in media, advertising and design, by dint of working as 'cultural intermediaries' are taste-creators. Their own preferences tend to be in marginal culture such as the jazz, cinema and painting of the avant-garde. As such, these particular professionals tend to be the people who mediate 'cutting edge' cultural forms to a wider audience.

This identity may bring these 'cultural intermediaries' into conflict with any aspiration for solid, professional recognition, for, as adherents to this 'new petite bourgeoisie', designers only half-heartedly aspire to a *conservative* professional status. There is something of a self-marginalization going on here that runs through design's educational and commercial system. In their sociological analysis of British art and design school culture, Frith and Horne (1987) note that, unlike other subjects in higher education, art does not lay emphasis on academic qualifications (e.g. GCSEs, A-levels) for its entry requirements. Instead, much emphasis is laid on the student's portfolio and interview as evidence of their creative potential; beyond the basic skills of drawing and visualization, greater emphasis is laid on personality attributes in the selection process. Once the student is enrolled, the relative lack of strict timetabling, the provision of personal studio space instead of classrooms, and the emphasis on individual creativity alongside the cultivation of a group, studio-based atmosphere conspire to produce a working practice 'which assumes the status of lifestyle' (Frith and Horne 1987: 28).

As such the art school ethos separates itself from other educational cultures and actively resists incorporation into the mainstream. This has certainly been the case through much of Western Europe and the USA, but in the UK it has been particularly pointed. Frith and Horne argue that successive governments have attempted, and failed, to make art and design education more vocational, more 'responsive' to the needs of industry. Instead, the art school experience continues, largely, to promote a Romantic, marginal vision of itself, celebrating 'the critical edge marginality allows, turning it into a sales technique, a source of celebrity' (Frith and Horne 1987: 30). Thus the art and design education system itself is a sociologically determined recipe for the manufacture of Bourdieu's 'new petite bourgeoisie'. It continues to reproduce and promote specific attitudes to what being an artist or designer means and how their lives might be lived.

It is important to reinforce here that designers draw on this system to differentiate themselves from other professions and educations, to identify and distinguish themselves and their skills. But they are also involved in constant manoeuvrings to differentiate themselves from each other. This differentiating system draws on myths of individuated creativity inherited from art education in particular and fine art culture in general. I self-consciously use 'art' instead of 'art and design' for, in the first place, the design student's first contact in post-school art and design education is in the more generalized art-and-design foundation studies. Here the majority of tutors come from a fine art background and draw on individual (largely male) artist myths as a motivating factor (Clegg and Mayfield 1999). Furthermore, as we shall see in the next section, the system of design curatorship, publication and thus stardom draws predominantly on a fine art tradition of representation. In both these cases, the search for and production of novelty and difference are important.

Differentiation is also necessary for the commercial survival of design consultancies: after all, they are competing with each other in order to achieve market share. Ultimately this results in design consultancies who position themselves as brands rather as if they were products or services in a competitive market (Barnard 2000). This may be done through their reputation for thoroughness, efficiency and cost-effectiveness, their experience, breadth and depth of knowledge, but they may also use their creative profile. They have to be recognized as taste-makers. One of the techniques towards this aim is to 'curate themselves' through the production of catalogues, books and exhibitions about their own work. Similarly, Wally Olins suggested in an article entitled 'Getting New Business' in 1981 that an effective design consultant should ensure that they published articles 'in influential publications like *Management Today* or *The Director*' (Olins, quoted in Baker 1989: 276). Consultancies might also develop their own slogans (such as Elmwood Design's 'There Is No Finish Line') or mission statements as part of this self-identification process, or highlight a specialism within their own 'corporate' approach to designing. So, for instance, in 1998 design consultancy The Partners began to promote itself as a consultancy which offers 'third brain thinking': mixing the logical (left brain) with the intuitive (right brain). They claimed that designers are adept at combining these two characteristics and subsequently developed this 'third brain' concept for recruitment and teambuilding the consultancy for clients (Valentine 1998). Meanwhile, design consultants Michael Wolff and Piers Schmidt developed 'The Fourth Room', aimed at using creative design principles to help companies plan future strategy (Thackray 1999). In doing so, designers and design consultants are not only curating themselves, but also effectively writing their own histories: 'historicizing' themselves.

HISTORICITY AND MODERNISM IN DESIGN DISCOURSE

Much of the history of design has been written and disseminated to effectively support this system of professionalization and differentiation. Many of the earlier design history texts focused on the successive attempts at public recognition of design as both a profession and a product (e.g. Carrington 1976), and this turns the narrative into a discourse of 'pioneering modern design heroes' in the face of a largely uninformed public. Part of the point of many of these texts was, then, to *inform* them and build a respectable status for their profession. This has privileged a particular process and product in design: the account of design has been progressively separated from the reality of its practice.

Central to the historiography of design has been the emplacement and refutation of modernism. This dates back to Nikolaus Pevsner's *Pioneers of the Modern Movement: From William Morris to Walter Gropius*, first published in 1936. It traced a linear, progressive perception of design history, a steady development of architectural style, based on the work and aspirations of individual architects and designers, from the historicism of William Morris and the Arts and Crafts movement to the 'machine aesthetic' of Walter Gropius and the Modern Movement. In this book, Pevsner established the canon of 'form follows function' as the governing design ideology of the 20th century. His view no doubt reflects the dominance of German art and architectural history wherein, as Gropius himself professed, architecture is the leading edge in the development of design.

Pevsner's text is essentially teleological in that it strives to explain everything in terms of an historical inevitability. This again is derived from Pevsner's Germanic training. A Pevsnerean account therefore requires a selective, straight-line approach to history. Clearly his text privileges modernism as the apotheosis of design: the narrative builds towards its conclusion at the Bauhaus where the resolution of conflicts between art and industry are resolved. As Heskett remarks, '*Pioneers* imposed a linear interpretation upon an age that was diverse and plural in nature, taking part of a complex picture and representing it as the only significant element' (1986: 7). It should be noted that Pevsner was not neutral in this account: he was an editorial member of *Architectural Review*, a journal largely dominated by the modernist canon from the 1930s. Interestingly, as if to reinforce the 'design = modernism' equation, the book was published from 1949 as *Pioneers of Modern Design* rather than *Pioneers of the Modern Movement*.

While many subsequent texts rework Pevsner's narrative through different routes, the structure remains the same. Sigfried Gideon's *Mechanization Takes Command: A Contribution to Anonymous History*, published in 1948, eschew's Pevsner's great designers' view to foreground the history of industry, technology and social customs. Nonetheless, the notion of progress towards a maturity guides the narrative. Likewise Reyner Banham's *Theory and Design in the First Machine Age* of 1960 reworks notions of functionalism, but still discusses the same objects, people and lineage as Pevsner.

This system supports what John Walker calls 'the canon of design', whereby 'the baton of genius or avant-garde innovation passes from the hand of one great designer to the next in an endless chain of achievement' (Walker 1989: 63). Meanwhile, Richard Buchanan (1998b: 260) reminds us of the vast void between the aspirations of some reforming designers and the activities of the consuming public: the acres of publications on William Morris, the Bauhaus and so on, do not explain that public taste often went in quite the opposite direction! For example, while the design of tea-sets was a frequent design exercise for modernists (see Julier 1998), it does not explain why the world's biggest selling product of this type was Harold Hadcroft's distinctly historicist 'Old Country Roses' – featuring floral patterns and a neo-Roccoco form – which has sold 100 million pieces since its introduction in 1962 (Woodham 1997: 217).

The representation of design has been dominated by the achievements of individuals in the first place; second, by the aesthetics and ideology of modernism; and third, via specific objects of a certain type. Product design in general only accounted for 8 per cent of design business in 1995–96 (*Design Week* 1996) and yet it has dominated the pages of design history books and the minds of design historians alike. Moreover, this narrow account is in itself dominated by the discussion of furniture design.

The cabinet or bureau was a standard exercise of the 19th century, when furniture was the preserve of cabinet-makers. In the 20th century the chair had taken its place: it had assumed an educational and emblematic status. The design of a chair's success can be judged both by the volume of production and sales and also by its 'publishability'. A highly successful chair, which returns to the designer between a 1.5 and 6 per cent royalty commission, can ensure a steady income to a studio. Furthermore, a chair may be readily turned into a two-dimensional photograph for publication in magazines. Indeed, a designer has admitted to me that he photographs his chair prototypes to see what they look like 'on the page'. Another product designer has agreed that he only does furniture to achieve some public profile for himself in order to get his name around. Designers use objects to ensure and mark their place in the 'canon of design'.

Certain events and locations conspire to support this system. The various international furniture fairs such as at Valencia, Cologne and, in particular, Milan provide an opportunity to reinforce a star system of designers rather like the film festivals of Cannes and the Oscar awards. Each of these events includes design awards, the presentation of new designer products, and are heavily marketed to design journalists. The system resonates into design curatorship. The Vitra Design Museum, opened in 1990, is exclusively dedicated to exhibiting the furniture of 'name' designers. Significantly, the museum's collection of over 1,200 chairs included few examples of industrially produced office chairs, which form the major part of global chair production. Instead, it was mostly devoted to more experimental forms that are manufactured on a small scale. London's Design Museum has mostly featured monographic shows, which furthermore support a modernistic conception of design: itself supported by the heavily retro-modernist 'white cube' of the building's architecture. Finally, the design shelves of high street bookstores are dominated by glossy monographs which reinforce this curatorship. One bestselling publication is an exhibition catalogue entitled *Pioneers of Modern Furniture* (Fischer Fine Art 1991), picking up on the Pevsnerean tradition. For its mediators, for its writers, journalists and curators, design comes to mean modernism, or even, modernist furniture. Thus in her round-up of a year's style, Abrahams suggests that 'the public are finally coming to appreciate the value of good design' (1998: 52). Her examples of 'good design' were all pieces of furniture that exist in the modernist pedigree of Charles Eames and Robin Day.

In all these cases the object of design is progressively reified. In other words, all aspects of the design, production and distribution are concentrated in the object as if they exist *in* it. The material form stands in for these invisible processes. Acknowledgement or analysis of these need not be explained otherwise. This reductionism in turn builds myths of design history by stripping 'its subject matter to an unproblematic, self-evident entity (Design) in a form that also reduces its historical specificity and variety to as near zero as possible' (Dilnot 1984: 7). Interestingly, a favourite motif in monographic design books and exhibition catalogues is to place the photograph of the object alongside a curriculum vitae of the designer. Subsequently, all one is left with is the designer's career situated within the historical 'canon of design' as a way of legitimating the present.

Thus the system of design publishing is exploited for the designer's own ends. More broadly, this form of self-representation can be called 'historicity': the designer is building on the way history is written in order to provide a discursive framework for and legitimate his or her own activities. Victor Burgin has called this 'history-writing as underwriting' (Burgin, quoted in Blauvelt 1994: 209). 'Historicity' is a term used most lucidly by the French sociologist Alain Touraine. He uses it to define 'the set of cultural models a society uses to produce its norms and its domains of knowledge, production and ethics' (Touraine 1995: 368). Thus it is concerned with 'the creation of historical experience, and not of a position in historical evolution' (1995: 369). It is therefore subjective and open to contestation.

Meanwhile, Poynor argues that graphic design is either excluded from the history or 'gets a limited walk-on part' (1999: 7). Where graphic design has been represented, again this has been according to the Pevsnerean model. So, for example, Meggs's history of graphic design (1983) concentrates on the influences and styles of individuals, building a narrative tending towards the development of modernism and its dismantling in postmodernity. This process of history writing serves to separate graphic design out as a profession, as against its 'vernacular' activity carried out by anonymous contributors (Blauvelt 1994). It also provides a self-legitimatizing structure for individuals to take up a moral position. For example, a letter from a graphic designer published in *Design Week* complained of 'design's very breath of life ... suffocated by perpetual mediocrity and highly questionable work' (Argent 1998). This despondent correspondent then went on to cite the work of 'design-greats' Paul Rand and Abram Games as inspiration for the revival of its 'integrity'.

Classical approaches to design history and discourse are thus restricted and restrictive in approach and the objects of its study. Walker raises the rhetorical question as to why design historians don't study military weapons, police equipment or sexual aids – surely three great domains of user investment in a planned product (Walker 1989: 33). Furthermore, as we have seen in the Chapter 2, the vast majority of designers are involved in the planning and implement-ation of communications. Design is about concepts, relationships, ideas and processes. It is also a collaborative venture which is supremely intradisciplinary in that it unites specialists in two- and three-dimensional communication, visual and material culture, and it is interdisciplinary in that it brings different professional domains together. As Victor Margolin notes:

> Design history ... has not had much success in engaging with current practice. These issues involve new technologies, innovative collaborative efforts among design professionals, a concern with the impact of complex products on users and the relations between the design of material objects and immaterial processes. (1995b: 20)

SECOND MODERNITY VERSUS DESIGN MANAGEMENT

It is interesting to note how the most virulent critiques of the way design history has been written – ostensibly by British design historians – have come from American-based critics (see Dilnot 1984; Blauvelt 1994; Margolin 1995b; Buchanan 1998b; all cited above in this chapter). It seems that they are sharply sensitized to the tensions between theoretical positions and prac-tical action in design.

There is a manifest separation between the actual practices of the design profession and some of the discourses that are mustered to explain and legitimate itself. On the one hand, there is the complex, multidisciplinary industry, accustomed to teamwork, stylistic and oper-ational flexibility and active in a broad range of domains of use and exchange. On the other hand, individual biography focusing on the designer's creativity and the modernist canon as a benchmark of ethical and formal development predominate in the articulation of historical experience. This may explain how the same design critic can write, along with others, in the academic *Design Management Journal* about the need to develop a design education system which eschewes individual creative genius in favour of nurturing teamwork and collaboration (Morris et al. 1998), while in the professional weekly magazine *Design Week* he gives a top ten of the century's best designers, apparently seeking homage to just those values rejected in the earlier article (Myerson 1999).

During the 1980s, some critics close to the design profession attempted to revise the 'canon of design' approach in the context of theoretical and commercial developments of that decade. An example of this was the publication of *Design after Modernism: Beyond the Object* (Thackara 1988), which amalgamated a wide range of essays dealing with technological and social changes and their impact on modernity, the city, questions of functionalism, manufacturing systems and design practice. It opened up a range of issues which the Pevsneristic reading was not equipped to consider. Perhaps given the breadth of subjects covered and writers contributing, this publication did not reach a consistent position. Nonetheless, the book clearly honoured the diversity of practices and positions available in design by this date.

At the same time in Italy a focused group of designer-cum-commentators developed a stridently coherent ideological stance and expressed it in a refined and sometimes impenetrable language that championed a second modernity in the void left by the retreat of modernism. This was most thoroughly articulated by Andrea Branzi (1984, 1988, 1989, 1993). In his published texts, Branzi acknowledges the end of the era of modernism as a unifying system of ideology, technology and aesthetics. Nonetheless, he does not relinquish the idea of modernity altogether, but rather he envisages its transposition into an 'ecology of the artificial'. In this 'second modernity', Branzi embraces the attributes of a post-industrial society – that flexibility, differentiation but also industrial internationalism will prevail. This productive system provides a basis for the exercise of a 'new tribalism', an 'ensemble of linguistic families' (1989: 38) in which cultural preferences – and thus tastes in design – are independent of ideological and national structures. The outcome is a 'new functionality of objects, that has to correspond to uncontrollable parameters of poetry, psychology and spiritualism' (1989: 38). Furthermore, he champions the Italian *Nuovo Design* (discussed in more detail in Chapter 5 and of which he was a practitioner), which was based on small-scale production of goods with new technologies as emblematic of an appropriate response to this demand (1993: 127).

No doubt Branzi was attempting to develop a discursive field for design which acknowledged the ideological, industrial and commercial shifts of the late 20th century and which was not shackled by the need for any 'homage to modernism'. His American critics point out that while he identifies new criteria for designing, both in production systems and consumer demands, his proposals for a design to meet these are rooted in a Eurocentrism and that it is laced with a paternalistic bent (McDonough 1993: 129; Buchanan 1998a: 6). Flexible specialization, supported by information networks, may well cater for diversity of taste but Branzi, they opine, still suggests a design response from a position of high cultural goods. Buchanan points out how Branzi describes his second modernity 'as an artificial system based neither on the principle of necessity nor on the principle of identity but on a set of conventional cultural values that somehow make it possible for us to go on making choices and designing' (Branzi 1988: 71, and quoted in Buchanan 1998a: 5). Both McDonough and Buchanan are therefore wary of Branzi's position, interpreting the 'us' in Branzi's statement as 'we designers'. To put it bluntly, the view is that market segment-ation and diversity is okay as long as it falls within the taste parameters of a particular, refined aesthetic sensibility: you can have any shape kitchen implement you like as long as it comes from the catalogue of a north Italian manufacturer.

It is interesting that Branzi's critics come from a self-consciously declared American position. Both Buchanan and McDonough regard modernism as somewhat alien to the American concep-tion and practice of design. Their objections are founded in a conception of the culture of design as being a differentiating and responsive activity in which overarching theorems are untenable. McDonough speaks of 'design's lack of theory, its vulgar link to real people's lives', and con-cludes that 'Design is, almost by default, too vast, too fragmented, too chaotic a system for benign management, for organized reform' (1993: 131).

While these American commentators come from a broad range of opinion and backgrounds, they do seem to promote a more pragmatic vision of design. Buchanan (1998a: 10) in particular draws the debate away from Branzi's linkage of culture as an expression of ideology to rein-troduce it as an activity, as cultivation. He is therefore interested in the processes of design as a search for understanding and values. As such he emphasizes that 'the history of design in the twentieth century is not merely the history of products or of *personal styles of expression* or even *of broad cultural ideas*. It is also the history of the *character and disciplines of design thinking as they are formed through encounters with new problems*' (Buchanan 1998a: 13, original italics). In this way he sees design as being engaged in rethinking the nature of products in the context of action.

Buchanan is not necessarily specific about what he sees as 'products', stating that they can incorporate communicative symbols and images as well as physical objects (Buchanan 1998a: 13), but he also goes on to consider design in its role as shaping systems, environments, ideas and values. In this mature state it may be involved in the external presentation of goods and services to the public, but also in the internal systems that manage their development and distribution. He is thus shifting the debate from material form to immaterial processes, from design as a purveyor of objects to the shaping of structures and relationships.

There are some resonances with Buchanan's argument in Ezio Manzini's elaboration of the concept of 'dematerialization'. Manzini (1992, 1998) explores ways by which material goods may be supported or even substituted by immaterial systems (hence dematerialization). He proposes information-products (typified, for example, by internet-based entertainment), results-products (where their efficiency is measured by the 'absence' of other material products), community-products (for example, collective kitchens organized in the form of clubs) and duration-products (where, for instance, the manufacturer plays a role in the recycling or disposal of products) as strategies for integrated products and services (Manzini 1998: 50–7).

Manzini's position is blatantly forward looking and contains a strong dose of social and envir-onmental advocacy. It is also tempered by an extensive understanding of materials and inform-ation technologies. By comparison, the rhetorics of much American design discourse, at least as evidenced in the *Design Management Journal*, are driven by pragmatic desires to maximize market share and profit. But in common with Manzini, there is a clear enthusiasm to move bey-ond the object to consider a range of interrelated communicative and material relationships. In the former case this might be expressed in terms of ensuring brand authority, loyalty or engage-ment through the careful ensembling of marketing, design and advertising. In the latter, Manzini demands intervention 'on the strategies that determine the social and environmental quality of the changing world' (1998: 57). In whichever case, design is not regarded just as a profession or an historical result, but is seen as something that requires management. Its effectiveness is judged more in achieving the most appropriate combination and use of different disciplines and the best relationship with end-users. This contrasts obliquely with a discourse that invests its values solely in the formal characteristics of the object.

SERVICE DESIGN

The backgrounds and overall aims of Branzi, Buchanan and Manzini discussed in the previous section are varied. What binds them is the consideration of the relationships between material, immaterial and human elements. In their different ways, they have tried to attend to shifting roles for design within contemporary economic, social and environmental realities. More specifically, these include a move to more flexible and responsive production methods, the impact of digital technologies and the fragmentation of social groupings and lifestyles. In their texts, they analyse, describe and develop a language for talking about design in these circumstances.

Their concerns are in shifting the discourse of design beyond products. But this doesn't mean to say that that they envisage the total replacement of tangible with intangible items. Rather, their work has grown out of an increased interlocking of the material and immaterial in contemporary life. As described in Chapter 2, the rise to dominance of the service sector in post-industrial economies has been particularly important in reframing what design can do. It is mostly to do with this fact that these authors' considerations have come about.

Services are typically described by what they are *not*. Services are not like goods that can be exchanged and moved through various locations; they are regarded as involving processes (such as interacting with your bank) or performances (for example, going to the cinema or the theatre) rather than being about owning specific objects. They only come into being in their use (Morelli 2002). This contradistinction between goods and services is problematic, however, for it often implies that services are concerned only with intangible or immaterial elements (Vargo and Lusch 2004). All services involve material elements, though. These may be the tightly orchestrated within a brand identity, for example within fast food where the staff training systems, provision of ingredients, design of the kitchens, point of sale, customer seating, buildings as well as graphic communication elements all entail paying careful attention to the coherence of its material parts. Alternatively, the provision of stockbroking services, while dealing in the relatively intangible movement of money, still takes place within a constellation of objects and spaces, including office furniture and equipment (Mackenzie 2009).

From around 2000, a new specialism called 'service design' began to be defined. A strong literature on service design emerged (e.g. Saco and Gonsalves 2008; Kimbell 2009; Stickdorn and Schneider 2010), testimony to the interest that was shown from a variety of sources.

The rise of service design may broadly be seen as a response to the growth of the service sector in post-industrial economies. Its pedigree lies in a range of related specialisms such as branding, interaction design (which includes the design of digital interfaces and systems) and product design. In particular, it analyses and designs the user's journey through a service provision, qualifying the important moments of that journey as 'touchpoints' where particular attention is given to the customer experience. These touchpoints may be, for example, the check-in desk or flight information provision at an airport. It therefore involves the orchestration of multiple artefacts (such as a combination of web, smart-card, products) and their positioning and sequencing. It is very much concerned with the *relations* and *exchanges* that go on between actors and artefacts within a system. In terms of design process, particular notice may be taken of small-scale innovations that users and producers of services create themselves, seeing that their 'unofficial customization' may be of significance and applicability that can be up-scaled.

Like branding, service design is often both inward- and outward-looking in that it attends both to the processes and experiences within the organization and its end-users, seeing that the interface between these two is highly important. However, service design takes the role of the design beyond a brand ethos to consider the interlocking of material design elements and the systems and structures by which a service is constructed and delivered more systematically. It follows, therefore, that in this model of practice design takes a more active role in corporate or public sector organization and their approach to management. While branding largely involves the production of organizational guidelines that usually have to be rigorously adhered to, service design's approach is looser and more iterative in its engagement with a problematic. The service design process involves lengthy periods of producer and user research, prototyping, and implementation as well as an ongoing adjustment of outcomes.

With regard to design discourse, the emergence of service design first demonstrates, again, the constant fragmentation and differentiation of design disciplines as new specialisms are developed. Second, service design takes design, in general, another step further in embracing considerations that lie beyond the discreet object and into the relations and arrangement of human and non-human elements. This more strategic role for design itself suggests a continual upgrading of the ambitions of its professionals as they seek not just further recognition for the importance of the forms they create, but also to be understood as consultants who intervene on the direction and structure of an organization, though very much as seen through the interface of service producers and users. Third, a fully resolved outcome is not always considered optimum in service design: as organizations, contexts and publics are in continual change, so is the design of services. This opens out the role and status of the designer in that it invariably entails longer client relationships. It also repositions the focal concern of designers to be in process and relationships.

DESIGN THINKING

Another way by which design has overlapped into different fields and discourses, and also opened out a conception of what design might be, has been through so-called 'design thinking'. This acquired greater visibility from about 2005, as it began to be taught in a number of business schools such as the University of Oxford's Said Business School, Stanford University's d.school and the Weatherhead School of Management at Case Western Reserve University, USA.

The adoption of design discourse in management schools may be read as an attempt to make themselves fashionable as design takes on an increasingly public significance. Alternatively, it represents an interesting admission that all management decisions are indeed design decisions. More compellingly, design thinking suggests that the techniques and formats of designing can be imported to management as a way of confronting challenges and stimulating innovations.

Kimbell (2011) provides a useful analytical taxonomy of theories of design thinking, noting that the term is understood in various ways and has quite a long history. First, she shows that design thinking has already been identified within theorizations of more traditional approaches to designing, for example in the analyses of Cross (1982), Schon (1991) and Lawson (1997). Here design requires a special kind of problem-solving ability, which is a skill in itself. This is where reflection-in-action is mobilized and the design problem itself gradually gets more refined through the processing of a project. Design thinking in this context is a 'cognitive style'; it is a way of perceiving, understanding and interacting with the world. It is what designers have always done, but it could be a skill that is taught in other fields.

Second, for Buchanan (1992), design thinking – as we've already seen in this chapter – forms part of a generalized way of grasping the nature of the modern world. Drawing on the work of John Dewey (1934), it is seen as an attitudinal framework that pays attention to aesthetic experience. Objects do not 'express'; rather, they are experienced. Buchanan opens out the field in which this takes place, although not necessarily being specific about what is experienced; but these can include signs, things, actions or thoughts. Furthermore, in this openness, the design problem itself may be constantly redetermined, as it is in itself under continual evolution. This notion is drawn from Rittel and Webber's (1973) notion of 'wicked problems'.

Third, Kimbell (2011, 2012) identifies a more recent wave of writing that distinguishes design thinking as an organizational resource to stimulate innovation. Martin (2009) sees design processes as a way of creating entirely new approaches and concepts rather than having to choose between alternatives. Brown (2009) is more specific about what designers do, claiming that their heightened sense of empathy allows them to understand what users find desirable, what is technically feasible and what is viable for the producing organization. In this paradigm, design thinking involves the processes of visualisation and prototyping, inferring a more exploratory approach through creatively trying out and testing ideas rather than being bound by the predetermined routines of process.

These three clusters of thinking on design thinking have, in common, a refusal to separate cognition and action. Thinking about something is embedded into doing something, and vice versa. As such, and according to Bauer and Eagan (2008), design thinking can provide a counterpoint to a perceived over-analysis that takes place in management. It was notable that design thinking should emerge from 2005, when it was increasingly recognized that traditional management teaching was not equipped to deal with the complex contemporary challenges of recessional economies, resource scarcity and climate change. Design thinking also represents a growing appreciation of the contributions that design can make to confronting organizational and global dilemmas, even if much of this potential still remains to be explored and identified. Finally, as we have also seen with service design, the discourse of design shifts here to reflecting and embracing it as a problem processor rather than the solver of more fixed and easily observable challenges.

CONCLUSION

While much of designers' work has been concerned with the prosaic rigours of running a business, on a larger level, some of their energies have been directed at establishing their occupation as a profession. In doing so they have reflexively constructed an image of themselves and the design they produce for public consumption. The Pevsnerist writing of design history has partially supported this system in giving primacy to the individual designer in the shaping of goods and in the privileging of particular forms and types of design over others. The reception, use and consumption of design are afforded little attention in these accounts, even though, again, we have seen that design practice is intimately bound up in an understanding of its audience and market.

As we saw in Chapter 2, the production of design, however, involves a more complex system of alliances between groups of professionals and is directed at a much wider range of goods, services and spaces than some popular accounts recognize. In the face of these changes some attempts have been made to develop alternative frameworks for considering design. These may attempt to update and adjust traditional conceptions to a contemporary reality of modern manufacture, distribution and social pluralism. Alternatively, discussion has shifted away from material objects to a more integrative view of design, which in turn may challenge the designer's traditional role.

Ultimately, the history of the discourses of design evidences a 'layering up' of what design is perceived to do, how it is practised and the roles and statuses available to the designer. In other words, it is erroneous to think of discreet phases of design, where specific types of professional practice supersede each other. Attempts to reduce the whole of design to single definitions and logics are therefore unviable. Rather, it is subject to an accumulation of meanings and significances as it fills out various corners of everyday life in different ways.

CHAPTER 4
THE CONSUMPTION OF DESIGN

Are consumers passive receivers of design objects and docile users of design spaces? Or are they actively engaged in redetermining meaning? Entering into such debates is important to thinking about how design culture functions. By isolating consumption from the work of designers and systems of production, much of the interest and complexity of contemporary design culture is missed. By contrast, Chapter 4 promotes an approach that places consumption in a dynamic relationship with issues of production and design. Further, it is useful for the study of design culture to think of consumption not solely in terms of the actions of individuals and using singular objects, but as a shared social practice that engages constellations of artefacts. Writing imaginatively, the experience of design objects and spaces can deliver insightful, even poetic, reflections on them. They can even help us in our enquiries into production and the work of designers.

While the majority of popular accounts of design remain unashamedly designer-centric, many critics and historians have sought alternative approaches to the subject. Some have been critical of the methodological and theoretical stance taken by Pevsnerist approaches, keen to challenge the dominance of modernism and point out alternative practices and approaches to design. Others have stepped outside the predominantly north-west European and American contexts to demonstrate that a straightforward application of modernism is not universally viable (e.g. Sparke 1988; Julier 1991; Boym 1992). Some have carried out detailed explorations of the activities of designers as part of a wider corporate culture, thus placing design more within a business history context (e.g. Heskett 1989).

Alternatively, several design historians have moved entirely away from a design and production approach towards foregrounding the role of the consumer in the biography of objects (Attfield 2000). Their interest has been in the taste, social customs and the role of objects and spaces in the forging of human relationships and self-identity. This approach has often been fuelled by a drive to challenge the complacency of designers and design students in believing that theirs is the only account. After all, the majority of design history has been taught in practice-based art and design departments, often to provide an alternative narrative to the day-to-day experience of the studio education. Thus they impart a recognition that no matter how much designers try, they cannot fully control the processes by which the public read, interpret or even straightforwardly use the objects, images and spaces that they shape. As Adrian Forty points out, there is a paradox here in that designers are both in command of what they do and at the same time are the agents of ideology, subcontractees to a bigger system. He believes that there is no answer to this, only that 'both conditions invariably co-exist, however uncomfortably, in the work of design' (Forty 1986: 242). Meanwhile, some design historians have ever more vigorously applied themselves to studying consumption to the point that critics such as Richard Buchanan (1998b), whose chief interest is in the processes of design, wonders whether they are in fact hostile to practice.

In order to open up the discussion concerning the consumption of design, historians have drawn from a wide range of theoretical discourses which have been developed in Cultural Studies, Social Anthropology, Sociology and Cultural Geography: a veritable 'spaghetti junction of intersecting disciplines, methodologies, politics' (Slater 1997: 2). These have largely focused on the qualitative analysis of consuming: how objects, images and spaces are valued, thought about or, more straightforwardly, used by their public rather than on the quantitative aspects of the size and the structure of markets. In their theoretical underpinning they share a range of key thinkers who have developed a series of distinctive positions on the nature of consumption. We shall review these, identifying the contribution that a critical understanding of their positions can make to studying design culture.

THE CULTURE OF CONSUMPTION

As we have seen with the term 'design', so 'consumption' is a broad concept which invariably requires qualification. Consuming entails the using or using up of something. It may involve the pleasures or un-pleasures of having an artefact, or it can be concerned with the acts prior to ownership: gathering product information, browsing, shopping and acquisition. Looking, listening, smelling or touching are also acts of consuming. It may also involve the consumption of time, as in the case of some leisure experiences or in the rental of goods. The various acts of consumption are experienced in a variety of ways, locations and moments.

Such prosaic activities of consumption express, knowingly or unknowingly, a wider set of cultural and ideological systems. At an immediate level, consumption is concerned with the struggle to control the visual, spatial and material fabric of everyday life. Consumer culture, then, concerns the larger picture that acquisition and use represent, the values and systems which are reproduced and articulated through consuming.

Some ground rules as to how we might view the general character of consumer culture in the West are usefully established by Slater (1997: Ch. 1). First, consumption is intrinsically a cultural process. While it requires economic exchange, it also involves the exercise of taste as part of a self-identifying act. Consumer culture includes the balance between a quest for achieving meaningful ways of life and the resources available to be able to do this. It is therefore about 'having' rather than 'being'. As such it is also the dominant value of capitalist society.

Second, Slater argues that consumption entails an exercise of private, personal choice within the market: the emphasis is on the acquisition and experience of goods and services which are not produced by the consumer him- or herself. It is also universal and impersonal in that, in principle, goods and services are not produced to individual commission; rather, they are produced to an imagined and unknown consumer. Access to goods is only limited by the ability to pay for them. It is open to anyone with the money.

Third, if consuming involves making choices, then consumer culture is identified as a culture of freedom and individualism. Thus consuming is declared as the exercise of private will, free of public intervention. Slater argues that it is also a private act which is consigned to personal pleasure rather than public good. In this highly individualistic mode it may even contradict notions of social order, solidarity and authority.

Fourth, consumer culture is founded on the constant expansion of demand. Indeed, economic organization is fuelled by an insatiable desire to produce more wealth, acquisitive power and therefore more consumption. So society must be highly rational and disciplined in order to deliver this, but at the same time it must foster irrational passions and desires in order to promote consumption. The tension between the two characterizes the cross-over from modernity (rational) to postmodernity (irrational) in contemporary society.

Fifth, in this post-traditional society, consumption becomes the leading device through which individuals construct their identities, suggests Slater. Whereas in pre-modern society identity and status were largely given and modes of consumption were subordinate to these, modern concepts of individualism require that the goods one acquires and displays momentarily define one's identity. As the order of society is unstable, however, so is the relationship between consumption and identity. Thus the meanings of appearances, the codes by which we read identities, are constantly changing.

Sixth, consumer culture incorporates virulent mechanisms for the production and representation of commodities as signs. They are increasingly mediated – through advertising, packaging, shop display and so on – and become aestheticized. Furthermore, increasing amounts and types of commodities are not material goods but representations (computer software, for example) and experiences (such as certain forms of leisure) – they are 'de-materialized' products. In view of this, there is a new flexibility in the relations between consumption, communication and meaning. Contemporary economics, commerce and politics are therefore driven by 'sign-values' – what things look like and how that image is interpreted. Culture, Slater concludes, takes up a leading position in the modern exercise of power.

DESIGN AND CONSUMER CULTURE

The above summary of consumer culture is useful for the observer of design in that it establishes a basis with which we can begin to compare specific contexts and modes of consumption and situate the discourses of selected objects therein. By considering specific design examples, Slater's outline requires some qualification.

First, his reduction of consumption to an anonymous act – that goods are not produced to individual commission – is generally the case, although we must be mindful of examples where goods and services are designed for customization. Bicycles, computer software and financial packages are often adapted to a user's specific requirements so that the consumer plays an active role in their shaping. Production and consumption invariably overlap to form what Toffler (1980) called the 'prosumer'.

Second, Slater's emphasis on consumption as a private, politically passive act ignores the reality that individuals also engage in a public realm with consumption. Much of Material Culture studies have been dominated by investigations of the private domains of consumption and the private individual. However, more public spaces are powerful loci for the articulation of both public and private modes of consumption. Where the public domain has been considered, it has mostly been within the framework of the commodification of that experience: shopping as a form of spectacle and expedition into modernity (e.g. Corrigan 1997); museums and expositions as the organization and classification of material culture for public consumption (e.g. Vergo 1989); heritage industries (e.g. Urry 1990) and the 'consuming' of public services (e.g. Keat et al. 1994).

By placing the consideration of consumption into a public realm, interesting questions are raised concerning the crossovers between private and public space, commodified and non-commodified goods and services, and the personal and the political. For example, voting in local and national political elections may be guided by preferences as to how councils and governments spend the money they gather through taxation. Tourism and leisure involves the consumption of some non-commodified services, such as museums run by volunteers, in a public or semi-public environment. Private consumption may also be directly guided by ideological beliefs that are articulated in a public way: the boycotting of goods from repressive regimes or which have a highly negative environmental impact illustrate this direct link between political will and consumption. More loosely, private patterns of consumption may be informed by a wider public identity concerning the aesthetic and utilitarian dimensions of the places we inhabit and use. Thus a poor public transport system may cause higher private car ownership. Consumption is not exclusively about the acquisition of individualized goods and services, then. It involves the interconnection of a range of actions through a chain of sites and times (Jackson and Thrift 1995).

Third, Slater, at least initially, builds a dualism between a rational society of production and irrational individualistic consumption. To characterize consumption as 'irrational' certainly pays due regard to the role of desire; however, this shouldn't be overplayed. Many, if not most, acts of everyday consumption are highly rational. They are based on the stringent calculation of need and value for money. Design may subsequently play to a rational/irrational split in consuming and may in turn blur or confuse the distinctions between the two. Some goods may be made from cheaper materials but still aspire to luxurious ambition in their form (as we shall see in Chapter 5); leisure spaces may be highly rationalized, promising their efficient use, yet give the impression of endless leisure time (as we shall see in Chapter 8).

PASSIVE OR SOVEREIGN CONSUMERS?

As an organizing principle, then, consumer culture is *the* culture of the capitalist age. However, to reverse away from this larger context, to investigate the fluxes, disjunctures and contradictions within it, the design and mediation of objects, spaces and images will require detailed attention. Circulating around all features of consumer culture is the tension between individual autonomy and consumption's wider role in promoting economic competition. On the one hand, consumption may be used as an expression of personal freedom and power; on the other, it concerns the manipulation of needs and wants by dominant institutions.

The idea that consumption might be a vehicle for the pacification, coercion and manipulation of the masses stems from a position taken up by members of the so-called Frankfurt School. Writing from the 1920s to the 1960s, they deliberately avoided romantic notions of creativity and individuality in the production of cultural artefacts and pursued the possibility that it was a coordinated, logical and calculated activity. Adorno and Horkheimer (1979 [1947]) used the term 'culture industry' to express the similarities between popular entertainment and mass manufacture. They suggested that their production became commodified and distributed just like any other artefact in capitalist society. They were consumed by a mass market which was passive in its uncritical tastes and reception of cultural goods. Thus an audience is duped into believing in the quality of the things they consume as evidence of the successful functioning of the state and its political economy. Equally, as Carr and Fusi (1981) explain, the mass consumption of popular entertainment and goods may be mobilized towards what they called 'the culture of evasion': in the case of Spain during the fascist Franco dictatorship, to which their discussion was directed, this involved the saturation of the mass media with low-budget musicals, bull-fighting and football, which in turn promoted passivity and avoided the remotest chance of the politicization of consumers.

This 'manipulation' theory is extended from entertainment to all goods by Galbraith (1958, 1967), who argued that the fundamental problem of advanced capitalism is the disposal of its surplus products: as we have seen, in order to grow and survive, capitalism must 'over-produce' in terms of current demand. So needs have to be created (the 'production of consumption') in order to deal with this problem. In design terms, this gives rise to advertising promoting 'false needs', as Packard suggests in *The Hidden Persuaders* (1957). Within this, we might even recall the very nature of the design profession, as I argued in the last chapter, which is required to create a need for its services.

This explains the strategy of obsolescence in which products have a limited life designed into them, either through their lack of physical durability or their quickly becoming unfashionable. Advertising helps brand loyalty so that consumers continue to buy within the range of products offered by the same manufacturer. Upon their respective goods becoming obsolete, consumers then climb a 'brand ladder' by buying the next product up the range.

At the opposite end of the scale to these manipulation theories is the notion of 'consumer sovereignty'. This effectively turns the manipulation theory on its head and argues that if corporations are in competition with each other, then they must respond to the expressed preferences of consumers. After all, what is to stop them moving between brands rather than buying into a ladder of same-brand products? Thus within this conception of sovereignty the consumer becomes an ultimate symbol of all other freedoms of capitalism. Even the most mundane act of consumption becomes an expression of individual freedom and honour. It is an image which neatly contrasted with the inability of Soviet systems to provide for individual desires from the Cold War until the collapse of socialism in the late 1980s. Complementary to the concept of consumer sovereignty was enterprise culture, which expressed the idea of individuals seeing consumption as an entrepreneurial activity in itself. Thus goods and services such as property and pension plans are appreciated for their ability to generate further capital. Similarly, entrepreneuralism within enterprise culture has a 'go-getting' quality; it is able to anticipate and exploit market opportunities. Both consumer sovereignty and enterprise culture suggest that an heroic individualism was promoted in the 1980s, as the neoliberal agenda in capitalism took hold.

Simultaneously, discussions of consumption as a resistant or empowering act have emerged. Social anthropologist Daniel Miller (1987, 1988) explored the dynamics of consumption in terms of alienation and de-alienation. His argument is that artefacts are intrinsically alienating: they come with little or no information concerning the conditions of their production and distribution and the consumer holds no social relationship to their producers. Consuming is, as we have seen, an anonymous act. Thus the consumer engages in the de-alienation of these of the material world through use and customization to their own needs. Among the examples he used to support this case is his ethnographic study of kitchens in a north-London housing estate. The fitted kitchens came as standardized installations in the flats and Miller therefore looked at how tenants made these 'their own' through making adjustments to them or through their complete replacement. By personalizing their living environment tenants were resisting the tastes handed down to them by their landlord. Through their own aesthetic preferences they were also making highly individualized statements about kinship, gender, memory, gift exchange and personal space. Such studies present the consumer as highly active in determining or creating the social meaning of goods, rather than as the passive receiver of given meanings.

Similarly, Hebdige (1979) in his studies of youth subcultures contends that 'street' music and fashion are involved in the re-appropriation of the material of mass culture through a process of *bricolage*, of do-it-yourself assemblage. Hence punk style took the stereotyped dress codes of mainstream gender roles such as the city gent or the streetwalker and altered and subverted them in ironic, playful or confrontational ways. Clearly Hebdige draws on highly spectacular forms of personal expression, but both he and Miller consider consumption in areas where its practice is less bounded by economic pressures. Along with Fiske (1989a, 1989b) and de Certeau (1984), they also open up a space for evaluating the meaning of consumption in 'real', everyday life as a creative, pleasurable activity. It thus becomes a productive process in itself.

As much as the sovereign consumer notion has been generated within neo-liberalist conservative ideologies, so, then, has it stood behind academic challenges to the Frankfurt School's conception of a docile mass audience and reinvigorated academic interest in the actions of ordinary citizens as creative and empowering.

One must approach the work of Miller, Hebdige, Fiske and de Certeau with a measure of caution, for, as Meikle (1998) points out, they have a tendency to romanticize the subcultures they investigate. Their accounts are often biased against the dominant cultures responsible for the design of commercial products and they do not address the majority of consumption which takes place in the mainstream (Meikle 1998: 197). If their aim is to remobilize a sense of dignity in the everyday, particularly in working-class life, one is left asking why, for instance, they haven't discussed the dress, chants and gestures on the football terraces or the effects of hire-purchase and home-shopping catalogues on taste and consumption patterns. These writers are important, however, because while design objects – kitchen hardware, fashion, music – are discussed, their main concern is to show how these enact social or ideological values. Their approach owes something to the work of Veblen and Bourdieu, whose interest was in the active role of consumption in articulating social relations.

Based on observations of the *nouveau riche* of the late-19th century in the USA, Veblen's *Theory of the Leisure Class* (1970 [1899]) was the first major contribution to the literature on consumption. He argued that this class displayed their wealth through the conspicuous display of non-utilitarian goods. Basing his theories on an extensive study of Parisian consumers, Bourdieu took a similar standpoint to Veblen in the notion that the culture of consumption was concerned with differentiation and identity: goods take on a symbolic role in this process. The key development Bourdieu makes is in suggesting that people distinguish themselves by the distinctions they make. The ability to make these distinctions is in their 'cultural capital'.

Veblen and Bourdieu both tended, on the whole, to separate consumption from production. It is, however, a pervasive strategy of contemporary commerce to re-appropriate the character of active consumption. Their theories will be interrogated in more depth in the next chapter, where we shall look at the role of producers in articulating the processes of differentiation for consumers.

DE-ALIENATION AND DESIGNING

Interestingly, the notion of giving back some active engagement through consumption to the public had been explored in various art and design practices from the 1960s. The verve for *happenings* in artistic practice of the early 1970s often included street performance, which encouraged the participation of audiences. This in turn encouraged the latter to build their own meanings and understandings of the event. A similar 'letting-go' was to be found in the radical proposals of the British architectural group Archigram. Their 'plug-in cities' proposed the use of inflatables and prefabricated modules as architectural elements fulfilling a range of services which could be literally bolted on to a structure in response to consumer demand and changing tastes. Out of these utopian, politically motivated movements came the development of modular furniture, which allowed the user to assemble seating, storage and other elements according to their personal preferences (Papanek and Hennessey 1974). Thus part of the design task was given over to the consumer.

Self-assembly, modular furniture obviously re-emerges in a commodified form in mainstream manufacture and retail, most obviously in the case of IKEA. As the world's largest furniture chain store, IKEA successfully established a brand identity based around the retail of particular design values deriving from its Swedish background. Among these was the promotion of flat-pack furniture which, as they explained to their customers, through their catalogues and in-store announcements allowed them to reduce costs in shipping and therefore make their goods cheaper. They also argued that the greater ease of transport of such items made them more environmentally responsible. By making these issues clear to customers, IKEA were effectively inviting them to become privileged participants in their corporate vision. This narrative of participation in a 'democratic' corporate vision was reinforced through their advertising, such as the 'chuck out your chintz' television advertising campaign devised by the St Luke's agency in 1997–98. It featured women ridding themselves of oppressive Victorian taste and heading for the libertarian halls of IKEA in a parody of political emancipatory movements. IKEA was being offered through this advert as the reasonable, democratic alternative to belong to. Thus 'freedom' of consumption is conditional on and conditioned by shopping at IKEA.

The IKEA case is a sophisticated example of a crucial challenge with which designers and marketers engage. In effect, among their jobs is the *de-alienation* of alienating artefacts. This means that they mediate the gap between production, in its crude form as the system for the origination and creation of goods and services, and consumption, as the user's engagement with them. The integration of design, marketing and advertising allows for a sophisticated construction of meanings to be supplied with the object and to be identified with it. Thus both the physical content of goods and their interpretation are considered within the production process. Simultaneously or alternatively, the consumer builds his or her own hermeneutical engagement independent of the producer. The designer, in combination with other professionals, must take decisions regarding the degrees and mechanisms of de-alienation. The designer can entirely hand over the object to be received 'as it is', to allow the consumer to build their own meanings or none at all. Or he or she can carefully construct an 'aesthetic illusion' around the product.

This dialogue between the producer and the consumer may not necessarily require complex marketing mechanisms. It may originate in the content of the product itself. A designer might develop ways by which the use of an article involves the building of a relationship with it. An example of this is in photocopier design carried out by King-Miranda for Olivetti during the 1980s (Barbacetto 1987). In designing their operating interfaces, they explored the incorporation of pictograms which required the user to adopt and master its own visual language. While these pictograms were derived from archetypal forms, the learning of the photocopier's language still required an intimate interaction with it. As a relationship with the product was built up, then so its alienating character, particularly in a new technology as it was then, receded. In the light of this example, Barbacetto explained that: 'Design is destined to incorporate … the cultural contents of the relationship between men and technology' (1987: 101).

COMMODITIES AND THE AESTHETIC ILLUSION

Consuming goods or services may pass through several different stages. After all, we have seen that it involves several sensorial activities along an extended continuum of time and in various locations. The significance of the object itself thus undergoes a gradual but continuous transformation, passing from future desire, to present achievement, to memory.

An extreme view would consider all things as commodities at all times, that they always are exchangeable and have value as such. Conversely, Igor Kopytoff (1986) argues that, in fact, objects can pass from a commodified to a de-commodified status. Thus something might be bought but then given an individualized identity which cannot be subsequently exchanged. Corrigan (1997: 36) uses the example of the cat to illustrate this: a cat might be bought in a pet store where it is a commodity; it is then singularized as a family pet and is unlikely to be re-commodified subsequently. Kopytoff claims that things can take on biographies whereby their status and meaning change according to different contexts and, of course, the writer of that biography. 'An eventful biography of a thing', he goes on, 'becomes the story of the various singularizations of it, of classifications and reclassifications in an uncertain world of categories whose importance shifts with every minor change in context' (Kopytoff 1986: 90).

Some attempts to understand the shifting meaning of objects through time stem from a reading of Karl Marx's *Capital: Volume One* (1957 [1867]), in particular his discussion of the commodity. In Marxist terms, the commodity is the object in the realm of the market. Exchange-value is the value of the commodity in the market, while use-value is the actual value something has outside the market. Once in the marketplace, commodities circulate independent of the labour that produced them; they are effectively alienated from the human conditions of their production and that labour is not visible. In feudal and communal contexts social relations were directly reproduced by the exchange of goods. Broadly speaking, contact with the producers of goods was direct – you knew who baked your bread or cobbled your shoes. In capitalism the products of labour are separated out from the relations of labour. After all, under capitalism, objects are placed in the marketplace where the consumer is unknown, just as the consumer is unlikely to know the producer or much about the systems of their production. The division of labour further ensures this anonymity. As a result, according to Marx, social relations through labour are replaced by relations between things; commodities *stand in* for those relations and only relate to each other or in relation to money which, itself, abstractly represents all commodities.

This process leads to what Marx called 'commodity fetishism'. A fetish is something that is believed to have a supernatural power. Thus commodities become fetishized in that they are thought to embody the power of human relations (see Figure 4.1). Once the commodity is divorced from its productive base, then it is free to take on a range of cultural values beyond itself. Thus through advertising, display, branding, salesmanship and other forms of mediation, it is conferred with myths which in turn appear to be 'natural' to it. Semiotics is a methodology used to decode these myths and explain how they are constructed.

In this respect mention should be made of the work of Jean Baudrillard. Baudrillard (1988) played a key role in stepping away from the Marxist conception of commodity fetishism being an expression of citizens' alienation from each other as producers. His interest was in the notion that the desire to consume is not directed at specific objects; rather, it is a generally produced condition. Hence it is more accurate to talk about consumer culture than consumption. He suggests that as signs, goods are free to take on any association or meaning as a play of signifiers. This doesn't mean to say that production is unimportant: both production and consumption are caught up in a system in which each becomes a simulation.

Considerable attention has been given to the role of advertising in constructing myths around commodities (Dyer 1982; Williamson 1988 [1978]). Meanwhile, Schudson (1993 [1984]) argues that advertising is not as important a force as these critics make out and usefully draws our attention to other forms by which product knowledge reaches consumers; these would include word of mouth, mass media other than advertising, direct marketing and promotions. Leiss et al. (1990: 36–9) suggest that advertising is a largely reactive profession which follows market trends, and

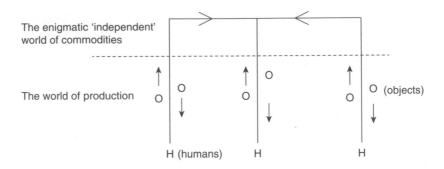

Figure 4.1   Market society (adapted from Cohen 1978)

that it is more successful in giving information than actually manipulating consumers into unwittingly buying things they do not want. (The limitations of advertising are discussed further in Chapter 10.) The inference here is that advertising participates in a wider orchestration of values and is not solely responsible for any mythologizing processes. Therefore we have to look to other features in which design intervention is made along the system of provision.

Haug (1986) presents an argument which forces us to consider the intersection of a variety of visual, textual and material forms in the development of 'commodity aesthetics'. He argues that artefacts in the market have to promise a use-value once they are sold: they have to appear to be useful before they actually are. This 'aesthetic illusion' is established through the appearance of commodities themselves, through the semantic of the product itself. Thus a 'technocracy of sensuality' runs through the origination, shaping and promotion of products and in turn shapes consumer expectations. In part his text may be linked to the styling of products through the application of a 'second skin', an exterior surface that does not necessarily relate much to the interior workings. Thus, sports cars have to *look* as well as *be* fast.

This is important when regarding contemporary product design as part of a brand ethos and also in view of the increasingly sophisticated ways by which the design and marketing of commodities overlap into consumer culture. We shall see in Chapter 6 how the external appearance of products interfaces with their promotion. However, Haug's analysis suggests that commodity aesthetics refers merely to the externally applied, decorative effects of goods. In this case their performance remains the same while their external semiotic appeal changes (Wernick 1991: 190). The attributes of goods designed for promotion as commodities (exchange-value) may also provide the utilitarian content (use-value), however. Where promotion and function converge, for instance, is when chocolate is made to be sweeter or cars to be faster (Fine and Leopold 1993: 27). This is particularly the case in image-based goods such as CD-ROMs, video games, the interfaces of smartphones or newspapers and magazines, where the look of the thing is intimately bound up with the way it functions.

SYSTEMS OF PROVISION

Haug represents an important departure from other theorists in his demand for a vertically integrated analysis of material and visual culture. He does this by linking product form to its mediation to social signification in consumption. To follow this challenge demands that the cultural critic employs a variety of skills. She or he must act as business historian, semiologist, economist, sociologist, ethnographer, anthropologist and, above all, be visually literate. Few consumption theorists (e.g. Featherstone 1991; Corrigan 1997; Campbell 1998) actually approach the objects of consumption. Artefacts, visual or materially based, are rarely discussed and so we are left with observations that circulate around a void which requires filling.

One commendable exception to this general reluctance to approach the object is Hebdige's classic essay on the Vespa motor scooter (1988: Ch. 4). Hebdige identifies production, mediation and consumption as three key 'moments' in the object's biography. He skilfully rides it through these, first taking us to the scooter's origination in post-war Italian reconstruction. He then considers the marketing strategies in introducing this new typology in two-wheeled transportation, but also forms of product mediation outside the Piaggio motor scooter's remit, such as owners' clubs and word-of-mouth reputation. Finally, he explores questions of gender and sexuality within its accumulated social meanings. Through this, he reveals both the continuities between production and consumption and the mutability of the object – the possibility of different, even conflicting meanings through its various moments. Importantly, however, he does not lose sight of the object; instead, he brings together a sense of the Vespa's visceral presence, its various representations and the discourses that accompany these.

Another strength in Hebdige's approach is that he clearly acknowledges the fact that he is dealing with forms of consumption particular to his central object during a given period. Again, this is at variance with many texts which approach consumption as if all its forms were the same, as if the conditions of acquisition, use, storage and memory of luxury goods were the same as for, say, staple goods.

An alternative methodology to generalist theories of consumption is proposed by Fine and Leopold (1993; Fine 1995) in their 'systems of provision' approach. They argue that commodities or groups of commodities are structured by a chain or system of provision that unites a particular pattern of production with a particular pattern of consumption. This approach therefore looks for the specific ways that production and consumption are brought together according to the goods or services under analysis rather than a generalized view of patterns in this process. They identify distribution, retail and what they call 'the cultural reconstruction of the meaning of what is consumed' (Fine and Leopold 1993: 4) as devices for connecting production to consumption. The mediation of the relationship between product, production and the consumer is paramount to the work of the designer and links back to their work in de-alienating commodities. As Gardner and Sheppard put it, 'The designer is out to achieve what Marx believed was ultimately impossible under capitalism, to bridge that yawning gap between private production and public consumption' (1989: 74). They describe this as the 'holy grail' of the designer in their perpetual attempt to make products 'meaningful' by getting the right fit between production and consumption. It seems appropriate to adopt Fine and Leopold's 'systems of provision' approach in the face of this.

The designer is involved here in fashioning and controlling the 'flows' of material, visual and textual information of a product. This idea of 'flows' has been promoted by Spanish sociologist Manuel Castells (1996). He argues for a reconfiguration of cultural geography, calling for an analysis of information interchange along networks rather than the discussion of identities within discreet spatial boundaries. Conceptually, there is some resonance in Raymond Williams's notion of 'flows of images' in his discussion of television and cultural form. Williams (1974: 87–9) reconstituted the critical analysis of television by challenging us to think of it not as a sequence of individualized moments but as a flow of image and sound. I wish to generalize the concept so that, in design terms, objects are not abstracted from contexts into a reified, modernist canon (the single-piece exhibit, mediated by the expert's caption). Rather, they belong to a never-ending stream of visual and material narratives running in a series of directions. We might begin to think in terms of 'flows of artefacts' both material and visual through a circuit.

CIRCUITS OF CULTURE

Through their critiques of earlier theorists, some academics have recognized the need for a more complex approach to studying the culture of production and consumption. The classic model would be to arrange production, distribution and consumption in a straight, sequential line. Johnson (1986), however, loops this chain back into itself to describe an endless 'circuit of production and consumption' (see Figure 4.2).

Johnson's diagram is useful in a number of ways. First, it suggests a link between the public and private domains of consumption, as well as ideological conditions and personal action. Second, it emphasizes the interpretative nature of consumption, suggesting that the objects of production become 'texts' which are then 'read'. This reading then feeds into lived cultures; it informs the way that everyday life is articulated, which then provides information upon which production then acts. Third, we may then begin to appreciate design as both articulating and enacting social relations and human action.

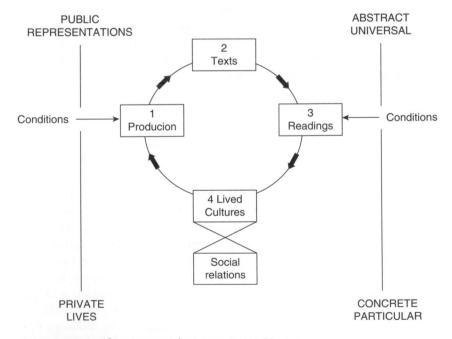

Figure 4.2   Johnson's 'circuit of production and comsumption' (1986: 284)

Du Gay et al. (2013) push this model further by suggesting that different stages in the circuit all interact with each other (see Figure 4.3). Their argument is more specific in terms of the qualities involved in the production and consumption process. They claim that both production and consumption inform social identities, the way that objects are represented and their systems of regulation. By regulation they mean the way that norms are established in order that the product is consumed in conformity to specific patterns and meanings. Furthermore, they may be encountered in different formats through this circuit – as primary functional objects, as represented in promotional material, at the point of sale, and so on. Their meanings are subject to constant transformation and rewriting by both producing agents (e.g. designers, marketers and distributors) and their consumers. Through their critical and exhaustive study of the Sony Walkman, they continually return to the overlapping and interactions of different nodes in their circuit of culture.

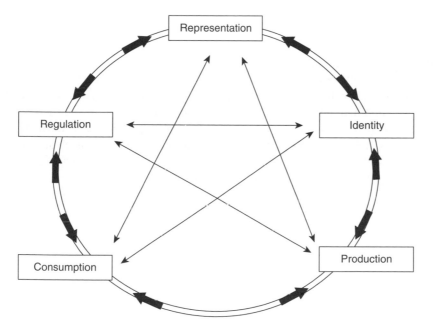

Figure 4.3   du Gay et al.'s (2013) 'circuit of culture'

DESIGNERS AND THE CIRCUIT OF CULTURE

Johnson (1986), Fine and Leopold (1993), Jackson and Thrift (1995) and du Gay et al. (2013) all provide models or suggestions for considering the production/consumption relationship that are applicable in different ways to different objects, spaces and images. Rather than assume a universality in this, they honour the diversity of actions and experiences involved between distinct cultural and commercial forms. Thus for instance, so-called fast-moving consumer goods (FMCGs) – goods such as foodstuffs which are subject to repeated repurchase – will be treated differently from consumer durables. Products may be moved through the circuit, or the system of provision, in different patterns and speeds according to the many variables along its route. Certainly, design may act as a laxative for this circuit, helping to move goods faster through the system (Reavley 1998). In other words, design promotes an insatiable appetite for newness, variety or 'the next thing'.

As we have seen in Chapter 2, market research for major brands often combines quantitative data through surveys with qualitative research undertaken, for instance, through focus groups. The account planner then develops this information into a detailed brief for designers. As such, he or she is attempting to anticipate consumer expectations as well as develop future desires. The account planner is in a position therefore to orchestrate some measure of the flow through the circuit of culture.

There are various methods by which design production appropriates the realms of consumption. At one end of this scale, consultancies may employ designers who represent their target market as consumers themselves. In Britain, this was particularly the case during the mid-1980s when design consultancies eagerly employed young graduates who had an instinctive feel for trends in the youth market for retail and consumer items (York 1988). It was assumed, effectively, that by designing for themselves they would be designing for their peers. At the other end of the scale, brand and identity specialists will promote complex design systems in order to ensure that all aspects of consumer behaviour are mapped, accounted for and anticipated as part of the design process. Thus while marketing gurus Schmitt and Simonson (1997: 143) criticize open-ended, theoretical discourse on consumption, they are keen to promote models such as a particularly convoluted one devised by design methods and marketing specialist Peter Bloch aimed at 'Seeking the Ideal Form' (1995). This model networked cultural, situational and psychological domains in order to explore different levels of consumer response. Schmitt and Simonson stated that Bloch's article, which outlined this model, 'could be a forerunner to a potentially useful line of research in the area of product aesthetics and identity' (1997: 44).

Despite Schmitt and Simonson's positivistic and somewhat anti-intellectual stance, it must be noted that increasing numbers of designers and design students engage with theoretical discourses in the social sciences and humanities as a way of deepening their critical perspectives on consumer culture. This has led some to observe that they are better versed in 'French philosophy' than in the technical intricacies of design (Kinross 1997: 202)!

WRITING ABOUT THINGS

The rise of interest in consumption has indeed been accompanied, if not prefigured, by an artistic response to the growth of consumer culture. During the 1950s the Independent Group – a collective of artists, critics and architects – and other pop artists explored consumerism, in particular through the impact of American popular culture. The collages and paintings of Richard Hamilton revealed the relationships between product appearance, advertising and sexuality in subtle ways, which have led John Walker to describe his work as that of a 'knowing consumer' (1983: 32). His contemporary, the critic Reyner Banham, wrote many lively essays on product design and popular culture, such as 'Power Plank' (1996 [1973]), an essay on the semantics of clipboards, and 'The Great Gizmo' (1981 [1965]), on electronic gadgets. His penchant for gizmos and gadgets was expressed in a largely formalistic way; the main concern was for the physical attributes of commodities and his relationship to them as a consumer. Thus his approach was similar to that of an art connoisseur looking at design, except that he vastly extended the border of what the design critic might look at beyond the modernist canon to all mainstream everyday objects.

Fiction writing opens a pathway by which description and specialist descriptive terms may be celebrated. Nicholson Baker's first novel *The Mezzanine* (1988) follows the journey of an office worker through his lunch hour as he considers the minutiae of his material surroundings: the shape of a stapler in relation to locomotive trains; the shift from paper to plastic straws; why one shoelace should break before the other; the labelling of a packaged sandwich as 'Cream Cheese and Sliced Olive' ('why *sliced*?' he asks). Through such obsessive interrogations he links them to memory, showing that 'our relationship with material things, and our awareness of their gradual but continuous transformations, provide a measure of much of the meaning of our lives' (Meikle 1998: 197). Similarly, David Guterson's detailed explanation of trawler-fishing equipment (1995: 346–7), Slavenka Drakulić's discussion of laundry (1988: 43–54) or William Gibson's description of a 'chunker' (1994: 9) show that articulating the material can provide poetic, beautiful results. In each of these examples the narrative of the novel is momentarily grounded in the visceral reality of the everyday. Likewise, Patrick Suskind's bestselling novel *Perfume* (1987) features a protagonist with extraordinary powers of smell: using this device the reader is navigated through a unique perspective on space and the relationship between sensory perception and place.

In addition to their ability to expand the poetic potential within descriptions of the everyday, such novelists observe the interrelationships between their characters and the objects, spaces and images of their fictional environment. Indeed, their observations are more than 'scene-setting' because they also act as devices to propel their respective plots. Guterson's novel engages a forensic approach to solving a suspected murder; doing laundry in Drakulić's account opens out a discussion of the challenges of collectivization during the Soviet period; the weaponry described by Gibson forms part of a futuristic cityscape where materiality remains more useful than virtuality. In each of these depictions, things, spaces or systems are embedded alongside everyday, routine actions to form practices that have their specific logics according to their narratives and their consequent settings.

CONSUMPTION AND PRACTICE

The adoption of a 'systems of provision' approach that leads on to thinking about 'circuits of culture' helps us conceptualize the interrelationships between productive and consumer activities. We have seen that distinct types of goods and services engage varying systems of provision and are therefore encountered differently – they have their own sets of 'rules' that are configured through their specific circuit of culture.

Developments in the sociological consideration of consumption have also led to a greater sense of connectivity and specificity that provide compelling structures for investigating the role of design in society. The critique of particular approaches to Visual Culture expressed in Chapter 1 focused on its insistence on over-concentrating its attention on the ocular transaction between individual visual artefact and individual viewer. Equally, we have seen in this chapter that approaches to consumption that foreground it as an individual expression of private will leave out the fact that consumption is also socially constituted.

By thinking in terms of consumption as 'practice', we can begin to explore an alternative conception that considers the specificity of its various modes and locations, the possible interrelationality of objects, spaces and images and the ways by which rules of engagement act.

For Reckwitz:

> A 'practice' … is a routinised type of behaviour which consists of several elements, interconnected to one another: forms of bodily activities, forms of mental activities, 'things' and their use, a background knowledge in the form of understanding, know-how, states of emotion and motivational knowledge. (2002: 249)

A consideration of practice therefore brings together material and immaterial processes. Practice is supported both by designed artefacts – for example, things that are used, spaces that define activities or images that communicate information – as well as shared ideas as to how those practices may be carried out or what they might mean. Practices are 'filled out' by a multitude of individuals and products that act as their carriers. They are therefore socially constituted.

Practices may be conceived in terms of various forms of consumer activities, each with its sets of rules and norms. Bourdieu (1992) developed the notion of 'field' as an extension of practice. He was more concerned with explicitly competitive versions of practice wherein the field provides the setting for its rules (Warde 2004). Analogously and quite literally, many sports take place in fields and require specific and agreed rules for them to be carried out. They also include designed hardware that provides the focus for their play, supports their rules and facilitates their spectatorship. However, even sports involve a combination of competitive-based rules and noncompetitive considerations and their successful function requires the combination of these. At one level, there are the formally created procedures that allow the sport to be played fairly; at another, there are socially understood elements to the game – such as sportsmanship – that make it affable and entertaining. Thus, in generalizing this notion, it is necessary to go beyond a competitive conception of field – where all actions are strategic – to embrace a more nuanced understanding of practice.

Schatzki (1996: 89) argues that practices work as both coordinated entities and are performed. In the former case, rules are explicitly formulated in order for practices to coalesce and be understandable. This may be implicit in terms of the tacit, shared 'doings' and 'sayings' within a practice or it may be explicit through rules, principles, precepts and instructions. In the latter case, practices can also become regimes in that they regulate behaviour and thought. Finally, this may exist through what he calls 'teleoaffective' structures, in which a shared aim defines how a practice is carried out and thought about. But practices are also sustained through their performance. Regular enactment of practices tests and reinforces their norms.

The emphasis in using this approach to practice is thus on the relationality of people and artefacts. Value is not perceived to reside in products or services themselves, nor in the meanings attached to them (e.g. through product styling, branding or advertising), rather it emerges in practice itself (Shove et al. 2005). Economic value is only as much as people are prepared to actually pay; the environmental value of a 'green' product is only realized upon its use; the emotional value of a brand requires a shared frame of reference among its participants. Artefacts give focus to, facilitate, mediate and explain norms of practice, but they only have value in so far as their consumers are prepared to engage with them.

This leads Warde (2005: 141) to suspect that 'the distinct, institutionalized and collectively regulated conventions' of practices insulate their carriers from 'the blandishments of producers and promotional agencies'. The routines of everyday life as well as institutionally imposed rules make consumers of products and services unchanging in their habits. Since practice involves networks of contingent elements, consumption may be more conservative than some proponents who celebrate it as being in constant change and development think. Changing to a different smartphone, for example, requires learning how it works. It might require you to download new support software onto your computer. It might make transferring stored information from one to the other (addresses, photos, music files) complicated and frustrating.

Nonetheless, while practices may indeed display facets of normative action, they are also continually evolving. This may be in response to external stimulae such as climate change, environmental legislations, rising interest rates, the threat of terrorist attacks or war. But corporations are constantly devising ways of moulding existing practices or creating new ones. Thus in introducing new products or services, producers seek to *destabilize* established practices (Slater 2002).

Practices do not exist in isolation from one another. Indeed, they may be mutually dependent or in conflict. A professional football match has its norms and artefacts on the field, but it also depends on a set of practices – fandom, televization, corporate hospitality – that support it but may also exhibit conflicts between and within them. Each will have its own understandings, actions and artefacts. Thus producers may develop products and services that resolve conflicts between them which in turn produce new practices and destabilize routines. For example, to encourage people out of their cars and resolve the tension between environmental concerns and personal transportation practices, better public transport information services supported by digital wireless networks may be provided. This destabilization of practices itself requires habituation and assimilation, a process that may be managed through design as well.

Producers are competitively focused on installing just the right balance of stabilization and destabilization in their products and services so that they are able to retain recognition in the marketplace while not alienating consumers or being irrelevant to their practices. American industrial designer Raymond Loewy coined the acronym MAYA – Most Advanced Yet Acceptable – to describe this balance (Trétiack 1999). Callon et al. describe this balancing act accordingly:

> The singularization of a product, which allows its attachment to a particular consumer, is obtained against a background of similitude. The difference that enables a product to capture the consumer always involves the prior assertion of a resemblance which suggests an association between the consumer's former attachments and the new ones proposed. ... Capturing, 'attaching' consumers by 'detaching' them from the networks built by rivals, is the mainspring of competition. (2002: 203)

By considering consumption in terms of practice, the analysis is shifted away from thinking about the transactions between individual user and singular object. Instead, one is encouraged to consider different activities as constituting a network of people and products. Equally, it should be remembered that design itself is a practice, with its own rules, understandings, skills, meanings, personal and collective professional aspirations. Thus it is also affected by its own lens in the way it intervenes on practices.

CONCLUSION

It is not insignificant that the growing interest shown by sociologists, anthropologists, cultural geographers and historians in matters of visual and material culture and its consumption has emerged in an era where ideological and commercial primacy has increasingly been given over to consumers within systems of liberal democracy and market capitalism. However, given the broad range of academic disciplines with an interest in consumption, it is hardly surprising that a wide variety of positions regarding its value, meaning and practices have been adopted. Broadly speaking, these may be divided into three camps. To perhaps oversimplify, first, there are those who frame consumption as an essentially docile activity over which producing agents dominate (Frankfurt School, Galbraith, Packard, Haug); second, those who adopt, at times, the notion that consuming can be emancipatory or even resistant (Hebdige, Miller, de Certeau, Fiske); and third, those who view it as neither of these but as an expression which has its own, often spectacular, postmodern logic (Baudrillard, Eco). Finally, and more recently, academics (Schatzki, Shove, Warde) have considered consumption as more networked and contingent activity that involves constellations of artefacts and socially constituted norms and activities. As subsequent chapters in this book argue, the culture of design conspires to overlap these positions, making consumption both active and passive, meaningful and meaningless at the same time. Consumer empowerment, ironically, may sometimes mean an ability to accept given situations as they are with both distance and engagement. It is perhaps more useful to consider *how* the exchanges of production and consumption take place.

Consumption stands at the intersection of different spheres of everyday life, between the public and the private, the political and the personal, the individual and the social. It represents and articulates these relationships but is also active in reproducing them. Given its ubiquity, the study of consumption need not privilege certain goods and services over others; it promises an open-game where the most prosaic interaction with material and visual culture is laced with significance. Equally, Veblen, and later Bourdieu, remind us that we must be aware of the symbolic-value that they hold, that despite the promise of democracy of consuming within market capitalism, it may also be an act of differentiation and distinction.

Theoretical explorations of consumption have provided useful conceptual frameworks for the interrogation of the exercise of taste. Some literary and artistic creations develop a lively vocabulary to express the visceral immediacy of our visual and material environment. Both of these pursuits again remind us of the polysemic nature of consuming – that it can mean several things at various levels. Nonetheless, while there may well be levels of interpretation and significance that reside independent of the values which are generated by productive interests, design practice is increasingly concerned with refining and controlling the flows and patterns of meaning that pass from production to consumption. Again this points to the intrinsically reflexive nature of design. Consumer information, both quantitative and qualitative, is filtered, interpreted and recycled in an endless circuit. The intervention of design on practices both uses and interprets them, but also acts to destabilize them or even create new practices. In respect of the multiplicity of practices, different types of goods and services are also moved through this circuit at different speeds and each with its distinctive manner. Understanding the exchanges that take place along this continuum requires the mobilization of a range of theoretical frameworks and cognitive skills.

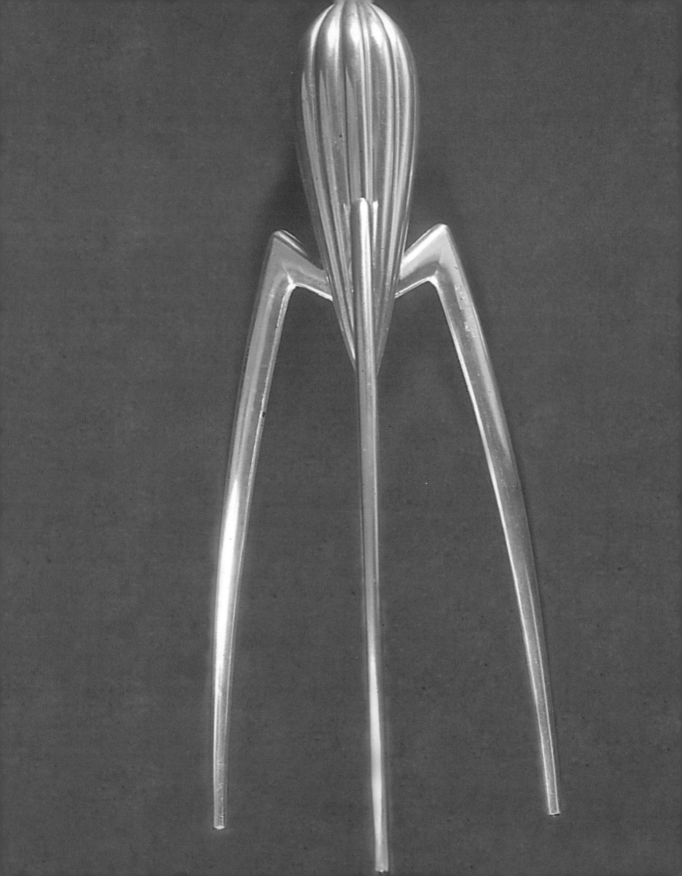

CHAPTER 5
HIGH DESIGN

Of all the categories presented in this book, high design is perhaps the most forceful in its influence on public perceptions of design and designers. Chapter 5 discusses how high design is produced and consumed. By production, we do not just imply the manufacture of design objects but also how their meanings and, indeed, those of high design in general are constructed. Here the focus is, in part, on mediation. This includes how design objects are written or spoken about, but also, indirectly, how the image of their designers is sometimes portrayed. Consumption refers to how these objects are physically utilized; but this also extends to how they are understood. Indeed, we see that their 'uselessness' or wastefulness contributes to their significance. This is bound up with social practices that have to do with cultural capital and conspicuous consumption. In the final section of this chapter, the relationship of certain practices of design to art is discussed, showing how these not only extend but also challenge this idea of high design.

Three slender legs rise from delicate ankles. Bending at an impossibly high knee they sweep back to a fluted, central teardrop form. These aeronautically profiled, arachnoid supports lift the object heavenward for the admiring gaze. Perfectly fashioned for maximum 'look', this tripod holds aloft the raw nature of the implement's bulbous, phallic head.

It requires both skill and strength to use. The lemon-squeezer gives slightly as one bears down, rhythmically twisting and pushing on the fruit. Your hand is left messy with the detritus of your labour as the lemon disintegrates beneath it. Channelled by the fluting that adorns the head, juices glide lazily down the side to meet at a tip on its underside. From there they stream into a vessel beneath, giving off the glistening flow and satisfying sound of micturition.

Once cleaned up it is then returned to a shelf, a cabinet or its box. There it will sit, poutingly hermaphroditic, insouciantly demanding.

ANOMALOUS OBJECTS

Besides its strangely transsexual aspect, the Juicy Salif lemon-squeezer exhibits several other 'in-between' characteristics. As a utilitarian kitchen implement, it only half works. It delivers lemon juice in an enticing, amusing fashion straight to a glass, but you also get the pips and some pith with it, which may then need straining out. For the novice, juice splatters about: it is only after one learns the correct body posture, the optimum conjunction of limbs and the requisite force needed, that this problem recedes. As if to underline this connoisseurship of function, the instructions supplied with the object include copious advice and detailed drawings on its use and cleaning. They also tell us that upon its first use, a chemical reaction takes place between the lemon juice and the aluminium, rendering the first squeezing redundant. Equally, the metal discolours, losing its shine.

So is this an object of use or of contemplation? Should it be consigned to the kitchen cabinet or the lounge shelves? Certainly it fits alongside a range of odd kitchen gadgets which are brought out on particular occasions: pasta-mills, artichoke plates, avocado dishes, fresh herb shredders. And the tacit psychomotor skills which are mastered in its use become ritualized acts in the same way that the stirring of a Christmas pudding mixture becomes an annual event. They mark time, repetition and familiarity.

Alternatively, its shininess allies it with a typology of silverware reserved for the cabinet of 'special things'. Since the 17th century, the family silverware has functioned in several ways. First, it has had a use-value in being brought out and employed for important occasions such as festive banquets, christenings and weddings. Second, it has had exchange-value in that, besides real estate, it has acted as a fixed asset for families, its value on the market being more stable than cash. Selling the family silver then becomes a last resort in times of dire financial circumstances. Third, silverware has symbolic-value in that it is used as a gift and heirloom, thus reinforcing kinship. Fourth, it has sign-value in representing the cultural tastes of its owner.

As its designer remarked of it:

This is not a very good lemon squeezer: but that's not its only function. I had this idea that when a couple get married it's the sort of thing they would get as a wedding present. So the new husband's parents come round, he and his father sit in the living room with a beer, watching television, and the new bride and mother-in-law sit in the kitchen to get to know each other better. 'Look what we got as a present', the daughter-in-law will say. (Starck, quoted in Lloyd Morgan 1999: 9)

Retailing at around £45 a piece, the Juicy Salif is absurdly, disproportionately expensive in the same way the silverware of a family of the lower gentry in the 17th century was often worth more than their other effects put together. Its exchange-value may appear to far outweigh its use-value. Nonetheless, it's only made of aluminium.

If its visual references combine both male and female bodily attributes then it also reminds one of Buck Rogers style-science-fiction imagery of the 1950s (a decade when aluminium in consumer items was coming of age). The teardrop shape of its head is also redolent of the Arabic designs which found their way into late-medieval architectural details, the name 'Juicy Salif' reinforcing this association. Thus it is both popular and 'exotic' in its referents. Neither male nor female, but both. Useful and useless. Refined and trashy. An object of display and yet it is too damnably singular to fit in with anything else. Perhaps these anomalies are what hold the object's fascination. Lévi-Strauss (1969) argued that in the West, we structure our world around binary opposites as a universal sense-making process, hence male/female, culture/nature, domesticated/wild. Each acts as 'other' to its partner. There are, however, 'anomalous categories': things which transgress the binary divide and as such hold a particular interest and/or disgust. On a lesser level, perhaps, then, the Juicy Salif functions as an anomalous object.

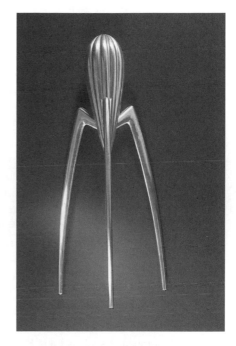

Juicy Salif lemon-squeezer, designed by Philippe Starck, manufactured by Alessi Spa from 1990
Photo: Guy Julier

HIGH DESIGN

The Juicy Salif lemon-squeezer was designed by Philippe Starck and manufactured by the northern Italian producer of tableware, Alessi Spa, from 1990. It has become emblematic of both its designer and its manufacturer, given a leading role as an image in monographs published on both (see Sweet 1998: 9, 1999: jacket image; Lloyd Morgan 1999: 8). Along with perhaps the Alessi-produced Richard Sapper-designed 'Kettle with a Singing Whistle' (1983), the Juicy Salif lemon-squeezer has for some become synonymous with the excesses and pretentions of the 1980s in particular and design in general. Both have been lambasted for the high ratio of price to functionality. Meanwhile, design 'guru' Sir Terence Conran tells us that 'it's intriguing, tactile and desirable, and even though it squirts juice all over your shirt, it's fun to use' (cited in Sweet 1998: 36). More soberly, design-buyer Craig Allen suggests that 'there's more to this than getting juice out of a lemon' (Allen, quoted in Russell 1996).

Having seen that the object does not fit comfortably into historical typologies, it is also interesting to consider how it fits in with contemporary hierarchies of design. At one end of the scale we might establish 'anonymous design' as a category wherein objects, spaces and images are conceived and shaped by professional designers or people from other backgrounds taking on a designer's role, but, crucially, the etiquette of the designer is not formally recognized. Pencils and zippers may be examples of 'anonymous design' which have been subject to painstaking, if not obsessional, historical research (see Friedel 1994; Petroski 1996). At the other end of this scale we find 'high design' where conscious designer intervention and authorship, along with the price tag, play a large role in establishing the cultural and aesthetic credentials of an artefact.

Design critic Peter Dormer (1990) provides a useful discussion of 'high design'. He divides the concept into two categories: *heavenly goods*, being objects designed for the rich to buy; and *tokens*, objects bought by the 'wish-they-were-rich'. Heavenly objects combine astonishing high performance with exclusivity. However, there is always a limit to the degree of performance that most products can be taken to: industrial design and manufacturers in the contemporary age deliver goods which cannot be bettered, unlike 100 years ago. Beyond a certain, relatively low price, the rich cannot buy a better performing camera or home kettle than the wider public. Thus, Dormer argues, exclusivity has to be invented by the inclusion of unnecessary details. Precious metals, unusual leathers or exotic timbers may be incorporated into the product to boost this quality. As in the case of the Aston Martin Lagonda motor car, it may be unnecessarily hand-built in an age when computer-controlled manufacturing may give a much higher standard of workmanship: 'The power to have the exclusive rights to another person's labour is appealing because the possession of someone else's time is an absolute. All the other aspects of an object can be copied and mass produced and, horror of horrors, popularized' (Dormer 1990: 124).

There are other devices in design origination, branding and distribution by which heavenly goods maintain their exclusivity. For example, the car manufacturer Porsche also has a separate design company which collaborates with lighting, furniture and accessories manufacturers to develop products for the seriously rich; thus the Porsche design brand is 'lent' to other products. While producers of luggage and accessories such as Louis Vuitton have historically maintained an exclusive status, in recent years companies such as Land Rover and Rolls-Royce have moved into this market, transferring the brand value of their core product into other objects which in turn act as advertisements as much for the corporation as for the owner's status. This is known as 'brand-stretching'. Finally, sophisticated retailers such as Dunhill or Harvey Nichols may reinforce the values of heavenly goods by turning shopping into an exercise in socio-economic differentiation.

However, as we slip away from the material qualities of heavenly goods and consider their mediation, we begin to overlap with the realm of token goods, for they are scenarios of participation of the 'would-be-rich'. Token goods provide imitations or intimations of the lives of the seriously pecunious and represent a much bigger industry. They are affordable for the professional classes with disposable income or access to credit but maintain an aura of discernment.

The places where token goods may be bought nestle within the habitat of the very rich. (I have bought two Juicy Salifs, one for research purposes from Oggetti and the other as an expensive tongue-in-cheek wedding present from the Conran Shop. Both these outlets are in London's Chelsea where you can also buy Rolls-Royces or exclusively tailored coats.) Shopping for these goods becomes a form of tourism as you venture into the territory of exclusivity to claim a token souvenir of that momentary experience.

Alternatively, since the 1980s we have witnessed a partial de-differentiation between museum curatorship and retail and, indeed, between high art and the high street (Lash and Urry 1994: 272;

Whitely 1994; Urry 1995: 151; Zukin 1995: Ch. 4). Museums which display modern design, such as the Museum of Modern Art in New York or the Design Museum in London, also have a nice shop attached. You can peruse the exhibits and then go to the museum shop and 'buy a relic, a token of what cannot be yours' (Dormer 1990: 117). Likewise, designer objects are displayed in shops as museum pieces. Lees (1997: 79) notes that Alessi retail sites invariably display a single example of each product, suggesting their uniqueness and preciousness, just as museum objects have traditionally been curated. In other outlets, such as Harrods or John Lewis, the Alessi range is displayed together in the same way that museums often maintain 'families' of objects. Smaller museums, Lees notes, with reduced space and funds, will invariably use Alessi products as 'a shorthand for describing 1980s design and postmodernism' (1997: 79). Thus Alessi, in cooperation with museums and retailers, are able to effect an interchange around their objects: they achieve 'museum status' while being affordable and buyable.

High design can thus be defined in relation to other goods. If by falling into the category of 'heavenly goods' they may be the same as other products, they are given further value by, for example, their use of materials that have no relation to actual performance. If they exist as 'tokens', their value is partly generated by reference to the other goods around them. This may be the objects in a museum or on display in shops nearby. In other words, the notion of high design is not exclusively intrinsic to the object; it is also contextually determined.

DESIGN CLASSICS

Within this process, the term 'design classic' has emerged as a way of labelling products which sum up the best of their time but equally whose appeal surpasses their immediate historical context. This is a problematic term, not least because there are certain objects that may offer the best design solution to a functional and aesthetic problem which may not last as a problem. This is particularly the case in the design of corporate identity, capital goods or certain technologies that respond to immediate economic and cultural circumstances which subsequently change and render them obsolete (there is unlikely to be a classic telex-machine design, for instance). Conversely, then, the 'design classic' label privileges certain functional goods over others. Basic activities like sitting, lounging or eating remain unchanged: chairs, chaises longues or tableware more readily receive the 'design classic' accolade.

Certainly there are cases of a brand receiving the 'design classic' status. The most obvious of these would be Coca-Cola, which appears with monotonous frequency in books on branding (Murray 1998). The inference in much of the discourse of the design classic, as made evident in Sudjic (1985) and more recently in the *Phaidon Design Classics* publication (Terragni 2006), is that there is something intrinsic to the artefact itself which gives it that status. In the same way we have seen that objects are subject to commodity fetishism – that the social conditions of their production are magically imbued in them – so then 'design classic' augments the reificatory processes. Thus we must remember that in the case of Coca-Cola, the corporation itself has energetically marketed its brand as historical by featuring the earlier bottle shape on the side of its cans, but less subtly through exhibitions and catalogues tracing the development and applications of its brand identity. In this way the company legitimates itself, reproducing its own myths in order to be both historical and contemporary – timeless, in other words – and thus a 'design classic'.

Again the process may work in the other direction. In 1990, London's Design Museum exhibited a 'Flexo' lamp as an example of vernacular Spanish design to coincide with a season of Iberian events. By 1995, the retailers Habitat were selling the lamp, telling the consumer via a label stuck on its base that it was 'a classic of Spanish design' and that there was one on 'permanent display at the Design Museum in London'.

As part of this historicizing process since the late 1970s several international furniture companies, including Aram, B.D. Ediciones de Diseño, Cassina, Knoll and Santa & Cole, have re-edited historical pieces by 'hero designers' such as Antoni Gaudì, Le Corbusier and Marcel Breuer. This inserts the corporations into the canon of design by aligning them with proclaimed historical figures. Subsequent new products draw their status from this circumstance. Likewise, Alessi began to manufacture historical designs such as Marianne Brandt's 1925 tea set from the early 1980s. Unsurprisingly, the Juicy Salif later gets described as an object which 'pushed design to new limits and instantly became a cult classic' (Sweet 1998).

Objects become the token goods of high design through association within a complicated system of mediation and distribution. In an essay entitled 'The Work of Art in the Age of Mechanical Reproduction', Benjamin (1970 [1936]) argues that the development of systems for the serial production of images such as colour printing has not devalued the originals; rather, it has bestowed greater importance and aura on these (which explains why despite huge growth in art-book publishing, the public still flock to galleries).

Since the 1980s, the distinctions between the design object as curated in the museum and the design object as displayed through retail have been blurred; acquisition of the mass-produced artefact is a way to borrow back some of the aura of the original.

MEDIATING PRODUCTION

The object analysis delivered at the beginning of this chapter is contentious, based on the restrictions of the author's personal experience of it. Clearly, responses to it will vary according to differing socio-economic and cultural backgrounds. However, further consideration of the circumstances of its production suggests that its readings are indeed restricted or pre-empted by its manufacturer, Alessi Spa, and its designer, Philippe Starck. Alessi moved from being a manufacturer of 'anonymous design' household products to incorporating designer goods into its catalogue in the 1980s. An event that marked this step was its Tea and Coffee Piazza project, in which it invited world-famous architects such as Hans Hollein, Robert Venturi and Michael Graves to each design a tea set which went into limited production of 99 pieces each in 1983. The designers' individual processes were published in a book edited by Alessi itself (1983), which served to reinforce the 'greatness' of the authors and, by association, the manufacturers involved. Alessi is an extraordinarily media-friendly company. To promote the brand image and its products, Alessi uses Di Palma Associati for its public relations, one of Italy's foremost publicity agencies which specializes in the promotion of design. It produces and distributes a plethora of gift mailings, press releases and publications, which get readily reproduced in design journals (Lees 1997: 81).

Since the Tea and Coffee Piazza project, Alessi has published several book-length discussions of its own work which give both basic product information concerning size, weight, materials and so on of its goods, and often turgid postmodern deconstructional essays on the 'meanings' of its products (e.g. Gabra-Liddell 1994). There is an interesting irony in the way that the analysis is derived from the theories of poststructuralism that are mustered to deliver a pre-packaged meaning for the consumer. Poststructuralism contends that meanings of textual, visual or material artefacts are multiple according to the consumer's position, rendering authorship effectively dead. In the instance of the Alessi publications, the strategies of pluralism and multiplicity of meaning are re-appropriated into the producer's ownership. Interpretation is self-generated, articulated and disseminated as a pre-emptive strike on the consumer before he or she makes his or her own mind up.

This not only legitimates the otherwise banal nature of many of Alessi's products by giving them intellectual status, it is also a form of rationalization. By publishing the designers' development sketches, photographs of consultants on the factory floor and employing a philosopher or sociologist to write on the significance of all this in the modern age, we can see where the money we spend on their products is going. The brand image of Alessi as wacky, honest, thoughtful and committed to high production. Design values are reinforced while at the same time the consumer is drawn into its corporate culture.

CONSUMING POSTMODERN HIGH DESIGN: VEBLEN AND BOURDIEU

As we have seen, buying tokens such as the Juicy Salif may be an act in the performance of 'design tourism': it is the souvenir bought at the end of a day's cultural sightseeing. Connoisseurship and a measure of privilege are both mobilized in the process of purchase. The link between leisure, consumption and social distinction was elaborated by Thorstein Veblen (1970 [1899]) and later developed by Pierre Bourdieu (1984).

Veblen first defined leisure as time consumed non-productively rather than the space outside paid employment; after all, many household activities, such as washing, cleaning and cooking, are not considered to be leisure activities. Leisure is created from a sense of the unworthiness of productive work – for some there is no need to work all the time, and for a privileged few there is no need to work at all. Leisure, then, becomes evidence of one's pecuniary ability to afford not to work. Out of this basis Veblen coined three key concepts: conspicuous consumption, conspicuous leisure and conspicuous waste. *Conspicuous consumption* involves the possession of goods, which in turn demonstrates one's leisure time and economic status both to acquire them (in terms of shopping and choosing them) and to appreciate them (in terms of understanding their cultural value). This inherently involves a degree of *conspicuous leisure* in that the consumption of goods, and leisure activities one must add, means that one is seen to be using time non-productively but also that one is employing others towards non-productive ends. Thus shopping, tourism and hobbies all involve the labour of others such as shop

Selling/curating high design: part of the Alessi range as seen in (above) Peter Maturi & Sons, Leeds and (below) interior of Domane, Leeds
Photos: Guy Julier

assistants, waitresses or gamekeepers in supporting non-productively used time. The final piece of this matrix entails the *conspicuous waste* of goods and services. The artefacts and activities of conspicuous consumption do not fulfil a utilitarian purpose, but often they *emulate* utility. The rich do not need to hunt or fish in order to feed themselves, but they do like to play at it; necessity is turned into sport.

The Juicy Salif clearly fulfils all three of these criteria of conspicuosity. We have seen how it has been marketed and placed in a way to ensure its consumer status. We have seen how its lack of efficiency compared with more standard models encourages its contemplation and use in a somewhat non-productive manner: it doesn't squeeze lemons very well and mastering its use may be considered a 'waste of time'. It is interesting to note how much of the Alessi promotional material emphasizes the craft ethics of the company and the incorporation of craftsmanship into manufacture; thus the labour of others is obviously secured for the consumer. Finally, while being an object of display, the object nonetheless proposed a utilitarian purpose as a kitchen gadget.

Interestingly, the tension between the banal conspicuosity and the potential use of such high design objects is expressed in an Alessi publication. In 1996 its research centre published *L'oggetto dell'equilibrio* (the balanced object) as an updated Alessi manifesto. Speaking of the 'unbalanced object', which the company seeks to avoid, Bruno Pasini described it as:

> an object which refuses to 'soften' in the passage from the showcase to the home; an object so highly charged with personality that it cannot be personalised. It is an object whose identity becomes confounded with its advertising, which doesn't age yet falls out of fashion. It is often merely an imitation of something truly functional: an object that doesn't invite use, but whose similarity to one that does serves as an alibi of its decorative essence. … From the second half of the 1980s onwards these objects have crowded our stores, our magazines, our homes: indistinguishable, narcissistic, self-aggrandising, pretentious, unjustifiably authoritative: objects which wear you out just looking at them, which you're afraid to touch, which fail to suggest their own purpose. (Pasini, quoted in Lees 1997: 87)

As Lees observes, Pasini could as easily be talking about Alessi's own products, or even the Juicy Salif.

Bourdieu's seminal study was developed from a highly systematic quantitative analysis of the real-life tastes and pursuits of a broad range of French consumers. He adopted a starting point which said that social relations first and foremost are cultural rather than economic. In other words, what we have, and what we do in our leisure, define us in class terms more accurately than the jobs we are employed in.

Bourdieu's interest was not exclusively in *what* people acquired or did, but in *how* they made distinctions between different types of cultural goods. Thus distinction was a key concept: it denotes both the process of identifying differences as well as the way by which goods and their meanings are used to achieve difference. Within this Bourdieu draws up clear categorizations of high-brow, middle-brow and low-brow culture. The process of distinction requires what he called 'cultural capital', this being one's measure of that ability to distinguish between the cultivated and the vulgar. Finally, he employs the idea of the habitus as an umbrella concept, drawing together individual action and social relations through the exercise of taste and cultural capital. In design terms, the habitus is a useful concept – though it is often confused with 'lifestyle' – for it demands the consideration of non-explicit activities in everyday life. It refers to habitual, customary activities, such as squeezing a lemon; it binds these to the body, showing that the processes of distinction and cultural capital are acted out. Thus the bodily pose adopted when squeezing that lemon, the ease or self-consciousness felt in undertaking this task, are expressions of our breeding.

As a broad basis for his systems of distinction Bourdieu drew on Kant's notion of the aesthetic as the taste of the dominant class and contrasted this with an anti-Kantian aesthetic (see Table 5.1). The Kantian aesthetic differs from Veblen's emphasis on a strongly conspicuous form of consumption by suggesting that it is more detached and that, indeed, the overt display in itself is considered to be vulgar by those of 'high cultural capital'. Their interest, then, is in cultural goods which are 'difficult' to appreciate and which do not promise immediate pleasure. Consumption, in these terms, is an educated, informed practice. Conversely, the anti-Kantian aesthetic is more highly conspicuous and promises a more immediate, sensual pleasure.

There are several problems with Bourdieu's methodology and conclusions. First, his survey was carried out in a way almost identical to quantitative marketing surveys; thus he missed out on much of the looser, qualitative experience of consumption which interviews or focus groups may provide. Second, he then set himself the task of grafting his data on to pre-established social groupings: working-class, bourgeois, upper-class, and so on. This meant that other possible groupings are ignored – gender is not discussed, for instance. There is a tendency to stereotype the consumption behaviour of groupings – thus working-class taste is presented as based in the 'choice of the necessary' and is somehow 'unclouded by ideology' (Slater 1997: 163). In this version, the working classes are perceived as an authentic humanity, fulfilling a particularly Romantic vision. By extension, the tastes of other classes are more elaborated, self-conscious and positional.

Miller suggests that an alternative approach to studying the relationship of consumption and social groupings might be found in observing the divisions which pertain to 'object domains' (Miller 1987: 158). Alternatively, then, groups are clustered around particular forms of consumption and stylistic tastes which may be identified. The study of the goods themselves provides evidence

Table 5.1   Kantian and anti-Kantian aesthetics (Corrigan 1997: 29)

Kantian aesthetic	Anti-Kantian aesthetic
Higher cultural capital	Lower cultural capital
Elite culture	Popular culture
Cultivated, abstracted appropriation	Immediate pleasure
Mind-centred (understanding)	Body-centred (sensuality)
Representation as convention, esoteric, formal	Representation as naturalistic
Subtle, detached, inconspicuous form of display readable only by those sufficiently cultivated or civilized.	Overt display of wealth and consumption readable by anyone
Preferred photos: cabbages and car crash	Preferred photos: sunset and first communion

of the significance of the social divisions between these groups. In turn, as Miller admits, if one is to interrogate goods to this end, one cannot separate production and consumption, as Bourdieu (1984: 230) assumed.

To return to Alessi objects, then, it is clear that many of them intentionally combine attributes both of elite culture and popular culture. In Bourdieu's terms they blur the line between a Kantian and an anti-Kantian aesthetic. Thus the contribution of American architect Robert Venturi to the Tea and Coffee Piazza project resulted in a teapot which combined the proportions of classical architecture in form with an overtly kitsch graphic element in decoration. At one level, there is a cultural commentary concerning the way in which urban fabric incorporates both the serious and the banal, from spectacular buildings to poster boardings. On another level, Venturi is providing an object which requires a degree of specialist understanding to appreciate – some knowledge or experience of classical architecture would help in 'reading' the object – but at the same time, the tea set has an immediately sensuous appeal. Likewise, the Juicy Salif, by very dint of its poor utilitarian performance, forces one to stand back from it and think about it as an aesthetic object. Having demanded a distanced, intellectual engagement, it then delivers a set of banal referents in its form. In this way, the Alessi objects oscillate between different categorizations. Their polysemy – the possibility of their occupying different, changing and contradictory meanings – is the one theme they hold in common.

This polysemy, however, is not unlimited. The objects do not promise an endless set of readings. They are carefully orchestrated through a series of movements which may indeed give the impression of a limitless freedom to derive personal significances, but which in reality are constantly self-referential.

HISTORICITY

It is perhaps useful at this point to place the Alessi objects in the context of Italian postmodernism in order to pinpoint the 'historical baggage' they come with. Modern Italian design came of age in the period of reconstruction immediately following the Second World War. For many of its protagonists it was ideologically focused on the home as a site for the personal, moral and social reconstruction following the failure of fascism. The design and production of modern furniture and, in particular, the 'lighting object' (highly sculptural illumination drawn from an abstractionist aesthetic) established international recognition for the new Italian material culture. Meanwhile, the gap between the practical demands of mass social housing of the post-war period and the idealized Italian home widened. Designers were caught between their ideological ambitions of providing affordable design goods for a mass market and a combination of high production costs, even for plastics-based objects at the time, a growing middle class and the lure of international recognition as mediated by lifestyle magazines such as *Abitare*, *Casa Vogue* and *Interni*. Modern design, in other words, became appropriated into 'a predetermined "culture of the home", associated with a particular middle-class, consumerist life-style … turning all Italian objects … into highly desirable, élitist artefacts' (Sparke 1990: 194).

Given this tension, avant-garde designers – in particular Ettore Sottsass – sought to destabilize the canon of high design. The anti-design movement grew up as part of the general crisis of the late 1960s, typified by worker strikes and student protests. Radicals among the Italian design fraternity turned their attention to the development of micro-environments rather than perpetuating object fetishism. Within this project designers re-appropriated the imagery of mass culture into pieces so that they became a form of meta-design – design about design. Thus, for example, Sottsass designed the 'Mickey Mouse' table, which was produced by Bonacina in 1972. By featuring the graphic imagery and form of the Disney character he returns the 'message' of the table to the fact that, like Mickey Mouse, it is a mass-produced object for global consumption. The potential aura of the object, then, is deconstructed for you. The postmodern collapsing of distinctions between high and low culture is undertaken, however, with a political point to it. Nonetheless, this enthusiasm for democratization of design in many of the projects undertaken by radicals in the 1970s ultimately found its way into the high-design galleries of the 1980s. Equally, the Alessi objects reside in this tradition of Italian high design: witty, ironic, charged with theoretical intention and which harbour self-effacing luxury.

MODERN DESIGNERS/MODERN CONSUMERS

The oscillation of the designer between radical intention and reactionary outcome, between discomfort with the conditions of high-design production and compliance with its consumption is somewhat characteristic of Italian design discourse, but not exclusive to it. Indeed, it may even be a condition of European design stardom of the late 20th century.

Of this mould, Philippe Starck is perhaps the most known. Like Alessi, he has been highly media and public friendly. Like Raymond Loewy, an earlier French designer, he has a media personality that is wholly Gallic: he claims to drink only champagne and even wears a beret. His personal contradictions are well cultivated: he speaks a highly educated French but dresses grubbily; he speaks with intelligence and self-effacing irony. His press interviews have been consistent and well turned out for instant media reproduction; public lectures become energetic, theatrical performances. Monographs and articles often feature as many photographs of Starck – usually in witty poses – as the objects he designs. No doubt he is a designer of considerable talent. He is noted for combining a prolific output – by 1986 he was modestly telling interviewers that he had 97 projects on the go – with a sincere design rigour and understanding of technical problem solving (Aldersey-Williams 1987). His designs span from the interiors for exclusive clubs, through furniture to foodstuffs and fashion. The apparent ease and speed with which he applies himself to such various projects – he claims to design chairs inside 15 minutes – completes the image of flamboyance and decadence.

In 1997 he announced that he would give up designing altogether in order to devote his time to non-partisan political, socially-orientated causes. This collapsing of the house around him and walking away from it was an ultimate utterance in a career made up of smaller gestures. He told a professional journal in 1986: 'I have not one single theory. I have no ideas about aesthetics, and I don't give a damn' (Starck, quoted in Aldersey-Williams 1987: 51). A decade later he was telling another: 'There is no place for the deified products of the past decade. … All those fashion victims are so pathetic – they come home at night and have an apartment full of fashion items made by designers for designers but not for the public', completing this tirade later with, 'I don't have any aesthetic assumptions. The Starck style in the market is a waste of time' (Starck, quoted in Capella 1997: 56).

This punk 'gesture towards a nowhere' resonates in the Juicy Salif. The beautifully dysfunctional lemon-squeezer offers a paradigmatic objectification of this attitude. As Miller tells us, 'Objectification describes the inevitable process by which all expression, conscious or unconscious, social or individual, takes specific form. It is only through the giving of form that something can be conceived of' (Miller 1987: 81). Thus the cultural baggage of designerly euphoria, its achievements, excesses and wastages converge in the Juicy Salif. In this context, the Starck signature conspires to brand the object. Indeed, one commentator has suggested that Starck may be the last great 'designer hero', but that he is also a brand (Hollington 1998).

It is perhaps less the individual biographical details that generate some of the object's meanings as the way in which they are marshalled up and presented to a consuming public. Whether Starck's self-presentation is genuine or a mere pose in order to generate media, and thus public interest in him, is not a useful question. What is at stake here is that there is a coherence between the object and its production, designer and consumption.

This coherence exists within a highly refined and reflexive network of producers and consumers. Starck's accusation concerning 'items made by designers for designers' is telling. By briefly returning to Bourdieu, we are reminded of his so-called 'new petit bourgeois' class, many of whom are employed in creative professions and whose tastes lie in cultural goods of the avant-garde. He identifies their task as 'cultural intermediaries' in that they broker modern ideas and aesthetics, both in the work they do and in the way they consume. Thus the acquisition of high design is a necessary component in the particular system of distinction to which this class adheres. Specific objects and designers subsequently become a shorthand for the knowledge and values inherent in this system. There is, in Bourdieu's words, 'a correspondence between goods production and taste production' (1984: 230).

DESIGNERS, RISK AND REFLEXIVITY

This process of destabilizing convention within the parameters of the market is apparent in some other design objects and processes. In certain quarters of graphic design a similar self-destructive attitude has mediated its high design and designers to their public. Since the early 1980s a highly localized strain of high design has emerged within graphics clustered around a handful of specific individuals.

Interestingly, this discourse has emerged mostly within the discipline of typography. Typography has historically achieved a dominant professional and academic status in relation to other specialized disciplines within graphic design as a whole. Unlike illustration, which draws much of its working procedures and stylistic norms from fine art, or packaging design, which draws from advertising and branding, typography has developed a stronger academic tradition of its own. Numerous key texts, such as those by German typographer Jan Tschichold, established ground-rules as paradigmatic reference points for its practice and debate. Several scholarly journals, such as *Typos* and *Visible Language*, have existed to disseminate research in typography as well as maintain its intellectual legitimacy.

In addition to this scholarly activity, typographers have developed their own historical canon of designer heroes. A key text that helped to establish this canon, echoing Pevsner's seminal title, is Spencer's *Pioneers of Modern Typography* (1969). The educational and working processes of typography also promote a star system. In the same way that the chair has been a standard exercise as well as a way of creating design which becomes emblematic of the designer, so, traditionally, typographers have applied themselves to the origination of typefaces to perform a similar role. Like the chair, the typeface design has not necessarily addressed a specific utilitarian outcome. In the same way that the chair may be specified by other designers – it may be chosen to complete an interior design – so other graphic designers will employ specific typefaces. What furniture is to industrial design, typography has, at least until recently, been to graphics.

Through a combination of scholarly discourse and popular publication, then, typography in particular and graphic design in general has produced its own celebrity system. Among these one might name Malcolm Garrett, Peter Saville, Neville Brody, Erik Spiekermann, Rudy Van der Lans, April Greiman, Dave Carson and the design groups 8vO and Tomato. Among these in London, Neville Brody, in partnership with critic Jon Wozencroft, founded the Fuse project in 1991, which published typefaces on CD-ROM by well-known, cutting-edge and almost exclusively male designers. It also established an annual conference to extend its discussion. A similar print-based project had been headed by Rudy Van der Lans in California under the title of Emigré from 1982.

While it is difficult to generalize about their graphic style, with perhaps the exception of Erik Spiekermann, all of these adopted a highly expressive typography. In this mode, the letterform was not merely seen as a vehicle to mediate something else (i.e. the sound of a word) but became a medium of expression in itself. Through the 1990s many of them pushed the limits of typography by deconstructing both the historically accumulated rules of legibility in both layout and typeform. The Fuse project in particular set out to consider and even challenge the applicability and use of typography in a post-print world, sometimes to the point that the legibility of typefaces was considered not an issue.

These designers have all published their work widely; of them, *The Graphic Language of Neville Brody* (Wozencroft 1987) and *The End of Print: Graphic Works of Dave Carson* (Blackwell 1995) became cult works for the 1980s and 1990s respectively. And as if to reinforce the 'constant reinvention' narrative of design, each of these publications had sequels added to them in 1994 and 1997 respectively in order to update followers. These have functioned as *catalogues raisonnés* of Brody's and Carson's work but are also design artefacts in themselves.

How do such books function to become high design objects? While much of their content is in the reproduction of highly commercial graphic design projects, such as magazine layouts and advertising campaigns, it is distilled and refined into the book that subsequently becomes a high-design artefact. By editing their own *oeuvre* and repackaging it, their authorship is given

Cover of *The Graphic Language of Neville Brody* (Wozencroft 1987)
Photo: Neville Brody

precedence over the original client's importance as the design commissioners. Furthermore, by taking designs away from their original function, their formal qualities become fore-grounded over their effectiveness in shaping the editorial content of a magazine or in selling a product. The artistry of a typeface or a layout becomes the content. Through this process the patina of low culture is packaged into high design. This demonstrates that while Veblen assumed that all taste would filter on a 'trickle down' basis, from upper to middle classes, there can also be a 'trickle up' dynamic, from subcultural roots into the ambience of high graphics.

Such publications have mostly been bought by other designers and design students. As such, a simulacrum of risk, art-lifestyle, but also of negation is being communicated to the world of the design student by representatives of the profession to which they aspire. We have seen in Chapter 3 how students and professionals in design celebrate the marginality of their own prac-tice. The following quotation, drawn from a design magazine article about Tomato, a London-based collective that worked across several communications platforms, may be read as typical of the 'attitude' that accompanies this process:

> clients include Coca-Cola, IBM, Levi's, Nike, Pepsi, Sony and Thomson … Tomato first 'happened' in February 1991, when a group of graphic designers and an ambient-rock-techno band, Underworld, began working together out of the London flat of a music business man-ager. … The members of the all-male group (with one female assistant) dress casually, make constant jibes at each other and are impossible to pin down. … 'The name Tomato means nothing', Warwicker told me over coffee in the East Village. 'You can put lots of mean-ings into it but there are none. A bit like our work really.' … Tomato provides a look that appeals to Generation X: fast cuts, layered imagery and distinctive blurred flickering and dancing typography. … Freedom is a movement, as the Nike slogan goes, and the members of Tomato are ferocious devotees. … 'We're not easily employable.' (Hall 1996: 78)

So how are we to begin to theorize this? First, while the surface of much of the work of Tomato (and indeed Carson, Van der Lans and later Brody) seems to be expressing an un-meaning, it still exists within a framework of meaning-production. The individual words and letters may be dislocated and impenetrable in the way they are distorted and layered, but there is a confluence in the narratives regarding the designers themselves. We have learnt that Tomato 'are not easily employable'. We are reminded frequently that Dave Carson does not have a formal training in graphics, but was a surfing champion and failed secondary school teacher (Blackwell 1997). Indeed, Emily King (1995) points out that both the Fuse team and Carson's 'End of Print' thesis may refer to the replacement of paper-based communication with digitization, but can also sug-gest that there is nothing left to say.

This apocalyptic nihilism as a principle of modernity becomes their core theme. It is, broadly speaking, self-conscious wherein 'modernization … is becoming its own theme' (Beck 1992 [1986]: 11). If, according to the sociologist Ulrich Beck, one of society's key contemporary fea-tures is that rather than being economically positivistic or technologically determinist, it also possesses the ability to calculate positions on the basis of varying data. Likewise, designers may calculate avant-gardist positions for themselves within the parameters of the market. Their romanticism is reflexively constructed. Or, to put it more bluntly, *appearing* to lie outside the mundane structures of everyday life, to be 'edgy' or 'contra' may be a carefully thought-through decision that nonetheless helps to make their work sellable.

Second, this process allows for other forms of risk to be inhabited. Beck (1992 [1986]) and Giddens (1991) both identify risk as a key concept in reflexive modernization. Giddens identifies a progression from a state in which hazards were incidental and intrinsic to experience to a society in which the calculation of risk parameters is a determining influence on activity (1991: Ch. 4). According to Beck, these risks are not so much recognized physically but 'mediated on principle through argument' (1992 [1986]: 27). Many of the newer risks (nuclear or chemical contaminations, pollutants in foodstuffs, diseases of civilization, bankruptcy, repossessions) completely escape human powers of direct perception. In terms of design practice, risk becomes aestheticized, reflexive and often deliberate. It has become firmly entrenched in the rhetoric of high design whether in its objects or in their mediation. Thus 'cutting edge', 'experimental' and 'intuitive' became familiar descriptive terms among designers, design students and design writers of the 1990s. This attitude finds its way into mainstream design practice too. Design commentator Jeremy Myerson has noted how designers can seldom resist claiming a job to be a 'breakthrough and a radical departure'. He adds: 'I can't imagine a firm of solicitors completing a conveyance and saying "we really subverted the context with that one"' (Myerson, quoted in Whitely 1993: 43).

This may have been carried out in a direct challenge to modernist notions of legibility in graphic design. This is done through the disintegration of the historical, modernist canons of Jan Tschichold or Stanley Morison to incorporate a multi-layering of images and type, collisions of typefaces and multidirectional text reading which seem to invent their own private visual languages. This may be a deliberate ironic subversion or designed to entice the reader into a form of 'decoding'. As Ian Cartlidge said in 1991, 'If the type is laid out in an intriguing, playful and entertaining way, the reader may be immediately stimulated and then begin to break down the type until the message is received' (Cartlidge, quoted in Poynor 1991: 34).

This entertainment of negation and denial suggests a kind of punk inheritance among such designers. While talking of punk aesthetics, Hebdige develops Julia Kristeva's notion of 'positioning in language'. In the punk context this is achieved through a refusal 'to cohere around a readily identifiable set of central values. It cohered, instead, elliptically through a chain of conspicuous absences'. It gestured, 'towards a "nowhere" and actively sought to remain silent, illegible' (Hebdige 1979: 120).

If 'punk will never die', then it is in this realm of babble, denial, conspicuous absence and illegibility. At a wider level of popular culture this was evidenced in the denial of authorship through sampling, blending and layering in 1990s dance music. Origins and authenticity were obscured through distortions such as scratching or modifying the tempo. To the classical musicologist, techno music may have been impenetrable. Questions of theme, development, recapitulation seemed irrelevant. The traditional 'rules' of song-writing are torn up and thrown away. And likewise in graphics. Structure, grid, referents, rhythms and the space on the page are distorted, dislocated, compressed, destroyed, made 'dangerous'. We may term this 'an art of danger ... [within] ... a politics of safety', to rephrase Cousins (1994: 423).

F Code image designed for Fuse 6 for Neville Brody 1993 as seen in *The Graphic Language of Neville Brody 2* Photo: Neville Brody

CRITICAL DESIGN

Within this viewpoint high design appears to be affirmative of the status quo despite any claims that it is edgy or avant-garde. It suggests that its practitioners are merely playing in the safe context of the mainstream marketplace rather than proposing something more critical of it or that produces some kind of alternative to it. This may seem harsh but I wanted to show how the disruption of content and the near denial of utility themselves produce further meaning. To dovetail this with my earlier argument, the obfuscation of legibility in some graphics or the deliberate refusal to design something that works fully on a practical level are common tactics in high design. Uselessness implies, in Veblen's terms, a form of conspicuous waste, itself suggesting an ability to entertain the fun, reverie or subversion of the artefact. It can open up the imagination. At the same time, it can also indulge a refined, particular and self-referential process of design culture. To turn back to the discussion at the beginning of Chapter 3, this is where design culture produces its own discourse and a way of justifying its own existence.

Before concluding this chapter, however, I'd like to take the discussion into two highly refined, yet much discussed fields of design practice that have received considerable media attention since the 1990s. I do this because they both incorporate interesting additions to the arguments presented thus far. The first one, called 'critical design', goes in the opposite direction in terms of its relationship to utility in that it focuses very much on possible uses, albeit that these might be previously unimagined. In doing so, design is indeed used as a language to critique the status quo of the marketplace. The second field, called 'design art', is a more commercial practice, and yet its objects are invariably fashioned to make a commentary on material culture. While being oriented differently towards their audience, both of these may be understood to occupy their own critical space between high design and fine art.

The term 'critical design' was originated by Anthony Dunne in the late 1990s at the Royal College of Art in London. His concern was with the way that product design – particularly of electronic goods – constantly looked to the optimization of form through giving attention to such considerations as human factors and product semantics (a concept that is discussed further in the next chapter). Instead, he aimed to create objects that were 'post-optimimal' (Dunne 2005). This means that he pursued a tactic of defamiliarizing objects through a focus on poetics and fictions. By creating a series of 'what ifs ?', possible, unthought-of situations for everyday life are imagined and objects designed in response to these questions. In so doing, Dunne and Raby use design to critique the assumptions that are made about economy, environment, culture, politics and society that are embedded into objects.

Critical design is often presented through a range of outcomes. Dunne and Raby's Placebo Project of 2001 explored people's responses to electromagnetic fields in the home, challenging the notion that domestic gadgetry will give us more control over our lives. The resulting objects were exhibited at London's Victoria &

Tableau of Electro-Draught Excluder, part of Placebo Project (Dunne and Raby, 2001) Photo: Jason Evans

Albert Museum. They were also photographed in everyday settings to create tableaux that rein-forced the psychological drama that they were invoking, the photos also being exhibited. The project also resulted in the publication of a book (Dunne and Raby 2001).

Dunne and Raby themselves state that there have been several other designers working in a similar vein without calling their work 'critical design' (Dunne and Raby 2012). These would include Krzysztof Wodiczko, Natalie Jeremijenko, Jurgen Bey and Martí Guixé. Likewise, the work of these practitioners appears in a variety of contexts, from installations in galleries, to films (as in the case of Noam Toram), to performances or objects placed in the public realm. What dis-tinguishes these works from other objects discussed in this chapter is that they do not circulate as commodities. They are not for sale, at least through retail outlets. Instead, they are presented as a series of destabilizations of everyday contexts including the museum itself.

Works of critical design therefore appear – although not exclusively – in contexts where we also might find fine art being placed. Indeed, they could be included under the broader term of 'design art' that was employed in the late 1990s and 2000s. However, it is important to note that Dunne and Raby themselves stressed that their intention was not that their work should be seen as art (Dunne and Raby 2012). The focus of their work is on design and material everyday life; all their works are utilitarian, although not necessarily in ways that we immediately would expect. Importantly, much of the work within the critical design rubric has been undertaken as aca-demic enquiry through particular institutions, including the Royal College of Art and Goldsmiths College, both in London. Discussion of its relationship to art, its critical dimension and its con-tributions as academic enquiry is, by now, extensive (e.g. Seago and Dunne 1999; Mazé and Redström 2009; Ericson and Mazé 2011; Malpass 2012).

DESIGN ART

Design art gathered pace in the 2000s as the global art market itself went through exponential growth (Thornton 2009). It was typified by highly expressive furniture or lighting that often made references to well-known historical or everyday objects or included visual twists. Alternatively they were highly valued for their technical innovations or prowess. They were usually produced and sold in limited editions.

The financial boom of that decade, at least until 2008, left collectors pursuing investment opportunities in the art market and thus it spilled over into design objects. These were sold through specialist galleries such as the Carpenter's Workshop Gallery in London, the Moss Gallery in New York, Vivid in Rotterdam and Contrasts in Shanghai. They were also exhibited at trade fairs like Design Miami/Basil and, in a secondary market, through auction houses such as Sotheby's, Christies and Phillips de Pury (Taylor 2011). Finally, they were also collected by institutions such as the Victoria & Albert Museum in London. Prices ran, for example, from $25,700 for Gonçalo Mabunda's 'Elegance Throne' (Beard 2008) to $293,000, reportedly paid by Brad Pitt for a Jeroen Verhoeven 'Cinderella Table' (Barreneche 2008). Thus, design art should be read as much as a function of a particular commercial circumstance as a desire by some practitioners to poeticize design.

One might also interpret the rise of design art as a kind of crossover with certain fine art prac-tices. There had been an ascendance during the 1990s of artists such as Tracy Emin, Sarah Lucas,

Damien Hirst and Gavin Turk, whose work very much depended on material things such as mattresses, cigarettes, plastic chairs or metal containers (Archer 1997). Here materiality is brought to work on concepts, so that the familiarity of these things is disturbed through their arrangement, juxtaposition or referencing to other things or ideas. The use of found objects wasn't by any means a new artistic technique. After all, it could be found in the work of pop artists in the 1950s and 1960s and traced back to Dadaists, Surrealists and Marcel Duchamp in the 1910s and 1920s. However, the more recent work in this mode functions in a particular, contemporary mediascape in that, for example, the stories that circulate about the artists or the dramas that unfold about this or that gallery exhibiting them feed in and out of the art objects themselves. Meaning flows within a structure which is more than the artwork itself (Lash and Lury 2007; Taylor 2011).

Where design art might cross over with the kind of art just described is, rather obviously, in its engagement with the material. Again, we must note that the arrangement of found objects as a design technique can be traced back to designers such as the Castiglioni brothers in the late 1960s, so-called 'adhocism' in the 1970s (Jencks and Silver 1972) or the 'creative salvage' work of Ron Arad and Tom Dixon in the 1980s. Each wave of this had its own set of motivating factors. With regard to design art, the ordinary, everyday stuff of life is gathered up and re-used to suggest a story or, more straightforwardly, enhance its beauty. Tejo Remy's series, beginning in 1991, of assembled drawers entitled 'You Can't Lay Down Your Memories' invites speculation on collecting and travel. Rody Graumans's '85 Lamps', first designed in 1993, takes the very utilitarian-looking lightbulb and fitting and clusters them to form a glowing chandelier.

Work by Graumans and Remy was included in the Droog collection. Droog was founded in 1993 by art historian Renny Ramakers and designer Gijs Bakker in the Netherlands. It subsequently functioned as producer, publisher, exhibitor and retailer of the work of Dutch designers associated with it. In effect it became a brand for this collective, through which

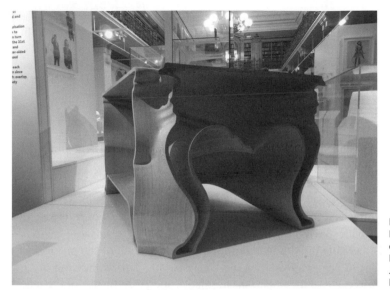

Design art as seen in the Victoria & Albert Museum: (left) Sebastian Brajkovic's 'Lathe chair', 2008; (middle) Tejo Remy's 'You Can't Lay Down Your Memories', 1991; (right) Jeroen Verhoeven's 'Cinderella table', 2005. Photos: Guy Julier

narratives to surround the work could be generated, as we have seen earlier in this chapter with Alessi. However, the re-use of everyday objects, which became something of a signature for the catalogue of Droog, itself draws further possibility for narrative. We are invited to speculate on where the components that make up the piece came from and what other 'lives' they have had. Furthermore, and crucially, to compare with the discussion of the artists such as Emin and Hirst above, the Droog objects remain as design objects so long as they are available to own or are placed alongside other objects that are quite clearly about design, not art.

At the end of the day, these are still working pieces of furniture or lighting. By contrast with the Starck lemon-squeezer, for instance, they are, in fact, more recognizably utilitarian. Their utility demands that we consider what it would be like to have or use them. In so doing, they suggest that we pause and (re-)consider our material world and what makes it. Critical design and design art both exist conceptually in a space between high design and fine art. They draw characteristics from them both while maintaining their own specific ways of operating. It should be stressed that both critical design and design art represent, at least in their more public form, the work of some very specific practitioners who are connected with very particular educational, cultural and commercial institutions. In turn, these give further legitimacy to their practices. In addition, their existence testifies to the constantly fragmenting qualities of the culture of design, as new practices and discursive fields for design are generated.

CONCLUSION

Cultural creation in high design is mediated through language. We have seen how the Alessi/Starck brands are carefully orchestrated through a variety of channels, each reinforcing the other.

The denial of utility in these and the high graphics of Carson and others is self-referential. Their forms allude to the conditions of consumption – commodified yet purporting to unmarketability. They also draw on a central theme of design production – risk, or more accurately, its minimization. This is high design's apparent radicalism within the structure of deeply conservative institutions. Critical design takes a further turn with its proposal of new functions that ask questions about the dominant market systems. Meanwhile, design art indulges the marketplace while commenting on value and utility, if ironically at times.

Slater argues that each 'stable' object makes an incision into the world, 'cutting out a set of relations and oppositions'. Destabilization merely involves the creation of new sets of relations and oppositions. The challenge, for the producer, is in hiding the processes of production, in making it appear that the stability or instability arises from the object itself rather than from the 'agencies that cut it out and bind it together in particular forms' (Slater 2002: 101). There is the object itself, on to which attention is focused, but then there are the systems and contexts that give it meaning. Some are visible and readable. Others are obscured.

Ultimately, high design is therefore providing a more spectacular version of the processes of the wider marketplace. That is, it engages in wilful acts of destabilization. In the case of high design, this is just more intensely concentrated into the aesthetics and performance of the object but also into its systems of mediation. In terms of the object itself, this may be through raising its performance value, or, as we have seen, it may also emerge from precisely the opposite – the denial of utility. But such narratives are also told through other channels, such as the way its designer presents him/herself in the media or the way that an object is given particular readings and thus specific historical orientations. In any such case, the kind of high design we have looked at in this chapter can be said to be reflexive in that it is both the output *of* and comments *on* the economic and cultural system that produces it. Ironically, then, any deliberate act of obscurity or any conscious negation within high design tells us something about the bigger picture of value creation.

CHAPTER 6
CONSUMER GOODS

The relationship between external appearance and technical performance is a recurrent point of discussion in consumer goods. With its focus on consumer goods, Chapter 6 initially focuses on product styling and how this is used to communicate how a product works. It shows how a concern for the surface appearance of consumer goods also influences the ways by which they are represented, both within the design process itself and through the way it is frequently pictured in design magazines and books. We also see how some designers employ techniques to understand how consumers in different cultural contexts live with their goods. Market segmentation and the rise of product semantics as central to the design of consumer goods have gone hand-in-hand with the growth of flexible and short-run manufacturing systems. Nonetheless, it is important to recognize that product design also involves a kind of craft activity, where individual decisions and judgements on form are made. Finally, we return to the consumer experience of products, looking at psychological engagement through 'flow'. Then we look at the process of habituation and how the efficacy and meanings of consumer goods are reliant on networks that include other objects, human activities and knowledge.

An image of a product designed by Josep Lluscà
Photo: International Design Press Agency, Barcelona

In each photograph an object floats in the half-light, its dark background stretching to an endless space. It could be a power-tool, a palm-top computer, or some medical equipment. Any utility is stripped away by the picture – the product is reduced to a tasteful conjunction of surfaces, textures and tones. At the front of the picture-plane a point on the artefact's surface catches the glare of the studio lights. It is close to us, in our space, touchable. And yet, it is isolated on the page. The only one. Unique. Special.

IMAGES

Within the design profession a minor subspecialism exists in the photography and presentation of new products. Design consultancies or their clients commission skilled photographers to create images of the objects they have designed. These are processed into high-quality digital files which are in turn handed on to journalists and critics for inclusion in the pages of their magazines or books. Otherwise, they are used in their own promotional brochures or websites.

We saw in the last chapter how retailers will display goods to make them appear like museum objects by showing them individually in their shops. In product design a language of representation has evolved which partially fulfils the same ends. By picturing the product on its own, it becomes that singular object of desire rather than one of many identical mass-produced commodities. We are asked to appreciate it as it is, without the interference of other products to compare it to, its packaging or other users. The loss of these contexts and its actual physical presence is compensated for by playing up the colour and textural qualities in the image.

This form of representation has some resonances in the still-life oil paintings of the 17th century Dutch masters. Berger (1972: Ch. 5) makes a persuasive argument that oil painting was employed because it reproduced as faithfully as was then possible the 'thingness' of things; but in the same token, by the act of that reproduction, by presenting ordinary objects on canvas in a frame, they were bestowed a feeling of aura.

Three hundred years later, pop artists on both sides of the Atlantic explored the effects of this representation of products. In New York, Andy Warhol's silk-screens of soup cans or detergent boxes deconstructed the aura that advertising was intending to give them. By reproducing multiple images of the same product Warhol reminds us not of their uniqueness, but of their seemingly unending serial reproduction in the capitalist system. Meanwhile, as with many British pop artists, Richard Hamilton was interested in the representation of commodities. From 1957 he developed a series of paintings which explored the surface forms of products both as they were and as they were mediated through advertising. His painting entitled '$he' impressionistically described the forms of domestic products such as toasters, vacuum cleaners and fridges. In doing so he revealed both their stylistic similarities and the linkage between the exterior form of consumer goods and their representation in advertising. To underline this point, he drew allusions between the exterior surface of smooth curves in these products and mainstream representations of female bodies. The connection between product to be looked at but also sold and consumed and mass media representations of women is reinforced in the title: $he. Thus Hamilton was interested in what Haug (1986) later called the 'aesthetic illusion' of products: the promise of their use-value – in this case as flashy, sexy objects of desire – conveyed in their image and in their status of exchange-value. His investigation was into the 'second skin' of the styling of consumer goods and the values this carried.

Interestingly, Hamilton was working on this painting as Roland Barthes's seminal book *Mythologies* (1983 [1957]) was first published. This collection of short essays explored the social and ideological significance of everyday objects and events ranging from 'steak and chips' to 'striptease'. Through these case studies he showed a variety of ways by which Western society sustains, sells and identifies itself while at the same time obscuring its own truth. Like Hamilton, his interest was in exploring what values lay beneath the surface of objects, beyond their external image. His discussion of the Citröen DS car, for example, exhibits the same fascination with the literal exterior of the product. Here he draws attention to the perfection of its smooth surfaces to the point that this automobile takes on a magical or even religious aura.

SURFACES

Warhol, Hamilton and Barthes all concentrate on the external design values of products. None of them is concerned with their actual performance. They are, in effect, approaching the objects as graphic communication – as adverts of themselves. It is noteworthy that both Hamilton and Warhol worked in graphic design as well as fine art. They were also working at a time when colour photography was becoming increasingly cheaper to reproduce in magazines. Thanks to the development of photolithography in the post-war years, advertisers and magazine editors began to replace illustration and accompanying copy with colour photographs of modern products. Furthermore, developments in manufacture and materials gave increasing prominence to the 'external skin' of objects. The so-called 'Detroit styling' of American cars, which fascinated Richard Hamilton so much, was made possible by the development of chroming and steel rolling in the post-war period. Similarly, plastics had been in use since the mid-1800s, but it wasn't until the post-war period that we find their widespread acceptance in consumer items.

Subsequently, more than any other material, the use of plastics has revolutionized the way designers and their public perceive consumer goods. The advantages of plastics, such as cheapness, lightness and the ability to mimic other materials, also go some way to explaining a century's resistance to public acceptance. In the English language, 'plasticky' is readily connected to 'rubbishy'. Dormer (1990: 63–4) has pointed out that among many other features, plastic fails to age gracefully, unlike, say, wood or leather. Rather, it is prone to discoloration and scuffing. It either looks brand new or ready to be thrown away. It also shatters or cracks on extreme impact, making it impossible to repair. Equally, it can only be recycled or reused by experts. Apart from fibreglass, most plastics are unlikely to be found in the workshop of a do-it-yourself fanatic. Thus a set of values are attached to this material and are thrown into relief in contrast with other more 'traditional' materials.

This line of thought is also pursued by the design theorist Ezio Manzini. In his book *The Material of Invention* (1986), Manzini points out that the majority of 20th-century design has concerned itself with the structure of objects. Thus, for instance, in using tubular steel, modernist designers such as Marcel Breuer were able to reveal the physical framework – the skeleton – that supported the sitter. With plastic, the outer skin shows nothing of its internal physics, the make-up of its polymers. We are only presented with a two-dimensional surface. Its light, smooth and shiny aspect effectively *dematerializes* the object.

The commercial and cultural values of plastic lend itself ideally, then, to its use as an outer casing. In terms of many domestic consumer items, such as radios or hairdryers, it clothes internal workings, and perhaps only indirectly tells us something about the functioning of that object. Elsewhere, it is used to mimic graphic imagery. Thus in children's toys it is often used for cartoon characters. The loss of a sense of internal structure is compensated for in plastic by the adoption of vivid colours or suggestive shapes. Not only is plastic a material of invention, it is also a material of *representation*. In this context Robin Kinross's statement that 'product design increasingly aspires to the graphic' (quoted in Huygen 1989: 90) is particularly apt.

DOING THE DYSON

Many consumer goods offer paradigmatic examples of this late-20th-century shift from structure to surface in product design language. Among these, the Dyson DC01 vacuum cleaner, first launched in 1993, provides a rich array of features which allow us to interrogate this effect. Discussion of this product has primarily focused on the originality of its invention and the problems its designer James Dyson encountered in taking the device to manufacture and market, including a monographic exhibition held at the Design Museum in London in 1996 entitled 'Doing the Dyson'. But no matter how engaging these aspects are, they detract from a full appreciation of the innovations to be found in the vacuum cleaner's semantics – in the way that product communicates its function and value. A detailed discussion of this product is fruitful, for it provides useful reflections on the relationship of internal workings to exterior skin and the ways by which utility is communicated. These observations can be transferred to the numerous subsequent models of the Dyson vacuum cleaner, for the basic design approach has been maintained throughout.

The Dyson DC01 vacuum cleaner is centred around the creation of a mini 'dual cyclone' (hence 'DC') and some understanding of how this works is necessary in order to understand its ramifications in terms of product styling. Vacuum cleaners work on the basis of a fan that in pushing out a stream of air creates a vacuum; in turn this sets up an equally powerful suction which draws air carrying dust particles and debris into the cleaner. Traditionally, this incoming air is filtered by a paper bag. Air inflates the bag and then filters out through pores in the fabric of the bag and back into the room, leaving the dirt behind. As these pores clog up, however, this system loses its sucking power. The alternative cyclone approach does away with a bag. Instead, the air is pushed into the wider, internal end of a cone. As the air works its way to the point of the cone, it speeds up – in the case of the DC01, this is from 20 mph to 924 mph. The heavier dust then flies outwards to the edges of the cyclone and the centrifugal force that is created gives each particle increased mass. It then easily drops out of the bottom, smaller end of the cone to be collected in a cylinder into which it fits. Meanwhile, the lighter air finds the quicker and easier route out by rushing back up the centre of the cone. This process is repeated in a slower cyclone which also makes up the outer casing and picks up the larger debris. By providing an alternative to the need for a bag, the dual cyclone avoids clogging and therefore supplies much greater efficiency in suction. Thus the central theme of the traditional vacuum cleaner, the bag, is replaced by another device.

Some historical knowledge of vacuum cleaner design is useful at this point. Following the vacuum cleaner's invention in 1901, the bag for traditional upright models was housed in a zip-up sack suspended from the handle. When the cleaner was switched on it would inflate, making the physical effect of air being sucked in immediately visible. The conjunction of a 'spine', in its column, and a 'lung', in its bag, gave it an anthropoidal character, its lung inflating as it 'drew breath'. Additionally, one could remove a cover on the base to see the motor band driving the fan. Thus its functioning could be directly viewed.

In the early 1960s, General Electric in the USA brought out its Dial-A-Matic (known in the UK as the Convertible), the first hard-bodied upright vacuum cleaner. By encasing the bag in moulded plastic, the workings of the appliance were increasingly covered up in subsequent models. Air being sucked in and blown out, the rotation of the fan and the inflation of the bag were increasingly hidden away. The streamlined styling of its exterior skin meant that its actual performance was only visible indirectly by seeing how much cleaner the floor appeared to be.

The DC01 gives back a sense of performance, but only indirectly. As with later versions of upright cleaners, apart from the brushes underneath the base, there are no moving parts to be seen. The effect of the cyclone is visible as dust and debris whizz round inside the transparent cylinder. But the creation and functioning of the declared 100 per cent suction are communicated, by a large measure, through visual association. The idea of a cyclone as the central theme of the product introduces the mental image of spirals of air, or in the case of the dust in the cylinder, concentric circles. This sets the principal motif for the product styling. From the top of the handle to the design of the plug, then, some 356 full- or part-circular lines are described in the object. The wheels, for instance, feature three concentric circles on their inside and a small 'mudguard' set at an angle, to suggest dynamic energy as well as echoing the idea of streaming into the cylinder at a tangent – the optimum angle for setting up the real cyclone. Clearly, some of these circles perform a real utilitarian purpose. The spiral casing of the hose allows it to be stretched. But when stowed away in the upright position, it bunches up to create a staccato stack of rings which are carried through to the circular motifs in the handle.

A range of secondary associations also emerges through careful examination of the product. In the handle itself we find an allusion to cooling fins, which do not perform any utilitarian purpose as such: there isn't any heat conduction through the plastic. Instead, they set up other associations with, perhaps, industrial machinery, motor transport or aeroplanes. The silver-speckled grey colouring of most of the vacuum cleaner makes a further connection to aeronautics while the yellow detailing is redolent of heavy plant machinery. The appliance is noisy. The motor thunders along accompanied by a satisfying rush of air being sucked in and pushed out. It has two basic pitches, which again suggest air travel. One is when pushing it along: a deep, industrial vibration created partly by the rotation of the brushes (take-off). The other when standing upright is a higher, more airy sound (landing). Through the air travel reference, connotations of efficiency, work, movement and progress spin out from the cyclone theme, to be communicated 'on the outside' of the machine, as it were.

DC01 vacuum cleaner, design by James
Dyson 1989–92, manufactured by Dyson
Appliances Ltd
Photos: Guy Julier

To stretch the machine–aesthetic association further, the typography used in Dyson products is derived from one originally designed at the German modernist design school, the Bauhaus. In the early 1930s, Herbert Bayer developed Universal as a typeface for use in publicity. The suppression of upper-case letters and the letterform's basis in circles rather than ovals were thought to make it easy to read at a distance. The Dyson logotype picks up on the circle theme once again, and for those with specialist knowledge of design history, an historicist association is made with the Bauhaus movement which promoted modernist ideals of visual and functional efficiency, fitness-for-purpose and other such 'no-nonsense virtues'.

PRODUCT SEMANTICS

The analysis made above of the Dyson Cyclone DC01 vacuum cleaner is loosely semiological. We looked at the shapes, colours, textures and sounds of the product and considered how these created content and meaning for it. In this way we identified the linkages between the thing itself (in semiological terms, the referent) and the sign. In semiology, the sign is made up of two parts: what it indicates (the signifier) and what it represents (the signified). Thus, for instance, we saw how the repeated circular shapes on the handle looked like (or in semiology-speak *denoted*) cooling fins. The idea of cooling fins used to draw off excess heat would indicate an attachment to a high-powered engine, perhaps a motor-bike or an aeroplane. This in turn *connotes* mobility, speed or even modernity itself. These connotations, then, are derived from mythical meanings in society, hence the connection between a particular shape incorporated into the handle and the product as evidence of our modern, efficient age. Again, this is how Haug's 'aesthetic illusion' is at work: the form indirectly tells us how well the product is going to perform. As its designer, James Dyson himself states that 'Good design, generated out of the function of the thing, will explain why it is better, and why it should be bought. If it looks "the business" ... then it will present the impression of its own effectiveness' (Dyson 1998: 206).

The rich layering of visual suggestions which are made in the design language of the object derives from a branch of industrial design known as 'product semantics', a term first used by Krippendorf and Butter in 1984. In short, this method may best be described as 'designing by association'. Designers will ascertain what emotional values they want the consumer to attach to the product. They will then develop forms that instigate the associations to, hopefully, inculcate those feelings.

Obviously there is always the danger of slippage between the meanings the producer intends and those that the consumer interprets. In the case of the Dyson Cyclone, the interpretation I have given includes some of its designer's ambitions for the product but also extends them. Dyson explains that the silvery-grey colour, made up of an almost transparent plastic with aluminium flecks incorporated into it, gave it a 'NASA look'. The yellow alludes to warning signs on building sites and the stripes of wasps and tigers, adding to a message of the machine as predator. The ribs on the front of the handle were included first as a lightweight way of making that point stronger, and second, to visually smooth the transition from the body to the handle. The suggestion of 'fin-cooling, a high-tech, motorbikey look' was what Dyson calls 'a design byproduct' (Dyson 1998: 199–200). Thus its principal designer claims that the semantic appeal is secondary to the resolution of engineering problems.

A second question that advocates of product semantics must confront is whether or not consumers actually want the associations they design into consumer goods. For example, design critic Hugh Aldersey-Williams complains of how graphics are arbitrarily and garishly applied to sailboards or ski-equipment to connote belonging to some kind of subcultural group through their ownership. Not wishing this enforced lifestyle association, he would rather erase the graphics from his own ski-gear (Aldersey-Williams 1993: 142).

The development of product semantics from the early 1980s has led to some ambition and optimism regarding its use. Some designers have considered its potential in ascertaining objective ways of designing emotional content into products. In South Korea, Hsiao and Chen (1997) developed a semantic and shape grammar-based approach to individual features of office chair design. They explored the semantic values of various forms abstracted from the basic typology of the office chair by marrying particular primary shapes with their associated emotional effects. From this they then produced a computer program which pieced together separate formal components according to the emotional characteristics they wished to imbue in the object.

In the Netherlands, Muller and Pasman (1996) followed a similar path. They sought to classify certain formal and associational features of chair design in order to provide frames of reference for the designer. They used three broad classifications that encompassed design considerations for products. These were 'prototype', meaning the utilitarian requirements; 'solution type', which referred to available and possible formal characteristics governed, for instance, by the parameters of production and materials; and 'behavioural-typical features', which took into account consumer experience and preferences and came closest to thinking about the semantics of consumer goods.

Details of the DC01 vacuum cleaner
Photos: Guy Julier

Subsets within this last category were 'socio-cultural styles' such as 'professional or recreational' and 'progressive and conventional', 'historical styles' such as gothic or classicist, and 'style articulation' using bipolar adjectives such as 'controlled and impulsive'. From these categorizations, they wrote a computer program which would then provide on-screen product images of chairs which had already been designed and corresponded to the matrix of design qualities required. This, they claimed, would then provide designers with a 'bandwidth' of visual reference points to then work from and an immediate designerly set of precedents to refer to.

Both the above cases allow for a genuine, considered interrogation of the possible cultural resonances which can be designed into products. However, they are both based on the rigorous classification of visual, material and linguistic qualities which are not necessarily fixed or stable. They rely on subjective definitions of concepts such as 'progressive and conventional' and their visual or material counterparts. Does it necessarily follow that one form is 'progressive' when it may be deemed 'conventional' to someone else? Classification often tells one more about the predilections of the classifier than the status of the things classified.

MOOD BOARDS

By creating a 'map' of various forms which respond to the range of demands made by a client in a brief, the designer is able to sketch out and structure a context for subsequent product development. Muller and Pasman (1996) are attempting to provide a more sophisticated, but ultimately more precarious method for undertaking this task. In professional practice this is more often done by the use of 'mood boards'. These involve the arrangement and presentation of images of related products, logotypes, environments or other design material on to blank sheets in order to construct an artefactual and associational context for the thing being designed. The designer's own drawings and photographs or samples of materials may also be introduced. Sometimes the designer might even produce a three-dimensional 'mood environment' or collection of artefacts. This is then used to fix an idea of the relationship of the object of enquiry to other artefacts for both the designer and the client. Whereas drawings, plans and models relate directly to the product under development, the mood board is entirely conceptual.

As such the mood board is a device used to communicate values at various stages in the development of a design project. Thus it might be used early on to clarify market information or the designer's intentions for him- or herself, or the client. It might involve a reflective component in assessing the impact of a design's development. Or it might be used to support a final client presentation. In this format, it provides a visual bridge between the linguistically based data of a client's brief or market research and the visual and material outcome of the finished product. Invariably the designer is not just classifying and creating a frame of reference for his or her direction through form alone, however. Human activities and comparative brands may also appear on the mood board. This means that the identity of a product is located in relation to other cultural and commercial identities which locate the product as a marketing proposition. As such it may also be produced as a visual map. Equally, as designer Steve Heron (1999) affirms, it can be used to explore the ordinary context of use for a product – how it fits in with the clutter of everyday life.

The mood board is, in fact, used throughout a number of design disciplines: to explore the ambience of a retail environment; to distinguish separate features of an exhibition space; or in conjunction with a storyboard for a multimedia presentation. It can then mediate between designer and client, but also express and explore values which lie outside the drawing board or the Computer-Aided Design (CAD) program. Design methods writer Tom Mitchell (1988) warns of the way by which working with forms on paper or on screen can divorce the designer from the day-to-day reality of the finished product in use. At its best, then, the mood board can bridge the gap in the design process between object as planned on the drawing board and the client's conception of the end-user.

Furthermore, this visual interpretation may be finally 'talked up' at client presentations. Clients and designers negotiate a shared understanding of the meaning of a drawing, a 'mood board' or a prototype or model through discussion. Thus even in the private relationship of designer to client, meaning is not necessarily stable and requires an intense exchange between the verbal and visual (Tomes et al. 1998).

This 'mood board' scenario, then, is strangely at odds with the final photographic presentation of products in design media and consultancy brochures as discussed at the beginning of this chapter: the first presents a contextual network of meanings around the product; the second reduces it to a singular, silent, reified form. The relationship between the two formats – one concerned with meaning, the other with pure form – strikes at the heart of problems in product semantics in particular, and the interpretation of lifestyles in general.

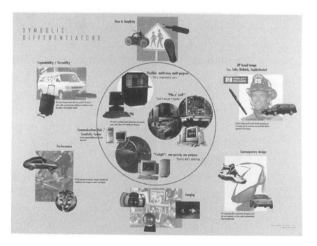

Brand map produced in a collaboration between Lunar Design, California and Hewlett Packard. This was developed in 1998–99 as part of a project to explore and visualize the brand image of Hewlett Packard 'Pavilion' home PCs. The collaboration aimed to mediate the gap between 'designer' intentions and the more mundane requirements of the marketplace
Photo: Lunar Design

LIFESTYLES AND DESIGN ETHNOGRAPHY

In 1957, the pop artist Richard Hamilton produced a collage for the Independent Group exhibition at London's Institute of Contemporary Arts which was called 'This is Tomorrow'. The collage, intended to be incorporated into the exhibition publicity, was entitled 'Just What is it that Makes Today's Homes so Different, so Appealing?'. Drawn principally from cut-outs of magazine ads, the collage presents a construction of a 'state-of-the-art' interior complete with modern domestic appliances and furnishings. A number of different discussions are available in this image: the media construction of the body, gender and domesticity, attitudes to the relationship of nature and technology. But overall, this represents a witty invocation of an ad-man's idea of lifestyle. After all, as Independent Group colleague Reyner Banham noted, the 1950s saw the emergence of brand image, consumer research and motivation research (the science of establishing the 'real' or subconscious reasons for buying one product or another) in advertising and design (1981 [1965]: Ch. 2.4) – all components which engage with consumer lifestyles. By extension, the collage could almost be read as a designer's mood board. Certainly, the title of the piece ('Just what is it ... ?') smacks of an open blue-skies design brief put before a consultancy.

Hamilton's collage also illustrates the idea that consumer groups may be clustered around object domains rather than being categorized simply by class or demography. This idea resonates with Miller's suggestion, mentioned in the previous chapter, that rather than accepting given class identifications, as Bourdieu had, social groupings are clustered around particular forms of consumption (Miller 1987: 158). As such they may be more fragmented, segmented and fluid. Goods and the way they are arranged, displayed, worn or used become symbolic markers of lifestyle not just to reflect social position, but also to enact cultural distinction.

Discussion of consumer culture and lifestyle in Sociology and Cultural Studies has largely focused on this symbolic role of goods (e.g. Hebdige 1988; Featherstone 1991; Lury 1996). The emphasis has been on how they are used to say something about an individual's or a group's relationship to other style groupings or their own, and thus their own social standing. Celia Lury calls this 'positional consumption' (1996: Ch. 2).

Sometimes mood boards can look more like clichéd storylines for an ad campaign rather than a genuine attempt to explore user needs and desires. Often, the images of individual objects within the scenario are themselves lifted from magazines, advertisements or trade photographs, thus adding to this effect. By arranging a set of products onto a flat surface, designers order and classify them into a specific circumstance. In presenting them in a two-dimensional world, much of their status as objects of use is lost as they are turned into imagery. This process may promote a viewpoint of consumption as being purely 'positional'. Furthermore, mood boards may often tell us more about the designers' self-idealization or habitus than the real needs and desires of their end-users.

The use of mood boards may also reinforce what McCracken (1990: Ch. 8) described as the 'Diderot effect'. He describes this as 'a force that encourages the individual to maintain a cultural consistency in his/her compliment of consumer goods' (1990: 123). This may operate in maintaining consistency in the 'family' of goods a consumer assembles and to exclude inconsistencies; it might force, by the acquisition of something, the individual to adopt an entirely new ensemble of lifestyle accoutrements; it may be that consumers deliberately buy goods which do not complement each other in order to consciously disturb the Diderot effect. So where designers make mood boards look more like the pages of a store catalogue, they conspire to assume levels of complementarity in the assemblage of goods that make up the lifeworlds of their end-users. Again, this may ignore the highly personal, seemingly irrational approaches that people harbour in their own value systems regarding the choices they make in the consumption of goods (see Csikszentmihalyi 1991).

Alternatively, then, by the late 1990s, some product designers were using ethnographic research in order to get beyond the restrictions experienced when undertaking market research from a corporate environment perspective and to view human behaviour and interaction with consumer goods in situ. Design ethnographers Salvador et al. (1999: 37) argue that individuals will adopt the strict parameters of corporate cultures when they leave home for work; this, consciously or unconsciously, will always feed into and affect the way they conceive of products to be used in domestic life; market observation and analysis is also affected by the 'corporate effect'. By engaging in participant observation with end-users in their own environments and becoming part-time anthropologists – or 'deep hanging out' as they also term it – they may discover patterns, customs and attitudes to consuming which focus groups or market surveys do not reveal. This may be particularly useful when considering how global product concepts or brands fit in with or may be adapted to local contexts. The final stage in this process is where the anthropological activity is articulated into descriptive data or narratives about their subjects and then becomes ethnography. At this point the designer draws back from immersive, participatory involvement (in anthropological terms, the 'emic' element) and sits outside the scene, as a detached observer (the 'etic' constituent) (Tso 1999: 72). Their description of events may then be communicated through mood boards or visual maps.

This approach suggests that designing products is not exclusively about positional goods for positional consumption. By reducing the design-thinking down to details of texture, colour or semantic association and exploring their relationship to human behaviour, designers are exploring consumer goods, not as they might appear to others, but the patina, quirks, ticks and irrationalities that they perform in the everyday lives of their users.

Lifestyle trends research therefore provides useful data from which designers can work. It is small wonder, then, that many design consultancies incorporated specialists in this area into their practices in the 1990s. For example, the American consultancy Design Continuum listed three key areas that they build into the design process: knowledge, product and brand. Within their knowledge-building services they included 'Consumer understanding', encompassing 'direct observational research' and 'professional immersion and noticing' (role-play, in other words) and 'Context analysis' through, for instance, 'cultural assessment', 'archetypal profiling' and 'segment opportunity mapping' (Design Continuum 1999). In 1998, retail and leisure consultants Fitch bought the Paris-based Peclers, a styling agency specializing in forecasting future trends in fashion. They also developed their '4D' approach, that is 'Discover. Define. Design. Deliver' (Fitch 1999). The first two of these refer to the gathering of market intelligence and its articulation into design briefs for clients.

Whatever jargon consultancies use to explain their offer to potential clients, the point is that it evidences the fact that design consultancies may not only exist at the interface between producer and consumer but may also move downstream to carry out consumer market research and upstream to provide strategic product management for clients. Scenario planning, including the use of mood boards to articulate lifestyle perceptions, is one tool used in this process.

While quantitative data regarding lifestyle preferences may be mustered through market surveys, the partnership of ethnography and design may yield innovatory results. A well-known example of this is in Sony's development of portable televisions. The American company General Electric had conducted a survey by judging people's responses to mock-up televisions to estimate demand for a small portable television, the conclusion of which was that the 'people do not place a high value on portability of the television set' (General Electric, quoted in Lorenz 1986: 34). By contrast, Sony looked at people's behavioural patterns at home and the number and type of television channels available. Using these data they anticipated that a portable television would actually suit changes in these patterns. Following the success of their portable television, they then went on to do precisely the same with the video cassette recorder, the Walkman personal stereo and the Watchman flat-tube television. Thus, lifestyle research for design consultancy becomes a form of cultural analysis, ethnography or design criticism in itself.

BACK TO THE WORKSHOP

But how is all this research for design translated into actual artefacts? The incorporation of lifestyle trends research into a design consultancy may be consolidated in order to promote its professional standing with clients, but, ultimately, these data have to be used towards the shaping of material objects. Clearly, visual mapping aids the synthesis of data into formal characteristics. In the course of drawing or pasting-up images for this, the material qualities of weight, density and surface texture are lost: again the emphasis leads towards the exterior, graphic qualities. Designers may therefore brainstorm with conjunctions of objects in their quest to achieve the optimum form. For example, multinational product design consultancy IDEO keeps a box in each of the company's six major offices in San Francisco, Palo Alto, Grand Rapids, Chicago, Boston and London. Each box contains five drawers holding 200-odd objects which are tagged and numbered. There are related websites on a company intranet which then give further materials information, including their manufacturer and previous use in other products. Designers rummage through the compartments and play with the items, which include tiny batteries or miniature switches, in quests for inspiration (McGrane 1999).

There are times, however, when designers may be exclusively absorbed in technical and formal development in the workshop and where the intuitive manipulation of forms without the intellectual baggage of research data takes precedence. James Dyson devotes much of his autobiography to explaining the many hours spent in workshops manipulating mock-ups of his cyclonic vacuum system, emphasizing the 'hand and heart' aspects of designing. Indeed, many consultants will claim that despite the increased conceptual complexity of the job, there is still an artesanal element to design (Hollington 1999a).

Writer and designer David Pye made a useful distinction between different modes of craft and design practice. One is 'workmanship of risk', where the exact formal qualities of an object are not determined before its production – a situation normally allied with craft making. The other is 'workmanship of certainty', where the finished outcome is preconceived and which we would identify in most product and interaction design (see Dormer 1990: 144–5). There are artesanal moments in much product design where 'workmanship of risk' exists, but it forms just one of several stages in an overall research process. Ultimately, precision and certainty dominate in the development of consumer goods. This is due not only to the importance of synthesizing front-end consumer research, but also to the various restrictions of production tooling. The belief of 19th-century reformer John Ruskin that the best design was the product of the faculties of head, heart and hand accurately describes the demands made of modern designers (Frayling 1999).

PRODUCT SEMANTICS AND FLEXIBLE MANUFACTURE

Product semantics emerged in the early 1980s for a number of historically specific reasons. One was due to the growth of microchip technology for products, which allowed for the miniaturization of the internal workings of many electronic goods. Henceforth, the form of such products did not have to be so tightly determined by their internal workings. But it was also derived from a theoretical discourse on both sides of the Atlantic, which was perhaps over-optimistic in its practicable ends but reflected the wider ideological and commercial shifts of that decade.

At the Cranbrook Academy of Art in Illinois, USA, Michael McCoy and his students explored the potential of product semantics to the hilt during the 1980s. Many of their projects explored visual languages for information technology hardware and consumer electronics. This led them to consider the kinds of software they processed. Thus in designing a CD player, students Kevin Fitzgerald and Scott Makela considered hip-house and 'house music' and the way they collaged excerpts of music together. By extension, they saw this as metaphor for the street lifestyle where these genres grew up and where appropriation was necessary for survival. These 'street' themes were then introduced into their design so that the CD player featured welded-steel speaker horns and a body constructed of the wood used in baseball bats. McCoy claims that this process means 'that designers are moving closer to their audiences, the people who use the technology. They are trying to understand and empathize with a particular culture and needs' (McCoy 1993: 136). It must be remembered, however, that Cranbrook was working as an educational laboratory for ideas, and that while these proposals did much to challenge hitherto accepted norms in design language, in the so-called 'real world' their products would probably only appeal to niche markets. The flexibility of manufacture required to realize these designs would push them into a 'high-design' category.

In Italy, the Memphis projects of Milanese designers from 1980 were concerned with the ironic, playful and colourful re-rendering of the exterior of household products. The practitioners and theorists of this 'new Italian design' were closely bound up with the family-run workshop networks of northern Italy. The dominance of small-sized neoartesanal industries allowed for the steady flow of batch production objects of desire to turn the theoretical ambitions of Milanese designers into material artefacts. Thus a close link between a semantically informed design approach and its ready translation into products could be forged: just as language is flexible, so could its manufacture be. In this climate, leading designer and commentator Andrea Branzi was able to extol the virtues of 'new handicrafts' as the basis of a 'second modernity' (Branzi 1984). According to Branzi's argument, product design could return from its wilderness years as a department of alienated corporate capital to a workshop of ideas and their making. This, in many respects, was a re-vindication of the Arts and Crafts ideals of a hundred years earlier.

During the early 1980s, this euphoria was matched by an emergent discussion on flexibility in the political economy of the West, which was evenly matched in its optimism by both right- and left-wing observers. Within this, the example of the so-called 'Third Italy' was frequently invoked by progressive writers on economic sociology (e.g. Berger and Piore 1980; Sabel 1982). The notion of small manufacturing businesses innovating both luxury and high-technology products for an international market was seductive. In the workshops of the Veneto and Emilia-Romagna, artesans developed and batch-produced either exclusive fashionware and furnishings or capital goods such as machinery, tooling or specialized equipment. Here, then, was William Morris's ideal of the amalgamation of intellectual and manual labour made real (Sabel 1982: 220–31). And what is more, their products kept pace with fluctuations in market demand. For those who supported the concept of consumer sovereignty, then, the flexible manufacturing system, like that of the Third Italy, complemented and exonerated the dominance of a market-driven political economy. It provided ample proof of the correspondence of enterprise culture and consumerism in the 1980s (Block 1990; Jessop et al. 1991). Seen in this light, Branzi's socialist-driven intentions – his so-called 'radical design' – may, in fact, be seen to unwittingly conspire with the economic ambitions of neo-liberal proponents of the free market system.

The flexible manufacturing system that Branzi and his cohort drew on is just one form of it, however. It was probably apt for short-run, high-design products but also for capital goods and certain components – short-run, specialized, capital-intensive products, in other words. But for mainstream consumer goods, this could not provide sufficient scale in research and development or the cost savings in manufacture that large corporations could offer.

Much of the engineering demands required in even the most straightforward products draws on significant capital and human resources in their development. James Dyson talks of having developed 5,127 prototypes for the cyclone system over three years (Dyson 1998: 121). In 1996 the in-house design department of Hewlett Packard numbered 27 professionals in all. This was made up of six industrial designers who took care of product aesthetics and human factors, 16 mechanical design engineers responsible for the components that make up the product, five tool designers whose job was to add and modify features in order to facilitate component manufacture, and two plastics process engineers who provided specialist knowledge as to the behaviour of plastics in their various states of formation (Wood and Ullman 1996: 202).

Generally speaking, new product development absorbs around 15 per cent of the production budget, but commits 80 per cent of overall costs (Thackara 1997: 424). Thus while we have seen that the human resource costs may be substantial in the Dyson and Hewlett Packard cases, these are overshadowed by expenditure on tooling up, raw materials and manufacture. In view of this fact, it is vital for companies to achieve the optimum product development before actual expenditure on production 'ramp-up' is made. Furthermore, the resultant high overall costs must be met by high-volume sales.

The pressure on designers is not just to achieve the right 'fit' of aesthetic and utilitarian values in a product in order to satisfy the brand requirements of the producer or the lifestyle desires of the consumer and subsequently justifying tooling and manufacturing costs. To these demands, the question of product safety has added to the weight of responsibility on designers. In the UK, for example, the Consumer Protection Act of 1987 made 'the manufacturer or importer of a product with a design defect liable to compensate a person who suffers damage, without the sufferer having to prove negligence or a contractual relationship' (Abbott and Tyler 1997: 116–17). From 1993, the 'CE' marking in the European Union was established to signify that products conformed to all the various safety controls of the different member states: in other words, it acted like a 'passport' to be allowed free movement within the Community market (1997: 95). In addition, the EU General Product Safety Directive imposed obligations on producers and others in the chain of supply to place only safe products on the market. Such directives put the responsibilities for product safety and its testing on the producers and suppliers and, by extension, back to their designers.

Given these restrictions, it is not surprising that variety and flexibility in certain consumer goods, such as electronic hardware and white goods, is, in fact, reasonably limited and does not live up to the ambitions of some proponents of product semantics. There is also a range of associated features outside the flexibility of manufacture: the amount and type of retail space available and the need to cluster products around core brand identities rather than produce fragmented flights of design fantasy both contribute to this effect. A typical scenario, then, is for variety in a product line to be created by establishing a new product and then subsequently adding variations and additions to it.

In terms of the body design of products, computer-aided manufacture is limited in delivering flexibility. Van Hinte (1990) argues that its forte is in processing information, with which it can control other machines by switching them on and off according to consumer demands at its most basic. The computer is therefore most influential in carrying out simple operations in manufacture, such as in spraying or welding, or controlling variation in punching and drilling tools. By contrast, he reflects, three-dimensional data for moulds takes longer to process digitally than 'real' moulds. Variety as a means of catering to individual consumer desires is achieved less from computer-controlled machinery than by taking a modular approach to designing. This is typical in power-tool systems with a variety of attachments or in bicycle assembly. A glaring example of how product variety could only be expressed in simple details rather than in the main body was in the Nokia 3210 mobile phone. This product featured clip-on fasciae so that the user could customize it – within a narrow menu – to their favourite colour and finish. Otherwise, the hardware was relatively undifferentiated from that of other models.

In many consumer goods, flexibility of production is achieved through a combination of computerized information systems with relatively low-technology industrial arrangements. A classic and well-known example of this is in Benetton clothing. Its headquarters is in Treviso, northern Italy, and eight Benetton family-owned factories in the immediate region carry out design work, grading, marking and cutting. Labour-intensive assembly, pressing and embroidery are contracted out to small firms. Below them, these firms subcontract to a third tier of very small workshops – often non-unionized, low-wage setups – which carry out more specialized tasks. Benetton tightly controls demand down through these tiers according to market fluctuations. Upstream of the final assembly, the company only sells its products through franchises which bear its name. Each outlet is connected to automated warehouses and regional and world headquarters through a computer network. In this way, the company can receive information on customer demand. Of particular importance are data on shifting tastes in colours. Using information which originates in the retail outlets and is then downloaded through the Benetton network, computer-programmed equipment shifts from one colour order to another. The dyeing process for goods is held off as long as possible so that consumer information can be fed into production at the last minute (Harrison 1994: 89–95).

'United Colors of Benetton' is not just a slogan which expresses a brand identity, then: it is also shorthand to describe the flexible production systems it employs. As a company, Benetton itself is stripped down to its core competencies of design, marketing and assembly. It not only benefits from using information technology and flexible manufacture to close the producer/consumer gap, it is also free to concentrate on interposing itself at a variety of points on the 'circuit of culture' so that its identity in the marketplace may be bolstered via strident and well-known marketing campaigns.

The Benetton example is similar in many respects to the industrial structures of Japanese design-led corporations. Of these Toyota was the pioneer, it having stripped down to core competencies in the 1980s so that it relied on a tiered system of suppliers: 168 in the first tier, 4,700 in the second and with 31,600 suppliers in the third (Harrison 1994: 154). Equally, by the 1990s, 75 per cent of the production at NEC, Panasonic, Mitsubishi and Sony was contracted out (1994: 158). This contracting-out organization is a development of the *keiretsu* system, literally meaning 'societies of business', upon which the Japanese manufacturing sector thrives.

Sony was among the innovative Japanese corporations which modified this system in order to facilitate greater flexibility and creativity. In this climate, the Walkman personal stereo system was conceived, not through an orchestrated process of product planning, but, it appears, as the coincidence of a number of ideas and the need of the tape-recorder division within Sony to revitalize its prestige within the corporation (du Gay et al. 2013). The subsequent product and marketing mix was, however, highly organized and has allowed for subsequent developments of the Walkman in order to broaden its consumer appeal as well as reinforce its brand recognition. For instance, the Sony showrooms – located in major global cities such as Tokyo, New York and Paris – are furnished with 'lifestyle settings' such as bedrooms, offices and lounges, rather like the 'mood board' scenarios made almost real. Here consumers are encouraged to play with Sony products. Their behaviour and preferences are closely monitored by Sony staff. The showroom thus becomes a laboratory for analysing consumer reactions to different products. This information is then passed on to Sony headquarters, which then feeds into subsequent product research and development. As a result of such market research, Sony has gone on to manufacture over 700 versions of the Walkman. While maintaining certain basic features in the design, Sony draws on flexible manufacturing systems – either in its own automated technologies or in the way it contracts components production out – in order to reach particular lifestyle segments of the market. By catering to different and progressively changing tastes, it is able to spread and reinforce the brand across a wide range of consumers and global markets.

DESIGNING GLOBAL PRODUCTS

The Sony and Benetton examples show that, as Bennett Harrison (1994) argues, it is in fact the large, global corporations that have continued to hold the commercial initiative and economic power in terms of their ability to exploit the fit between detailed consumer information and flexible manufacture. The end of Fordism does not necessarily mean the end of large corporations. As

James Woudhuysen stated, 'if small firms may be able to go global more easily than in the past, the world still belongs to multinational corporations' (1998: 111).

Product designers have benefited from this situation. Chapter 2 pointed out the vast growth in interior and graphic design sectors since 1980 as Western economies has shifted more in favour of services industries. However, so-called de-industrialization has not meant a decline in product consultancy. Those manufacturing companies in the West who weathered the storm of the recession in the early 1990s were mostly those that were more predisposed to product innovation. From 1990 there was widespread growth in the number of in-house designers employed by manufacturers and service providers who take a central role in product planning and the commissioning and managing of external design consultants (NDI 1994: 7). This trend continued into the 2000s (Design Council 2010) as companies saw the strategic role of design as being of increasing benefit to them.

Furthermore, economic globalization creates a situation where design information is passed between different nodes on a global scale. This may be between separate offices of a multinational design company. Thus while large consultancies in the 1980s established offices abroad to tap into local markets, by the late 1990s the traffic was two-way. Since consumption patterns and taste in certain products exist on a global scale, market intelligence and design know-how are constantly passed between the nodes both to keep up with and subsequently intervene in the global flows of information. In 1995, Japan's Ricoh, the photocopier manufacturer, located a design studio in Taiwan. Woudhuysen (1998: 100) lists three advantages for shifting research, development and design (RD&D) offshore: first, the internationalist effect of this move means that such offices develop products which are marketed over a range of countries, thus providing economy of scale and scope; second, by linking RD&D in different time zones through information technology networks, firms move CAD results between sites on a 24-hour basis so that new products are developed more rapidly; third, RD&D sites can tap into local knowledge on competitors, the market and specialist expertises and share these features globally.

This last point effectively evidences the global–local nexus. It suggests that globalism and locality are not in tension, but are mutually dependent. As Kevin Robins suggests, 'Globalization is frequently seen in terms of the "disembedding" of ways of life from the narrow confines of locality. But, increasingly, we are coming to recognize that it is – paradoxically, it seems – also associated with new dynamics of re-localization' (1997: 28). This means that the global–local nexus involves 'a pragmatic compromise between the aspiration to expand market spaces and the realities of cultural gravity and resistance' (1997: 30).

PRODUCT DESIGNERS AND THEIR CLIENTS

Product designers generally address the demands of representing a client's brand aspirations and creating products for a wide marketplace. There are no standard norms as to how this is achieved, however. Just as the nature of design consultancy does not allow for standardization of practices, so clients will make different demands of designers depending on their own expertises, product, scope and scale. Here are some examples.

Except for the occasional assistant drafted in to work on specific projects, British designer Julian Brown works entirely alone. Yet his clients include global corporations such as NEC, Sony and Curver. In the development of products, he explores what he calls the 'prime forms' that make up the quintessence of the client's products. Thus in his domestic and office gadgetry for Italian company Rexite, he extended from a design language already laid down by Giancarlo Piretti over a period of 15 years. 'Good design', in his words, 'arises as an evolution both of the client's own development and of its relationship with the designer.' His quest, then, is to discover a client's particular cultural identity and develop products which act as 'attitudinal markers' of that identity. This kind of dialogue, he claims, puts design on to a 'higher plain' than mere problem-solving; it is a level which, he claims, 'cannot be calculating' (Brown 1999). This design approach may resonate with 'brand thinking', although the emphasis is more on the client, producer side rather than on complex consumer research.

This notion of striking an 'attitude' with clients as part of the design process is also inscribed into Hollington's approach. This British product and interaction design studio, numbering around 15 employees, is more explicit in taking on and developing a client's brand through products. In mid-1998 they began working with Kodak, in the USA, towards a new range of cameras. The first camera was introduced in mid-2000, an advanced photo system (APS), zoom camera called AdvanTiX T700. Development work used very specific information regarding camera purchase. Two key features were that traditional film was not going to be entirely replaced by digital photography and that a significant number of leisure cameras are bought prior to vacationing. Using these data, Hollington developed key features of the camera which accentuated these notions. First, these included a rugged, robust exterior with big, easy to use controls; the challenge was to combine this ruggedness – akin to luggage – with the 'precision tool' values expected of a quality camera. To do this they combined soft-feel materials and sculpted forms with instrument-like, crisp, metallic detail, and colour/material/finish consultants Barron Gould developed the grey-green colour palette which relates to travel clothing and luggage. Second, some external design cues that stress the qualities of the APS system, such as the facility to choose picture format (classic, HD television or panorama) were incorporated; thus the 'CHP' control is moulded in jewel-like opalescent green plastic, is large, and can be seen from the front of the camera, the point-of-purchase viewpoint. Third, the range of cameras incorporated a flash housed in a flip-up cover that protects the camera's delicate lens and viewfinder optics and enables the flash to stand well away from the lens and thus help avoid the perennial problem of 'red-eye'. This unique-to-Kodak design feature is also seen as a strong part of the product's brand identity. Hollington's clients call the basic physical layout and shape of the product 'form factor'. This is elaborated into what is commonly termed 'product design language' through combining the otherwise 'abstract' design considerations, such as ergonomics, fitness for purpose and design-for-manufacture, with a design idiom which adds to its brand identity (Hollington 1999b).

At times the language used to describe the product designer's work may appear rather more opaque, however. For instance, Richard Seymour of well-known design consultancy Seymour Powell states in an interview:

> The X-factor in the product is its essential personality, its desirability quotient, if you like – those intangible, emotional features, over and above function and efficiency.... We're constantly searching for that elusive iconography, the psychological bridge between consumers as they are and consumers as they'd like to be. (Seymour, quoted in Tomes et al. 1998: 129)

In each of these examples, the designers are establishing common frames of reference with clients, not just in the visual or strategic scenarios they envisage for them, but also in the verbal articulation of core ambitions. Language is thus not just a vehicle to mediate and explain ideas; it helps to shape the content of the product and, ultimately, its public meaning. It is small wonder that it appears to assume increasing prominence in the design process in an age of branded products, where semantic values are paramount.

PRODUCTS AND BRAND IMAGE

The narratives and themes set up in this dialogue between designer and client focus on the design process. They may also be extended outwards to provide content for other interventions to promote the brand. A designer's characterization of a product through identifying a key word or phrase to crystallize their aims may indeed sound like an ad slogan. For example, designers working for J. Walter Thompson on the corporate identity of Delta Airlines came up with 'Lufthansa with a smile' as a tag-line to centre their development work on – it meant that they wished to communicate their client's brand values as those of both efficiency and friendliness (Richardson 1999). These are for the internal use of the client and consultancy, but may find their way into the public realm. The key theme of the Dyson DC01 was dispensing with the bag through the invention of the cyclone system: Dyson's first advertising campaign used the words 'Say goodbye to the bag' (Dyson 1998: 231).

Indeed, the Dyson DC01 and subsequent models provide a tight-fitting case study not only because of the transparency of the product's values, but also because its designer was responsible for its manufacture and subsequent marketing. In this case, the story of its conception, shaping and the efforts made in taking it through manufacture and distribution becomes an integral element of its brand image.

The notion of 'brand image' is slippery. While the brand identity of a product involves the straightforward attributes given to it by its producer, brand image belongs to both producer and consumer. It refers to those values which are both created and communicated around the product; but these values are also subject to the fluxes of their possible meanings in society. Concurrent events may add to or detract from the public image of a brand. It is not surprising, then, that in the 1990s some design consultancies even joined forces with public relations companies (Richardson 1999). This helped ensure that the brand identity of a product could then be influenced in the public domain through the control of accompanying information. In the Dyson case, the analysis of brand image is made even more circumspect as, in the first place, the company is concerned to distance itself from mainstream marketing systems which promote brand identity. Throughout his autobiography, Dyson reminds us that the styling of the vacuum cleaner emerges in the first instance from

AdvanTiX T700 camera, designed by Hollington, produced by Kodak from 2000
Photo: Hollington

solving engineering problems and that the strength of its innovations do not need further dressing up through advertising or sales gimmicks. Nonetheless, the Dyson story interfaces with a rich set of cultural discourses that help to shape the brand image. In other words, Dyson the individual, Dyson the manufacturer and Dyson the product have their own mythologies which are both produced and consumed.

As an affable but retiring personality, James Dyson is well known. He is a genuinely philanthropic entrepreneur who has supported a range of charities and causes. Some of these relate to his own activities, such as his support of London's Design Museum. He has also been a vociferous critic of patenting systems, which due to their high costs, he claims, stifle the enterprise of many small-scale inventors.

The 'Dyson story' has been told through numerous newspaper and lifestyle magazine articles (e.g. *Sushi* 1999). It is also recounted in a small booklet given with each Dyson product, in the Dyson autobiography and on the company website. It is an heroic story of an inventor and designer who developed a range of innovative products for international export. Each product has its own chapter in the story in which a simple design idea is taken from the workshop, through struggles to find backers, to their eventual market success. Each successive business venture builds on the last one until the narrative reaches its apotheosis in the realization of the DC01.

This is a gripping story full of yarns and cliffhanger suspense. It has resonances in a long pedigree of British 'visionary' hero inventors. Many of these have not reaped the rewards of their own innovations: John Hargreaves, inventor of the Spinning Jenny, had his idea pirated and died in poverty; Charles Babbage, who built the precursor to the calculator and computer, died a disappointed man; Sir Clive Sinclair is more known for the failure of his C5 electric car than inventing the pocket calculator, a version of the home computer and the digital watch. The Japanese, reportedly, believe that 56 per cent of the world's greatest inventions came from the UK; yet at the same time an estimated £165 billion has been lost from British inventions going overseas (Crace 1999). There are nonetheless some members of this 'it's crazy but I think it'll work' school who have achieved recognition and have even gone on to become national icons. Among these one would include the 19th-century engineers Isambard Kingdom Brunel and George Stephenson, who, interestingly, is featured on the UK £5 note. Contemporaneous with Dyson, we must acknowledge the 'Bayliss story'. This has a similar narrative of an inventor, Trevor Bayliss, who came up with an idea for a clockwork radio in 1991 but had to work through a series of hurdles, including rejection from the British Design Council, before his invention got into production. By 1999, no less than 120,000 Bayliss radios were being manufactured each month. These are stories 'out there', fashioned in the public domain by journalists and television producers. But it is noteworthy that in his autobiography Dyson cites Brunel and Dan Dare (an equally 'knife-edge' hero of the boys' comic *Marvel* fame) as his two greatest inspirations. Both the Bayliss radio and the Dyson vacuum cleaner objectify these narratives. As mental images, the ratchets and springs in the radio and the chunky aspect of the vacuum cleaner resonate with notions of engineering of a bygone era.

The DC01 came on to the market in 1993. Historically, this was at the tail-end of one of Britain's deepest economic recessions. Just as the Vespa motor-scooter from 1947 signalled Italy's post-war reconstruction, and the Mini Metro car was supposed to mark an emergence from a decade of labour relations discord in the automobile industry (Johnson 1986; Hebdige 1988), so the dual cyclone vacuum cleaner represents a new entrepreneurial sensibility based on design-led innovation. To transpose from Hebdige's argument about the Mini Metro (1988: 82–3), reading the Dyson story involves understanding the 'official' fixing of the product's image (Dyson literature, advertising, packaging, press releases etc.). Whether that reading makes sense and has resonance depends on the reader's prior knowledge of and relationship to external, related factors of ideological issues and cultural codes. Consciously or not, the consumer is presented with not one object, but a series of objects born of different 'moments' in the circuit of culture.

Brand image is therefore something that designers and producers can capitalize on. Stories can be told around products to boost their reputation or clarify their identity. But this is also open to outside influences that can favour or detract from this process. At times, the significance or meaning of a product may be derived closer to home, in its actual use.

PRODUCT USE

This chapter has concerned itself primarily with the relationships between representation, design processes and manufacture, marketing and distribution. The discussion has shown how layers of meaning are built around consumer goods. A coalition of the fluid processes of design, market research techniques and flexible manufacture attempts to sustain brands, continually layering meaning while retaining the core product and brand identity. These processes involve cognition both 'inside' and 'outside' the product. In the latter sense, new product development is viewed scientifically, as a commodity with potential exchange-value. The majority of this chapter has focused on this foregrounding of the activities of design and production domains interpreting and exploiting consumer markets. But the designer, and indeed the user, also experience it as a 'thing', as a raw object of use. This penultimate section looks more closely at the Dyson Cyclone in use, in order, perhaps, to retrieve design values which lie beyond the brand and are more firmly embedded in the everyday use of the artefact.

An innovation of the Dyson Cyclone and its less known forerunners, the G-Force (1985) and the Iona SF7 (1988), was the inclusion of a transparent cylinder. Previous vacuum cleaners had steadfastly hidden the dirt collection away. With the transparent plastic cylinder, the DC01 proudly displays all the dust and debris it sucks up. Being able to see dirt whizzing round in the chamber reinforces the 'cyclone' idea. It also makes a 'feature' of the dirt and allows it to be quantified. Conventional vacuum cleaners physically and visually spirit dirt away. With the transparent cylinder of the Dyson Cyclone, the dirt is held in suspension. This can provoke both shock and disgust as the user sees what was in the carpet, but also satisfaction at seeing that it is now captured. The domestic labour of cleaning is neatly quantified in the level of dust and debris to be seen in the cylinder. On a small level, then, the results of traditionally invisible domestic labour are made visible and measurable.

At the same time, the actual use of the vacuum cleaner might become 'autotelic'. This is a term used by the behavioural scientist Mihaly Csikszentmihalyi (1975) to describe the intrinsic satisfaction of carrying out activities in their own right, rather than towards any goal. Autotelic experience is one of complete involvement in the activity where there is neither boredom with it nor worry about performance. It may require skills and skills development, but clear feedback on actions is given. There is therefore a rational cause-and-effect wherein the results of actions are realistic and predictable. The activity engrosses the participant, blotting out all other external stimuli. It centres the individual entirely in the present, rather than being laden by past knowledge or future expectation. These factors add up to deeply pleasurable, self-confirming experience.

Autotelic activities, or 'flow' as Csikszentmihalyi otherwise calls them, might include dancing, sport, navigating a computer game, or even using a vacuum cleaner. Cleaning may involve domestic drudgery rather than domestic euphoria. But reaching to corners of a room, moving furniture, choosing and assembling hose attachments while lost in the drone of the motor may draw the individual into an intense involvement with an external challenge. This might be the experience of using any vacuum cleaner, but certain design details in the Dyson Cyclone may engender this effect. The apparatus features many points of physical interaction. The cable has to be manually wound back on to the body rather than being sprung. There are no fiddly adjustment buttons. Rather, points of contact – the clips to release the hose and the cylinder, the filter holders, the button to switch it on – are flagged up in yellow against the grey body. The chunky aspect of its general form reinforces this physicality, as does the superior weight of the plastics used. As design observer Peter Lloyd Jones tells us, 'if a person's possessions are to be capable of stimulating lasting intrinsic satisfaction, it is clearly desirable that they are designed from the outset not only to provide emotional goals and perceptual challenges which stimulate flow, but to be moreover inexhaustible to this kind of contemplation' (1992: 69).

THE IPOD: CONSUMPTION, PRACTICE AND CONTINGENCY

Given its purpose of domestic cleaning, the Dyson Cyclone may be limited in terms of how 'inexhaustible' its ability to stimulate 'flow' might be. The Apple iPod, however, presents a paradigmatic example of how a product's success relies on the coincidence of a number of features that are both intrinsic to the product itself and extrinsic to the social practices that it engages. From its launch in October 2001 to early 2006, 50 million iPods had been sold. It was estimated that sales would outstrip the Sony Walkman and Discman's cumulative units of 309 million over 27 years by 2012, despite being in a more competitive marketplace than these products were (Credit Suisse 2006). The iPod's astonishing success is due to a number of factors, including the visual coherence between all aspects of its design and promotion. But this may also be attributed to the close fit between it as an object of individual use and as a social instrument.

Some of the product's compelling attraction is bound up in the careful mustering of intrinsic design features to the product. Much of this is achieved through the interface between the exterior surface and its interior capacity. On the outside we are presented with a sleek, modernist exterior that packages 'the ubiquitous white box of the modern art gallery into a handheld object, complete with streamlined curves and the use of minimal sans serif typeface' (Kristensen 2006). Indeed, its unyielding aspect is underlined by the fact that the object is hermetically sealed; there are no visible screws, there is no access to its interior. This 'mystery' of the exterior is reinforced by the knowledge that its designer, Jonathan Ive, rarely gives interviews and the Apple design studio in Cupertino, California, is run in total secrecy (Boradkar 2003). Little, if any, 'explanation' is given as to how its design was arrived at or where future developments may go.

The iPod's matt white front and chrome back contrasts a soft, absorbent effect with the harder, reflective material. Its seemingly unyielding aspect – the viewpoint given in most visual representations of the object – is broken when, through handling the iPod, a more varied experience of the product is encountered. Indeed, the optional addition to the product of the protective rubber sheath called the iSkin reinforces the sense of tactility. This 'expicitly connects the iPod to flesh, to being alive' (Kristensen 2006). If the sense of movement and activation in manipulating the wheel isn't sufficient, then an optional click sound is added in to reinforce the sensation of the product as machine. Thus an exchange between human manipulation and electronic responsiveness is embedded into the design of the product via the outer skin of the object and, in particular, via the surface of the click wheel. Cooley (2004), speaking more generally of hand-held electronic gadgets that include screens (otherwise known as 'mobile screening devices'), calls this process 'tactile vision'. The *fit* in terms of the relationship between eye, hand, body and listening extends the act of looking into a strongly embodied process. The design of the iPod therefore facilitates a transition from visual appearance, through tactile engagement, to aural immersion.

Fifth-generation Apple iPod, iTunes and other Apple paraphenalia
Photo: Guy Julier

The combination of these actions that the product instigates may be understood purely for their sensory power, but they may also be appreciated as part of a longer-term and expanded set of practices that the object facilitates. The iPod's 40GB capacity to store 10,000 songs or 700 hours of tracks – many more than the majority of its MP3 competitors – means that the object also becomes a sound archiving, ordering and display system. Again, at a sensory level, this means that users create playlists that help to 'narrate' their experience of spaces. Choosing specific sets of songs that complement everyday situations – jogging, commuting to work, washing up – colours these experiences (Bull 2005).

This analysis so far foregrounds the individual's sensory experience of the object, focusing on its affordances: that is, what it allows users to do with it. We might also explore the iPod in terms of the processes of consumption through the relationship of its commercial 'scripting' and the social networks that this activates.

In developing a theory for the process of acceptance of technologies into everyday usage, Roger Silverstone employs the notion of 'domestication' (Silverstone et al. 1994; Silverstone and Haddon 1996), itself a concept developed in British media studies in the 1980s. This concept takes as its starting point a rejection of entirely technologically deterministic views of goods to explore the aesthetic, moral and affective dimensions that influence their acceptance. In broad terms this means that a new technology shapes human actions, but these are also shaped through everyday contexts of use. Just as du Gay's 'circuit of culture' involves a continuous cycle of information and artefacts between the agents of production and consumption, so Silverstone conceives the processes of consumption as involving three stages that draw from and feed back into production. He calls these three stages *commodification*, *appropriation* and *conversion* (Silverstone and Haddon 1996: 62–5) and they provide a useful framework towards understanding the iPod's success.

'Commodification' is where the identity of a product or service is recognized and developed. This identity may be produced in part through the work of public policy-makers, regulators, market-makers and, of course, designers (Silverstone and Haddon 1996: 63). Here the industrial and commercial processes work to create material and symbolic artefacts and shape their meanings. But also, as we have already seen with the Dyson DC01, these also exist within ideological contexts beyond the object that contributes to their definition. For example, the regular media invocation of the existence of an 'iPod generation', representing 16–25-year-olds in the early 21st century stands in for a set of shared experiences, activities and outlooks of an age group (e.g. Brown 2006). Consumers engage in 'imaginative work' in piecing such meanings together. On one level, this forms part of the de-alienation of the object's processes where attempts to fill out a biography and identity for the object are made. On another, this will always be a frustrating experience because of the limits of consumption itself: if we are to follow Baudrillard's line (1988) that consumption engages desire that can never be satisfied – a necessary pre-condition for capitalism itself – then the process of de-alienation is never completed. Consumers move on, and this is fundamental to the iPod's maintenance of market share. In the case of the iPod, its replacement cycle is estimated at 1.5 years – a figure not dissimilar to the mobile telephone and the PC markets. With five generations of the product being released inside its first four years, these upgrades are carefully controlled in order to capitalize on consumption cycles so that just as one item 'wears out' (either in terms of the dedication and interest on the consumer's part or in terms of its technological functioning), so an upgrade is available. Indeed, as new consumer numbers are estimated to decrease from 2006, so the replacement market would become more significant to Apple's market (Credit Suisse 2006).

'Appropriation', according to Silverstone, is where enough of the publicly defined meaning that is articulated in the commodification processes is accepted for the product to be bought and then become part of the owner's private sphere. It has to fit into pre-existing practices and environments, but may also in turn produce new ones (Silverstone and Haddon 1996: 64). Obviously, as with all MP3 players, the iPod is dependent on computers of sufficient power to transfer audio files from CDs or the Web to the unit and by extension, skills, knowledges and networks that facilitate this. As such, the iPod is just part of a series of what Molotch (2003) develops in terms of what he calls 'lash-up'. To explain this term he uses the simple example of the toaster, explaining that its existence presupposes the supply of bread of a certain size – and by extension other material supports such as plates, jam and electricity. Objects are contingent upon the existence and successful functioning of others. 'Not just having a taste for toast, people *enroll*, as sociologist Bruno Latour [1987] would say, in the toaster project' (Molotch 2003: 2). Likewise, iPod users 'enroll' in an iPod/iTunes project. They adhere to the specific forms of purchase, collection, classification and exchange of digital audio files that MP3s promote, particularized practices of music listening and a wider cultural and commercial system that surrounds the iPod.

'Conversion' is where the private sphere of consumption 'reconnects the household into the public world of shared meanings' (Silverstone and Haddon 1996: 65). This is where goods may be discussed, compared, analysed or shown-off – where their existence and meanings, and the consumption thereof, are articulated. A proliferation of websites offer forums and blog spaces (including, for example, in late 2006 www.ilounge.com, http://playlistmag.com, http://blog.wired.com/cultofmac, www.ipoditude.com, http://blog.easyipod.co.uk) for technical and product release information, as well as for discussion and photos of iPod enthusiasts and their enthusiasms to be posted. It is also where the agents of production, such as marketing specialists, designers, advertisers and regulators, learn about consumer behaviours and attitudes. These are data that complete the 'circuit of culture', feeding information into further product development.

'Domestication' has come to be understood as not just concerning the acceptance of new technologies into the home, but also in terms of the 'taming' of wild things (Attfield 2000; Stewart and Williams 2005: 203). As consumers have become habituated to digital media in general, so the effort required in the 'taming' of new technologies has diminished. Moreover, with such confidence, consumers are able to act flexibly so that pre-existing media formats are reconstituted (Koskinen and Kurvinen 2005). Intended and unintended practices that engage the product are invented. In terms of the iPod, this would include the swapping of music files between friends. Personal playlists and iTunes libraries become signifiers of individuals' identity, tastes and lifestyles that are used as a shorthand for forming social groups. Making one's iTunes library available to inspection and use by others is both a self-identifying act and a socially bonding process. Such a constitution of social networks of mutually supportive individuals who are engaged with specific consumption practices instigated by a particular product has been termed a 'brand community' (Muñiz and O'Guinn 2001).

This process overlaps with the notion of consumption as practice, introduced in Chapter 4. Applying Reckwitz's (2002) definition of practice provides a useful synthesis of the social and individual of value iPods, while taking into account their network of objects, environments, systems and actions. By analysing the 'suites' of contingent objects on the one hand and the knowledge, understandings, bodily activities and states of emotion that are shared between users on the other hand, the designer may start from an enriched awareness. As Figure 6.1 suggests, there are first orders of contingency that make up 'suites' of objects.

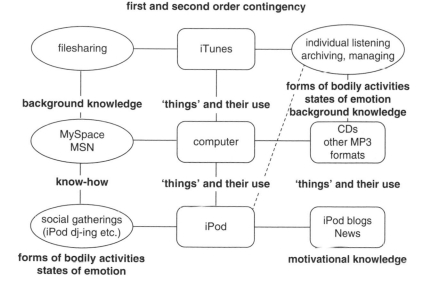

Figure 6.1 Reckwitz's (2002) definition of practice combined with first and second orders of contingency in the context of iPod use

These are objects that have a dependency on each other. Hence, at its most basic level, to function the iPod (or, indeed, the iPhone) requires a computer, cables, the iTunes software and Internet connectivity. There are also second-order contingencies that are not necessarily requirements for the primary object to function but they do facilitate an extended use of it: that is, objects for file storage such as external hard disks or CDs or speaker systems for iPod dj-ing. These secondary orders of contingency are often where the social questions of value, taste or connectivity may exist. To return to Molotch's 'toaster project', jam allows for shared appreciation of the individual's food enthusiasms. Likewise, social networking platforms like MySpace or Facebook are where teenagers display their personal music interests, after which music file-swapping subsequently might take place.

The connection between first- and second-order contingencies is not necessarily always intended by manufacturers. Users find ways of combining products in ingenious ways. These and many other systems of habituation lie both beyond and within the ambit of the Apple iPod brand. At one level, its consumers have expanded its range of uses beyond individual listening into a system that exploits the contingency of its technology into a social context. By relying on supporting computer-based networks for downloading and ordering music files, so these very networks provide a basis for discussion forums, swapping files or organizing social gatherings around music following.

Nevertheless, while other technologies may be used in these processes, the ease of use of the supporting iTunes program and a combination of the iPod's engaging design features and superior storage capacity continually refocus users back to the brand. By extension, the 'i' of iPod links to a range of other Apple products that share its general aesthetic, such as the iMac, the iBook, the iPad and the iWork computer program. Silverstone's process of domestication is not necessarily sequential in the case of the iPod. Constant upgrading, sharing and discussing by iPod users mean that 'commodification', 'appropriation' and 'conversion' overlap.

It would be questionable to assume that this iterative revisiting of the iPod and its associated products by consumers means that production and consumption are brought closer together in any meaningful way. Little discussion of the situations under which the iPod is manufactured in China is made (see Joseph 2006). Indeed, Negus (2002) argues that the work of cultural intermediaries, such as designers and branding specialists, conspires constantly to separate production from consumption. Branding may work to make consumers feel part of a corporation's identity and vice versa, but this closeness is confined to the production and consumption of *meaning*. On the back of my iPod I am told that it was 'Designed by Apple in California' (just as my cycle panniers that often carry it around tell me that they were 'Designed in Norway' but not where they were manufactured), but I am not told how it got from the designer's drawing-board to my desk. Meanwhile, the actual conditions of manufacture and distribution remain obscured. Thus Marx's classic notion of alienation and commodity fetishism – as discussed in Chapter 4 – is maintained. Meanwhile, this object implies an interplay of a generalized sense of brand identity and highly individualized consumption practices through the relationship of its exterior design qualities of its hardware and its 'interior' software that promises personalization. But it should also be noted that it is a highly social instrument in that its use is also performed through a set of contingent technologies and behaviours that extend beyond the individual user and individualized objects.

CONCLUSION

The Dyson vacuum cleaner is perhaps more unusual than many products in its consistencies between design, manufacture and mediation. This is not least because all these aspects have been centred around the efforts of one design entrepreneur. While specialist design critics or ordinary users may have genuine criticisms of the product's primary design – its weight, its noisiness, its overplayed styling – the coherent fit of product content and image, in a variety of representational forms, may well explain why it has been cited so frequently as an example of design excellence. James Dyson plays down the roles of branding and marketing to promote the integrity of the product instead. But even this contributes indirectly towards shaping a brand image.

There is no getting away from it. Consumer goods exist both as objects and signs. Design methods, in particular the use of the mood board, often ensure this attitude. The development of plastics has led to design values being concentrated on their exterior surfaces to the extent that they may be as easily considered as graphic symbols as haptic forms. They become semiotically loaded. It is on this exterior surface only that most domestic goods may be subject to specialist treatment so that a variety of consumer tastes can be catered for. However, while the initial sensory experience of a product may be visual, users may subsequently enter a range of other engagements, including tactile and aural. Generally speaking, the use of product semantics requires more design certainty than flexibility. Increasingly, they integrate both hard-edged market research and other academic disciplines, such as social psychology and ethnography, into their processes as a way of ensuring this certainty. Research and development costs, tooling up for manufacture and global distribution networks mean that economies of scale mitigate against any return to a romantic notion of small-scale workshops producing almost artesanally-conceived objects for a segmented market, at least, in domestic consumer goods. By contrast, the dominance of multinational corporations in the global economy makes them the prime clients for product designers, and the demands they face are therefore ever more complex and challenging.

Finally, it must be remembered that while consumer goods may often be represented through photography as singularized objects, they are in fact always contingent upon other objects and activities for their existence. No object is an island, but part of a never-ending constellation of things, people and practices.

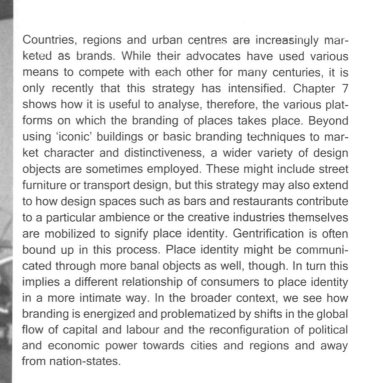

CHAPTER 7
BRANDED PLACES

Countries, regions and urban centres are increasingly marketed as brands. While their advocates have used various means to compete with each other for many centuries, it is only recently that this strategy has intensified. Chapter 7 shows how it is useful to analyse, therefore, the various platforms on which the branding of places takes place. Beyond using 'iconic' buildings or basic branding techniques to market character and distinctiveness, a wider variety of design objects are sometimes employed. These might include street furniture or transport design, but this strategy may also extend to how design spaces such as bars and restaurants contribute to a particular ambience or the creative industries themselves are mobilized to signify place identity. Gentrification is often bound up in this process. Place identity might be communicated through more banal objects as well, though. In turn this implies a different relationship of consumers to place identity in a more intimate way. In the broader context, we see how branding is energized and problematized by shifts in the global flow of capital and labour and the reconfiguration of political and economic power towards cities and regions and away from nation-states.

Various views of the Landmark Leeds project, 1991–92 designed by FaulknerBrowns
Photos: Guy Julier

In the city centre of Leeds a series of new urban furnishings appeared in 1991–92. The date is important, for two reasons. First, it coincides with the Department of Health and Social Security's move of its headquarters from London to Leeds, bringing some 1,500 employees and their families with it. For this metropolitan influx, the city was shifting its image as northern industrial town to major cosmopolitan centre. Second, 1992 was the year of full integration of the European Union, where internal trade barriers and passport controls would apparently disappear. The EU flag was proudly flown outside the Leeds City Council buildings.

The seats, lighting poles and balustrades were doing more than providing a perch or a leaning-post for weary shoppers, therefore. They seemed to be conspiring to redefine urban identity through their form. They are architectural detailing, but they are also part of a graphic treatment of the cityscape. They are about communication.

So what of their form? They were implemented as the redevelopment of a pedestrianized core of city-centre streets to connect a series of covered shopping plazas developed in the late 1980s. In addition to the basic seating and lighting, they included decorative paving, planters and a series of 'gateway' features. As focal points at junctions and places of repose they provided areas for buskers, street hawkers and political activists as well as ordinary shoppers to congregate. They not only served to physically break-up the street lines and remind us that this was an area that had been claimed back from vehicular circulation; they also provided a scenario for urban spectacle – entertainment as laid on by yet another Andean pan pipe band or the sellers of charity publications and political pamphlets. The multiculturalism, flows, inequalities and disunities of urban living are strangely harmonized in this seemingly modern space.

At first glance, the overall image of this scheme is generally 'European modern'. Powder-coated steel, aluminium tubing and granite provide a textural mix which would be equally at home in Düsseldorf or Rotterdam. The application of coloured, curvilinear decorative effects to some of the elements, however, causes some elements to recede into their immediate retailing context. Their slightly freehand signature is redolent of the many corporate identity and retail interior schemes that were developed in the late 1980s. Architectural critic Ken Powell described this scheme as 'out of place', 'meretricious' and 'a disgrace in a city full of fine Victorian craftsmanship' (1992). In the context of the Leeds City Council's ambitions, these criticisms may well be taken as praise. The project was very much the brain-child of the City Council's leadership and was, according to another of its critics, not the product of 'the normal process of public consultation' (Leeds Civic Trust, quoted in Smales and Whitney 1996: 209). As will be revealed in this chapter, it was precisely the client's ambition to be 'out of place', to be strident and to leave behind certain associations of being a Victorian city.

Discussion of such schemes does not belong exclusively to the architectural critic, however. Urban design projects suggest change in the conception and experience of city spaces and touch on leisure and urban planning studies. It also belongs to critical geography in that it is about the changing economic and cultural status of cities in a global context. These installations suggest new urban tastes arising from shifting class and employment patterns and may be studied by sociologists. By broadening the net of discursive contexts for such objects, we might achieve an enriched vision of them. But we can also find out more about their material and visual significance

'Leeds Look' architecture early 1990s: (above) Quarry House (Department of Social Services) and (below) Leeds Magistrates Court
Photos: Guy Julier

beyond their superficial forms and functions. We can explore the values and experiences to which the objects are connected and of which they give expression. In turn, we can begin to step away from a notion that the identity of urban centres resides solely in the exterior qualities of their architecture and adopt a more diverse approach to this question.

The cities of Leeds and Barcelona provide key case studies for this chapter. These are chosen as emblematic of changes that have taken place in many global cities. With a population of some 700,000, Leeds may be viewed as typical of many northern UK cities that has undergone a transformation in its employment base from a predominantly manufacturing base to a service economy since the 1980s. Urban design programmes such as the one just introduced were intended to recode the city centre, strengthening its reputation for retail and night-time entertainment. The shift to a service economy implied the rise of new forms of work and leisure to support it. The transformation of the Mediterranean city of Barcelona during the 1980s and 1990s, not least in its preparations to host the 1992 Olympics, provided a blueprint for many others throughout the world in marking out a new direction for a city and claiming itself as a significant place for the attraction of investment. In both cases, there is an intensification of the use of design as a promotional device by city authorities.

A direct result of this intensity is that 'place-branding', as a subspecialism of marketing, design and branding, has emerged. Place-branding is the process of applying the branding procedure as applied to commercial products to geographic locations and is a burgeoning activity within advertising and marketing (Olins, 1999). A more general interest in the relationship of product–country image is claimed as the 'most researched' issue in international buyer behaviour; there were, it was calculated in 2002, over 750 major publications by more than 780 authors who address this theme (Papadopoulos and Heslop 2002: 294). Against this background, specialist place-identity marketing and brand consultancies have emerged (e.g. Total Destination Management in the USA and Placebrands Ltd in the UK). 'How to do place branding' books have been published (e.g. Ashworth and Goodall 1990; Kotler et al. 2002; Morgan et al. 2002). An academic journal, *Place Branding*, was established in 2004.

Despite this verve for studying and orchestrating place-branding techniques, the complexity of urban agglomerations means that this is rarely, if at all, programmatic. Each urban identity is the result of the historical layering of social, cultural, economic and material elements over which planned branding systems are difficult to implement. Thus the process is not simply one of 're-branding' but more of 'brand management'. It is about the 'slow-moving husbandry of existing perceptions' (Anholt 2002: 232), drawing on what already exists and articulating its further trajectory. Therefore, in order to understand the diverse processes and potential limitations of attempts to muster place-brands, and the crucial role of design therein, as well as appreciate its often non-programmatic nature, it is necessary to take a detailed historical view of various case studies.

EVALUATING PLACE: BEYOND ARCHITECTURAL CRITICISM

Leeds City Council had played a significant role in shaping the architectural contours of the city centre immediately prior to the Landmark Leeds scheme. The inward-looking shopping developments that prefigured the Landmark Leeds project were not built on the same massive scale as seen in Manchester's Arndale Centre or Newcastle's Eldon Square in the 1970s. Large 'signature' developments did not dominate, therefore. Instead, a layering of somewhat chaotically and contradictory planning initiatives dating back to the pre-industrial revolution (Nuttgens 1979) provided an intact heart within which new developments had to function.

During the late 1980s, the city planning authority ensured that developers and their architects followed a set of unwritten design principles that came to be known as the 'Leeds Look'. This coincided with an unprecedented growth in office building: in 1987–88 new office development in Leeds rose from an annual 155,000 square feet to 275,000 square feet; by Easter 1989, 640,000 square feet were under construction with another 700,000 square feet in the pipeline (Barrick and Thorp 1989). This was partly motivated by a desire not to repeat the perceived planning mistakes of the past by allowing more assertive international-style office blocks to dominate the cityscape. The city's Planning Committee therefore 'tinkered' with those design details over which it had limited jurisdiction, such as the shape of fenestration or the pitch of a roof. Broadly speaking, this meant that new schemes reinterpreted the style of its riverside warehouses. This created a climate in which bold architectural statements would not be accepted and therefore not proffered. A series of prominent buildings were established exhibiting the same exterior usage of red brick, York stone for lintels, sills and other such details, slate roofs and Tuscan towers, pitch-roofs and window openings. These elements were not distinctive of Leeds in the late 1980s – a similar set of features could be found in office building throughout Britain in that period. The higher growth in building and the influence of the city Planning Office nonetheless conspired to concentrate this style with far greater density than elsewhere.

The 'Leeds Look' term was first coined by Ken Powell in an article entitled 'The Offense of the Inoffensive' (1989). Commenting on the influence of city planners on architecture, one critic described the city as 'Leeds: the smotherer of invention' (Kitchen 1990). Meanwhile, another claimed that the 'brick aesthetic ... seems to have been wrapped around most of the new buildings to prevent planning delays' (Whittaker 1990). These criticisms reveal that while the Planning Office did not overtly set about forging a particular architectural identity for the city, certainly the style elaborates a general aesthetic which was founded in aspects of its commercial heritage, but even this was a generalized typology. Nonetheless, both the response of its critics and the activity of its various producers demonstrate that the so-called 'Leeds Look' was, at the time, equating building with urban identity. More precisely, the exterior surface of a building, rather than its internal spatial arrangement and functional use, is privileged as the carrier of that identity.

This relationship between the built environment, its planning and design, and the visual consumption of places might be generalized further. Urry argues that novel modes of visual perception in the city were formed in the 19th century (1990: 136). Citing Marshall Berman's discussion of the mid-19th-century Paris of Charles Baudelaire, he links new urban forms and their experience by the middle classes through to the growth of photography as a way of seeing. Berman (1983) contends that the rebuilding of Paris in the Second Empire under the direction of Baron Haussmann brought forth a quintessentially modern experience of the city. The creation of wide boulevards was partly to facilitate rapid troop movements. But it also provided sweeping vistas of the cityscape so that each walk included dramatic visual effects. The boulevards became stage sets for an audience made up of the street-side cafés. The street provided scenery for the middle-class stroller to see and be seen in, the deprived and destitute having been removed from the action altogether. Here, the anonymity of the crowd gave both the security of private life and the stimulation of public action. In this world, the pedestrian (male) visitor – the *flâneur* in Baudelaire's terms – could observe without actually interacting with the objects or people of their gaze.

There is an indirect link, Urry therefore suggests, between this emergence of a cityscape designed for looking – both at it and its subjects – and the growth of photography. Just as the *flâneur* visually consumed all city sites, so the tourist photographs each vista on offer. There is the same detachment, the same pursuit of the picturesque in all things, the same wandering eye. The equation made between the built environment, the 'ordinary' stroller and photography stresses in each of these their visual consumption. Buildings, urban furniture and street layouts are valued solely for their external appearance; visitors merely look at them and each other within their scenography.

An extension of this attitude is to argue that the external appearance of buildings functions like advertisements (Crilley 1993). The public are spectators of a two-dimensional presentation of city; the exteriors of buildings act as triumphal displays of its historical, commercial and cultural resources. In their influential book *Learning from Las Vegas* (1972) the influential theorist-practitioners Robert Venturi, Denise Scott-Brown and Steven Izenour had encouraged architects to conceive their buildings as 'billboards', to concentrate on their exterior surfaces in conveying certain messages through the choice of materials, historicist quotation in design details and/or their allusion to other imagery. In turn, Crilley notes, architects learn their imagery from the findings of market research; they speak of 'taste cultures' and 'semiotic groupings' as would advertising executives (1993: 235). Finally, famous architects and artists may be engaged to design buildings and public artworks for a city. This acts to publicize its power and enlightened attitude as a patron.

In the light of large-scale redevelopment projects such as Canary Wharf in London, this analysis carries considerable weight. Cities whose built environment is significantly marked by the interventions of historically important architects, such as Mackintosh and MacMurdo in Glasgow, use their signatures to market themselves (Laurier 1993). Equally, the boulevards and vistas of Paris remain intact for the visitor to re-enact the strolling and viewing in the great city. But what if funds, public demand or conservation laws hinder large-scale redevelopment? What if a city does not possess the advantage of 'great architecture'? What if political or commercial demands require something less overt, of a smaller, more intimate scale? Here, perhaps, a different sensibility in architectural or urban design, but also in the conception of how a city is consumed, kicks in.

That this 'Leeds Look' period was soon superseded by the Landmark Leeds initiative demonstrates a significant turn from architecture to design as a key defining feature in the identity of a city. The Landmark Leeds project originated in pressure from shopkeepers and the Leeds Chamber of Trade and Commerce to regenerate the city centre. Despite the significant growth of office space in the city centre, retail and entertainment demand was falling. In the face of growing competition from out-of-town shopping centres and alternative nearby urban centres, the designers of the Landmark Leeds scheme, FaulknerBrowns, undertook a wide-ranging study of the city as a whole, reviewing transport, green corridors and key city-centre sites in order to revitalize its use. Out of this survey, the urban furniture scheme emerged as a way of recreating a sense of place in the heart of the city (Davenport 1999). Many design decisions were guided by pressure from the City Council to put in place a scheme as quickly as possible. Thus, as is often the case with projects of this scale and complexity, its various features were assembled in a piecemeal fashion.

The project coincided with a vigorous and swift campaign to position the city as a major European centre, an ambition which Leeds was not alone in harbouring. For its particular part, however, the City Council encouraged the establishment of the '24-hour city' notion (again not an entirely original initiative as, for instance, Manchester and Bolton had both adopted the same strategy). This looked to relaxing licensing hours for bars and restaurants in the city centre and supporting the 'night economy' (Bianchini 1995) of 'after-hours life'. It strove to kindle a continental European 'café culture', which was vigorously promoted by the local government tourist offices, regional news media and lifestyle magazines. The social life and visual constitution of Leeds could emulate Parisian restaurants, Barcelonese bars or the coffee-houses of Vienna. The identity of the city became design-dense. This effectively decentred its cognition. It shifted from the purely visual consumption of architectural exteriors (the 'Leeds Look') to the more holistic 'experience' of seating, signage, sounds and smells. It was also decentred in that it pursued an identity through assembling and arranging from 'a kit of dangerously fragile parts' to make itself up as a 'good European city' (Smales 1994: 51). Despite the potential dangers of this 'cut and paste' approach to developing a city identity, it is noteworthy that the more intimate, visceral experiences of eating, drinking, dancing and socializing – and the design hardware that surrounds and encourages these acts – are given greater prominence.

In terms of the management of city centres, in several instances the 1990s saw a clear shift away from foregrounding the architect, or at least repositioning him or her as the orchestrator of a wider range of urban activities. In Leeds, the chief city architect was reappointed as the overseer not just of the quality of individual buildings, but with a remit to manage the cultural use and infrastructure of its urban fabric. In 1999, the city of Hull appointed its first city 'brand manager', whose job was to coordinate all aspects of the city's image, ranging from its public architecture to its information leaflets. Between 1980 and 1984, Oriol Bohigas famously acted as Barcelona's City Council head of architecture and urban planning; he returned to public service at the beginning of the 1990s to take charge of the city's cultural planning.

In a critique of contemporary architectural discourse and practice, Martin Pawley (1998) reveals the dominance of visuality. He argues that criticism has been dominated by art-historical approaches: this is highly selective in what it considers to be of value and that selection is itself based on the discussion of purely formalistic values. In turn, styles are presumed to express the zeitgeist of an era (Pawley 1998: 99). Eras themselves are defined by the art historian. Thus a particular style is judged as 'typical' of its period while the art historian is also instrumental in defining these characteristics. By extension, this self-referential discussion leads to two key effects on architectural practice. First, it encourages a constant and uncritical replication of features that are assumed to express a particular age. In town centres, for example, where architectural heritage is 'preserved', historical façades are retained while redevelopment will completely alter the interior functioning and spatial arrangement of the building. Second, and more importantly, the majority of architects and their critics foreground the external appeal of buildings as the chief, or only, feature of value. As we have seen with products, buildings are presented in magazines or brochures via their superficial formal and semantic effects. They are shown as images of themselves.

Pawley suggests that the implications of breaking away from this canon of appreciation and practice are enormous. It would dispense with the fetishization of external form and embrace internal use. In turn, this will reveal the real import of buildings:

> In place of the city as the treasure house of civilization, it will expose the city as monstrous squanderer of resources. In place of the building as an investment, it will put forward the building as an expendable container. In place of aesthetic value, it will put forward the value of access to networks that annihilate distance, presence and want. (Pawley 1998: 93)

This suggests that architecture exists as the support for information exchange (as in computerized office environments), the distribution of material goods (as in warehouses) or the ebbs and flows of everyday life (as in urban furnishing such as the Landmark Leeds scheme).

Urry's analysis gives special prominence to the visual in the (tourist) cognition of places. It is one where looking at buildings, people and scenographies is the mainstay of visiting localities. By moving the emphasis away from the visual consumption of architecture, Pawley challenges us to explore alternative ways by which the built environment is experienced.

Other authors have suggested similar reorientations. Novelist Jonathan Raban (1974) provided a portrait of London which explored the city as a place of encounters and events. His 'soft city' of experiences, sometimes inhumanely violent, sometimes lovingly intimate, contrasted with the 'hard city' of urban planning and architectonics, financial and demographic statistics. Over a decade earlier, Jane Jacobs published an autobiographical journal of 24 hours in New York (1961). It affectionately dwells on the daily rituals of urban street life – the opening of shops, sweeping of streets, collecting of children from school, returning home from work. Marshall Berman eulogizes Jacobs' commitment to the vitality and diversity of urban experience. According to Berman, Jacobs' vision extends Baudelaire's interest in the visual spectacle of the city streets and is evidence of the continuous unfolding of modernity in the urban context (Berman 1983: 312–19). However, Jacobs also brings the experience down to a more immediate level. Her cityscape is not one of majestic vistas and building façades to create an heroic stage-set; it is a more chaotic, denser place of social exchange.

This kind of analysis opens out the internal organs of a city for inspection. It claims urban identity to jest not merely on the external appearance of its buildings, in the architectural look of a place, but also in the everyday attitudes and actions of its inhabitants. Both Jacobs and Raban, perhaps romantically so, suggest an emancipatory individualism in the city experience. They celebrate a triumph of the individual's will to determine their own metropolitan meanings. At the same time, the character of that participation is supposedly shared. Jacobs' and Raban's explorations reveal not just their personal viewpoints, but also a collective recognition of the social encounters or auditory rhythms in the city. Localities have their own stories and yarns to tell, which in turn communicate something about what one might expect of them. These are what sociologist Rob Shields (1991) terms 'place myths'. Subsequently, designers and marketing experts may appropriate these place myths or even originate them to position a city, region or even a nation against their competitors.

THE BARCELONA PARADIGM

Of all examples of the mobilization of design in the public context in order to position and differentiate a city, Barcelona has become paradigmatic. For example, it is cited as the source of inspiration for Rotterdam's extensive redesign work in the public domain (Hajer 1993: 64), and it was awarded a Royal Institute of British Architects' gold medal for recognition as a role model for urban regeneration in 1999. Russ Davenport, project architect for the Landmark Leeds scheme, had visited Barcelona several times before and during its development. He used images of urban design in Barcelona in his presentation to Leeds City Council clients and encouraged them to travel there in order to see the possibilities for themselves. Seeing what had gone on in Barcelona gave him and his team of designers 'a lot of confidence as to the possibilities available for an urban design project' (Davenport 1999).

Nonetheless, many of Barcelona's plaudits have ignored the several layers and networks of signification on which its redesign in the 1980s and early 1990s took place. Clearly a major impetus for development was given by the city's hosting of the Olympic Games in 1992. International 'signature' architects, such as Arata Isozaki and Norman Foster, were engaged to design major buildings, the indoor stadium and the communications tower respectively. The city's architectural heritage of Gaudì, Domènech i Montaner and Puig i Cadafalch was cleaned up and promoted. Public transport was extended and traffic circulation improved. Four kilometres of seafront were reclaimed and its portside was redeveloped.

Urban design in Barcelona 1980s: (top) Metro signage; (middle) waterfront; (bottom) Parc de l'Espanya Industrial; (top opposite) Moll de la Fusta waterfront; (below opposite) drinking fountain
Photos: Quod; Isabel Campi; Pedro Mandueño; Guy Julier

But much of the redesign of the functional and experiential apparatus of the city belongs to initiatives outside this event.

In Barcelona through the 1980s we find the confluence of a number of events which added up to produce a concerted reworking of the city's identity in a European context. During four decades of the right-wing dictatorship of General Franco, the infrastructure of Barcelona and most other Spanish cities was largely neglected. By the time of Franco's death in 1975, its urban fabric was marked by chaotic traffic systems and high levels of pollution, irregular public transportation, and a dearth of public amenities.

The subsequent transition to democracy ushered in the partial decentralization of state power to city councils and regional governments, which gave them greatly increased autonomy in their education, transport, public and commercial policies. In Barcelona from 1980 onwards, the socialist city council set about a radical urban regeneration, first of its metro system but also of its parks and plazas. Signage for its public transportation system installed a greater feeling of order and structure to the city chaos; paving projects and new public spaces gave back a sense of dignity to urban life (Buchanan 1986; Julier 1991: Ch. 4).

This emergent design hardware gave material form to some very specific metropolitan and 'nationalist' aspirations. They must be read not just in the context of the urban regeneration of a recently democratized locality and its preparations for a global event, but also as part and parcel of a wholesale ideological, cultural, commercial and, hence, aesthetic repositioning of a region.

The creation of the autonomous government of Catalonia in 1979 gave way to the establishment of complementary regional–national identities of ruralism and modernity. On the one hand, more conservative notions of tradition and heritage of the Catalan region were embedded in the rural economies, but the autonomous government also sought a position in a dynamic, federalized Europe. The latter required the mobilization of cultural models in order to communicate a notion of an enterprising, flexible, creative and technologically sophisticated workforce and economic infrastructure both internally to its own population and externally to prospective foreign investors (Julier 1996). This push came under the heading of 'normalization', in which both linguistic and cultural 'Catalanization' were advanced hand in glove. To be 'normal' meant that Catalonia's own language would be hegemonic and that at the same time cultural infrastructures and habits of cultural consumption would be comparable to those in Europe (Fernández 1995). In this context, design would be an apt signifier of the cultural sphere.

Taste is therefore linked with the process of identifying a city or region, and through the interrelationship of public architecture, design programmes and private consumer habits, so buildings, signage, urban design, fashion and home furnishings provide 'objectivated cultural capital' (Leach 2002: 283). In the Catalan case, this idea was promoted not just in terms of the imposition of modern street furniture or through vigorous regional support of design institutions (Julier 1995), but even when one turned the television on; the equation of 'Catalan = modern' was communicated through visual form. The first official Catalan television channel, TV3, brought together a team of young media professionals and graphic designers who shaped its aesthetic. As Catalan design historian Viviana Narotzky has commented:

With its carefully designed studio sets and animated graphics with minimalist music, its newsreaders' choice of clothes and hairstyles, and its selection of furniture, the visual world it brought into over 50% of Catalan households every day was a designer's world. Using the same didactic insistence with which it was promoting a habit in cultural consumption in Catalan, it normalized a certain type of visual and material environment: 'normal' Catalans spoke Catalan, listened to Philip Glass, dressed smartly and sat in designer chairs. How different were they from other Spaniards! One only needed to switch channels to see the proof. (Narotzky 1998)

Domestic taste and modernity was also linked to the changes in the fabric of the city via a television soap opera in 1992. *Poblenou* featured a family who, having won the lottery, moved from their run-down home in the Gothic Quarter to a brand new designer apartment in the Vila Olimpica (Campi 2003). In thinking about the role of architecture in the identification with space, architectural theorist Neil Leach takes us beyond the object to 'engage the subjective processes of identification' (2002: 281). We can begin this analytical approach, Leach argues, by considering Bhabha's concept of nation as 'narration' (Bhabha 1990). Here the meaning of nation comes into life through the language and rhetoric that articulate it. This narration is not abstractly independent of objects, however. Instead, what is said is activated by objects, while narration also contextualizes and gives meaning to them. Design objects and discourse are mutually dependent in generating belonging. In addition to this concept of 'narrating' place–identity, Leach also draws attention to how this is 'performed' by drawing on Butler (1990). Within this conception, identity is subjective. It can be played out through the reiteration of a set of norms. These norms, then, can be adopted or appropriated, used, used up and relinquished. The interchanges between design as experienced in everyday life and design as seen on television provided both the props and the plot for the performance of a new sense of modernity.

If modern 'cool' was frequently invoked to communicate the European, technocratic style-consciousness of the new Catalonia, then this was frequently balanced by messages of spontaneity and freedom. In many examples of graphic design in the 1980s, painterly gestures in primary colours that echoed the style of Catalan artist Joan Miró were frequently employed. Miró had been associated with anti-Francoist dissent, but the directness of his visual language was now being appropriated to advertise the freedom of the market rather than political emancipation (Satué 1997). This was evident in the *Barcelona mes que mai* (Barcelona more than ever) campaign visualized by Pepino García in 1984, an advertising campaign developed to inculcate civic pride. On a more international scale, Josep Maria Trias's identity for the Barcelona 1992 Olympic Games released in 1988 similarly expressed local identity. This identity programme was 'explained' through the pages of design magazines (e.g. Trias 1988) and later through the press. Catalans learnt that the logo incorporated 'Mediterraneanism' with its artistic heritage and were also told that the use of Times semi-bold in the typography evoked an antique Roman past. This process of 'telling it like it's meant to be' served not only to repeat certain place-myths as embodied in the graphic work, but also to reinforce the self-consciousness of their use in the public realm.

New design in Barcelona infiltrated all levels of everyday life by the late 1980s and continued to do so into the new century. The values of modernity, Europeaneity and technology as well as locality and creativity were invoked throughout the cityscape. Its significance was underlined by a series of interconnected ideological and cultural features: it contrasted starkly with Spain's immediate past by replacing national isolationism, conservatism and environmental chaos with internationalism, modernity and civic pride; it foregrounded new design as an amenity for a new civil society; it aspired to achieving a confluence between local identity, regional political will and modernity in a transnational context. Design hardware – the city's new bars, public spaces, street graphics – was deployed in an intensely public arena both in itself but also in its constant mediation and reproduction through the media. The circulation of new design through retail outlets and design magazines, its discussion in the local press and promotion through design institutions ensured its intense mediation. Furthermore, design became a matter of recurrent political interest among regional government, city council and civic associations. It served to bolster the emotional software of the city, promoting highly refined attitudinal aspirations and unity by linking nationalistic sensibilities, self-identity and place (Narotzky 2000). The consistency of its message in terms of taste and cultural capital gave the appearance of local cohesion.

The Barcelona paradigm presents a dense and complex network of individuals, agencies and institutions of design production and consumption, (see Figure 7.1) but it should also be understood in the context of global patterns in the redesign and marketing of place. Critical analysis of its developments, and those of many other locations, may be shaped, according to Booth and

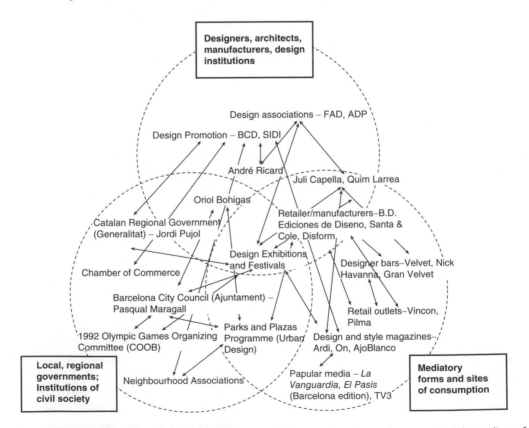

Figure 7.1 Domains of design culture that formed Barcelona's designscape, 1980s and 1990s: arrows denote lines of *direct* relationship and influence

Branding Barcelona: (left) *Barcelona més que mai* (Barcelona more than ever) promotion; (right) Barcelona 1992 Olympic logo
Photos: Ajuntament de Barcelona; Quod

Boyle (1993: 22–3), by three theoretical approaches. First, a regeneration programme and its attendant cultural policy may be seen as an attempt to cushion the effects of a slippage from an industrial to a post-industrial context. Second, it may be a local response to the globalization of capital and the demand to attract international investment. Third, it may be a way of producing an illusion of the cultural capital of urban unity for the benefit and reward of an upper- and middle-class commitment to urban living.

CULTURAL ECONOMIES, REGENERATION AND GENTRIFICATION

Between 1977 and 1993, the USA lost about 2 million of its factory jobs. Britain lost 3.6 million, a decline of 45 per cent over roughly the same period (Ward 1998: 187). Leeds saw a similar manufacturing employment drop from 33 per cent to 17 per cent over this period (Leeds City Council 1998). Manufacture as a percentage of gross domestic product dropped in Catalonia from 36.2 per cent to 30.4 per cent between 1986 and 1991 (Martín 1992: 39). In each of these cases, employment structure has come to be dominated by services.

In responding to the shift from an industrial to a post-industrial economy, or more widely, from organized to disorganized capitalism, urban centres engage in the development of cultural policies which are defined in economic terms. It is seen both directly and indirectly as a form of job creation, a way of attracting inward investment and in converting the existing labour force to new modes of employment and bringing in skilled professionals from outside. Culture is bundled up with business services, leisure industries and tourism in an effort to regenerate city-regions and therefore create wealth and employment (Booth and Boyle 1993).

The creation of events, services and attractions in order to regenerate and market places is by now well documented and discussed (e.g. Bianchini and Parkinson 1993; Kearns and Philo 1993;

Ward 1998). This includes the establishment of festivals, major sporting and cultural events and the development of museums and other visitor attractions. A commonly reproduced and even caricatured theme was the development of waterfront or dockland areas. Originating in Boston in the mid-1970s, this approach integrated high-class new housing, visitor attractions such as an arts complex, a major museum or theatre as well as new restaurants and bars.

Boston's regeneration was supported by a high-profile public relations campaign. In a similar vain the 'I ♡ New York' campaign was launched in 1977. In 1983 Glasgow brought out its 'Glasgow's Miles Better' slogan, which was followed by a plethora of similar attempts at boosterism by individual cities. Whether it involved substantial building programmes or the consolidation of advertising campaigns, all such manoeuvres are highly design-intensive.

In terms of employment, the support of cultural industries in post-industrial cities is not insignificant, and was given increasing attention by governmental bodies from the mid-1980s. In the UK, the total number of people directly employed in the cultural sector in 1991 was 650,000, 2.7 per cent of the total workforce. Its gross fiscal value was greater than either the mechanical engineering or the chemical industries (Policy Research Institute 1996: i). In Leeds, more specifically, the cultural industries were judged to reflect a similar pattern, but were also expected to grow significantly in terms of output and employment (Policy Research Institute 1996: 12). Individual cities, regions and nations sought strategies to boost this sector.

The cultural industries also came to be appreciated for their symbolic capital in contributing to the self-image of a place and its population as dynamic, creative and entrepreneurial (Julier 2005). Zukin (1995: Ch. 4) makes the same argument concerning the high contribution of the cultural sector to the New York economy. Reflecting Bourdieu's notion of 'cultural intermediaries', she observes that they work in a vanguard, trying out and exemplifying new trends both as producers of cultural artefacts and events as well as their consumers. More specifically, she states that:

> We owe the clearest cultural map of structural change not to novelists or literary critics, but to architects and designers. Their products, their social roles as cultural producers, and the organization of consumption in which they intervene create shifting landscapes in the most material sense. As both objects of desire and structural forms, their work directly mediates economic power by both conforming to and structuring norms of market-driven investment, production, and consumption. (Zukin 1991: 39)

Equally within the Barcelona paradigm during the 1980s, designers were invoked not just as signifiers of modernity, but also as energetic exponents of a new enterprise culture. Their internationalism, facility for commercial networking and technological know-how carried a high symbolic-value within the city's reassertion on a national and international stage (Julier 1996). Enterprise culture has to be 'made reasonable' in order to make direct sense to those involved (Keat and Abercrombie 1991: 10). By giving material and visual form to this notion, design and designers, as cultural intermediaries, were appropriated by politicians and journalists in this quest.

The conversion of focused pockets of the cityscape in turn supports this self-image. The new cultural economy of post-industrial cities is invariably located in 'gentrified' zones. Downtown areas which formerly housed warehouses, small-scale workshop units or struggling specialist shops are converted into night clubs, designer bars and restaurants, private art galleries or craft studios and offices for other participants in the creative industries. Numerous examples of such creative quarters exist to illustrate this: The Calls in Leeds; the Born district of Barcelona (Pibernat 1999); Hoxton in London (Benson 1999), Helsinki's Design District (Koskinen 2005) and Chicago's Wicker Park (Lloyd 2006). This concentration services the avant-garde visual and gastronomic tastes of those working in the creative industries. The spaces have a symbolic role too. They reproduce the relatively low capital investment on which creative industries are habitually founded. As befits this sector, they are also liminal: they cross between cultural experience and commercial entrepreneurialism; they extend from the working day into the night economy, reinforcing the 24-hour code of 'art is life, life is art'; and as former locations of urban degeneration, their heritage is visually and mythically hard-edged and low-life yet now harbours the 'higher' ideals of cultural production. Further consideration is given to this strategy and its effects in Chapter 10, where the role of design in shaping and communicating knowledge and social capital is given more attention. Meanwhile, just as place-branding serves to promote a reconfiguration of perceptions of the human resources available in a location, so it affects the way that spatial geographies are presented.

MUSEUMS AND POST-INDUSTRIAL PLACE-MAKING

With de-industrialization, the clear imagery of specific systems of production and particular products which could be associated with locations (Sheffield steel, Staffordshire pottery, West Midlands light engineering, for example) recedes into memory and museums. This heritage may be retained as a tourist attraction, by way of industrial museums or experience centres, becoming a major industry in its own right (Hewison 1987). However, the link between such initiatives and local history may be more tenuous at times. For example, as part of the regeneration of Leeds, the Leeds Development Authority secured the establishment of the Royal Armouries Museum, bringing in investment of £43 million. Aside from being the home of a First World War tank factory, Leeds does not have a history in the manufacture of armaments, unlike, say, Birmingham. Heritage, argues Ashworth (1990), is a contemporary saleable experience produced by the interpretation of history. It is defined by the consumer not by the raw materials, however; it is, in essence, a function of the market. The presence of the Royal Armouries in Leeds is only legitimated by consumer demand.

Conversely, museum and exhibition designers Event Communications insist that to ensure their success in terms of visitor numbers, it is vital that projects are tied into the local economy and culture (Phelan 1999). In the first instance this reinforces the historical identity of a place and lends greater credence to the attraction itself through that association. When in 1998 they came to design the Dynamic Earth attraction in Edinburgh, these associations had to be quite self-consciously underlined. The experience centre tells the story of evolution which was, needless to say, a global event. However, in its scripting, early connections are made with James Hutton, the 18th-century Edinburgh man who conceived the idea of geological time, and Arthur's Seat, the volcanic hill behind the centre. The linkage to Scotland is also forced in a more subliminal way. Scottish actor John Hannah is used to

Gastronomic infrastructure for the Leeds 'creative quarter' around The Calls: The Arts Café; Oporto; Metze bar/café;
Photos: Guy Julier

narrate film sequences within the exhibition, the scripts of which frequently refer back to Scotland as 'ancient land'. It is hoped, on the part of the designers and clients, Lothian and Edinburgh Enterprise, that by anchoring this sense of place into the experience and continually referring separate elements of it back to its immediate location, visitors will want to go out and discover more about Edinburgh and Scotland. The production process is also important in consolidating the attraction within the local community. A project of this size and complexity generates local interest and involves a large amount of subcontracting to tradespeople (Edwards 1999). It is therefore connected to the locality in very real terms. The development of places of consumption (such as the Dynamic Earth) produces 'multiple local enthusiasms' (Urry 1995: 2).

BEYOND NATION-STATES: CITIES AND REGIONS

While the creation of heritage museums and experience centres can have a significant impact in the regeneration and marketing of places, there is clearly a limit to how much heritage many urban centres can take. Other regeneration initiatives are marked by their homogeneity between different cities – the statutory waterfront development, 'continental' café culture, public art schemes, high-profile cultural events – which in turn fosters their sameness.

Meanwhile, the dual shift towards service industries and the globalization of capital means, though, that cities compete ever more vigorously to attract inward investment. In Europe, an estimated 300 smaller cities and regions compete with each other for investment and jobs. Internationally, 40–50 medium-sized cities of populations of more than a million vie with each other. In addition there is the rivalry between London, Frankfurt, New York and Tokyo as world financial centres (Thackara 1997: 129–31).

While improvements in transportation and communication technologies have facilitated the exchange of goods and information across national boundaries, the industrial and commercial agglomeration on cities and their immediate regions (the city-region, in other words) has increased. This is primarily because production and work depend on a dense and complex network of exchanges of information, skills and goods (Scott 1998). It results in focused regions of particular activities, such as Silicon Valley in Southern California as a hub of information technology industries or Milan and its hinterland supporting design-intense fashion and furniture development and manufacture.

Separate nodes of activity may be closely interlinked across national boundaries in order to share and exchange their specialisms. The film, animation, advertising and design industries of central London give a very precise example of this effect. Since 1995, they have been served by their own information technology network called Sohonet. This capitalizes on and further facilitates the dense system of subcontracting on which neighbourhood's creative industries. Using fibre-optic cabling, this network allows the rapid movement of video, audio and other data in digital form between interdependent studios. Furthermore, it is linked via transatlantic cabling to the Hollywood film studios. With the time difference between London and Los Angeles, material such as special effects animation can be worked on in Soho during 'down-time' in California.

Exchange between separate nodes bypasses the parameters of sovereign states. Geographer Allen Scott (1998: Ch. 8) contends that this has important ramifications for the organization of global political power blocs (see Table 7.1). This emergent political organization empha-sizes the strengthening relationship between regions and multinational blocs. If design acts at the vanguard of structural change, and indeed produces a 'cultural map' by which these changes can be recognized, then it deserves examination. We have seen how the Landmark Leeds scheme, and parallel developments in the city's cultural economy, aspired beyond the aesthetic borders of the nation-state in order to broadcast itself as a European city. Likewise, Barcelona design short-circuited any notions of 'Spanishness' in order to make the equation of Catalan/modern/European.

Aesthetically speaking, this confirms a notion of what Nederveen Pieterse (1991) termed 'fortress Europe'. Modern European identity has, in his estimation, developed a self-image as 'the cradle of civilization', seat of reason and the inheritor of the Enlightenment. According to Nederveen Pieterse, this ethnocentricism requires a 'barbaric' other, identified in the Islamic world of North Africa and the Middle East, that surrounds Europe. Simultaneously, if, as Spivak

Table 7.1   Global political reorganization (after Scott 1998)

Level	Example	Commentary
Global	United Nations (UN)	Coordinates agreement on global issues of health or environment, but politically weak.
Multi-national blocs	European Union (EU) North American Free Trade Association (NAFTA) Asia-Pacific Economic Cooperation (APEC)	Facilitates intra-bloc exchange. Not politically or economically strong but size allows manageability. Roles as centres of authority and influence will grow.
Sovereign states	Spain United Kingdom	Still the most potent bases of economic and political power. But regulatory power being passed upwards to supra-national blocs and functions of state passed downwards to regions.
Regions	Catalonia resund	Traditionally subordinate to nation-state. But ability to coordinate concentrated social and economic activity means that they will strengthen. Regions have direct, unmediated relationship with multi-nation blocs, bypassing sovereign state.

(1988) argues, the developed world now appropriates postmodernism and pluralism as a core value, then the celebration of a supposed culture of diversity also becomes a celebration of the West and the sophistication that this value entails (see also Billig 1995: 155). The ability of a city or region to be multicultural and to include people and lifestyles from various origins is therefore held as a positive feature: it demonstrates its openness and cosmopolitanism. Following on from this argument, by contrast parts of the world that lie outside this are seen as monocultural, lacking, impoverished and unsophisticated. European modernity, then, incorporates particular sanctioned forms of multiculturalism.

THE BRANDING OF CITY-REGIONS AND NATIONS

More benignly, this reorientation of political and cultural discourse towards regions musters some interesting results. As in the case of Catalonia, European regionalism allows for the retrieval of local identities. But technological and economic change may indeed create new regional identities. Such was the case of Øresund, where the building of a bridge linking Copenhagen (Denmark) and Malmo (Sweden), across the Øresund sound, would open up opportunities for the concentration of specific shared or complementary partnerships in a transnational region. The new region brings together Zealand on the Danish side and Scania in Sweden. Steps to their integration originated partly in an historical study of their shared past and cultures (Weibull et al. 1993). Making up a population of 3 million, the new region shares expertises in bio-industry, environmental technology, life sciences and food, tourism, trade and distribution as well as information technology, media and communications. The region is therefore constituted less in formal structures of governance – since these reside within their respective nation-states – than in their shared physical environments and human resource bases.

The Øresund Konsortiet, a consortium of organizations involved in the promotion of the region, engaged the London-based design consultancy Wolff Olins to develop a brand identity for it. The ensuing study consolidated an appreciation of the shared features of history, environment and economy. It also identified attitudinal factors to the region's personality – that is openness, inclusivity, responsibility and innovation – which flavour the brand. Eventually, all these facets are distilled into the Øresund marque. Here, two organic shapes and the palette of earth and sky colours represent the coming together of the two areas, but also the shared 'attitude and visual language of the region' (Øresund Committee 1999) in its natural environment and the human values of its population.

The use of 'attitudinal' factors to identify a city, region or nation is evidence of an emergent tendency by politicians and their design consultants to consider them as brands. Hans Arnold, working at Wolff Olins, developed a structure for identifying different levels of branding within a region which integrates place factors and human resources. The regional brand was equated with its overall 'attitude'. This is subsequently made up of: 'local brands', which incorporate its various environmental features such as its towns and cities; category brands, which describe its competences as evidenced in its economy and educational infrastructure; and, its product or service brands, such as specific leisure attractions, which are sold and consumed as part and parcel of the place (Øresund

Committee 1999; Vinogradoff 1999). These categories are then distilled into a central idea which provides a short-hand, by way of a slogan or a simple image, to communicate its essence.

Wally Olins, co-founder of Wolff Olins, reinforces the notion that governments can control the brand image, and thus the attitudinal markers, of an entire nation. In a report written for a British government think-tank, The Foreign Policy Centre, he stated that:

> Governments can create the mood and lead and co-ordinate the image. ... All countries communicate all the time. ... Collectively, all these millions of messages represent an idea of what the nation as a whole is up to, what it feels, what it wants, what it believes in. It should be the task of government – with a very light touch – to set the tone of these messages. (Olins 1999: 25–6)

Wolff Olins was highly influential in promoting the idea of rebranding places during the late 1990s. In November 1996 it approached BBC2's *Money Programme* with an idea for a programme in which it would develop a brand for Britain. Their research had shown that Britain's image and reputation were damaging the country's ability to compete in world markets. Furthermore, British people had a uniquely poor self-image of their country. They determined 16 key signals and values which 'encapsulate the essence and personality of a new brand for modern Britain' (Wolff Olins 1999a), these being: original; invest in; made in; educating; creative; leading; team; skilled; discovering; welcoming; diverse; innovative; strategic; exporting; popular; serving. Their recommendations were that the word 'Great' be taken out of Great Britain, arguing that 'New Britain will demonstrate greatness without having to say so'. The visual scheme in which they proposed to substitute the use of the Union Jack, which had become associated with football hooliganism, imperialism and right-wing politics, would not make particular emphasis on red over blue or vice versa. The brand, they claimed, was 'post-political'.

The resulting television programme, *Made in UK*, was followed by a report produced by the think-tank Demos, entitled *Britain™ Renewing Our Identity* (Leonard, 1997), and a pamphlet produced by the British Tourist Authority, *Branding Britain* (1997). They coincided with the emergence of the 'Cool Britannia' slogan, used liberally by politicians to describe this new Britain. The term 'Cool Britannia' originates in the title of a song by the Bonzo Dog Doo-Dah Band released in 1967, and was

Øresund marque in various applications, designed by Wolff Olins 1999
Photos: Wolff Olins

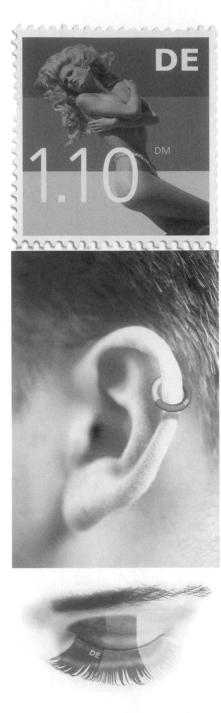

re-used both in a headline in *The Sunday Times* and in an ice-cream brand in 1996. In 1997, the British Council commissioned design consultancy Johnson Banks to develop a campaign to promote the 'New Britain' brand abroad. In each of these cases, the drive was to manoeuvre the national image away from historical associations of empire and cultural conservatism towards one of modernity and pluralism.

This 'softening' of national image through brand strategies clearly reflects the shifting status of nations in the new world order. Wolff Olins undertook a similar study to their *Made in UK* programme for the German television station ZDF in 1998, in which they developed proposals and sketches for a rebranding of Germany. The recommendations included redesigning the national colours by introducing the European blue in place of black and using a typographic signature of 'DE' to stand for 'Deutschland Europa' (Wolff Olins 1999b). The applications of this in the resultant television programme and an exhibition which opened in Berlin in January 1999 played up such values as tolerance, diversity, non-conformism, creativity and peace – values which are easily generalizable to other European nations. Pluralism, as we have seen, is readily appropriated as a core value in a (post)modern fortress Europe.

PROBLEMATIZING THE BRANDING OF PLACE

Unsurprisingly, attempts to create a cohesive brand image for a locality under relatively loose headings such as 'creativity', 'modernity' or 'multiculturalism' are easily problematized. In the first instance, it locates identity less in the unique characteristics of a focused place (if they indeed exist) than in a constellation of transnational shared values. This might immediately result in contestation as to exactly what those shared values might really be. But equally, where a localized 'flavour' is placed alongside such brand building, the contradictions between the two are immediately recognizable.

The Barcelona paradigm is powerful not just because of the strength of the sum of individual design interventions deployed in a single context. There was also a tight fit between different components of du Gay et al.'s 'circuit of culture' (2013). Local and global demand was met by design production. Local taste-makers, be they famous architects or television channels, effectively regulated the nature and scale of design culture. Specific design products satiated notions of self-identity. Looking at the Barcelona paradigm in terms of 'systems of provision', it is clear that the city and its industrial and commercial infrastructure provided a tightly woven and highly localized channel linking production, distribution and consumption, which was self-supporting, self-legitimating and self-authenticating.

This 'success', however, was not without its critics. Catalan journalist Arcadi Espada noted that the nation-building of the regional autonomous government so effectively reached all areas of everyday life (including its design) that one seemingly could never cease to be a Catalan (Espada 1997: 43). He questioned whether the very specific identity of Catalanism was truly inclusive of its population – a sizeable proportion of whom were not of a Catalan family background – and whether its claim to inclusivity was met in practice. For Espada, Catalan identity was constantly represented and reproduced through what he called *cultureta* (literally meaning 'small culture'). This placed cul-

Images used in the Deutschland Europa exhibition in Berlin as proposals for the rebranding of Germany 1999 (opposite and above)
Photos: Wolff Olins

tural 'normalization' at the level of the everyday (such as in the design of studio sets on the local television station), whereby national values and myths of nationhood were more insidiously inculcated.

Espada's argument coincides with what Michael Billig (1995) saw as 'banal nationalism' in action on a wider scale. While in liberal democracies the state could only dictate national values through minimal legislative means, so these were reproduced more effectively at a more domestic level: through language, the attitudes expressed in television soap operas, the commentaries made in sporting events or identities carried by particular food products. Equally, the branding of cities, regions or nations seeks to implement values at a 'banal', nuanced and symbolic level: through the subtle application of a logo to a poster or a product, through the provision of public seating of a particular aesthetic pitch or through inflections used in copywriting. It seems that attempts to communicate and promote cohesion are brought down to the everyday material and visual features of private and public life. Marxist geographer David Harvey (1989b) argues that the kinds of initiative to define, distinguish and broadcast the cultural capital of cities are merely a gloss. In appealing to bourgeois tastes and aspirations for urban living, it patches over class, racial or ethnic divisions.

This process, within which design culture plays a significant part, may even enhance these fissures. Gentrification may result in traditional communities being displaced. This indeed happened in a limited way around Barcelona's Plaça Reial as part of its renovation prior to the 1992 Olympic Games and continued in other areas subsequently (Balibrea 2001; Degen 2003). Zukin (1991: Ch.7) presents an equally critical viewpoint. She contends that the new middle classes of global, disorganized capitalism exercise cosmopolitan tastes as a vehicle of their cultural capital. She discusses how this has resulted in growth in the demand for international cuisine since the 1970s. The 'vernacular' of diverse immigrant communities (to New York in her discussion) is thus appropriated and consumed by this class, displacing it from its traditional function in serving its own community. Identities are served up or even themed for this new audience. In doing so, their original vernacular is superseded by a conformity to and coherence with the values of the marketplace.

Coherence, as indeed purveyed by the machinations of design culture in the city, region or nation-state, can only be momentary, or may only address particular levels of social experience.

This coherence may be understood as the result of refined and pervasive 'designscape', of a fit between different expressions and narrations of design through both its production and consumption (Julier 2005). Global cultural flow of ethnic groups, media, technology, finance and ideologies means that place and identity may equally be understood in several other dimensions. Their shifting nature and rapid movement continually disrupt the unity of economics, culture and politics, and challenge attempts to impose order and coherence through programmatic approaches to place identity. The disjunctures between these five elements are experienced and articulated in different ways, by different people and groupings in different micro-localities (Appadurai 1990).

Movement can also lead to hybridization, as distinct global cultural sections are assembled to present new identities. With the weakening of the nation-state, globalization can result in the growth of various modes of ideological and cultural organization so that groups and individuals may be represented at transnational, international, macro-regional, national, micro-regional, municipal and local levels. This ladder of representation is criss-crossed by functional networks of corporations, international organizations, and non-governmental organizations as well as professionals and even, simply, internet users (Nederveen Pieterse 1995).

Cultural coherence may therefore be destabilized by a range of organizations, conflicting flows and activities. And if designers and other cultural producers are mustered to protect that stability, they may as easily attack it. Commenting on the 'Cool Britannia' phenomenon and its incorporation into the British Tourist Authority marque, cultural critic Robert Hewison wrote that:

> What the Cool Britannia phenomenon does tell us is how symbolic goods – music, movies, food, fashion, art, design, architecture – all of which convey values over and above their value in exchange, have become vital to the moral as well as the material economy. But in the end, symbolic goods have to symbolise something and that is why the buzzword Britain has become so significant. When our evangelical Prime Minister Tony Blair uses the words Britain or British 53 times in his speech to the Labour Party conference he is not reinforcing our sense of identity, he is betraying a profound anxiety about it ... it is up to the creators of symbolic goods – the designers, artists and architect readers of Blueprint – to scribble all over [the marque], to break in from the margins of an ersatz, marketised identity and reveal just what our collective sense of ourselves could be. (1997: 31)

In 2005, the Leeds City Council unveiled its own city brand and a celebrity-filled launch in the city's famous shopping quarter. Conceived by a local branding and communications group entitled An Agency Called England, it featured the slogan 'Leeds. Live It! Love It!'. In developing this identity, the agency undertook a survey of Leeds residents to discern if the city was a person, what kind of person would that be. The research that came back was that Leeds would be 'a young male, friendly, your best friend, a really nice person to know, an ambitious person, living in a trendy apartment, driving a Volkswagen Golf GTi' (Scott 2005). This would be used to articulate the new Leeds brand. Having, as we have seen, run through a variety of options in terms of the use of design hardware to express the city's identity, its marketing machinery was clearly nailing its colours to the mast. In view of Hewison's, Appadurai's or Nederveen Pieterse's respective comments, whether these colours would stick requires further debate.

CONCLUSION

The emergence of disorganized capitalism has denuded many localities of their power to identify themselves through their traditional industrial bases. Instead, cities and regions compete with each other as nodes of information, capital and labour on the basis of the skills and infrastructure they have to offer, as well as their aesthetic profile. The architecture of a location may have a role in this, but is of decreasing significance in relation to the broader evidence of its cultural capital, which is to be found in an array of activities drawing on the creative industries. Within this, design therefore provides visual and material cues, but as a practice it also represents a certain 'attitude' pertaining to the human and creative resources of that location. Design and the image that design conveys may at times enmesh itself with other manifestations of the metropolitan habitus. This may mean that it is aligned with other qualities of the urban night-time economies of bars, restaurants, clubs or galleries. These are given further resonance by the transformative practice of gentrification, where the traditional and conservative industrial or working-class cityscape is appropriated, moulded and remodelled into the modern and liberal post-industrial or middle-class urbanity. The rhetorics of regeneration are considered to be enough to legitimate these practices. Equally, however, the enthusiasm to arrange all the material, spatial, textual and visual design elements, which go together to communicate the brand identity of a location, requires such consistency as to make its claim to any unique qualities, by comparison with its competitors, an ever more difficult task. As the message becomes more and more simplified, so it becomes increasingly open to contestation.

CHAPTER 8
BRANDED LEISURE

Leisure has become big business as the use of free time has moved toward more planned and pre-packaged activities in the postindustrial age. The whole conception and organization of time may have even changed. Chapter 8 is devoted to unpicking some key questions with regards design for leisure. The fact that these range across theme parks, short-break destinations, retail outlets and experience centres demonstrates both their commonalities and differences. Branded leisure demands even greater interdisciplinarity in terms of the various design specializations under discussion. It is necessary to review the leisure centres' 'software' in terms of their promise – mediated through promotion – and the way they interface with other cultural phenomena. Televisual thinking works in mediating, producing and consuming branded leisure. With regard to their actual hardware, many leisure spaces provide a veritable *gesamtkuntswerke* (total art) of experiences, an entirely baroque splendour of sensations, incorporating practically all design categories into one. We must journey through these spaces to be both open to and aware of their illusory power.

> [Leisure] spaces appear on first inspection to have escaped the control of the established order, and thus, inasmuch as they are spaces of play, to constitute a vast 'counter space'. This is a complete illusion. The case against leisure is quite simply closed – and the verdict is irreversible: leisure is as alienated and alienating as labour; as much an agent of co-optation as it is itself co-opted; and both an assimilative and an assimilated part of the 'system' (mode of production). Once a conquest of the working class, in the shape of paid days off, holidays, weekends, and so on, leisure has been transformed into an industry, into a victory of neocapitalism and an extension of bourgeois hegemony to the whole of space. (Lefebvre 1994 [1974]: 383)

So wrote the Marxist intellectual activist Henri Lefebvre in his seminal enquiry entitled *The Production of Space*. Originally published in 1974, this text explores the relationship between mental space as conceived and represented, for instance, by architects and planners and the spaces of everyday experience. Thus Lefebvre strove to reconcile the forces that shape the social meanings of places with the human and social activities acted out within them.

Lefebvre raises a number of interesting points in the above extract. First, he suggests that leisure spaces only *appear* to offer opportunities for play, freedom and pleasure as a flip-side to the restraints of ordinary working life. Second, they are conceived and shaped to give that appearance whereas in reality they are highly controlled – as controlled as all other spaces. Third, just as work is organized and industrialized, so is leisure. He goes on to list more specific ways by which the control and management of leisure space constrains: it has its own 'rituals and gestures' (such as sun-tanning); its own 'discursive forms' (what should be said or not said); and its own modulations and models (such as chalets and hotels which reproduce family order and private life) (1994 [1974]: 484). By extension, we might consider the possibility that design conspires to provide and maintain this illusion of emancipatory leisure, and in delivering 'value for money' against time spent, colludes in its commodification.

In the early 1970s, Lefebvre was writing at the tail-end of a decade of rampant development of mass tourism, in particular of the cheap package holiday to the Spanish costas. The idea that spaces could be produced specifically for leisure consumption on a vast scale would have been particularly evident in this context. Contemporaneous with *The Production of Space* was *The Golden Hordes* (Turner and Ash 1975), a vitriolic exposé of the environmental and social impact of mass tourism. In Lefebvre's terms, these attractions transform a locality into a space of consumption. But they are also consumed in a variety of ways: they are looked at and thus consumed visually; they are literally consumed, in that their resources are used up; and they can consume one's identity (Urry 1995: 1–2). The spaces of consumption therefore imply the consumption of space.

One can only speculate on what Lefebvre would have made of the range of spaces which have since been designed and produced for leisure. Certainly, through much of the world the amount of time devoted to work has decreased. The total number of hours worked per year in OECD countries dropped by nearly 5 per cent between 1997 and 2010 (OECD 2012). In China, the number of official days off work per year increased from 62 to 147 between 1978 and 2008 (Wei, Qu and Ma 2010).

In the UK, annual expenditure on leisure activities rose by 50 per cent between 1992 and 1997. By the end of the 1990s, British consumers as a whole spent more on leisure and tourism than on food, rent and rates put together (Rees 1998). Even through the economic recession from 2008, expenditure on leisure continued to grow (X-Leisure 2010). Leisure activities these days are more capital- and design-intensive than ever. However, despite an overall gradual drop in working hours since 1950 in the UK, Rojek (1985: 15) has argued that the amount of leisure time available has not increased dramatically. In short, many leisure activities entail short bursts of energy, spending and visual consumption. They require fleeting absorption in branded spaces and experiences as momentary and instantaneous as the flickering images on a television set.

FROM FORDIST TO DISORGANIZED LEISURE

Organized mass leisure was instigated by the industrial revolution. In the UK, the growth of railways provided easy access to tourist destinations of the seaside and spa towns. Subsequently, entire industrial towns would close their factories for specific fortnights – known as 'the wakes' – as its workers and their families headed en masse for Blackpool, Bridlington or Bognor. The 1844 Railway Act obliged companies to make provision for the 'labouring classes', and within four years over 100,000 people travelled from Manchester to the nearby resort of Blackpool during Whit week. By 1850 this figure had doubled (Urry 1990: 21). Seaside entertainment (music hall, amusement parks, piers) developed to cater for the concentrated demand for pleasure which these visitors brought with them. Just as work was rationalized and regulated by industrialization, so, then, was leisure.

Using their specific attractions, holiday resorts would compete with each other for market share – the length of their piers, the quality of the air – and through 'boosterism'. Advertising campaigns, often carried out by borough councils in conjunction with the rail companies, were mobilized to show off their special qualities. In this way, leisure spaces began to be conceived as brands. Thus, for instance, we find Bridlington marketed as 'Bright, Breezy, Bracing' from the 1910s.

Throughout the 20th century, the concept of holiday centres as a more tightly orchestrated commercialization under a single brand of what seaside towns had been doing in the previous century emerged. In the UK, the Butlins holiday camps, established in 1936, provided relatively luxurious facilities with on-site amusements and organized entertainments. They reached their heyday in the 1950s but had gone into sharp decline by the 1980s. During this period Butlins, and their rival Pontins, shifted their identities from 'camps' to 'centres', 'villages' or 'holiday worlds'. By the 1980s they had moved towards the provision of a more segmented market, offering different specialisms at the various centres. This indicated a move away from the mostly homogeneous, rationalistic holiday locations for an equally homogeneous market towards the creation of more varied and subtly developed leisure brands.

Whereas rationalized leisure, inherited from 19th-century industrialization, took place at specific times of the year and entailed fixed destinations and activities for tourism, the development of the Spanish costas in the 1960s ensured that holidaymaking was a more sporadic affair. By 1980, around 5 million off-the-peg package holidays were sold each year; by 1990 this figure had risen to 11 million (Urry 1990: 48). Tourism, and leisure more generally, has subsequently become a more fragmented but also more tightly managed commodity.

Rojek (1985: 18–23) identifies four key features of contemporary leisure. First, it is a privatized affair which has become increasingly focused on the home rather than the public sphere. No doubt this has been encouraged by the development of radio and television, and then teletext, video, internet and computer games. It is the job of leisure entrepreneurs to get people out of their homes, but also to give leisure spaces the same security, exclusivity and 'buzz' available at home. Second, leisure is more individuated: it is more subject to personalization. Leisure spaces must deliver a menu of choice without destabilizing the core values of the brand. Third, Rojek believes that leisure has become much more commercialized, becoming a major industry in itself. Fourth, leisure is more pacified: it entails more complex and encultured expression through activities that require learning, practice and mastery. Whether it's appreciating high cuisine or trying out a new sport, leisure activities are, in fact, more restrained and regulated than ever.

TIME-SQUEEZE AND PACKAGED LEISURE

As work patterns in the late-20th century have become more fragmented and varied, so has leisure. Paradoxically, while there has been an overall decline in the length of the working week, for those in employment the total amount of leisure time (that is, time spent in unproductive activities) has diminished. Leisure entrepreneurs increasingly take seriously the notion of 'time squeeze': in a Henley Centre survey published in 1998, 59 per cent of respondents agreed that 'I have never had enough time to get things done'. This is particularly so among working women. They report only 13.5 hours per week free as against the 60 hours average (Rees 1998). Equally, in the USA nearly a quarter of Americans surveyed in 2006 said that they felt rushed all the time, with 41 per cent of working mothers reporting this (Taylor, Funk and Craighill 2006),

The sense of 'time squeeze' clearly relates to the speeded-up world that is envisaged in the contexts of the New Economy, discussed in Chapter 2. Whether this has resulted in an overall reduction of leisure time is a debatable point. Southerton (2003) argues persuasively that the issue is not about the *amount* of leisure time available to adults so much as the way time itself is perceived and managed. He reveals that, in particular, middle-class adults increasingly allocate and organize their leisure time into blocks of activities of differing intensities. Typically, he argues, goal-orientated activities such as chores or work are costed into measured timeframes to 'free-up' timeframes that might be more expansive and, perhaps, more relaxed in their use.

By extension, we might regard the rise of personal organization technologies – from Filofaxes to personal digital assitants – as evidence of products that support and promote this effect. But it also extends to the design of leisure complexes and their contents. This may also have given rise to the development of one-stop leisure complexes, or so-called E-zones (E as in Entertainment), which incorporate a variety of leisure activities into one branded site. This allows consumers the most efficient use of their precious leisure time as they move from cinema to pizza restaurant to bowling alley or from swimming pool to tennis court to health spa. In such circumstances, some design consultancy work is dedicated to achieving the right constellation of retail and leisure brands within a single branded space. These would provide sufficient variety of resources while maintaining the overall character of the leisure complex. Here the designer is not just originating new shapes, colours and names, but is also working rather like an image consultant by advising on appropriate off-the-peg brands to combine into the leisure offer (within the design industry this is frequently referred to as 'brand marrying').

In a later discussion, Rojek asks whether all leisure provides is endless but temporary distraction. He argues that dedicated leisure activity is quite rare (1993: 216). Compulsive hill-walkers or serious amateur musicians stand out as exceptions to a general conception of leisure involving momentary engagements with cultural goods and environments. Thus the latest film, music recording or sporting fixture is as easily picked up on as relinquished, just as an evening out may take in a range of sites or a night in front of the television may involve continual switching between channels. As such there are no rules that legitimate one form of entertainment over another. A leisure facility might offer a menu of distinctive experiences to choose from, but movement between them is seamless and de-differentiated.

As locations and the entertainment they offer compete to provide something more distinctive, more semantically loaded, so their originality and 'authenticity' become progressively more packaged. An extreme case of this would be in the production of a 'hyperreality' in which the imitation of an original is so good that it exceeds it to the point that the original no longer matters. This is what the cultural critic Umberto Eco termed 'the absolute fake' (1986: 40) amidst his discussion of Disneyland.

THE DISNEY PARADIGM

For designers and cultural critics alike, Disneyland represents a paradigmatic extreme of the theming and branding of leisure spaces. As a European visitor to the American Disneyland, Umberto Eco discusses it in terms of its ability to deliver a faked reality which corresponds more lucidly with our daydream demands. Eco focuses mostly on the details of Disneyland: how, for instance, a themed Polynesian restaurant includes a fairly authentic menu and apparently authentic Tahitian waitresses so convincing that one would expect nothing but Polynesia to be outside it. It isn't that the real equivalent doesn't exist; instead we admire the perfection of the fake. Thus our desire for illusion is stimulated further (Eco 1986: 40).

Meanwhile, American sociologist Sharon Zukin takes a broader overview of Disneyland and Disney World. She illustrates how 'its size and functional interdependence make [it] a viable representation of a real city, built for people from the middle classes that have escaped from cities to the suburbs and exurbs' (Zukin 1995: 53). It offers a gated, secure environment where the unwanted underclass cannot gain admittance. It is an idealization of urban space: autonomously governed and controlled by corporate management.

The notion of Disney's simulation of an ideal stems from Walt Disney's enthusiasm to materialize his utopian dream for America. Equally, the Project on Disney (1995) skilfully illuminates how its public relations machinery, its layout and detailing, and the training of its staff are tightly assembled in order to maintain an unbroken surface so that the visitor may never get behind the scenes, so to speak, and experience anything of it as a producing system. *How* its spectacle is created is a consistently shrouded feature – the magic must not be broken.

Furthermore, Disneyland is packaged for visual consumption. Its early critics argued that it proposed too few rides and too much open space. But this was missing Walt Disney's point. In developing the first Disneyland in Orange County, Southern California, which opened in 1955, Walt Disney rejected the schemes of two architects. Instead, alongside one of his own animators, Herb Ryman, he set about planning it himself (Marling 1997). As a result, Disneyland was more acutely inscribed with the narratives and visuality of the Disney of cartoon fame. It promised the security of the idealized vernacular, as seen in Snow White or Mickey Mouse. Euro Disney, opened in France in 1992, takes this a step further. Zukin suggests that 'it was designed as though never seen by the human eye, only by a camera – either a director's movie camera or a tourist's VCR' (1995: 57). It reproduces all those elements of America that European tourists want to see: New York City, the West and even Disneyland itself. In this way, the artifice and object collapse into each other. Disney simulates places and events for the tourist gaze, including itself.

POST-TOURISTS

Leisure spaces may be consumed in a variety of ways. Weekend breaks or foreign travel may be undertaken with different expectations of their outcomes for the individual. A distinction may be made, for instance, between the traveller and the tourist (Urry 1990; Rojek 1993). Clearly, the Disney paradigm has nothing to do with the traditional identity of the traveller. Travel experience – from backpacking in the Andes to a month's usage of a student rail ticket to criss-cross Europe – involves a measure of self-realization. Hardship may be encountered but the traveller experiences this as a rite of passage, as a maturing process. The journey-ing involves a series of physical, mental and visual challenges, but the work put into this is rewarded through some form of personal education and growth. By contrast, tourism dispenses with such exertions. The right to leisure has already been gained; pleasure is readily sought. It involves a search for the authentic in unfamiliar territory, either at home or abroad, and the consumption of these sights. This gives rise to the tourist's obsession with photographing things seen in order to capture and authenticate that moment for themselves (Sontag 1978).

Maxine Feifer (1985) suggests, however, that we are now in the age of the 'post-tourist'. Here the quest for 'authenticity' is abandoned. Instead of expecting to see 'real' locals performing folk-loric dance as if it were part of their everyday life, the post-tourist knows that such events may be put on precisely for the holiday season. The post-tourist is not disappointed by this: after all, it is the quality of the show that counts. And if it is a show, it need not even be seen in situ. The post-tourist might enjoy such experiences through other channels: through the television or in a theme park. It is the quality of the experience that counts, not how authentic it might be. The post-tourist is also able to appreciate the irony of this and treat it playfully. If leisure entails divesting oneself of the seriousness and posturing of working life, then the post-tourist is unlikely to make these demands. Furthermore, the post-tourist is accepting of, or even delighted by, the overlap-ping of various levels of experience. Souvenir shops, for example, sell kitschy model replicas of an historical site just visited that are appreciated as an integral part of the post-tourist visit as a whole. Various levels of consumption in leisure are therefore de-differentiated: high and popular culture overlap or even trade places.

If indeed post-tourists are that knowing, if they are prepared to relinquish the pursuit of authen-ticity in favour of the richness of the experience, then this will make them increasingly demand-ing consumers. In design terms, this pursuit of pleasure has to be catered for in ever more complex and blatant ways. Retail and entertainment design specialist Mark Artus (1999) argues that even the Disney paradigm is unable to satisfy this demand. For Artus, Disneyland offers attractions that make reference to something that has already made its mark: a vignette of a movie or the contin-ual loop of a theme tune which may remind the visitor of a favourite film. Visitors, he contends, are looking for a direct sensory experience where they are physically and mentally stimulated and involved in the entertainment brand. Rather optimistically (and revealing the designer's belief that leisure and brand experience can be one and the same thing), he adds that it is

> at the point of discovery that everything should change for the consumer; the soul and personality of the [leisure] brand should kick in, stroking the senses, encouraging serendipity and promoting anticipation about what might happen, never allowing the narrative to finish but letting it grow through individual interpretation. (Artus 1999)

Designing for post-tourism must therefore involve a strong measure of self-conscious artifice. Situations, events or places may be simulated. At the same time, however, this trickery is deliberately incomplete. There is little point in pretending that the real thing is being delivered. Rather, the designer hopes that the visitor is sufficiently involved in the experience to appreciate its convenience and perfection in its own terms, rather than as the 'absolute fake' as described by Umberto Eco.

Furthermore, the visual and material arrangement of branded leisure spaces need not be as dense or cluttered as suggested within the Disney paradigm. They need not present a postmodernistic arrangement of surfaces for visual consumption in which visitors lose themselves and their own sense of identity. Some leisure spaces are designed with the promise of quite the opposite. They appeal to an appetite for retrieving a sense of personal identity and achieving, albeit momentarily perhaps, self-realization. As such they aim to combine all three notions of travel, tourism and post-tourism. Such is the case of Center Parcs.

NAKED AND NOWHERE AT CENTER PARCS

Center Parcs is the European market leader in the provision of short-break holidays, operating in the Netherlands, Belgium, Britain, France and Germany. It therefore provides a significant case study to explore some themes of how contemporary leisure is formatted and designed. It has been in existence for 30 years, its first venture being a small complex of 40 holiday villas and limited sporting facilities in the Netherlands established by sports entrepreneur Piet Derksen in 1968. It is now an international group of 20 holiday villages. Their average size is around 100 hectares, the sites being combinations of woodland and water, always located inland. There is an average of 650 villas in each village; Center Parcs is targeted primarily at the family market and the design and layout of these villas reflect this use. The focus of each village is a sub-tropical swimming paradise, but they also offer a range of indoor and outdoor sporting and leisure facilities and a selection of themed restaurants. The Center Parcs concept is commercially very successful: it boasts over 90 per cent occupancy levels throughout the year. In 1997 the company had over 3.7 million guests staying in its mainland Europe villages (TDR Capital 2012) and 1.6 million in the UK (Center Parcs 2012). The basic concept of the centres has remained unchanged throughout its history: as the Center Parcs 1990 Annual Report mission statement put it, the company's aim is 'the provision of year-round residential leisure'. What kind of leisure experience is constituted within the brand and, subsequently, through design briefs?

The design of Center Parcs forest resorts follows the philosophy of the first development at De Lommerbergen. From this, a generic concept and design guidelines have provided an overall model for all Center Parcs developments. Factors such as size, density and layout relationships are specified. Through this uniformity, principles and standards can be set that allow a consistent basis against which other variables may be measured. Differences in take-up between different Center Parcs resorts may be assessed in terms of regional or national variations in consumer habits, demography, disposable cash and other socio-economic factors. As such, the uniformity of the design helps to provide market feedback.

As Herrmann et al. (2000) argue, the approach taken in the design guidelines for the overall layout of each site is similar in idea to Alexander et al.'s *A Pattern Language*, first published in 1977. Alexander developed a design methodology which argued for a correspondence between the patterns of events and the patterns of space. His interest, then, was in the psychological and sensory experience of spaces, and using this as a starting point. Interestingly, Alexander et al.'s book was published three years after Lefebvre's *The Production of Space*, and they reflect common concerns. Alexander opposed a design method based solely on the imposition of geometric criteria and his philosophy provides practical measures for achieving Lefebvre's concern in reconciling mental and physical space. The 253 patterns he proposed range from the towns through to buildings and construction details. These were not to be read as rigid structures for designers to follow but proposed an 'inside out' way of designing whereby the user or consumer's experience of space provided the key criterion. Different spaces, and thus different experiences, could then be assembled into an orchestrated whole. Individual elements of their design conspire to establish an overall effect. Over 20 years later, this foregrounding of the experience of spaces is highly relevant to the Center Parcs model, and indeed is relevant to designing for and analysing branded leisure spaces in general.

Two key components emerge in a consideration of the Center Parcs leisure offer and are reflected at all levels of design intervention. The first is that their overall layout and many details create a spatial and temporal dislocation. Visitors thus find themselves 'nowhere' in relation to their everyday conceptions of place and time. They are also nowhere in terms of the idea of being in a Utopia (being the Greek word for 'nowhere'). This links to a second key feature:

Various views of Center Parcs' leisure centres, including a sub-tropical swimming paradise, villa exterior and boating lake
Photos: Chris Royffe

that of being 'naked', though not in a literal sense. The Center Parcs venues present a highly encultured version of nature which draws on a strong environmentalist theme both in their image and working practices. The woodland resorts are 'naked' in that they are apparently stripped of the normal detritus and complexity of everyday life. Design details continually refer back to this identity. As we saw in the Disney paradigm, theme parks may constantly make references outside themselves. At Center Parcs the thematic clothing of elsewhere is abandoned. Finally, the emphasis on physical activities means that these features become *embodied*. The dislocation from the outside world and the essences of nature – fresh air, greenery, a different pace – are physically consumed.

As part of its marketing, Center Parcs produced a promotional video to accompany its brochures. With the inclusion of a voiceover, background sounds and the camera's ability to rove through the site, this medium is able to take prospective visitors through a 'typical' day there. Thus some of the emotional appeal of the place can be filled in while also setting up a narrative for consumer expectations. The July 1998 version of this video begins with the scene of a stressed professional couple in a car, presumably on their way to Center Parcs, mobile phone blaring. Cut to early morning at Center Parcs itself; the couple with young children ride their bicycles gracefully through the woodland. 'It's an island with no sea, a state with no passports, it's Britain, yet it's abroad ...', the voiceover tells us.

Even if you haven't watched the video before making your booking, the experience of arriving, participating in and departing from Center Parcs ensures one's dislocation from the normal cultural referents of place. Two arrival and departure days ensure that there is regular turnover of temporary communities. Arrival becomes ritualized as clients move through the reception area, redolent of a border crossing with barrier and passport control booth. Vehicles are only brought on to the site to unload children and baggage before being left in off-site car parks, and without one's car the dislocation begins in earnest. Paths are deliberately laid out to avoid straight lines so that getting from A to B takes much longer than one anticipates. Low-key barriers and the planting of shrubbery dissuade one from taking short-cuts. As if to reinforce the messages of

being in nature and to therefore slow down, signage implores new arrivals to 'Beware of rabbits crossing the road'. The Center Parcs' leisure activities, such as five-a-side football, archery or the steam room, are subjected to a regime of time organization (Aitch 2003: 292) that differs little from Southerton's (2003) portrayal of ordinary 21st-century life. But meanwhile a Center Parcs' strategy contrasts the outside, 'hectic' world with the natural, 'carefree' state – albeit a highly artificial one.

Vistas are restricted so that one rarely gets glimpses of the outside world. Long views are mostly across water, being either across the main boating lake or small canals and ponds. Over 90 per cent of the villas are placed to overlook water; this enhances the calming effect of the landscape design and establishes a key motif for the villages. It also adds to the labyrinthine effect on circulation by providing further 'natural' barriers. The villas themselves are arranged in clusters but they do not overlook one another. Rather than effect temporary sub-communities by getting to know their neighbours, then, occupants are encouraged to form a relationship with the Center Parcs' village community as a whole, it seems. The villas themselves follow a format designed by Dutch modernist architect Jacob Bakema for the first village in De Lommerbergen in 1968. They have remained largely unchanged with their vaguely Nordic interiors which so steadfastly resist fashion that they are fashionable in themselves.

Regardless of whether you are in the Netherlands, Belgium, Germany, France or Britain, then, one's visual and material experience of Center Parcs will remain largely the same. As John Urry tells us, localities are constructed for the aesthetic gaze, which requires a level of decoding on the visitor's part:

> This … strategy requires an ability to locate one's own society and its culture and make aesthetic judgements between different natures, places and societies. Thus it also requires a certain semiotic skill … and to know when they are partly ironic. (1995: 167)

Simultaneously, growing aesthetic cosmopolitanism makes this gaze ever more demanding. In the Center Parcs' case, rather than pump up the sign-value to emphasize a specific cultural location,

Opening sequence to Center Parcs' promotional video
Photos: Center Parcs

place is stripped of referents. There is nothing intentionally ironic at Center Parcs, although the artifice of the place or placelessness is clearly visible.

In his intelligent discussion of the use of white space in graphic design, Keith Robertson states that:

> The presence of white space is a symbol of smart, of class, of simplicity, of the essence of refinement. The absence of white space is a symbol of vulgarity, of crassness, of schlock, of bad taste. … So the bourgeois aesthetic sought to hide the presentation of wealth behind a diversion of interest into areas supposedly *outside* the economic and necessary … [its] expression in material things is one of disinterest and detachment. Such an aesthetic focuses therefore more on the *form* of doing things rather than the material things themselves. (1994: 61–2, Robertson's emphasis)

One might easily translate this concept to Center Parcs, except that here we are dealing with green rather than white space. By denuding the visitors of their cars and own homes, by putting them in Nordic-style villas, by making them walk or cycle everywhere, and slowly at that, by offering a cultivated patch of nature, Center Parcs provide a gated, 'nowheresvillage' as a momentary creation of 'fortress Europe' (Nederveen Pieterse 1991) that only exists within the temporal and spatial boundaries of the weekend and the perimeter fence.

If the environmentalist agenda comes over in the form of Center Parcs, then this is matched by its content. In 1991, Bioscan (UK) Ltd and Landscape Design Associates began a series of rigorous environmental audits for Center Parcs which reviewed the village design and layout, including their flora and fauna, waste management and recycling, and energy consumption (including employment patterns and goods sourcing) as well as environmentalism within its corporate planning system. This would consolidate and extend the 'greening' of Center Parcs and its stated benefits would include cost savings, increased profitability, competitive advantage, compliance

Interiors of Center Parcs' shops at Elveden, Suffolk: 'Natural Elements' and 'The Tree House', designed by Fitch, 1998
Photos: Fitch

with environmental legislation (particularly in France, Belgium and Germany and in the future in the USA) and an enhanced corporate image (Landscape Design Associates/Bioscan (UK) Ltd 1992). And if the ecological theme is still missed, design consultancy CGI Ingleton Thomas wove it into the design of the corporate identity 'leafbird' logo for Center Parcs in 1996.

These initiatives have subsequently found their way from the brand identity of Center Parcs in the 1990s to their design and management. In the UK, just 5 per cent of existing trees are removed to allow for the construction of the villas and main buildings. The landscaping places the emphasis on screening of buildings so that they appear to be *in* nature. The restriction of changeover days to Mondays and Fridays restricts the impact of traffic movements on the locality. In 1994 the Longleat Forest Center Parcs' village was opened in Wiltshire. It was developed in Aucombe Wood, a site designated as an 'Area of Outstanding Natural Beauty' which, but for its by now well-publicized environmental strategies, would otherwise have been banned.

The low consumption level of the villages in general is a notion which is also transferred to its temporary residents. The village centre does include a sports shop (the continentally named 'Sportique'), a gift and toys shop and a confectionery outlet. But the general emphasis is away from Bacchanalian orgies of shopping, and excessive drinking is dissuaded in the guest rule book. Indeed, the redesign of the shops, by entertainment and retail design specialists Fitch in the late 1990s, reinforces the Center Parcs' brand message rather than referring them to the outside world of shopping malls (Wren 1999). Of the three existing stores at Center Parcs, Fitch created new names for two of them: 'Natural Elements' and 'The Tree House'. Both of these in name and in their interior design elements return the theme to the overall Center Parcs' concept of woodland holidays. Within 'Natural Elements' three categories were created: 'Family time', 'My time' and 'Memories'. These pick up on sub-themes of the Center Parcs' 'mood'.

While stress is laid on sporting and leisure activities at Center Parcs, the need to exceed personal targets or to compete is played down: the promotional video includes missed archery shots and sailing boats running out of wind. By stripping away the mass cultural detritus of everyday life and eschewing an environment for competition, leisure is returned to the body. Michel Foucault (1977) has provided an extended and reasoned discussion of the relationship of the body to power. To summarize briefly one of his key arguments, Foucault discussed the way that social and economic relations were *embodied*. He contended that a corollary to industrialization was that the body was subservient to it: it was machine-like, routinized and disciplined through the repetition of physical tasks. The working body is made subject to labour. It might therefore follow in leisure that it is shown to be active and liberated. Rojek argues that in leisure it does not necessarily follow that the reverse is true, however. Instead, leisure relations are also those of 'discipline, training, coding, and control' (Rojek 1985: 156). After all, as we saw with the quotation from Lefebvre at the beginning of this chapter, leisure is as regulating as work. Leisure is pacified as is work.

Conversely, one might approach the body as an instrument of consumption. Generally speaking, in Victorian times the sea was regarded as producing health and sexual attractiveness, hence the enthusiasm for bathing. Progressively throughout the 20th century, however, the sun has usurped the sea on this issue. For many white Western Europeans, a tanned body symbolizes health and the economic power to spend time under the sun. This attitude has been extended into a verve for fitness. The period 1992–97 saw growth in the expenditure on health and fitness clubs in the UK by some 60 per cent (Nutley 1998). Fitness club membership continued to grow a decade later (X-Leisure 2010). Whether sun-tanned, muscular or both, this represents a significant aestheticization of the body. The body is shaped as an object for viewing.

So where does the Center Parcs' offer fit into this? One of the Center Parcs' slogans is 'Where you take your body to free your mind'. The corporeal restitution promised by its environment and activities may work to retrieve individual and familial values as much as repair mind and body for more labour. Center Parcs provides a refuelling stop for, in Foucault's terms, the placid body. But with its fitness rooms, sunbeds and sportswear store, it also conspires with the consumeristic notion of the 'body beautiful'.

The combination of a utopian creation and environmentalism as a backdrop for the aestheticized body has a 20th-century historical pedigree. The idea of 'going into the woods' as weekend leisure is historically well established in Northern and Central Europe. More specifically, links have been made between both left- and right-wing political movements, personal purity, nature and, indeed, naturism in the 1920s and early 1930s (van der Will 1990). While one is encouraged, mostly, to keep one's clothes on at Center Parcs, the emphasis on sporting leisure, bodily reconstitution and nature has evolved from this general tradition of weekend nature. The important distinction, however, is that although their forerunners may have gone to commune in the wilderness, visitors to Center Parcs join an ecology which is part given, part created and maintained. Woodland space is inhabited, but it is also carefully planned and managed. As such, it becomes cultivated by technology. And while the Disney strategy conspired to cover up any productive system in its illusion creating, Center Parcs makes frequent reference to itself as both a site of production and consumption. Its promotional video includes several views and scripted moments of employees at work ('for your benefit'). Visitor handbooks include copious information relating to the maintenance of its forestry and animal life.

This strategy creates an interesting link between the notions of 'traveller' and 'post-tourist'. While Center Parcs only very lightly incurs hardship and discomfort in forcing one to leave one's car behind, nevertheless the travel themes of self-realization and personal growth through the experience appear. At the level of the post-tourist and given the enormous commercial success of Center Parcs, its consumers accept that a certain level of artifice is at play and they are willing to go along with it.

As Marshall Berman put it, 'to be modern is to find ourselves in an environment that promises adventure, power, joy, growth, transformation, disintegration and renewal' (1983: 15), words which could easily come from a Center Parcs' brochure. Perhaps Center Parcs isn't the kind of modernity Berman was thinking of, but its techno-ecology suggests that modernity, these days, is in fact about going, albeit very slowly, naked and nowhere.

TELEVISUALITY AND DESIGNING LEISURE EXPERIENCES

If Disneyland and Center Parcs have one prominent feature in common, then it is that their public must leave their cars behind before making their visit. In his discussion of Disneyland, Umberto Eco remarks that by doing this, visitors give up their ultimate symbol of their individual identity. They therefore give themselves over to the power of the leisure space they enter. Following on from this, he points out how 'its visitors must behave like its robots. Access to each attraction is regulated by a maze of metal railings which discourages any individual initiative' (Eco 1986: 48). The speed of consumption at Disneyland is regulated. Once the visitor has paid that waiting price, they then go into an attraction which compresses a series of temporal or spatial phenomena together: the entire history of the US presidents in 15 minutes, a dizzying roller-coaster ride through 'Frontierland'. Conversely, Center Parcs stretches, rather than compresses, time and space by its twisting paths and frequent water features.

This time and space compression or stretching has resonances in television and cinema (see Harvey 1989a: Part III). These media use powerful ways to escape chronology. Through the techniques of slow motion, freeze frames, fast forwarding and rewinding, the passage of time can be compressed, expanded, reversed or frozen. They can also put us, the viewers, in several points in space at the same time by quick cutting or screen dividing. Television sports reporting can put us in several points in the stadium at the same time, giving us several viewing points. It can also give us a range of narrative structures to follow – we follow the game, an individual player or the spectators, but also the commentators' interactions with the match and each other. We also get flashbacks to pre-game interviews or review highlights afterwards. We are watching a narration of both the factual and fictional components of the event. There is the time of the thing told and the time of the thing telling (Metz 1974).

Developments in exhibition and museum design from the mid-1980s have shown a stridently televisual approach to the arrangement of interior spaces. During the 1990s, the number and scale of these attractions rose dramatically as lottery funding was allocated to the creation of new centres or the further development of existing facilities. Millennium Commission projects stepped up this pace further. Notably, many of its key figures have come from a background in television production. John Sunderland, chief designer of the Jorvik Viking Centre, the White Cliffs Experience and the Oxford Story, previously worked in television, as did Cel Phelan, founder of Event Communications, a multidisciplinary consultancy devoted exclusively to museum, exhibition and experience centres. As such they emphasize the need to script the experience of such attractions. One key difference from television scripting is that a broadcast requires a linear narration of events (though, as we have seen, not necessarily chronological); scripting a museum, exhibition or experience centre is multi-vocal (Janson-Smith 1999). Visitors are of different age groups and engage with the exhibit at a range of levels and so the storytelling for these spaces must work on several different levels at the same time. In this context, it is often necessary that the interior is visually dense, multi-layered and sign-heavy, providing visitors with a choice of routes through which to pick their way. As we will see in the context of many examples of interactive media design in Chapter 9, exhibition design provides both immersion and detachment. On the one hand, visitors are engaged at an immediate level in the sensory experience of the presentation (the time of the thing told), but are also involved in following the narration of the experience (the time of the thing telling).

Designers of some retail and entertainment spaces therefore take on a televisually informed approach to their planning. During the 1980s, architect Nigel Coates pioneered this attitude in his design work for the interior spaces of bars and shops. Coates recognized that the function of a building had less to do with its architectonic structure and was more dependent on virtually invisible elements such as electrical cabling and radio waves. By extension, the hardware of a building merely functions as a framework for exchanges of energy and information. His primary interest, then, was in the software of architecture – how it invokes experiences and provides narratives (hence his group was called NATO, meaning Narrative Architecture Today). Part of Coates's philosophy is extended from a notion that television and other mass-media events have changed the way we live for good. Citing the influence of Jean Baudrillard, he contends that:

> Instead of progress, we tend to heroicize what is normally hidden, to play up the differences, to encourage a society in a simultaneously primitive and advanced state of flux, in which adopted narratives and roles are able to reactivate the otherwise empty social stage, which television as a phenomenon (but not as a language) appeared to have forced us to abandon. (Coates 1988: 98)

Architecture, he continues, must face up to and confront this change. His own interior design work went on to incorporate rich textures of images and objects. He claims that, in developing a project, 'drawing has to contain a filmic hypothesis … [to identify] … key pictures of the action even bigger than the building' (Coates 1988: 100).

DEDIFFERENTIATION/DISTINCTION

If the visual and temporal language of television provides structures and forms for the design of some leisure spaces, then these centres may become dislocated. In the same way that the images and sounds on a television screen may come from any global location and be viewed almost anywhere, so experience centres or shopping malls can provide environments which are hermetically sealed away from their immediate locality. A sense of place is replaced by a simulation of elsewhere.

This is acutely noticeable in themed restaurants and shopping malls. In America, the theming of such spaces has reached intensive levels and is well discussed (see, for instance, Hess 1993; Gottdiener 1997; Betsky 1999, 2000). These were pioneered by John Jerde at San Diego Horton Plaza and then the Rouse Corporation at Faneuil Hall, Baltimore at Harborplace, and New York at South Street Seaport (Betsky 2000). Jerde's Horton Plaza drew from the architectural forms of the Italian Renaissance in order to invent a sense of history and permanence for it, while the plan emphasized meandering lines to stimulate a sense of 'wandering through' rather than hierarchy and order. Amidst the cacophony of shops, food courts and cinemas, plazas and cul-de-sacs were incorporated to provide points for social gathering and repose.

As such, shopping is repackaged as a 'retail experience'. Browsing in shopping centres is invariably associated with Charles Baudelaire's *flâneur*. His late-19th-century dandy gravitated towards the street cafés of Paris to consume the visual spectacle of the city. Baudelaire was writing at the time of the growth of department stores, which offered not just a range of goods under

NikeTown in London, opened in 1999, designed by Building Design Partnership
Photo: David Balfour

one roof, but also opportunities to meet socially and be entertained by the spectacle of the site. A crucial difference, however, is that Baudelaire's *flâneur* rarely bought anything. Instead, in the late-20th century, retailers hope that this perusal will eventually end in a purchase. Thus the 'retail experience' is designed to provide a stimulation to acquire by linking to other mediative forms of the brand value. The patina of the goods, the adverts and the shop interiors all link together to produce 'similar coded lifestyle values' (Ellwood 1998). The leisure of 'just looking' in the themed shopping mall, of being 'elsewhere', and of then identifying with particular lifestyle forms as mediated within the individual retail units is consummated in the purchase of goods.

The distinction between leisure and retail has become blurred in many cases. Some retail developments have moved towards the provision of leisure activities (so-called 'retail-tainment') in order to spread their brand offer. The supermarket Tesco Extra at Pitsea in Essex offered a fast-food and takeaway area, mooing imitation cows and roller-skating customer services assistants (Rees 1998). Specific brands have also extended into the leisure sphere: the Volkswagen Autostadt in Wolfsberg, Legoland in Windsor or Cadbury World in Bournville, and NikeTown in New York and London all provide visitor attractions which subsequently reinforce product identities. Significantly, investment for the Nike 'brandlands' comes from global advertising budgets rather than capital revenue. NikeTown interweaves a sportswear store with a museum, telling the story of Nike products with visual and architectonic recreations of the Nike brand experience. The last of these is made by reference to the core themes of its marketing strategy. This sportswear company had made a concerted effort to equate their Air trainers with 'rags to riches' stories of members of American street youth cultures making it to sporting stardom (Flusty 1997). This narrative is subsequently laced into the design of the brandland through a cacophony of projected images, taped sounds, video walls and stage-set architecture to produce an ersatz and generalized simulation of Bronx street life, or its many other global equivalents. Thus advertising, company museum and department store merge into each other. The chief designer of Nike's in-house team who developed the NikeTowns has said that he wants 'the experience of the shopper from the moment they see the Nike commercial on TV to the point where they are wearing the shoes when they come out of the store to be completely seamless' (Henry Beer, quoted in Betsky 2000).

This strategy of de-differentiation between retail and leisure conspires also to blur distinctions between the public and the private. Shopping malls themselves are, of course, both public *and* private spaces. Operated by private companies, they employ security guards to exclude unwanted elements – vagrants, buskers, street-hawkers and so on. They are invariably locked up at night. Equally, as museums since the 1980s have received progressively less state financial support, they have become increasingly dependent on sponsorship funding from private corporations.

This presents designers with a difficult challenge as a large part of their job is to *differentiate* the object – to make it distinctive or even unique. There is a limit to the amount of gimmickry which can be mustered to achieve this, however. Designers of more traditional leisure spaces, such as parks and museums, therefore have to separate themselves out from this highly branded and thematized ambience. At Trentham Gardens near Stoke-on-Trent, Fitch sought to strip away

Dynamic Earth experience centre, Edinburgh, opened in 1999: architecture by Michael Hopkins, exhibition design and development by Event Communications
Photos: Event Communications

any hint of theming, playing up the historical and environmental qualities of its brand image. As if to emphasize this 'innovation', they trademarked their approach to this project as 'anti-theming™' (Fitch 1999).

At the Dynamic Earth attraction in Edinburgh (introduced in Chapter 7), Event Communications played up its educational content by linking up with the national educational curriculum. With architect Michael Hopkins, its value as a public space and resource was also emphasized by opening up its vestibule and surrounding area to general public access. In this way its designers strove to distinguish the attraction from highly branded leisure centres where space is more rigorously privatized and the content is often more tightly tied in with corporate or brand promotion (Phelan 1999). By re-appropriating a notion of 'publicness' into the project, it seems that the quest to differentiate through design pushes the nature and practice of leisure into newer and perhaps unexpected territory.

CONCLUSION

The development of branded leisure spaces requires a painstaking coherence to all design features. This ensures a seamless progression between the brand image as purveyed through marketing strategies through to the actual consumption of their products and services. As such they are tightly scripted as a flow of experiences. This owes something to a televisual approach in their conception, but they also provide multilinear routes through them. They conspire to compress or expand the cognition of temporal and spatial dimensions within themselves. That said, the consumption of branded leisure spaces does not necessarily entail total immersion in them. Visitors may read them on a variety of levels: they may be highly engaged in the artifice of the occasion to the point of suspending disbelief, but equally they may knowingly 'play along', either critically or uncritically, with the illusion. Many of the themes of branded leisure emerge in the context of digital interactive media, considered in the next chapter.

JURASSIC
144–156 MYA

IGUANODON

120 MYA

Desktop Horse

CHAPTER 9

ON-SCREEN INTERACTIVITY

How does digital design change the way we read and interact on screens? What 'freedoms' does it promote? How does it challenge designers? Chapter 9 is concerned with the tensions that exists between expectations of design for digital media and its realities for users. It focuses on the minutiae of navigating interactive software - clicking on hyperlinks, moving through virtual spaces, waiting for downloads - in order to address the limitations and challenges that both its designers and consumers face. The rapidity with which the various platforms for on-screen design have developed has left designers struggling to ascertain a critical discourse and language for it, while at the same time their job has been to act as its technological and cultural intermediaries. This means that at times, the discourse is wildly enthusiastic about the immersive possibilities that are afforded in digital interfaces. At the same time, everyday experience tells us that they have to be rigorously structured and controlled in order to be readable and understandable.

I'm flying through the solar system and deciding which planet I want to have a closer look at. No, wait a minute, I'm re-mixing Peter Gabriel's latest opus on a weeny four channel desk and, hey, it's sounding better already. No, I'm swooping out of the stratosphere to look at the oil fields set alight by the Iraqi army as they retreated from the Gulf War back in 1991. Then I'm having a gun-battle with a would-be assassin inside a film I'm trying to watch. And I'm doing it through a television screen. Welcome to the world of interactive multimedia. (Horsham 1994: 25)

A flat, glowing screen and a disk spinning in the CD drive. And I'm waiting for a picture to download while I 'stand' in the virtual basement of a virtual dinosaur museum. It looks like how I remember natural science museums from my childhood: mysterious, echoey hallways, rough edges and didactic exhibit captions. The difference is that these dinosaurs are not silent, stuffed full-size reproductions, but animated, roaring beasts. Meanwhile, I have a map to find my way through the maze of exhibition rooms, but I'm not sure if I'd just prefer to get lost.

In the first of the above extracts, design critic Michael Horsham was reflecting all the optimism and enthusiasm for immersive digital environments in the early 1990s. They promised role-play and movement between distinctive, futuristic scenographies, but also the interruption of the traditionally one-sided flow of cultural production. The second is drawn from notes I wrote during my first encounter with the Dorling Kindersley *Dinosaur Hunter* CD-ROM at my local library in 1998. Here the restrictions of screen and software and the possibility that the experience is never fully immersive are acknowledged. Navigational aids are necessary. In addition, the design language employed may seem at odds with the medium – it exploits new technology to provide the virtual environment, but it is an environment more redolent of a 19th-century museum than a new interactive experience centre.

Both of these descriptions refer to relatively early iterations of interactive digital media when computing power was still comparatively restricted. Indeed, given the exponential development of digital technologies since then, these and many of the other examples I discuss in this chapter may seem outdated or quaint, even. Yet the analysis of such early examples also reveals some qualities whose change has been marginal since.

By 'on screen' in the title of this chapter, I refer to the smaller rectangle of the video display unit (VDU) as opposed to the larger cinema screen, and I am concerned with the interactive applications on screen, such as hypertext, CD-ROM, internet and convergent media. It is often difficult to separate out these different platforms, however, as technological and commercial development conspires to fuse more often than distinguish them. Two examples bear this out. In October 1999, Sega released its much anticipated Dreamcast, a computer game console (usually supported by ordinary televisions) that plugged into a telephone line and allowed users to challenge other players worldwide via the Internet. This was closely followed by Open, a new service offered by Sky, the satellite broadcasting company, that allowed digital television viewers armed with their television remote control to shop or check their bank accounts from home and send emails. These innovations anticipated fully convergent media where the boundaries between areas of digital cultural production disappear. Likewise and relatedly, commercial developments tend towards their integration rather than compartmentalization. January 2000 saw the merger of AOL (America On Line), the internet service provider, and Time Warner, the entertainments conglomerate. Again, this points towards the continued integration of broadcast media and interactive systems. Further convergences that were facilitated by mobile technologies such as smartphones are discussed in more depth in Chapter 11.

From the early development of human computer interfaces for personal computers to convergent media, designers have played a crucial role in shaping their content. The demands of the medium have provoked, to some degree, a reconfiguration of their role, requiring them to work in collaborative networks with a wide range of professionals and to regard the relationship with their end-user differently.

COMPUTERS AND GRAPHIC DESIGN

Within graphic design, the growth of desktop publishing since the mid-1980s facilitated a reconfiguration of the relationship between designer and client. Before the advent of the Apple Macintosh, artwork and copy for a piece of design for print would be specified and marked up by a graphic designer, and then the typesetter would prepare the finished graphic work for printing using either metal type or photosetting. However, the launch of the Macintosh personal computer in 1984 made a desktop computer accessible to many designers. Its key feature was its PostScript page layout system, developed by Adobe, which, unlike IBM compatible software, faithfully showed what was to be finally printed (such as the shape of distinct fonts) on the screen. By allowing the designer to input copy and arrange it on screen, the need for specialist typesetters was dispensed with. In taking out a layer of production, designers and clients were one step closer to the finished article within the design process itself.

The growth of computer technology as a design tool provoked a flurry of debate among its commentators and educationalists, which continued through the late 1980s and well into the 1990s (see, for example, Kinross 1997). Some of graphic design's traditions were directly translated from their metal-based origins into the digital format as Apple and its followers adopted much of the traditional terminology inherited from typography. For example, we still use the term 'leading' to describe how tightly or loosely the individual characters of a word may be set together, a term inherited from typesetting wherein lead spacers would be introduced to separate characters. On the other hand, the new production system was much faster, implying that it might become a less contemplative act than hitherto. More shocking to traditionalists was the fact that the software came with a repertoire of basic shapes, layouts and fonts to choose from. The designer could therefore assemble elements on screen according to pre-ordained patterns. It was feared that those traditional 'hand and eye' skills, such as drawing, which were thought to be the bedrock of design and thus invention, would be overrun by 'quick-fix' graphics which were tied by the parameters of the software available rather than the imagination and creativity of the designer. This alarm was further compounded by the fact that desktop publishing allowed non-professionals access to design tools. The graphic design profession was no longer protected by its own technology which required specialist training in order to use.

This debate was partially superseded by the fact that in addition to being a design tool, computers became a design medium. This was precipitated by the introduction of hypertext, via Apple's release of the HyperCard system in 1987, which allowed designers to write multimedia programs. Rather than functioning as a conduit towards print graphics, the computer screen itself became an immediate context for viewing by the end-user. Hypertext refers to software capabilities which allow readers supposedly non-linear forms of access to information via personal computers and terminals. It contains authored links which the user may follow and that create associations between different instances and forms of text. The term 'hypermedia' is conventionally used to describe hypertexts which incorporate other media, such as video, photographic images, sound, graphics and so on. Crucially, then, it is computer-mediated and thus remains in an electronic format.

The arrival of hypertext instigated a more profound set of changes for the graphic designer. On the one hand, it offered the restricted format of the video display screen itself, in its early days usually not much bigger than 28 cm × 21 cm. On the other hand, the designer now had to consider the structure and organization of elements to make up a document and the way the user would navigate through these. Obviously, these are questions which also confronted print graphics. By the arrangement of graphic elements on a page – the relationship of type to images, the emphasis given to different parts of the copy and so on – the designer is structuring the reader's experience of it. There is a time element involved in moving from page to page or scanning a layout. But while a book or magazine normally involve a progressive linear narrative for the reader to follow, a hypermedia document provides a multi-linear format where the user may move through a variety of pathways. The physical make-up of print media gives the reader an idea of the position of an individual part of it in relation to the whole. As separate 'pages' of a hypermedia document appear on screen, then previous pages are often obscured. In addition, by combining a range of media into the document – text, graphics, moving images, music, voiceover and so on – the designer has to consider their relationship to each other and how the narrative unfolds. In other words, the designer takes on a larger and more challenging role in the editorial arrangement of content. Production and distribution costs may be dramatically cut in digital media, but with the integration of moving image, music, narration and other forms, there is often more intense investment in the origination and editing of content. Finally, the designer's relationship to the client changes. Often the designer may only be providing an overall structure for the client to then fill in or update the detail. Ultimately, though, what either the designer creates on screen or what the client fills in is what the end-user gets. Production and distribution processes do not intervene to modify the look of the article. This has led some commentators (e.g. Myerson 1997) to equate computer interface and software design with craft. The digitized commodity may be serially reproduced, unlike in craft-making, but the designer has the same direct relationship with the end result as, say, potters have with their wares.

TECHNOLOGICAL DEVELOPMENT

Opportunities for developing, distributing and accessing hypertext products of increasing sophistication subsequently facilitated enormous growth in this sector of the design industry. The introduction of the CD-ROM provided a format on which a much greater volume of interactive material could be stored and accessed than could be achieved on floppy or hard-disk drives. For ordinary home consumers, the CD-ROM delivered the most powerful format for integrating different media into the interactive experience throughout the 1990s. It was nonetheless limited. A CD-ROM disk could only store less than an hour of compressed video; as a result they used a lot of text, stills and some sound, but only short and often low-resolution video clips (Holtzman

1997: 161). By 1995 it was widely accepted that stand-alone CD-ROMs would largely be unprofitable (Herz 1998). The range and depth of skills required in their development mitigated against their widespread commercial exploitation.

By contrast, less elaborate interactive entertainment could as easily be put on the Internet. Notably, then, the CD-ROM continued to be used only in specific markets. In the music industry, promotional video and sound could be repackaged into a visual/audio format of CD-ROM. It also favoured large-scale documents, such as encyclopaedias, which involve multi-linear navigation. It was used for promotional means to be given away, where the data already existed – thus designers use it to show-off the outer limits of their work. Finally, it maintained its market among children's multimedia: its contained nature, as opposed to the open network of the Internet, meant that parents would be reassured that their offspring did not stray on to 'unsuitable' material and that specific material deemed suitable by parents could be chosen. In practically all cases, children's CD-ROM titles were linked to other merchandise within its brand.

As internet technology developed, so it began to supersede or, at least, stand alongside the CD-ROM. In the later 1990s, the 'hybrid' CD-ROM emerged which combined its strength with the Internet network. This meant that users could interact with other people or information online in combination with the offline format of the CD-ROM.

The establishment of the World Wide Web (WWW) in 1991 provided the first global hypertext environment. The Internet was the result of a steady development dating back to the 1940s, which is well documented (e.g. Kitchin 1998: Ch. 2), and was largely exploited for military and academic purposes. With the possibility of two-way communication across a network, it should be likened more to the telephone than the radio or television. The Web allowed for the transmission of text, images and sound across its network. It also supported hypertext documents so that users had a direct link to other relevant sites. In the same year, Gopher, a system for searching and retrieving information, was circulated. This was soon followed by Mosaic, an internet interface which by 1993 became the standard on-screen format for the Web. Netscape Navigator, which was, for a while, to dominate web-browsing software, was released in 1995.

Internet authoring software, such as Dreamweaver which was introduced in 1997, allowed ordinary PC owners to design their own web pages within a dictated format. More importantly for professional designers, internet growth was fuelled by business use. Throughout the 1990s the number of business personal computers in Europe with internet access outstripped home PCs (Thackara 1997: 388).

PROFESSIONAL PRACTICES

With the growing complexity and size of corporate and institutional websites and the increased consumer use of the Internet, a digital media design industry had emerged by the late 1990s. In 1998 a reported 24 per cent of British design consultancies offered 'multimedia' design among their services (CITF 1998). By 2007, this had climbed to 56 per cent (British Design Innovation 2007). In the majority of cases this was an add-on feature to the multidisciplinary offer of a consultancy, often in response to client demand. A typical scenario would be that a client would ask for a website or a multimedia station to be designed as an extension to a material-based project, though often there wasn't a deep rationale for this except the feeling that they ought to have one.

Theoretically speaking, the design consultancy could subsequently apply their understanding of the client's brand values to the patina of a website, thus extending them further into another domain. A more advanced instance would be where, say, a website or an intranet system would be integral to the strategic development of the client's internal communications being undertaken by the design consultancy.

While the majority of design consultancies may include individuals drawn from a range of design disciplines, the digital media teams are invariably more open in their constitution, sometimes incorporating software programmers, musicians, artists, video-makers, writers, architects, psychologists and traditional designers. The range of skills which are drawn from in this area means that it is more common for individuals to work in flexible networks according to the demand of particular projects. This typifies the post-Fordist system of design practice which emerged after the early 1990s recession. It also reflects the need to constantly reconfigure working practices in the face of voracious technological development of the medium and the attendant changes in demands made by clients. Even Britain's largest and best-known digital studio, Deepend, with 120 employees, was organized into flexible and continuously changing subgroups according to both the particular medium – be it, say, website or convergent media – and/or the demands of specific projects (Waterfall 2000).

An understanding of the client's brand is important to the design process, but few designers within digital media undertook systematic brand development; this was more frequently left to brand strategists. While on-screen design for a known brand certainly will no doubt modify its image, generally speaking designers in this domain provided a mixture of technological know-how and narrative creativity (good storytelling, in other words) rather than a more holistic market research and product management strategy.

Thus, to extend from Bourdieu's proposition, designers become both cultural and *technological* intermediaries. They serve to broker new developments in electronic media and indeed its own development requires them to be constantly at its cutting edge – or at least just behind it – as access grows. As Steve Grand, British designer of the Creatures program, which generated virtual pets that were maintained online, stated, 'I'm rushing to capitalise on [the innovation] ... before increases in computer power make the problem so easy everyone will be doing it!' (Grand, quoted in Schofield 2000).

CRITICAL REFLECTION

It may hardly be surprising, given the rapidity of change in the technological platforms of design for digital media, that in its growth years it was marked by constant articulation and self-analysis by its practitioners, although, like their practice, this was largely restricted to the discussion of what was happening on screen rather than the wider commercial or ideological ramifications of cyberculture. In the 1990s, during the earlier period of the establishment of digital media as a design specialism, many of its figurehead designers and consultancies regularly published essays or journals – almost entirely on the Internet – which explored their medium. This would include Andy Cameron, founder of the London-based collective Anti-Rom (see www.hrc.wmin.ac.uk/), the Amsterdam consultancy Mediamatics (see www.mediamatic.nl/magazine), or the American consultant Jakob Nielsen (see www.useit.com/alertbox). This section gives some of the history of discourses that surrounded digital media in the 1990s. These evidenced the tensions between technological capability and creative aspiration.

This enthusiasm for critical reflection on practice can be read in several ways. First, it may merely have been a reflection of the access that these specialists have to digital publishing, which may at times have been less subject to the editorial controls of traditional print media. Second, it might be seen as a self-legitimating approach in a nascent profession anxious to promote itself and its intellectual capital. Third, and more benignly, it was born of a consciousness that normative discourses were still being established (Dew 1999). In the words, in that period, of digital media communications consultant Kevin Lycett:

> We are producing this stuff, but we are also constantly thinking about what it is. It is an alien thing we are designing on and for, and so we need to get to grips with it, in our working practices, our technological know-how, but also in how we conceptualize it. (1999)

Or as interactive media designer Nico Macdonald wrote, 'Developing a language to criticize and understand design in this media is the basis for moving it forward' (Macdonald 1997: 6). Similarly, Andy Cameron, of Anti-Rom, explained that 'We have found that designing for a medium so new that it has not yet evolved into a cultural form, or a language of its own, is almost impossible' (Cameron 1998a: 7).

Overarching positions on digital media within the design profession, such as they are, ranged from the optimistic, if not utopian, through the pragmatists to the hopelessly pessimistic. Parallel positions could be found in a wider discussion of the social and cultural impact of information technology systems and are discussed towards the end of this chapter.

The optimists regarded digital media as a liberating format where technology could be exploited to limitless effects. For some, such as designer David Collier, this optimism underlined its potential both as a communicative and interactive tool to the extent that it literally becomes embodied. He explains:

> Interactivity is the sixth sense that we're now developing and beginning to explore and use. We've had sound and vision and all those tactile things; interactivity is actually the first sense that really engages your mind. (1993)

For others, the possibilities of this technology seemed to be constantly just around the corner. In his book *Digital Mosaics: The Aesthetics of Cyberspace* (1997), Californian digital media designer and writer Steven Holtzman also claimed that new forms of cognition would arise with this technology. He looked to a future where he imagined himself to be 'curled up in bed with laser images projected on my retinas, allowing me to view and travel through an imaginary three-dimensional virtual world' (1997: 186). As if the technology, however, was somehow separate from ideological or social influences, he demanded that the reader 'Keep in mind, these digital worlds are not bound by the laws of the real world. All bets are off. Anything can happen' (1997: 101). Thus utopianism, futurism and technological determinism were melded into a single, seemingly science fiction-driven belief system which was expressed in a semi-mystical way.

For many rank-and-file designers for the small screen, there was a clear realization that the day-to-day realities of developing interactive digital media did not offer such scope. Designers may have access to sophisticated authoring software, but they know that their end-users will generally make different demands. In terms of websites, it was claimed that average users will spend less than one second on a homepage and would be reluctant to pursue the information they seek if it is more than four links away (Lycett 1999).

Even today, logging on to the Internet is a private act, not requiring the niceties of ordinary social interaction; it is a brutal relationship. In this sense, the consumer is sovereign. Moreover, ordinary home computer users rarely possess the software for rapid and trouble-free viewing of sophisticated graphics. For example, the then dominant web-browsing system Netscape was released in successive upgrade versions in the late 1990s. But as the total number of internet users grows, it was assumed that an increasing majority were in fact less likely to upgrade to versions which can handle sophisticated online data. Early internet users were more technologically sophisticated and demanding; later arrivals were, however, less concerned with and less interested in upgrades. According to web design consultant Jakob Nielsen (1999), Netscape 5, launched at the beginning of 1999, would never get more users than the Netscape 4 which pre-dated it by more than two years. In turn, he advised that advances in web design can only be incremental. Formal developments, such as greater use of moving image and interactive sound, would have to be put on hold. Free downloadable software, such as Flash or Shockwave, which supports moving image, was readily accessible, but was nonetheless slow and cumbersome for many domestic users who owned low-specification computers. In the meantime, improvements in content, such as better writing, could increase a site's usability (Nielsen 1998).

For Nielsen, the call to minimalism in website design was based on the pragmatism that 'the user is always right'. For others, such as New York-based digital media designer Jessica Helfand, it contained an implicitly Modernist stance which eschewed ill-conceived decorative effects and promoted a more rationalistic, geometric approach. Indeed, she cited the Dutch interwar movement De Stijl as inspiration in the way they deal with 'the relationships between structural form and transient content, between cyclical time and infinite space' (Helfand 1997: 9).

In whichever case, this tempered approach to on-screen design was not only at odds with the more aesthetic ambitions of some designers, but also conflicted with the corporate client's desire to weave something of the 'brand experience' into a website. While moving image clips and sound provided a scene-setting mood for a site, this may have, in fact, detracted from the motivation of visitors who merely wanted to get at basic information or make purchases. Nielsen criticized the American bookseller Barnes and Noble as a company making this marketing mistake on its website. He suggested that:

> They weren't focusing on how to buy a book, they were focusing on building their brand, which is so arrogant. They were saying: 'Because we are a famous bookstore, you should buy from us and not [Amazon].' Everybody who tried the two sites decided it was enormously easier to buy the book from Amazon, so that's what they did. (Nielsen, quoted in Schofield 1999)

Finally, the pessimists did not eschew digital media. Rather, these designers envisaged a highly limited role for themselves in this medium. This was starkly apparent in the declarations and activities of the groups of well-known designers involved in the Fuse project, as discussed in Chapter 5. It was driven by a philosophical position, influenced not least by Jean Baudrillard and Paul Virilio, which identified digital technology in its militaristic roots and claimed its impoverishment of everyday life as an instrument of surveillance, commercialization and banality (King 1995). Virilio (1997) in particular presented a bleak picture of social destruction brought by the loss of geographical spaces, distance and intimacy as the result of information technology. But the Fuse position was perhaps also driven by a realization that the days of the celebrity graphic designer were limited in the face of the widening of access to their tools, the growing consumer sovereignty over the design process and the range of specialisms required to deliver substantive digital media design products.

AUTHORSHIP

The crisis expressed by the Fuse members was symptomatic of a wider problem facing typographic designers concerning control over authorship. Before digitization, typefaces had been held in material form, for instance, as metal type in its traditional format or, from the 1970s, in Letraset. This allowed type foundries – the companies that manufactured and distributed these – to control their circulation. In turn, typeface designers could benefit from the return of royalty payments on sales from these foundries. However, with digitization a number of its characteristics confound copyright laws. These include the falling cost of reproduction and increasing speed by which 'perfect' copies can be made, the interconnectedness of machines which means that works can be transferred with impunity and without the knowledge of their creators, and the ability of computer software to mask original authorship. To put it another way, fonts can freely be downloaded from the Internet.

By focusing on the designer's role as an originator of typefaces or other primary forms, the Fuse team seemed to be missing the point as to their potential role in a digitized age. Since these were instantly accessible on the computer desktop, the designer would now be more involved in the *selection* rather than the *creation* of forms (Manovich 1997: 293). An extreme example of this is in a website which consists entirely of links to other sites. The designer arranges an environment within and through which the user navigates. Authorship resides less in the object but rather in the presentation of a situation, in the provision of structures, sets of relationships and possibilities of narratives and flow which are experienced through them.

Design process expert Tom Mitchell (1988) locates historical precedents to this attitude in the composer John Cage and painter Robert Rauschenberg. Cage's composition *4'33"* involves four minutes and thirty-three seconds of silence, while Rauschenberg's *White Paintings* consist of seven canvases, each of which is uniformly covered with white house paint. In each case the audience is left to experience the silence or space left in their own way. The musician or artist gives up their traditional role as the provider of the prime object of contemplation. Having set the situation up, they hand over the management of the aesthetic experience entirely to their viewers or listeners. In a similar spirit, from 1995 onwards, artist/musician Brian Eno developed software with Tim Cole which produced ever-changing interactive music. This is part of a long interest in a systems approach to composition. He had written in the sleeve notes to his album *Discreet Music* in 1975:

> I have always preferred making plans to executing them. I have gravitated towards situations and systems that, once set into operation, could create music with little or no intervention on my part. This is to say I tend toward the role of planner and programmer, and then become an audience to the results. (Eno, quoted in Mitchell 1988: 213)

More specifically in relation to visual interactive media, Andy Cameron has suggested that design work should be considered more in terms of a model than a proposition. In his estimation, the designer's voice is displaced (1998a: 7). Thus the designer may provide the language and its syntax, but users find their own voice within these frameworks.

READERSHIP

By providing a model for the user to navigate through and interact with, rather than a sequential narrative, the author/reader relationship is modified. Some commentators (e.g. Poster 1990; Landow 1992; Lanham 1993) explore the possibility that this indeed frees users to determine meaning to the extent, in some cases, that they actually become authors themselves. Among these, Landow is particularly vigorous in arguing this case. In the first instance, he aligns the emergence of hypertext and its implications with elements of poststructuralist theory. He notes how Jean Baudrillard, Jacques Derrida, Jean-François Lyotard and Marshall McLuhan all argue against the future importance of print-based information technology. For Landow, Derrida (1976 [1967]) in particular points to how 'new practical methods of information retrieval extends the possibilities of the "message" vastly' (Derrida, quoted in Landow 1992: 29). This process contributes to the 'decentring' of the message so that not just one, but several messages may be configured by the reader. He also draws attention to Roland Barthes's notion of 'writerly' and 'readerly' texts, first articulated in S/Z (1975 [1970]). Barthes suggests that readers react to written texts by, in a sense, producing their own text through reading, deriving a multitude of readings from it: polysemy, in other words.

For Landow, hypertext is an 'embarrassingly literal embodiment' of Derrida's and Barthes' theories (1992: 34). From this position he pursues a vision of hypertext as a liberational medium by arguing that the various on-screen blocks of texts – or 'lexias' as he terms them – and the links between them allow for a radical repositioning of the reader's status. Lexias disperse and atomize any possible sequentialism so that users are free to assemble their own meanings. Hierarchy, in terms of what are the important points of a document and what takes precedence, is destroyed, thereby making hypertext a democratized medium.

Such optimistic and ambitious claims, however, are problematic. McHoul and Roe (1996) in particular take issue with Landow. They point out that in the first place, the parallels he draws between hypertext and poststructuralist theorists are premised on a misrepresentation of their argument. Roland Barthes, in McHoul's and Roe's estimation, was concerned with exposing the fact that readers are slaves to a tyrannical text. Any amount of reading does not allow access to writing per se. In this vein they go on to note that hypertext authoring programmes, such as Authorware Professional, Macromedia Director and Toolbook, do not come cheaply. Likewise, Derrida was discussing the general preconditions of writing rather than outlining a manifesto for the reader's liberation. Finally, they point out that reading may be undertaken in several ways. They cite Wittgenstein (1968) in arguing that reading, even of the most uniformly arranged printed page, is not a singular process with a particular 'essence' to it. Instead, reading may be performed in a variety of ways – from word-for-word to scanning – and may be experienced in different ways regardless of the medium which is read.

In the light of these objections to a 'libertarian' view of hypertext, one might be guarded in claiming any particular qualities for interactive digital media. Nonetheless, some tentative suggestions may be made which point to a middle-ground between either the author's or the reader's sovereignty.

CONSUMING INTERACTIVITY

A non-interactive form of cultural production usually only allows space for interpretation and reaction on the part of its audience. Interactivity, however, involves a dialogue of control and feedback between a user and a program. It means that the user is able to intervene in the representation itself. Thus, in a mature form, 'interactivity allows narrative situations to be described *in potentia* and then set into motion – a process whereby model building supersedes storytelling, and the what-if engine replaces narrative sequence' (Cameron 1998b). Importantly, the user is not presented with an entirely non-linear situation. The linearity of traditional storytelling is substituted by a multi-linear network through which the audience navigates.

A hypertext document presents a variety of pathways through it. One chooses the route at specific junctions within it by clicking on links. Rather than a strictly textual presentation, a spatio-temporal representation may be offered – often described as 'Virtual Reality' – in which the user moves through a series of virtual spaces. In this instance, a 'real-time' simulation of moving through them is provided: doors open, brickwork and floor-tiling trail past, sound grows on approach and recedes on departure. The user has, albeit momentarily, something of the sensation of actually being in this virtual space. This is what is commonly described as the immersive experience.

Clearly, the user's relationship to the interface changes in the immersive situation. In the traditional narrative of cinema or theatre the user is outside the time of the narration, unable to control the speed of its flow or its direction. In the interactive environment, the user is inside the time of the events being described and is able to dictate their movement through it by pausing to take decisions, moving backwards, sideways, diagonally as well as forwards. Indeed, while in modern literature, theatre and cinema the audience watches the plot being built around the interaction and tension between characters, in the immersive environment, the narrative is driven by the spatial movement of the user (Manovich 1997: 290–91).

This is particularly noticeable in computer games where often the player is encouraged to role-play into the hero or heroine's viewpoint. Their progress is measured in terms of their movement through different levels, each featuring tasks to perform in order to move on. In discussing video games, Fleming argues that objective, environmental detail is invariably stripped back so that there is just enough to suggest movement through it (such as exploring caverns or leaping over crevasses) (1996: 191). It is a cartoonesque world with the outlines and geometry of objects given, but little of their texture or hues. The player thus does not focus on the detail of this virtual world. Rather, he or she appreciates its geometry. It is a framework for movement. This environment of immersion is not unmediated, though. Instead, simulation is encoded, planned and structured by its designer.

In these gameworlds, one's success depends on a degree of mastery over its geometry at two levels. Intensive and frequent engagement with its systems, rules and structure builds a set of intuitive responses (Weinbren 1995). If repeated without progression, it becomes either addictive or uninteresting. But often the player's interest is maintained by the unexpected appearing (Fleming 1996: 188). Working up an overall sense of how both the obvious features and the unexpected elements function is part of the game's challenge. It is perceived both from within, as the player discovers more about it through playing it, and outside it, in the way the player conceptualizes its overall configurations. Computer games designer J.C. Herz describes this process in terms of 'hacking' the game:

> And what you're doing, what I'm doing, what a lot of kids are doing, when they play video games is there's a certain amount of model making that goes on. What you have in a video game is a system, it's a model of some reality, someone's reality. And what you have as a player is a model that you're making in your head about how the game works. And when the model in your head matches the model in the computer, then you figured out the rules of the game, you figured out the system. And a lot of people actually don't finish playing computer games because to a large extent, the process of figuring out how it works is the game ... you've cracked it, once you've hacked it. (1998)

In a simpler way, a hypertext document encourages a similar approach. Skilled copywriters approach the hypertext medium with this in mind. Copy is shorter as there is less space to get the reader's attention. As copywriter Carol King states, 'what is written may only be a path to getting the reader to go somewhere else' (King, quoted in Jones 1999: 30). By contrast, traditional narratives employ techniques to associate concepts together through, for instance, contrasting sections ('however'), consolidating ideas ('for example') or extending arguments ('moreover'). Hypertext links are rarely so explicit about their function. If overused they can merely assemble interconnected text fragments in a meaningless trail of 'ands' (Mason and Dicks 1999). They carry meanings: for example, by the very act of associating one page with another. But the emphasis in building narrative is passed to the reader. First, readers find their way through and 'master' the data given, then they structure their own mental map of the various pages given and routes between them.

Manovich (1997: 297) observes that when web-surfing, a typical user may be reading a page while waiting for another to download. The user keeps checking the progress of this communication by looking at the toolbar which gives the percentage of download achieved. This act of communication – sending and reading the information that tells us about bytes being transmitted down wires – in turn becomes the message to supersede the web-page information. Likewise, virtual reality simulations constantly remind the user of the system in use. These three-dimensional environments are often designed so that the faster one moves through them, the less visual detail of objects is given. QuickTime VR, which by morphing a set of images of a space together allows one to navigate around a panoramic view, similarly 'deconstructs its own illusion' (Manovich 1997: 298). The more one zooms in to view objects, the more one is left with oversized pixels. This reveals the artifice of constructing on-screen images. Rather than give over more quidity to the viewer, instead we are confronted with apparently abstract shapes which we know are assembled to represent reality. Overall, then, the illusion of another free space on the computer interface is constantly jammed by menus, icons, texts, pixels – information telling us about what is happening in terms of the program and which returns us from the three-dimensional virtual world to the flat, glowing screen. Human computer interfaces can never be totally immersive. Instead, cognition lies on two levels, between concentration and detachment, between the status of user and viewer.

CYBERNETIC LOSS

In moving from the real to the virtual world, losses have to be acknowledged and compensations devised. Since the launch of the Apple Macintosh computer in 1984 and the Microsoft Windows operating system for IBM computers and their clones in 1985, these systems and their descendants have provided the user with an array of visual devices for navigating and reading the computer interface. On the Mac, for instance, we have a trash can (dustbin) icon which tells us where and how to throw away files; in Windows XP, more bizarrely, we have a 'recycle bin'. Buttons appear to be raised in relief, notepads have their spiral binding, communication is represented by a quaint old-fashioned telephone. This interface encourages the user to find his or her way round it by trying things out, clicking on what seems to be the appropriate icon and working through menus. Navigation, using a mouse, is essentially a two-dimensional act as one moves between applications. As Turkle observes:

> The user was presented with a scintillating surface on which to float, skim, and play. There was nowhere visible to dive. Yet strictly speaking, a Macintosh, like all computers, remained a collection of on/off switches, of bits and bytes, of traveling electrons ... (1997: 34)

By contrast, previous operating systems, such as CP/M and MS-DOS, required the user to type in instructions to the computer in order to access and open files or modify data. The experience was decidedly un-visual, and yet by being forced to learn and speak a specific computer language, the user was drawn into the idea that they were actually interacting with and commanding the software system. Turkle (1997: 36–47) likens this practice to a modernist conception of computer interfaces wherein the user has access to and a measure of the aesthetic/intellectual experience of the machine's functional workings. It was something that the user could control and modify. It follows, in her estimation, that the Macintosh interface is postmodern in that all the user gets is surface and simulation to be enjoyed. By extension, she compares the 'modernist' IBM corporation, whose personal computers ran on MS-DOS systems (and indeed, whose corporate identity was developed by arch-modernist Paul Rand) and the 'postmodernist' Apple corporation in the same way. Ultimately, the Macintosh model of the computer interface has prevailed. From 1995 the Windows interface provided the same basic features as the Macintosh, but, until 2000, was an overlay on to the MS-DOS system. This allowed the best of both worlds in giving access to the operating system, while those who sought greater ease of use could remain on the surface.

In either the Macintosh or the Windows interfaces, the metaphors of trash can, file, briefcase and so on serve to fill in for what has been lost in a process of dematerialization. Tasks which had previously been undertaken in a more material form – such as writing a book, involving the textures of paper and ink, the scratch of pens or the clatter of typewriters – are transferred into a digital format. In essence, this information consists of a binary code of noughts and ones, of the tiny electrical impulses of microchip technology. In shifting away from the material world of weight, texture, smell or incidental sound, much is lost. On screen this 'cybernetic loss' (Thackara 1988) is compensated for by giving a heightened allusion to materiality. This may be in the icons to be seen (as in the trash can), but also in the array of clunks, thuds and whirrs that the desktop sound system delivers. Make a mistake on a Macintosh and you get the sound of bedsprings or a toy trumpet; pull down on a menu in Windows and the dull thud of a chord played on a marimba accompanies you. We saw in Chapter 6 how the widespread use of plastics in product design meant that much of the communicative function of objects was thrown on to their surfaces and how, in turn, this gave way to an increasing sophistication in the use of semantic encoding.

Associative imagery is likewise heavily inscribed into the computer interface as a way of explaining and enabling some experiential cognition of what cannot be seen, or at least what has been lost in the transfer to digitally based representation.

Similarly, the worlds inhabited by the heroes and heroines of most video games are densely material and textural. Sonic the Hedgehog in the Sega series, or Super Mario of the Nintendo games, both work through a world redolent of H.G. Wells or Jules Verne, where the ordinary mechanical laws of leverage and elasticity, weight and gravity, momentum and force are still present. They inhabit a two-dimensional environment filled with springs, ratchets and pulleys that speaks in exaggerated tones of the industrial material culture of the near-past rather than William Gibson's science-fictional cyberspace of lightness (Weinbren 1995: 403).

The representation of material reality connects the interface to the more known world of everyday life. It takes a language which is already understood and then sets it up on screen. But it is also exaggerated, made hyperreal. Often this is not so much in the forms presented – we have already established that the digital domain will strip textures and detail down to leave one with geometry – but in their content. The Mac interface presents us with a trash can drawn in outline form with little textural detail, but it alludes to a heavy old-fashioned one, rather than a plastic wheelie-bin.

The designers of the Dorling Kindersley *Dinosaur Hunter* CD-ROM went to extraordinary lengths in order to make the virtual museum environment believable. In particular, the detail of the spaces is pre-rendered as opposed to live-rendered (Harris 1999). 'Pre-rendered' is when a detailed computer model is rendered at high quality a frame at a time and is stored as a series of picture files or a quicktime movie. Each frame takes many minutes or hours to render, allowing greater detail, but the finished rendered pictures can be called back quickly in succession to give the impression of a walkaround, for example. 'Live-rendering' uses a more basic, less detailed, but 'on-the-fly' approach to render a computer model from any angle the user chooses. It allows for more interaction with an object, as opposed to pre-rendering, which has a fixed number of views to choose from. Television graphics, such as flying logos and title sequences, use pre-rendering. VRML (Virtual Reality Modelling Language: a system which allows users to navigate virtual spaces on the Internet, conceived in spring 1994) and CD-ROM-based games like *Quake* and *Tomb Raider* use live-rendering. The *Dinosaur Hunter* CD-ROM is therefore sold partly on its technological capital. Its packaging boasts '30 interative 3D consoles ... 15 video segments, 340 fully rendered views, 650 screens and pop-ups' and appreciating the extent of its high-technology crafting is integral to the consumer experience.

The product has interesting coincidences with the visual hardware and thematic software of the international expositions stretching from the Crystal Palace Great Exhibition of 1851 to New York's World's Fair of 1939. Their common attributes included the fetishization of their own technology, their mixture of education and entertainment and their encyclopaedic content and format,

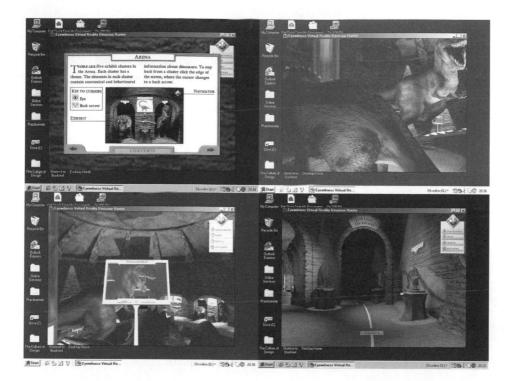

providing scenarios where all knowledge is knowable and measurable (Greenhalgh 1988). Both the CD-ROM product and its historical forerunner of the international exposition indulge in presentation of Umberto Eco's notion of the hyperreal (Eco 1986). Exhibits in both contexts were/ are presented to be more visceral, authentic and compliant to the viewers' expectations than their original (in the case of the dinosaur, this is perhaps inevitable, given its extinction). What is lost in moving from nature to its representation is compensated for by upping the aesthetic pleasure of looking. Pre-rendering the virtual environment helps this effect along.

A rendered look would have allowed the user greater freedom of movement through, and indeed scope to get lost in, the museum. Instead then, the user may be immersed in distinct environments – once they've downloaded – but also maintain their own mental map of its cybernetic architecture, backed up by on-screen navigational aids such as a museum plan. Likewise, expositions involved guidebooks, route-planning and signposting through a set of discreet situations.

Digital interactive environments frequently oscillate between delivering an immersive fantasy or imagined world, but also alluding to the raw qualities of the real world. A prime internet-based example of this is AlphaWorld, which first appeared in 1995 (formerly at www.worlds. net/alphaworld, subsequently at www.activeworlds.com) and prefigured several other virtual 'worlds' such as Second Life, established in 2003. This was a multiple user domain (MUD) where visitors could 'chat' with each other. It was configured in a virtual reality format so that participants could choose an avatar to represent themselves; they could then claim their own plot of land within a virtual neighbourhood and construct a homestead for themselves. In the

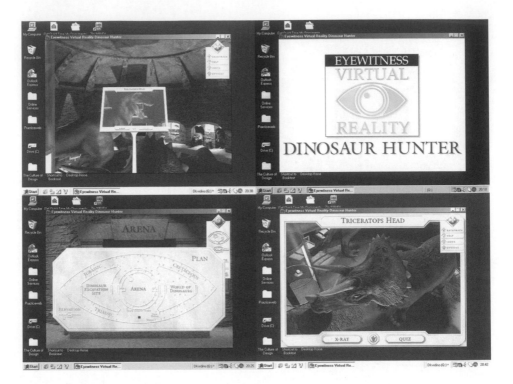

Views of *Dinosaur Hunter* interactive CD-ROM by Dorling Kindersley
Photos: Guy Julier

process, they could get to know their neighbours and interact with them. The scenario was clearly similar to that of a frontiersland of the American Wild West made up of an unplanned space measuring 655 square kilometres – more or less, significantly, the same size as California. It was progressively colonized by people, their homesteads, ranging from ranch-style tract homes to impenetrable stone fortresses to underground caverns and services such as bars. Users could create their virtual structures using objects from a library of more than 3,000 objects and textures. As of 30 June 1999, users had placed more than 30 million building blocks on AlphaWorld. The open space scenario contrasts with the fact that users actually construct their fantasy environment through the sweat of their brow and the click of the mouse.

LIBERATION AND REGULATION: THE BIGGER PICTURE

In its early days, AlphaWorld could be read as a metaphor for the pioneering of cyberspace in general on the World Wide Web (Huxor 1995). There were the same myths of unregulated space into which individuals could stake their claim and the same infinite possibility of constructing a world afresh. Just as the user was free to navigate through AlphaWorld, talk to whomever they wish, build whatever they fancied, untrammelled by planning consent or aesthetic norms, so in some quarters the Internet and other hypermedia forms are seen to provide some form of liberation.

Such claims resonate with a wider ideological position which views electronic information technology as decentralized and open. This attitude was particularly prevalent during the early years of the Internet (Sassen 1999). It was promoted by the California-based *Wired*, a magazine which glorifies the latest technological breakthroughs, the corporate spirit of leading-edge information technology industries and the hero worship of (nearly always male) software developers and business whizz-kids. Furthermore, much of its editorial content ascribes the technology and its content with a certain sense of autonomy. Its position is epitomized in the words of one of its columnists, John Perry Barlow, who claimed that 'Information is a life form ... information wants to be free' (1994: 89). Drawing from Richard Dawkins' notion of 'memes', he argues that information is self-reproducing and adaptable to the environments it inhabits. This implies that it can escape the normal structures of power and inequality and that, more ordinarily, technological platforms (such as the agility of web-browsers) or consumers' motivation (or lack of it) do not actually constrain its circulation. Such politically utopian views are matched by economic aspirations, held particularly strongly in the USA, that offer the prospect of the Web providing the basis for a new, democratic free market. Indeed, one time Vice-President of the USA, Al Gore, famously declared at a world congress on information technology in 1994 that 'families and friends will transcend the barriers of time and distance', and that also 'it will make possible a global marketplace' (Gore, quoted in Schiller 1995: 17–18).

The disembodying of information in the context of digital media and its treatment as apparently independent of any productive system smack precisely of Marx's notion of 'commodity fetishism'. Here we might call it 'info fetishism' (Henwood 1995). The difference, then, is that while in the first volume of *Capital* Marx wrote about how the relationship between commodities in the market appears to stand in for social relations, in the digital context, the information fetish appears as a relationship between bytes. Needless to say, the hypertext system on the Internet, of endless links between pieces of information and whose relationship appears to be unstructured and unregulated, may well encourage such a conception. Any productive activity seems to reside in the consumer's domain: surfing between sites becomes the labour, waiting for downloads is time spent. The real producing agents who design and upload the website, or even those who lay the fibre-optic cables to convey the information, are strangely invisible.

In parallel with the view of information technology facilitating economic freedom is one which regards it as a space for personal liberation. In cyberspace, some claim (e.g. Plant 1993; Turkle 1997) that individuals can experiment with identities, posting messages, joining chat groups, colonizing virtual worlds anonymously or under guises. It can also allow, as others argue (e.g. Rheingold 1994), for the creation of new networks of groups and individuals, through, for instance, the foundation of internet discussion groups.

Access to digital media is still governed by traditional spatial and social divisions. In the first instance, before any digital software can be viewed and interacted with, the user requires the hardware on which to run it. While a market for second-hand, low-specification computer gear may put it within the financial reach of many people in the developed world, Kitchin reported that even in the USA 50 per cent of all internet hosts were located in just five states (1998: 111). Even into the 2000s, computer usage was dominated by white, middle-class males from Western nations who spoke English (Intel 2012). Thus cyberspace is, in fact, concentrated along geographical, demographic, gender, class and cultural lines.

It is not just access to computer hardware or the cultural biases of its software that exclude users. It is also dependent on the hardware of cabling to deliver significant bandwidth. Particular geographical nodes, such as major cities of New York or London, are relatively well served in this respect. Consequently, the nodes that are well connected become information rich. Meanwhile, locations that lie outside these nodes and the lines between them are left as information poor (Graham and Marvin 1996: 189–206). It seems, then, that just as life 'on screen' is in fact restricted by the available formats and technologies, so it is also constrained and regulated by a range of issues outside the box.

BYTES AND BRANDS

In reality, the topography of electronic space 'weaves in and out of non-electronic space' (Sassen 1999: 62). This is the case as much for the social divisions relating to information technology as for the pragmatic organization of managing branded digital spaces. For example, from 1995 companies began using the Web for communicating with customers, partners and investors, leading to the enormous growth of electronic commerce in 1999. In some cases, strings of information may be channelled through corporate alliances which connect up advertisers, products and media. Helen Nixon (1998) discusses how in 1996 Australian snack-food brand Twisties was promoted in conjunction with a 'Cyberheads surf the Net for free' ad campaign. Associative links were made through packaging and advertisements between 'Net surfing' and surfing and skateboarding, both of which are central themes of Australian youth culture. The campaign was run by Smith's snack-food company in partnership with Compaq, the world's number one PC-systems retailer whose end aim was the promotion of the Compaq Presario, a personal multimedia computer aimed at the home market. By tying the use of information technology up with a practice of everyday life, in this case the consumption of snack-food, then it is instituted into the cultural norms of youth. Rather than being free-flowing, information is directed along specific routes between corporations and niche markets.

In the case of the Dorling Kindersley *Dinosaur Hunter*, the product constantly reconfirms the generic brand identity of its publishers. It refers 'back' to other products being sold with a 3-D press-out stegosaurus skeleton and a free copy of the DK Pockets series *Dinosaurs* book. It extends outwards in that the disk is a hybrid CD-ROM, meaning that it can link to an online website which gives access to further dinosaur information and activities. Visually, the product coincides with the DK design ethic, using the same typography, palette and high production values as all its publications. The virtual museum is structured in the shape of the Eyewitness 'EYE' logo created for Dorling Kindersley interactive packages.

For its proponents, electronic commerce was expected to fulfil a strong role in bridging producers and consumers, and thus develop brand awareness. In the same way that we have seen how on-screen design facilitated a more immediate relationship between designer, client and end-user in the design process, so e-commerce effectively took out layers of mediation between the marketer and the customer. Rather than the traditional channels of distribution, media and sales forces, the marketer–customer gap could be replaced by an electronic 'market space', according to Nicholas Rudd of marketing communications consultancy Wunderman Cato Johnson (Rudd 1999). This facilitates a more direct relationship so that consumers may have in turn a more direct relationship with the brand and can, indeed, personalize their relationship with it. For example, in 1997, global management consultants Ernst and Young launched a service which gave unlimited consultancy advice online to small businesses for an annual fee of just $6,000. It used an internet system which was configured to route questions to specific, appropriate experts within the organization (Morris 1997: 28–9). This leads some commentators to place great emphasis on the design of interfaces as they are perceived to be the only point where the product, customer relationship and brand personality are defined (Hanna 1997: 35).

Other specialists in the design and marketing of internet products and services foresaw the medium as an effective tool for consolidating brand experience. Michael Moon, President of GISTICS Incorporated, a high-technology market research company based in California, argues that while traditional media such as television, direct mail and print can be used to create brand awareness, websites can create one-to-one relationships with customers (and indeed collect market information on them) (Moon 1999: 63). Websites can become what he calls 'deep gravity wells', which offer 'bright compelling cyberspace destinations around which stakeholders can take orbit' (1999: 61). He goes on to suggest that websites can also act as 'theater', functioning as a stage and offering performances that keep audiences coming back. Other media, such as mailshots or emails containing hyperlinks, can be used to 'drive people into the deep gravity well' (1999: 64). The language Moon uses is revealing in the way it refers to customers or visitors as 'stakeholders', implying their greater participation in and, perhaps, ownership of the brand. The notion that these 'destinations' are 'compelling' implies that engagement is immersive and inevitable while, at the same time, subtle strategies have to be adopted in order to induce consumers into visiting and revisiting branded websites.

CONCLUSION

It appears, then, that specialists in the design of commercial websites demand that they be both informational and inspirational. On the one hand, they exist as points for the interchange of data between corporations and their public. On the other hand, they must convey the emotional appeal of the brand. This double-edged exigency runs throughout interactive digital media. Like the exposition and guidebook, they promise both immersion and detachment, random sensual chaos and structured mediation and regulation.

The immediacy of the medium forces designers to adopt the role of the user – what they see on screen the user gets, and vice versa. This has the potential for reconfiguring the performer/ audience divide. Users can partake in the forging of personal aesthetic pleasure and identity. Or they can access corporate information and entertainment relating to their favourite brand articulated in a highly visual format. And yet it also remains a flat, glowing, sensorially encrvated image on a small screen. The loss of artefactual information (smell, tactility, presence) can only be made up for by a dense packing of artifice.

CHAPTER 10

COMMUNICATIONS, MANAGEMENT AND PARTICIPATION

As well as end-users in the public sphere, design and branding are also concerned with 'upstream' contexts. Organizations such as companies or educational establishments have features that are not normally seen by the general public, such as training events or internal documents. Sometimes, though, there is an indirect effect intended as design is used to establish ideas, attitudes or even language amongst members which are then communicated through to their clients, customers or end-users. In turn, employees themselves become 'consumers at work' as they internalize enthusiasms for their own corporate brand. Design is used to engage workers in emotional or aesthetic dispositions. Chapter 10 is therefore concerned with the role of design in internal management and communications as well as in engaging various forms of participation. It goes on to analyse how, in the context of creative quarters, contexts might be consciously left 'undesigned' to engender a sense of informality, if you will, and in order foster something of a creative ambience. Finally, we look at how the public itself is engaged in urban design processes in order to build their long-term commitment to a locality and its communitarian value as well as a way of facilitating attitudinal change and building aspirations. Thus we see that the culture of design can permeate organizations and locations in ways that are not necessarily obvious, and that the object of design might not be material or digital, but behavioural or attitudinal.

It's a party. And yet the guests are in their office gear: suits, skirts, ties, shirts, lapel-badges. In other words, then, it is a corporate bash. This is no ordinary occasion, however: each event may combine such features as artists' installations, illusions, interactive technology pieces, psychologists, light and laser sculptures, reflexology practitioners and a stylish array of cocktails and canapés to produce a multi-layered creation. Guests wander through a series of spaces, each one rich with extraordinary displays and surprising encounters. Even the bartenders and cooks wear specially designed outfits and turn the serving of food and drinks into a performance in itself: a virtual waiter wall where individual canapés are dispensed from perspex windows; an eat me wall where boxed puddings are plucked from a velcro surface. It's almost as if a 1960s alternative *happening* has gatecrashed a corporate board meeting.

These are not gratuitous entertainments, however. Each party is orchestrated around corporate messages such as 'virtuality', 'liquidity', 'borderlessness' or 'transparency', which are then threaded through the scenography and performance of the event. To underline the more serious aims of the party and reinforce product by-lines, an introductory speech is made before the event gets underway. 'Enjoy yourselves and Xpand your Horizons', announces the host. He is Dr Francioni of Deutsche Börse Group, Europe's leading facilitator of equity capital.

From 1996, when the Deutsche Börse Group established an office in London, these events have been organized by Vamp, a consultancy specializing in the design and implementation of one-off productions. Vamp seeks out empty warehouses or office blocks – neutral spaces – turning them into multimedia environments that 'embody the corporate culture' of the client (van den Munckhof and Dare 2000). In the case of the Deutsche Börse Group, Vamp deals with a multinational organization comprising three divisions. Collectively, these provide an information technology-based cash and derivatives market trading system and a range of information products and consultancy to players in financial markets. Its core business is therefore entirely built around online services and products which, by their very definition, seem intangible. It is also a complex organization with several layers and types of activity. The Vamp events provide an opportunity for the Deutsche Börse Group's international marketing and sales teams to meet with other group members and outside corporate partners. They usually coincide with important announcements such as new product launches or mergers. The parties offer an environment to encourage corporate bonding while

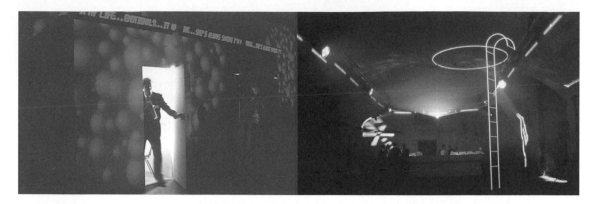

Views of parties for Deutsche Börse Group organized in London by Vamp from 1996
Source: Vamp

immersing guests and employees in visual and material manifestations of company values. These aims and objectives are constituted in more direct and simplified forms than are usually experienced in their workaday lives. At the same time, it is hoped that the cultural capital of the organization is reinforced and that values of modernity and creativity are communicated both externally to guests who have come from outside the company and internally among its professionals.

The Vamp/Deutsche Börse Group parties are perhaps an extreme example of a nascent arena of design intervention from the late 1990s where consultancies are directly involved in the formulation of strategies to develop the corporate culture of a client. This focuses on the 'below the line' elements of a company: that is, the parts that ordinary customers do not see. In design terms, this may embrace the aesthetic environment of a company, but in turn it is expected that this has an attitudinal effect on the way employees see themselves, interact with each other and with their clients and customers.

INTERNAL BRAND BUILDING

Traditionally, corporate identity has been regarded as a design tool by which both employees and their public relate to an organization. This is where the overall 'personality' of a company – its values and attitudes, its 'ways of doing things' – is communicated through a range of signifying data: logos, uniforms, letterheads, buildings and so on. Internal brand building draws a closer relationship between the employee and the products or services it purveys, and ultimately a closer relationship to its audience. It may therefore put the employee in the shoes of the consumer. Put otherwise, it aspires to inculcating an emotional investment in, as well as intellectual knowledge of, what it is hoped that the consumer eventually experiences.

As such, internal brand building represents an attempt to achieve coherence between the products or services of an organization and their mediation at all levels. This is effectively done through the collapsing of a series of boundaries. In the design profession this is done in some instances through amalgamating advertising, communications and design consultancy. For the client company, this strategy may be seen as part and parcel of the shifts in management theory and practice instigated in the 1990s. An important effect of this is that traditional distinctions between producer and consumer are increasingly blurred. In turn, for both the employee of a company and the end-user, the domains of 'public representation' and 'private life', as articulated in Johnson's 'circuit of culture' (see Chapter 4), appear to converge. The rest of the chapter explores the background to these changes and some further examples which illustrate them.

THE END OF ADVERTISING

Among many large corporate clients in the 1990s, responsibility for brand development and management ceased to rest solely in marketing departments, and by extension with their advertising agency. By 2000, a survey of 200 senior UK managers revealed that 73 per cent anticipated restructuring their companies, putting the brand at the heart of the organization and building its working structure around it (Manuelli 2000). With a greater fluidity as to the internal ownership of brands, it may subsequently be anticipated that corporate consciousness of it and action on its behalf pervade the organization more fully.

Despite this development, statistical indications are that advertising expenditure by no means receded during the 1990s – economic expansion and emerging global markets ensured continued growth for Western advertising agencies (CITF 1998). However, much has emerged to challenge any assumption that advertising is the sole guardian and mediator of brand values. (Within this discussion we must be careful to separate the notion of pure sales from brand values. Sales are dependent on a range of issues, stretching from product origination through advertising to promotions, positioning and pricing – all those elements of the 'marketing mix', in other words. Brand values refer more to the qualitative elements of recognition, emotional response, aesthetic appeal and, indeed, aesthetic illusion.) Schudson (1993 [1984]: 74–89) presents a convincing picture of an advertising industry which is fraught with divisions as to the efficacy of different techniques, in particular the question as to whether ads should be informational or emotional. Following his discussion, it appears that scientific approaches to the creation of ads, which would include market surveys or the pre-testing of ads on focus groups as part of the planning, vie with questions of intuition and artistry; this is typified by the creatives-versus-researchers tension in ad agencies. In turn, a lack of clarity as to what actually works and what doesn't calls into question advertising's efficacy. This leads to the often quoted and widely attributed remark on the part of a client that 'I know that at least half of my advertising money is being wasted. My problem is – I do not know which half' (quoted in Schudson 1993 [1984]: 85).

Schudson goes on to consider the consumer's information environment: that is, the methods by which the audiences receive data about products or services against which they set their advertising. His list of nine resources begins with the consumer's personal experiences of products or related products and ranges through government reports and consumer group information through to their interpretation of price (1993 [1984]: 90–1). This sets up powerful and constantly variable criteria by which consumers may challenge the claims of an advertisement. The growing sophistication of consumers in piecing together and interpreting different aspects of their respective information environments means that ad agencies have an ever-increasingly difficult job in producing plausible ads. This may lead them to be increasingly explicit and reflexive by developing a language which comments on the mechanics of advertising while purveying an ad at the same time (see Williamson 1988 [1978]: 7). Another response has been to deliver advertising in unexpected or novel contexts – ambient advertising as it came to be known in the late 1990s – such as by projecting it on to the sides of buildings or printing it on the back of bus tickets. In either case, it seems that some ad agencies began to take some desperate and extreme measures to get their message seen and talked about by an increasingly critical audience.

In order to defend this financial basis of their existence, but also their own integrity and raison d'être, representatives of the advertising agencies campaign hard sell the idea of publicity. This may not necessarily be in the face of any perceived threat from other practices in the creative industries, including design consultancy. More often this is directed at other elements of marketing used to secure brand loyalty, such as product promotions or customer loyalty schemes (see, for instance, Bond 1998; Crosthwaite 1999). Equally, however, letters to the professional design and communications press reveal considerable discomfort with the shift of some design consultancies repackaging themselves as brand consultancies (see, for instance, Massey 2000), with many arguing that the need to integrate marketing, strategy and design requires more than mere repositioning but considerable internal restructuring instead.

BRAND AND COMMUNICATIONS CONSULTANCY

From the 1990s representatives of sectors within the creative industries would provide evidence and counter-evidence to maintain their market share. On the other hand, fragmentation of working practices within the creative industries allowed groups to reconstitute their professional aims and the constellation of skills required to achieve these. This was matched by changes in internal brand ownership among clients and perceived developments in terms of the public reception of brand identity.

To focus on just one example as evidence of this shift, one might cite the communications and brand consultancy Circus, founded in 1998. With some 20 employees, Circus was not set up to carry out the specific making of design work themselves; rather, they formed partnerships with a network of some 50 other design studios and consultancies in the creative industries. Their aim, then, was to bridge the gap between 'thinking' and 'doing' – and thus between strategic knowledge and design action – by carrying out design auditing, project development and, more straightforwardly, developing design briefs alongside clients. As such, the design outcomes of these collaborations would be characteristically diverse, according to the desired end-results, and require the consultancy to partner with a broad range of design and communication disciplines. Circus could therefore stray across professional demarcations between design and advertising.

In this way consultancies conspire to broaden the means by which brand values are held, managed and mediated. To return to the example of Circus, just as their working practices were mixed by collaborating with a wide range of other consultancies, so the design platforms on to which solutions were placed varied. In essence, they worked from a model which involved the exploration of the relationship between the brand and its 'community'. Between the two, it took into account notions of 'place' (meaning the forms by which the brand was communicated), 'voice' (being the various details which make up its content) and 'structure' (the systems, both internal and external to a company, that manage the communication of the brand). As such, a complex matrix of relationships linking both the hardware (for instance, anything from a company's corporate logo to its buildings) and software of a client (such as the organizational structure of a company or even the way its products are viewed by its workers) are considered (Mottram 2000).

Shifts away from either advertising or design in their traditional senses towards communications and branding infer that an artefactual outcome (in the shape of an advertisement or a new retail scheme, for instance) does not always predominate. If, after all, the ultimate role of a consultancy in the commercial arena is to maximize profits, then it is incumbent on it to seek the most effective device in order to achieve this. An example of this is in Wolff Olins' development of a brand identity for the mobile telephone group Orange in 1993. In positioning the company in a highly competitive market they identified Orange's proposition as being 'outstanding value' and 'futureproof', supported by five values that were meant to describe the way customers should experience the brand. These were: 'straightforward', 'refreshing', 'dynamic', 'honest' and 'friendly'. The consultancy originated a tightly managed visual identity to reflect this. However, a key feature of the brand positioning was in advising that Orange adopt 'per second billing'. At the time, Orange's competitors all used billing systems which rounded call-time up. The insistence on 'per second billing' not only gave the brand a 'unique selling proposition' it also served to reinforce the brand values in the way the company did its business (Hamilton and Kirby 1999). Thus a 'weightless' solution was employed to consolidate the client's external brand image. In turn, this innovation served to re-invigorate the reputation of Wolff Olins among its own competitors as an organization that delivered imaginative and holistic brand consultancy (Vinogradoff 1999).

In other instances, highly artefactual design interventions may be mobilized in order to create brand awareness internally to a company's representatives so that this may be directly communicated externally. Imagination employs up to 400 professionals to specialize in the creation and management of events, environments and experiences. Their activities include communications planning, retail and leisure design, project management, television productions, films, touring shows and theatrical events. They therefore move fluidly between the upstream elements, such as the staging of corporate events and training, trade shows or conferences for companies, to the downstream public face, such as retail environments and experience centres. In doing so, Imagination strive to achieve a coherent fit between brand identity as understood by a client's representatives and brand image as perceived by end-customers.

One of Imagination's important long-term clients is the car manufacturer Ford. As with all automative producers, Ford experienced increasingly refined competition for market share in the late 1990s. In part this can be attributed to production outstripping overall demand, particularly in Europe. But it was also because by this stage – after nearly a century's development – potential buyers took it for granted that a modern car was safe, well-equipped, economical and reliable. Small cars perform beyond what is actually required, while extended warranties even made the few less-reliable cars still attractive. Within product types, many makes have become almost indistinguishable in their overall look and performance. With a level playing field between manufacturers in terms of product performance, distribution networks and post-purchase back-up, they are therefore forced towards using branding strategies more intensively than ever before. Part of the strategy for ensuring this was massively increased spending on publicity. In the mid-1990s, industry analysis calculated that between £200 and £600 of the cost of a new car was attributable to the manufacturer's advertising budget (Copps 1996). However, given the limitations of advertising as the sole guardian of brand identity, other systems of diffusion had to be sought.

The Aurora Project: developed by Imagination for Ford Europe, Berlin, 1998
Photos: Imagination

Into this context Ford launched the Cougar and the Focus cars in 1998. For this, Ford and Imagination developed the Aurora Project in order to establish awareness of a set of new brand identities for the corporation. The cars were featured on Imagination-designed stands at the major European automobile trade fairs throughout that year. In addition, however, they set up a major event in Berlin during July of that year which was visited by 20,000 representatives of the Ford dealer network of franchises throughout Europe with the aim of instilling brand awareness upstream, among Ford's salespeople.

Staged in a disused factory, visitors entered the site via a 65-metre bridge. A bridge was also used in the trade shows to signify the continuity between the heritage of the Ford brand and its future as embodied in the new Ford Focus. In an area of 25,000 square metres, the Aurora Centre comprised a presentation arena, four areas which featured audio-visual shows, computer stations and sculptural arrangements carrying the brand message (brand 'DNA rooms' in Ford parlance), offices and meeting rooms, a restaurant and kitchens. It was also surrounded by a kilometre-long drive familiarization circuit (Imagination 1998).

In common with all franchise systems, the core corporation's job is not just to market products to customers, but also to provide its distributors with the necessary knowledge and experience of it in order to make all aspects of its provision appear seamless. While part of the Aurora Project was to provide basic product information for its sellers, it was also to train them up in the appropriate 'brandspeak'. To this end the primary Ford brands (being 'design and package', 'driving dynamics', 'ingenuity' and 'accessibility'), which make up its 'DNA', were translated into the artefactual data of the Aurora Centre. Direct experience and knowledge of the cars was layered with visual and textual metaphors which would communicate the emotional appeal of the brand to its human mediators – the dealers themselves. In addition, through careful copywriting of speeches and textual information, they would be given a language of description which could subsequently be used on prospective customers in the selling process (Pickering 1999).

EMPLOYEES AS CONSUMERS

In the case of the Deutsche Börse Group events created by Vamp, we saw how the informal context of the company's party was used to facilitate business networking and reinforce corporate messages. In doing so, the boundaries between the public representation and the private life, both of a company and its individual employees, are relaxed. Guests from other firms are invited to the parties; they are fed something of the inside atmosphere of the group and see its members at play; but this is also within the parameters of the corporate event. Equally, the highly textured, sometimes intimate patina of the events, with their heady mixture of interactive features, encourages subjectivity and, to some degree, self-actualization; but again, this is mustered as an integral aspect of the corporate culture. Paul du Gay (1997: 316-18) lays emphasis on how a consequence of the globalization of finance has meant that, in fact, elements of communications, display and presentation have become more important. Transactional relationships of trust and affability between corporate players are highly valued. Financial networks are therefore, in essence, socio-cultural networks.

This example is also indicative of a shift towards a more complex and, indeed, aestheticized worker–employer relationship. This is where management interest has extended from creating and controlling the basic activities of work (what people do in their jobs) into managing its *meaning* with increasing vitality. Management has always entailed an element of ensuring its 'morality', as Salaman argues, but now 'they [also] seek to define the workers' emotions and relationships' (1997: 239–40). This therefore entails the development and management of 'meanings', 'feelings' and 'beliefs' which are important to the quality of service they deliver (du Gay 1996: 130). This evidences a shift from an authoritarian JFDI (Just Fucking Do It!) culture to one which is calculated to motivate employees into a personal engagement with and self-actualization within the attitudinal framework of the company. Furthermore, since the early 1980s this practice has been supported by the theories of corporate culture consultants such as Peters and Waterman (1982) and Deal and Kennedy (1982). They have advocated a 'hearts and minds' approach to corporate management in which the attitude and voice of employees are sought, won over and made loyal. Corporate culture therefore entails the self-conscious production of particular relationships between workers and the company, its products and services, and between each other.

Similarly, the Aurora Project to promote the Ford brand among its dealers was concerned with building enthusiasms and belief structures around a brand. A key feature, however, was that these ideas were being sold to them, albeit in a more spectacular fashion, as the dealers sell the product to their customers. This system of internal branding might have been done through direct mail or presentations to convey the key messages but, as the project's originators declared, 'it would have fallen short of delivering the essential degree of motivation' (Imagination 1998). So momentarily, members of the producing system become consumers. Again, the scenario of the event focuses on building emotional ties between corporation, product and employees. Within this process, subjectivity, normally associated with consumption, is found within the productive sphere. As du Gay states:

> The relationship to self that the employee is expected to develop builds upon and extends the identity he or she is deemed to have as a consumer: both are represented as autonomous, calculating individuals in search of meaning and fulfilment, looking to 'add value' to themselves in every sphere of existence, whether at work or at play. (1996: 79)

By taking part in the construction and implementation of systems, environments, ideas and values within organizations that communicate to and on behalf of individuals, design consultants are indulging in what Buchanan (1998a: 14) calls 'fourth order design'. In his estimation, this evidences a mature state of design practice. In first- and second-order design, practitioners are engaged in problem-solving towards the creation and implementation of signs, symbols and images ('first-order design') and physical objects ('second-order design'). In 'third-order design', they are involved in a more strategic decision-making mode which originates activities, services and processes for their client. Within 'fourth-order design' they ensure systems for the incorporation and functioning of those decisions. Both the Vamp and Imagination practices aspire to this fourth level: they are instrumental in ascertaining particular management messages but also devise ways of making them work.

The distinction between third and fourth order is fine. The former may provide a set of goals but does not necessarily guarantee their achievement. Fourth-order design, however, proposes enabling a transition with the organization towards those goals. This transition 'depends on discovering the core idea, values, and thought which organize a culture or system and propel it forward in a new search for expression in appropriate activities and products' (Buchanan 1998a: 16). Ultimately, this form of design practice does not exclude the other three; rather, it is hoped that it integrates all four orders in a complex, interdisciplinary approach which extends through preexisting systems of provision and circuits of culture and, in doing so, alters their configuration. It follows, then, that if either Vamp or Imagination were to extend their service further back towards originating and shaping core products for their clients, then they would be covering all four of Buchanan's bases.

AESTHETIC LABOUR

The Vamp and Imagination examples demonstrate the depth to which design culture extends. We have seen how products such as the iPod produce new practices and how, indeed, consumers themselves invent new practices around the product. In these cases the 'rules' of these practices are, arguably, not so overtly formulated as compared with situations where corporations are directly training or influencing their staff. Here, design is mobilized to develop a vocabulary of understanding, either for its sales staff in terms of the products the corporation sells (in the case of Imagination/Ford) or in terms of its core values (in the case of Vamp/Deutsche Börse Group).

At times, highly localized and specific instructions for workers are developed and implemented in order to assist in the materialization of a brand. Hochschild (2003 [1983]: 5–9) wrote of Delta Airlines' insistence that flight attendants *smile*, and smile as if they really meant it. According to her account, the smile was considered to be the company's greatest asset, itself reproduced as a smile-like strip of paint on the nose of each of its planes. She called this very conscious addition to the performance of more mundane tasks of in-flight service 'emotional labour'. Workers were required to act out a feeling that might directly affect the passengers' own sense of comfort and ease, but this 'emotional labour', as she called it, would also communicate the airline's brand.

Similarly, Pettinger (2004) writes of how sales staff in clothing retail are invariably required to wear the same brand clothes as the shop they represent. They should embody that particular style not only through what they put on to go to work, but also in their personal enthusiasm for and knowledge of the clothing lines. By contrast with Hochschild's account, there is a shift from the exposition of a particular feeling that comes from within the emotional resources of the worker to the adoption of an aesthetic disposition. The shop worker literally puts the 'uniform' of the clothing brand on in order to promote it, but also so that the clothes themselves are identified with the kind of people who work there. Witz et al. (2003) explore this notion in relation to a hotel chain that has a strong emphasis on its modern design values. They found that staff were hired not so much according to their experience in hotel work, but more for their potential to have the 'right image' and embody the hotel's designerly values. How they spoke, wore their hair or addressed guests would have to be nuanced towards the overall aesthetic of the organization. Training is directed at fashioning workers as 'animate components of that corporate landscape' (Witz et al. 2003: 49).

In the case of both the retail and hospitality examples, this kind of work is therefore described as 'aesthetic labour'. Work is extended into a signifying practice that integrates cognitive, motivated and embodied dispositions, or, as Bourdieu (1984) would have it, a particular *habitus* is designed, produced and managed. This effect has considerable resonance with a wider discussion of branding that sees it as way of exploiting common social world to create surplus value. Arvidsson (2005) argues that by getting consumers to take an interest in, exhibit or talk about brands, so corporations are effectively harnessing their labour for free in that it is they who are helping to promote them. Brand management is about developing techniques to promote this process.

Thus just as the subjective processes of consuming are melded into the worksphere within aesthetic labour, so the processes of consuming are appropriated towards productive ends.

DESIGNING FOR CREATIVITY

This blurring of the distinctions between consumption practices and the milieux of production has become a recurrent trope in the design of work environments, particularly where creativity is a key value to be promoted. Most iconic among these was the example of St Luke's (Law 1999). This London advertising agency, created through a management buy-out in 1995, dispensed with a traditional office system to provide lockers, cordless phones and shoulder bags for its creatives. The assumption was that advertising requires that teams work on various projects, each of which would have a dedicated room.

Similarly, the new British Airways headquarters near London, designed by Niels Torp and opened in 1998, incorporated several features to encourage less hierarchy and greater flexibility into its working culture. Hence a central walkway linking six small office blocks, which apes an English village street (complete with cobbles and trees), runs through its building. Workers are obliged to use this thoroughfare when arriving or to get to the canteen and thus ease of informal communications is promoted. In such ways, workplaces are designed around a 'geography of circulation … that promotes the "flocking" … of people around particular creative intensities, on the principle [that] innovation often comes from taking ideas across boundaries' (Thrift 2005: 150).

This marshalling of 'creative intensities' also finds its way into urban planning and design within regeneration and place-branding strategies. Here, the creation of cultural or creative quarters (introduced in Chapter 7) within cities or large towns has often been motivated through a tourism strategy. But this has also come from a desire to harness, encourage and communicate the creative resources of urban centres. They engage a mixture of functions and activities that are arranged in a variety of ways. They might restrict themselves to specific stand-alone museums or galleries that nonetheless create a ripple-effect of cultural production and consumption activity around them (e.g. Guggenheim, Bilbao; Tate Modern, London; Baltic, Gateshead), or to larger building complexes that incorporate a range of cultural institutions, such as opera houses, galleries and artists' studios (e.g. Bute Town Docks, Cardiff; Lisbon's Bairro's Alto and Chiado), or include entire quarters or networks of locations featuring galleries, bars, restaurants but also a dense clustering of creative industries such as design studios, ad agencies, media companies, artists' studios and craft workshops (e.g. Temple Bar, Dublin; Northern Quarter, Manchester; Jewellery Quarter, Birmingham; Veemarktkwartier, Tilburg; Lace Market, Nottingham). In 1999, O'Connor counted in the UK some 50 local government authorities developing creative quarters and districts. They have been adopted in local government planning in diverse locations including Lewisham, Folkestone, Nottingham, Dublin and Adelaide (O'Connor 2001).

The overlap of production and consumption in such areas is a conscious element in their planning. Most noteworthy in the formulation of this strategy has been the work of Comedia cultural consultants, whose work has influenced policy in several European and Australian cities. Its founder-director, Charles Landry, traces the historical background to this correspondence to the period of the Viennese Secession (1880–1914), where café culture provided the basis for the networking of ideas within a creative milieu (Landry 2000). A romanticism for such a past is evident elsewhere. Phil Wood, also of Comedia, typifies creative quarters in that they 'combine cutting-edge producers and demanding streetwise consumers in a self-reinforcing 24-hour economy' (Wood 2001). Elsewhere, singling out Manchester's Northern Quarter, he claims that

> so far as the cultural industries are concerned, [production and consumption] are one and the same thing. It is in the very process of consuming sounds, images and symbols of the city that today's creative producers are evolving the sounds, images and symbols which will be tomorrow's creative products … and on it goes in an endless cycle. (Wood 1999)

The aforementioned Northern Quarter in Manchester demonstrates both the strength and brittleness of promoting creative quarters. This area, measuring 56 hectares, is located close to Manchester's city centre and yet this creative quarter typically exhibits much of the louche liminality that has come to be associated with such areas. The building stock is made up mostly of former textile workshops and storage that now house a range of independent bars and restaurants combined with some 105 creative industry firms (Drivers Jonas et al. 2003). A 'Public Art Scheme' was developed from 1996 to encourage artworks that expressed its identity for the area. This was coordinated between the Manchester City Council and the Northern Quarter Association, representing stakeholders in the area (McCarthy 2006). Both its internal workings and its external appearance have been subject to careful scrutiny and an element of managed development (Wansborough and Mageean 2000).

These kinds of development represent, for urban planning studies, something of a 'cultural turn'. Mommaas (2004) believes that the conscious creation or nourishment of these clusters or 'milieux' is becoming an 'archetypal instrument in the urban cultural planning toolbox'. This moves the use of culture in regeneration to a more nuanced level than its more spectacular use in flashy museums, theatre complexes or festival agendas. Here the refined, horizontal relationships of key actors become the main driving force of decision-making as regards regeneration. Thus the facilitation of human and cultural capital go hand in hand. We might even fuse these to produce the term 'human cultural capital'. This would take Bourdieu's term of 'cultural capital' one step further. Instead of an individual's or group's ability to distinguish on the basis of cultural products, human cultural capital involves a distinction on the basis of cultural actors: who is active within a certain milieu, how they act and how their action is harnessed symbolically.

Creative quarters are promoted for their agency in urban regeneration. They come to represent a wider identity of transformation and the entrepreneurial selfhood of the city. In developing brand values for Manchester, Hemisphere Marketing and Design stated in their report that 'Market Street may be the economic engine of Manchester's retail scene but it is the independent and quirky Northern Quarter that is seen as most epitomising "Manchesterness"' (Hemisphere 2003). This is expressed within the values of 'attitude/edge/enterprise'. Thus as the Northern Quarter materializes notions of creativity, difference and entrepreneurialism (or, one might therefore say, reflexive modernization), so this becomes emblematic for the city of Manchester. 'Manchesterness' is mediated through design outcomes and by the wider design culture of the place. Attention is focused towards the 'flows, processes, mobilities and "horizontal" connections' (Edensor 2002: 30) that make up a place and its wider identity. The Northern Quarter's network sociality, its louche avant-gardism and its inhabiting of liminal spaces are made to symbolize that identity. Thus the Manchester case ultimately exhibits an attempt to appropriate a pre-existing designscape into an officially sanctioned marketing ploy.

However, while the creative intensity of the Northern Quarter was judged to provide a useful cue for Manchester's transformation, interesting tensions in the implementation of a design policy for the area emerge. The Northern Quarter was seen by consultants Drivers Jonas, Regeneris Consulting and Taylor Young to Manchester City Council as important to the Manchester Knowledge Capital Prospectus (Manchester City Council 2003). This outlined the centrality of the knowledge economy – with the usual attendant notions of 'innovation' and 'creativity' – to the city. Within this strategy, the Northern Quarter figures for its contribution to this process. They held that 'very few other locations elsewhere in the UK are able to boast this concentration of *both* creative production and cultural consumption' (Manchester City Council 2003). The Northern Quarter (or N4 as it has more recently become) has a strategic role in the wider re-imagining of Manchester. Hence it was argued that 'The ambition is for much wider national and international recognition of the unique qualities of the N4. The N4 will be increasingly seen and promoted by all our partners as a fundamental part of a growing global city' (Drivers Jonas et al. 2003). However, in the detail of their regeneration recommendations, they were understandably coy, wishing to maintain its edge and atmosphere. They argued that:

> Certain aspects should, however, remain unchanged. The Northern Quarter will retain its own distinctive identity as a location for the independent sector, where residents of Manchester and visitors can experience something different and soak up the atmosphere of a truly 'working quarter'. (Manchester City Council 2003)

Thus recommendations for small-scale improvements to lighting, street furniture and signage were made. But developments involving larger-scale building schemes were eschewed. These were seen to be a threat to the maintenance of that area's 'distinctive' and 'unique' character.

This awareness of the need for sensitive intervention or non-intervention no doubt indirectly stems from the widely understood threat of gentrification of such areas (Zukin 1989; Lloyd 2006). In short, the trend involves de-industrialization, bohemianization, gentrification and then the inflation of land values. The original trail-setters, ironically, are then squeezed out as rents become too high for these creative types of people.

The radical urban planning group based in Rotterdam, Urban Unlimited, takes this argument a step further by arguing for 'free zones' in cities. They suggest that for creative milieux to thrive, areas should in fact be left deliberately unplanned. In other words, 'cities can be saved from design in the name of creativity' (Thackara 2005b: 271). Furthermore, however, they argue that, in any case, the creative milieux are not so much arranged around places as around networks (Urban Unlimited 2004). The Northern Quarter, judged in this context, may be promoted on the romantic myth of place-bound network sociality rather than a more open understanding of the dynamics of creative industries.

This precarious balance between human capital and urban fabric, or, in other words, creativity and its materialization, has a long pedigree. The notion of identifying and promoting certain cultural milieux within a framework of urban policy harks back to the 1980s. In the UK this was formulated by a number of Labour-dominated councils (significantly, the Greater London Council), while in the USA the not-for-profit organization Partners for Livable Spaces focused on developing urban cultural infrastructures as a way of building local communities, citizenship and economies. Within this, Stevenson notes that an attempt is made to 'reconceptualize cultural activity as encompassing dynamic and pervasive processes rather than as a static range of artistic objects and products' (2004: 123). In other words, the new emphasis is on the social, knowledge networks that produce cultural activity rather than on the privileging of certain aesthetic outcomes within a hierarchical format. More recently, of course, this thinking emerged in the work of Charles Landry in the UK (2000) and Richard Florida in the USA (2002) to play a highly influential role that brought the promotion of cultural, social and knowledge capital together under a single rubric within policy circles.

This turn away from hierarchy and from objects and products means that the core identity of creativity has to be rendered invisible or virtual. The flagship or landmark building that works as a trigger for a place-brand in other locations (again, for example, Bilbao's Guggenheim) cannot play its operational part here. Instead, the demands for a liminal aesthetic, where creativity might always be about to happen, mean that the Northern Quarter will always be required to slum it.

SOCIAL PARTICIPATION AND DESIGN ACTIVISM

All the examples explored so far in this chapter involve the use of design within relatively rarefied corporate or civic contexts. Their ultimate aim was in enhancing productivity through, basically, the inculcation of particular values into a specific labour force or population. Acceptance and performance of these values involved a balance between disciplining and autonomy. On the one hand, they had to be embodied. Whether it was wearing the clothing correctly or using the right vocabulary, their dispositions and sensibilities had to be agreed, adopted and acted upon. On the other hand, they also encompassed and were dependent on a shared sense of enterprise and creativity. With possibly the exception of the Northern Quarter example, the processes of development and implementation of these values was largely a top-down affair involving the use of expert consultants to determine what they might be, how they might be mobilized and who would be most appropriate to carry them out.

The movement of design into Buchanan's (1998a: 14) 'fourth order', where designers are involved in developing the implementation of management strategies, resonates with the idea of design culture as 'encultured practice'. This understanding of the term, which has been introduced in Chapter 1, is one of several notions of design culture as action, but it perhaps best captures an ambition towards greater complexity both in terms of the outcome and the interdisciplinarity of design practice. Maier-Aichen refers to a 'Utopia of less … *but better*' that requires creatives not only to create compelling design products, graphics or interiors, but also 'to find innovative ways of communication, materialising and dematerialising things' (2004: 10). The emphasis here is on developing design as a transformative process or as a way of reconfiguring routine and outlooks.

Design culture as encultured practice may also extend beyond the orchestration of new consumer–producer relationships within corporate frameworks, to a process that works to transform everyday, public lives and aspirations. In the UK, Huddersfield-based 'creativity activists' Heads Together work strategically as catalysts by putting communities at the centre of the decision-making process in the regeneration of their localities. Their role is not in deciding the end-form for improving neighbourhoods, but in facilitating the

interface between end-user and a constellation of creative experts. This involves the flexible, slow-moving negotiations of relationships and expectations so that ordinary people become empowered to take a lead in the decisions over their environments. They are media-agnostic in that they do not prescribe a particular creative platform in response to situations; rather, whichever is most appropriate to address a context and issue will emerge from discussions. It might be the foundation of a community radio station or making a film to represent the lives and aspirations of a neighbourhood. Here, creative practice is about socially engaged, highly networked activities that are process- rather than object-centred.

The Methleys comprises 300 terraced houses in a suburb of Leeds in the UK. The area suffered from an unstable and transitory residential population, with attendant problems of crime and vandalism. With no gardens, the only outdoor space is the streets themselves, though these were largely considered as thoroughfares rather than the meeting-place of a community. From 1994, neighbours had begun to develop street activities during the summer months, including, in 1995, an outdoor movie screening. In the summer of 1996, local activists making up the Methleys Neighbourhood Action Group, aided by members of Heads Together, found funding and sponsorship from a mixture of public and private institutions to lay 800 square meters of turf through the neighbourhood's main street. This created a temporary 'park space' for a weekend, during which the 'Methleys Olympics', displays and even pony rides took place. The aim of this was not as an end in itself, but to open up an imaginative sense of possibility among residents (Sinclair 2006).

With a new feeling of neighbourhood vitality achieved, the next step was to establish the area as a 'home zone'. This concept had existed for over 25 years in Germany and the Netherlands. It is where neither pedestrians nor vehicles have priority, but street-use is reconfigured for neighbourhood conviviality. Heads Together's new role was in heading a campaign to establish the Methleys as Britain's first Home Zone. They were commissioned to make a film about the concept, while they also coordinated neighbourhood involvement in persuading the local council and national government to fund the initiative. The film has subsequently been used by hundreds of community groups in their campaigns for safer, better-designed residential streets (Sinclair 2006). By 1998, the UK government had pledged £30 million to establish 60 more home zones nationally (Biddulph 2003).

The Methleys (above) turfed for a week, 1996; (below) launch party of Methleys Home Zone, 2002; (opposite) seating and signage, Methleys Home Zone
Photos: Methleys Neighbourhood Action; Empics; Lizzie Coombes/Heads Together; Katy Hayley/ Heads Together

The Methleys' home zone itself was achieved through a range of design features, including: gateway treatments which incorporate custom-made artwork that make non-local drivers aware of the changed environment; the use of road paving to indicate a shared pedestrian space; and traffic-calming measures that also functioned as communal garden space. A detailed survey of residents' attitudes and changed uses 'before' and 'after' the Methleys' home zone's development provided evidence of improved quality of life for residents (Layfield et al. 2003). The issue of improved community relations was less evident in the survey. However, it should be recognized that engaging residents in developing ideas, and through that process creating a problem-solving community, took place over several years and may not be evident through a 'snapshot' survey. While a reduction in crime or road traffic accidents is easily measurable and discernible, attitudinal change can remain more hidden. However, it is perhaps significant that it now has its own website, and street events continue to be part of its annual calendar.

The emphasis in all of the Heads Together projects is on the transformation of communities as much through the end-user participation in the development process as through the end result. Within such processes, the role of the designer is altered towards a facilitative approach. This should not necessarily disempower the designers, whereby their role is simply to carry forward, project manage and materialize the unfiltered desires of groups or individuals. Instead, their expert role is to locate and build on their potential, to open up possibilities, to challenge the collective imagination and to help in the fashioning of new dispositions. In doing so it reconnects people, practices and place.

Through 25 years of activity Heads Together evolved their own working methods, moving through a range of creative practices, including theatre, photographic projects, radio production, curating and programming community events through to facilitating and managing design projects as we have just seen. This kind of socially motivated design draws the large majority of its revenue stream from non-commercial sources such as arts funding, local or regional government regeneration budgets, European Union grants or charitable organizations. The flexibility of skills and approach of a group like Heads Together matches its range of supporters and their expectations. There are pragmatic demands of such work in demonstrating relevance and effectivity to potential demanders. Nonetheless, such work is also driven by political desires that not only aim for democratic engagement with the processes and outcomes of creative practices among citizens, but in these, also seek a transformative effect on their everyday outlooks. As such, this may be termed as 'activist design'.

Design activism may be identified and interpreted in distinct but overlapping ways. Thorpe (2008) lays emphasis on design activism in the production of artefacts within social movements such as campaigning graphics or products that proclaim adherence to ecological values. Fuad-Luke (2009) views it as a way of shifting the aims and methodologies of design so that its processes are adapted to the foregrounding of social, environmental or political values over commercial ones. DiSalvo (2012) discusses the possibility of design as being 'adversarial' in the way it can create an iterative set of contestations such as objects that challenge the dominant status quo of urban life, or even provide citizen tools for revealing its more harmful aspects. Markussen (2013: 38), drawing on Rancière (2004, 2010), sees a role for design activism that, 'is not a boycott, strike, protest, demonstration, or some other political act, but lends its power of resistance from being precisely a *designerly* way of intervening into people's lives.' As it involves the development of artefacts that exist in real time and space, it is situated within everyday contexts and processes of social and economic life and impacts on it. It is nonetheless disruptive and destabilizing.

The example of the turfing-over of a street by Heads Together may be interpreted within all the frameworks of design activism given in the last paragraph. It seems most forcefully, however, that the way it disrupts the routinely accepted notion of the street (as a place to park cars and as a conduit for them between places beyond it) leads on to an intervention on the affective domain of its users. This is a designerly intervention. By rapidly and dramatically turning it into a secure space for play, alternative bodily dispositions in the street emerge (children turn cartwheels or adults put out picnic blankets). Outlooks – in terms of what the street could be – are changed not just through representation but also by physical engagement.

CONCLUSION

The motivations of the creative practitioners discussed in this chapter are diverse: corporate clients may afford designers large budgets to realize their creative ambitions; within local regeneration strategies, activist designers might be able to nudge on their political aspirations. However, the examples discussed in this chapter all show how design can be used to blur the line between above- and below-the-line elements and between traditional conceptions of producers and consumers.

In the case of the Deutsche Börse and Ford examples, we saw how employees are, in a way, reconfigured as consumers of their own organizations. Events are designed as ways of informing employees about their products or reinforcing a sense of corporate belonging. Visual and verbal cues are worked into these so that employees adopt a common language of description, or even shared enthusiasms and attitudes within that corporate culture. In its turn, this process turns labour into an aestheticized practice where the tastes, bodily dispositions and emotional expressions of workers are also drawn into and become part of the brand. Here very personal attributes of behaviour and identity – traditionally associated with the subjectivity of sovereign consumers – become appropriated into the sphere of work.

The use of design to signify and promote certain forms of labour and attract interest is also discernible in the creation of so-called 'creative quarters'. Again, design is mobilized to produce a certain, refined milieu where the distinctions between producing and consuming again are, to a degree, concealed. In a bid to encourage the clustering of creative workers in urban centres, a mix of work and leisure spaces are planned that are attractive to cultural intermediaries, including bars and restaurants, but also appropriate workspaces. We saw in the example of Manchester's Northern Quarter how a careful decision-making process was applied to the public realm in order to preserve a certain air of avant-garde 'edginess' for the area. In turn, this also fed into the city's brand identity. In this case, and similar ones, creative quarters fulfil a double function: they provide locations for the fostering of enterprise and communicate certain values of modernity about a place.

The development of the urban realm in the Methleys in Leeds demonstrates a further example of how design takes it beyond the fashioning of objects, images or spaces and into the domain of people's outlooks and experience of the world. By involving members of a neighbourhood in a slow-moving, decision-making process over the design of their streets, the results are not just an improved quality of life for dwellers, but also, it is hoped, a transformation in their aspirations and demands as citizens. Ultimately, in all these cases it should be noted that design objects are active agents. They function materially within the social relations that make up a corporation, a workplace or a neighbourhood. They also work to signify, or articulate, these various assemblages. In the next chapter, we shall pursue these ideas of assemblages, articulations and networks further.

CHAPTER 11

NETWORKS AND MOBILE TECHNOLOGIES

Smartphones, tablets and laptop computers contribute to the substantial changes in social practices in contemporary life. Chapter 11 considers how these mobile technologies are active in the creation of networked patterns of commerce and the everyday world. We review how the growth of mobile technology runs in parallel with specific economic arrangements of the late capitalist world and the information age. Design is a foundational element in this, not just in the differentiation of products and services but also in the control and organization of content provision by third parties. We see how leading corporations are involved in scripting or the configuration of metadata for other designers to use and the importance of intellectual property rights in maintaining their monopolies. From a user perspective, we see how mobile technologies engage a range of hybrid spaces and bodily dispositions and activities. Actor-network theory (ANT) is explored and related concepts explained to help us understand this fluidity of social practices that exists through and around mobile technologies.

Occasionally, to pass the time on a rail journey, I play a banal game I made up. I call it 'smartphone noughts and crosses'. If I see three people sat in a row, placed either horizontally or vertically down the carriage, using their iPhones, I give myself two points; if the row is broken by someone with another brand of smartphone, I just get one point. I invariably score quite highly.

These regular commuters sit and manipulate information with their fingers, performing intricate gestures as eyes flicker, frowns appear or faces light up to meet the information they conjure onto their screens. Muscle-memory builds as they open up apps to play video games, view share prices or book additional rail tickets. They peer at maps, check their email, scroll through their music list, browse through photos. They search for a forgotten piece of information on the internet, watch a movie clip or text someone to let them know that the train is running late. A new prosthesis, these handheld devices take them to another place.

Between their world and mine (I always choose to sit in the quiet carriage where passengers are asked to not to make cellphone calls), a simple switch mutes the iPhone. This is a design feature that, in itself, is the subject of lively discussion on internet blogs. Located on the side of the 3GS model of the iPhone, you'll find a satisfyingly clunky switch that turns its speaker off. As you do this a pictogram of a bell appears on your screen and the iPhone vibrates to reassure you that muting has been achieved. The 4S model's mute switch is disappointingly smaller. Nonetheless, this detail splendidly marks a boundary between the analogue and digital environments that are occupied while on the move.

But in *their* world – right now – where are they? Are their imaginations immersed in toil or pleasure? Which way are they orientated? Toward their work or their homes?

The train might be taking these commuters across the physical boundaries between work and home. But meanwhile, their mobile technologies may be blurring those distinctions.

IPHONES AND SMARTPHONES

The impact of the iPhone in particular and smartphones in general is fairly unmissable. The year 2012 was dubbed 'the year of the smartphone' as mobile web usage jumped by 82 per cent in the USA (Nielsen 2012: 3) while smartphone sales in China also grew by 137 per cent (Wang 2012).

The integration of mobile telephony and messaging, locational services, photographic, sound and computing into one handheld device has afforded a range of novel uses. In turn, this has produced new sectors in the development of digital products and combinations and dependencies between these sectors. The iPhone's general design features should be regarded in the context of a longer product evolution of mobile telephony. But the iPhone also included a number of refinements that made it particularly distinctive.

The first iPhone was unveiled at the Macworld convention in San Francisco in January 2007. It was launched onto the US market six months later, with the UK, France and Germany following in November of that same year. It was by no means the first smartphone to hit the market. Indeed, the concept dates back to 1973 when Theodore Paraskevakos introduced the idea of combining data processing, visual information and telephony while working for the multinational technology company SITA. The BellSouth Cellular Corporation's Simon Personal Communicator, marketed in 1994, combined telephony, fax and email with simple applications such as a calculator, calendar and an electronic note pad. In 1996 the Nokia Communicator provided a 'clamshell' design that opened up to feature a QWERTY keyboard and a high-resolution display. In 2000 Ericsson released the R380 Smartphone which greatly reduced the weight and size of such apparatus and converged a personal digital assistant (PDA) with the functions of a mobile phone (West and Mace 2010). This was the first mobile phone to be called a 'smartphone'.

A number of features distinguished the iPhone from its antecedents, though. While to the seasoned iPhone user it may be rather obvious to list these, they need drawing out in order for us to move to a sophisticated understanding of the relationship of their design and social significance.

First, although other providers were often offering the apparatus for free to encourage users to tie into their associated mobile phone networks, the first Apple phone retailed at $599. This reflected their confidence that it would be a 'must-have' device for early adopters. Previously, mobile coverage providers largely dictated what handsets were made, their design and cost (Vogelstein 2008). Apple had turned the tables in a contract with AT&T to foreground their design approach as a producer of both hardware and software. This high-entry cost was reduced to $399 within a year, but in the USA users were still tied into a two-year network provision with AT&T costing a minimum $1,400. This allowed a pre-paid mobile internet plan which encouraged casual usage. Thus a combination of a design-led approach to the handset and its capabilities along with a consumer payment plan adjusted the wireless carrier to producer relationship while also providing a new framework for its use.

Second, then, the iPhone delivered superior online capability through its Safari web-browser. Prior to this, the most successful converged phones were business-oriented email devices led by RIM Blackberry where mobile internet usage was less distinguished. In other words, the iPhone provided a platform rather than a phone, prompting technology journalist Lev Grossman to observe that 'computing doesn't belong just in cyberspace, it needs to happen here, in the real world, where actual stuff happens. The iPhone gets applications like Google Maps out onto the street, where we really need them' (Grossman 2007).

Third, the iPhone included in its functioning a high-end iPod music and video player linked to the iTunes system that had already been launched with the iPod. Its 480 × 320 pixel screen resolution allowed for a larger image than any other model in 2007 (though this was later superseded by Samsung). Thus it came ready for users to take advantage of Apple's content network and, subsequently, third-party content through applications.

Fourth, again while the touchscreen was not an Apple invention – Samsung and LG in Korea had already begun incorporating this into their phones by 2007 – the iPhone fully integrated the touchscreen without a stylus or retractable keyboard. Apple added the ability to pan through, stretch or enlarge images, to flick through pages or change the screen orientation by turning the iPhone sideways. Using it became a more bodily act both in allowing you to take or find 'your' information anywhere and in the extended range of physical interaction with its information that it facilitated. Those gestures of iPhone use, performed by modern commuters of this world, unite. The user is not an 'appendage of the machine' as Karl Marx and Friedrich Engels had it (Marx and Engels 2004 [1848]). It's not fully the other way around either: the machine (or read here 'the smartphone and its network') and the user exist together.

CYBORGS

Historically speaking, the concept of this fusion of human and machine has been well-established as a trope in science-fiction film and literature. It may, for example, be found in Mary Shelley's *Frankenstein*, first published in 1818. More recently in the popular imagination, the television series *The Six Million Dollar Man* from 1973, films like *Blade Runner* (1982) and *RoboCop* (1987) or Isaac Asimov's 1976 short story 'The Bicentennial Man' posited the idea of bodies that were enhanced by cybernetic additions or were entirely synthesized – thus, technically, being androids. However, the possibility that the blending of cybernetics and organisms (hence, the term 'cyborg') could be made real was claimed by Clynes and Kline (1960). In theorizing possibilities for the NASA space exploration programme they suggested that 'Altering man's bodily functions to meet the requirements of extraterrestrial environments would be more logical than providing an earthly environment for him in space … Artifact-organism systems which would extend man's unconscious, self-regulatory controls are one possibility' (1960: 26).

The cyborg idea allows for interesting flights of fancy in the fictional world, speculations on space travel, explorations of bodily limits in artistic practices or spectacular advances in medical restorative technologies. It is also interesting to step back and reflect on how everyday mobile digital technologies act to produce cyborg-like ways of living. How do smartphones or tablets conspire in the reconfiguration of daily habits? Where is their efficiency as instruments located? How does the design of these instruments effectively re-design the body?

In her far-sighted essay 'A Cyborg Manifesto: Science, Technology, and Socialist-Feminism in the Late 20th Century', Donna Haraway (2006 [1985]) considered social changes that were coming about as life developed through digital technologies into the post-industrial era. The text primarily sought to push socialist debate beyond traditional Marxist thinking where the subject can only be known through labour, contest feminist discourse that assumes an essential quality of being female, and counter psychoanalysis that is so rooted in familial narratives. All of these suggest a fixed set of understandings about gender, experience and identity. Instead, her philosophical position was aligned with a flexible, polyvocal, hybrid and polymorphous idea of identity and lived experience. Thus she begins by describing three loosenings of boundaries in the information age, these being: between human and animal; between animal-human and machine; and between the physical and non-physical.

Seeing this broadly stated scenario as a backdrop, it is useful to then recount her observations on the material conditions of an information age. Of the machine, she notes the progressive miniaturization and ubiquity of electronic gadgetry so that it becomes practically invisible. Further, the artefact becomes absorbed into the qualities of networks and systems. Thus, in terms of objects, she states that 'one must not think of essential properties, but in terms of design, boundary constraints, rates of flows, systems logics, costs of lowering constraints' (Haraway 2006[1985]: 129).

When one thinks of smartphones in the context of this sentence, their physical detailing becomes subordinated to their role as interfaces such as their efficiency as tools in accessing and delivering information, their ability to work in different locations or their accessibility for various software systems. Haraway also notes the transformation of work in which the limited working day as a clear timeframe is undermined. She uses the idea of 'home working', itself derived from cottage industries, as being a particular way by which, particularly for women, the locus of labour is dispersed. This is meant literally but also symbolically as notions of caring and stewardship get borrowed back into the work sphere. (You may wish to refer back to the discussion of 'emotional labour' in Chapter 10.)

Behind and within Haraway's argument is an intriguing sense of both oppression and liberation. On the one hand, she points out how information technologies and this cyborg notion come through military developments and strategies and are absorbed into systems of control and surveillance that are also employed through bureaucratic structures. Logging on, being connected and available makes you visible to others at a distance. On the other hand, by understanding these processes that are afoot, alternative possibilities for political mobilization that use the same technologies may be generated. Mobile technologies connect people around concerns and provide a place to generate new actions. However, throughout her essay Haraway emphasizes a sense of mutability and flexibility in identity and everyday practices. The cyborg, as a fusion of the technological and the biological, consistently blurs distinctions. Equally, as we shall see in the next section, the software tools, design activities and business arrangements that exist around smartphone and tablet applications move between closed and open systems, and between commercial control and facilitating creative freedom.

CLOSED AND OPEN NETWORKS

As with the iPod, while the iPhone appeared to offer a panoply of uses and content access, it was also a relatively closed system in its software. Zittrain (2008) points out the irony that when the Apple CEO introduced the Apple II computer in 1977 it was completely reprogrammable by users. Indeed, much of its success is ascribed to a spreadsheet application called VisiCalc that was created by a third party, Dan Bricklin, a year or so later. By contrast, the iPhone does not allow any reprogramming. Indeed, Apple did not even allow third-party web applications on the first iPhone. In March 2008, its proprietary software development kit for designing apps was released. These could only be marketed through Apple's App Store, which was launched four months later.

While designers could set the price of the apps they created, Apple took a 30 per cent cut on their sales through their App Store and retains the right to approve or disapprove them. The app design industry itself mushroomed with more than 125,000 app developers operating by September 2009 and with 85,000 apps available for download from the App Store (Rowan 2010: 2). By January 2012 there were over 500,000 available; meanwhile, by mid-2011, the Google Android market had reached 250,000 apps (Mureta 2012: 8). As of July 2012, the world's largest free app store, GetJar, boasted on its website over 458,000 registered developers with over 613,000 apps and games available for Android devices. Furthermore, alongside this growth has been the establishment of a range of well over 70 software platforms for their design, each with their applicability to different devices and distinct capabilities. And so the statistics go on.

The point here is to take note not only of the rapid growth of this design sector, but also of the varied nature of the smartphone and tablet app development tools and outlets. Within this, the issue of the degree of proprietary control over development and distribution by the different corporations (Apple, Google, Nokia, Palm, Samsung etc.) was varied, with Apple maintaining a higher level of jurisdiction over these.

For app designers themselves the degree of profitability of their products is precarious, with only the top 10 per cent actually making significant amounts of money (Laurs cited in Rowan

iPhones and Apple software in use
Photos: Guy Julier

2010: 7). Start-up costs for the creative development of apps are very low: Apple, for instance, does not charge for its software development kit and asks only a small amount for testing the app. These two points put together mean that app design is invariably undertaken as a 'sideline' to other professional activities and, moreover, not necessarily by design or even app design specialists with particular training in the crafting of these wares.

The app icon functions like a book cover, as something to be discovered, but with what's behind it as being more important. This sector of design bears another resemblance with the book publishing industry where capital costs for the originator are low and profits really only reside at the top 10 per cent end. Equally, a large number of 'enthusiast' writers feed into the low profit or loss making remainder of its profile (Thompson 2010). While distribution mechanisms have changed with the advent of ebooks, this structure in terms of origination continues. A significant difference with book publishing is that app designers can rely on consumer feedback to tweak and upgrade their product content. All apps invite customer reviews. Thus they are in a continual, iterative loop of product development. Part of this, rather like fiction writers, is achieved by encouraging a porosity between professional and amateur practices. App design may be both a commercial pursuit or a hobby. In turn, this creates a dense network of practitioners working across digital platforms, supported by online discussion boards and advice websites as well as the design software itself. The design business model for Apple and other platforms is in encouraging and facilitating high numbers of app designers to be involved in producing niche products. A fragmented but high-volume range of suppliers where their investment is relatively low-risk in terms of capital matches a global marketplace of heterogeneous desires.

In all aspects, smartphones, their software infrastructures, their apps (not just the products themselves but also the tools and employment base for design and distribution) and the entire business models that drive them exist relationally to each other. They occur as parts of a web of contingencies and dependencies, with each part in a process of 'becoming' as continual modifications are made, new content is delivered and new uses are discovered. Being peraps the most controlled and stringent, Apple's 'lash up' of these also makes their strategy and objects the most easily readable. In turn, this feeds its intensive, recognizable brand image.

CULTURAL RELATIVISM AND TECHNOLOGICAL CHANGE

Before proceeding, a brief word on cultural and technological relativism needs inserting here. So far, I have largely been talking about smartphones in the global marketplace but outside the Far East. The history of smartphone development in Korea and Japan has been markedly different: mobile internet browsing has been much more commonplace in these countries for longer. Tolerance of low internet bandwidth in wireless services has previously been higher in these countries. The design and content of smartphone applications have been highly refined – indeed, simplified – as appropriate to this situation. This is coupled with the fact that the Far Eastern markets required more language-specific content, in turn cutting out Western content and promoting culturally- and linguistically-targeted mobile usages. By contrast, Western developers were attempting to transplant fixed-line levels of richness and complexity to the mobile market before its infrastructure could actually cope with these, making the shortcomings of content obvious. Interestingly, while in the West smartphone usage only took off once that high-performance mobile services had been attained, the reverse was true for Japan and Korea. The limitations of the technology and its content led to much greater adoption of mobile internet browsing and, therefore, smartphones (Funk 2001).

The examples of Japan and Korea demonstrate how even for such global products as smartphones, the marketplace, and therefore design, can be segmented. This effectively works against global corporations having a 'one design fits all' approach. But this doesn't deter their efforts to monopolize sectors on a global scale.

THE COMPETITION OF MONOPOLIES

Corporations like Apple are constantly trying to achieve maximum market share within the bounds of a legal setting that regulates against the monopolization of these. This is demonstrated by the litigation cases that are brought between corporations against each other or by states working in the public interest in their efforts to show up any evidence of unfair trading. An example of this was the ongoing case taken by the US Department of Justice in 2012 and 2013 against Apple Inc., and publishers Penguin and Macmillan regarding the alleged price-fixing of e-books to squeeze Amazon out of the market.

At the same time, and more pertinent to the discussions of this book, the defence of copyright, trade marks, design patents (which cover the look and feel of a product) and utility patents (which cover technological innovations) is of immense importance to such corporations. Again, Apple has taken out several litigations to defend these. They include, for example, an unsuccessful case brought against New York City in 2008 for its use of a 'big apple' logo to cover its sustainability programme.

Apple CEO Steve Jobs put his own name to over 300 patents for Apple in his lifetime, most of which were design patents. This even included the glass staircases to be found in Apple stores and white plastic power adapters for Macintosh computers. Jobs' enthusiasm to appear on design patents may be read as a way to market the idea of the corporation's 'visionary leader'. However, a patent may be invalidated if it can be shown that a name put to it wasn't involved in the product's development. More likely, this shows his deep involvement in much of the detail of Apple's design (Helft and Carter 2011).

The famed secrecy that surrounds Apple, its Cupertino headquarters in California, the work of Steve Jobs and its head of design, Jonathan Ive, certainly adds mystique to the Apple brand. Apple employees are bound by strict commercial secrecy requirements (Cheng 2012). Meanwhile the release or announcement of a new Apple product is made via highly scripted and staged 'events' such as at the annual Macworld Fair and Conference. In the electronic industries, the careful managing of corporate image through the strategic timing of product releases also helps to boost share value (Aspara 2010). This secrecy also helps Apple to maintain market position by keeping its design and business model innovations ahead of those of its competitors. It allows their products to become established and commonplace before competitors can catch up with similar models. This isn't just in terms of the look and feel of an object, though these are highly important; it is also about establishing routine usage of all the related software features, such as the App Store or iTunes.

On a wider level, these practices evidence a key feature of neoliberal commercial practice, namely, the competition of monopolies (Lash 2010: 113). The liberal period of capitalism (roughly from the 1850s through to the late 1970s) was characterized by a diversity of firms whose accumulated value took the form of property and capital. Property law was important to this period. The more recent neoliberal period sees the expansion and consolidation of many more firms onto a global scale where their value is defended by intellectual property law. Put more crudely, this may be summed up illustratively by the following examples: Samsung v Apple; Sony Ericsson v Philips; Ford v Toyota; Coca-Cola v Pepsi; Unilever v Procter & Gamble; Zara v Benetton; Exxon v BP v Shell; Virgin Airways v British Airways; Goldman Sachs v Morgan Stanley; Wal-Mart v Tesco and so on.

In all of these, the competition is not just between products or services for market share but between brands. Each of these has a monopoly over, for example, specific supply chains and/or particular distribution systems, software platforms, retail networks and/or other features. Some of these may be facilitated by straightforward financial and contractual arrangements. But it is hardly surprising that the rise of neoliberal capitalism has been accompanied by the rise of intellectual property law since the late 1970s. For these corporations, design and technological innovations form important elements of this monopoly system and have to be legally protected.

There is a paradox of how, in the neoliberal period, competition between businesses, now on a global scale, has increased and become more intensive while 'nearly every industry is concentrated into fewer and fewer hands' (Foster et al. 2011: 1). This is felt at all levels of commerce: manufacturing, the retail trade, transportation, information and finance. It has transformed our high streets and shopping malls, the banking system, our food systems and the very look and experience of work and leisure. It has also added new roles for design.

In helping to maintain monopolies, design claims territories. So how does it do this?

SCRIPTS AND METADATA

Products are scripted (Akrich 1995; Fallan 2008). They are inscribed with intended use and meaning. The script is like an 'instruction manual' that is embedded into the object. The blank screen on an iPhone suggests that it should be switched on. The recessed, circular button beneath is the only responsive feature at this point. The screen lights up. A *trompe l'oeil* effect of a recessed groove appears (prior to iOS7 in 2013) with the words 'slide to unlock' and an arrow on a 'button' pointing from left to right. You're in and now you are already used to manipulating the touchscreen. A series of icons appear on the screen that invite further pressing. And on you go. Thus, how this smartphone is to be used is inscribed into the design of its interface. This scripting of use, so particular to the Apple design, therefore establishes routines and habits.

Design also works to script the way a corporation and its brand are organized across a range of sites and products. In the context of the former, these *meta*-scripts would include the design of corporate identity or brand manuals that are used to ensure adherence where the design is then subcontracted for deployment. Additionally, franchising operations involve the deployment of strict guidelines on product and service delivery. The design of uniforms and equipment as well as training and management guidelines conspires in the tight scripting for the franchisee.

A similar example is the creation of 'metadata' in the Hollywood movie industry (Sutton 2009). Since the 1940s, Hollywood has experienced a shift from centralized film production where the making of a film took place within a studio to complex networks of outsourcing. Furthermore, intellectual property rights have also extended into franchisee arrangements that produce such things as television spin-offs, comic-books and graphic novels, fast food tie-ins, gifts, toys or video games. Metadata provide a digital coding for subcontractees and franchisees to employ on whatever aspect of the movie or related merchandise they are working. Here a film's aesthetics, such as its colour pallet, its key forms or its sound quality, are synthesized into a digital package that guides the detailing.

The bigger and more powerful a corporation is, the more investment it is able to put into devising these scripts and their legal protection. In this way, design is intensified. It plays an increased role in ensuring the coherence and monopoly of a corporation and its products that is distributed across networks. Again, this isn't just about its 'look' and its ability to be recognized: it also conspires in the legally enforceable differentiation of that corporation from its competition by helping to create a monopoly over its particular way of providing products and services.

At the same time, it is well to remember that there is a co-dependency between the corporation and the networks of content designers and innovators who are associated with it. Studies have emerged with regard to the role of digital technologies in reconfiguring knowledge networks (e.g. Castells 2001) and the development of 'communities of practice' (e.g. Tuomi 2002; Thackara 2005a). For the corporation, the metadata afford sufficient space for entrepreneurs and enthusiasts to bring their resources together or to work in ways that bring the value of the core corporation while facilitating the tools or equipment for them to act with sufficient independence that harness their creativity. This is where a discussion of *agencement* and *dispositif* may be useful.

AGENCEMENT AND DISPOSITIF

In their multiple functions, smartphones link a range of practices, each having their particular associational supporting networks. However, the smartphone is not a static node in these. It is, in itself, designed to be in constant development and, indeed, its user is expected to always be finding new uses for it. It is scripted, but in such a way that this doesn't make it immutable.

As we have seen, the design of smartphone or tablet apps is rarely a finished process. Upgrades take place as customer feedback is responded to or new content possibilities become apparent. Equally, the smartphone is a platform for which the user constantly discovers new functions by adding apps, finding fresh ways to store information, interact with others and so on. As such, it is, as Knorr Cetina (2001) might describe, an unfinished object. It is unfinished because it is constantly subject to an upgrade or replacement with a newer model. It is unfinished because its functioning is only possible through its combination with other objects, technologies, networks, people or corporations. It is unfinished because it is always open to new possibilities. Its value is constantly *in potentia* but also defined by the possibilities it promises. It is in an endless state of becoming.

A shorthand way of describing this quality is as an *agencement*. This French word translates both as 'equipment' and 'arrangement', 'fitting' or 'fixing' (Phillips 2006; Mackenzie 2009); or to fold these two meanings together, we might think of something as an 'agent' – it is an entity but it also transforms other things. The use of this term in social philosophy derives from the work of Deleuze and Guattari (1988), who see the term relationally. It is the arrangement of something in relation to something else that gives it its sense.

In terms of its meaning and how it functions, it is more productive to see the iPhone as an *agencement* than Foucault's use of *dispositif*, though the distinction is useful here. Foucault (2007) uses this expression to denote 'apparatus', which carries a stronger implication of an ability to control (Legg 2011). Human activity follows prescription in this sense rather than inhabiting, exploiting or realizing possibilities.

It is interesting to bring together this distinction between the two terms of *agencement* and *dispositif* with my earlier discussion regarding the corporate activities to secure a monopoly and the role of design in scripting. By controlling the way the iPhone apps are designed and distributed through their proprietary software development kit and its App Store, Apple creates a stringent script for the realization of subsequent related products. In effect, at the production end their concern is with apparatus or *dispositifs*. In a broader sense, however, there is a sense of *agencement* also functioning here as app designers share knowledge between themselves and with their publics that in turn changes them. At the consumer end, the iPhone becomes an *agencement*, a piece of equipment that also carries arrangements with other equipment. Apple's control is largely upstream in that it is concentrated at the production end while consumers are given (at least the illusion of more) choice.

ASSEMBLAGE

Foucault's use of *dispositif* and Deleuze and Guattari's use of *agencement* overlap. They also coincide in their translation from French with the word 'assemblage' (Phillips 2006; Legg 2011). In their writings and lectures they all used both terms. Deleuze and Guattari's work reflected on Foucault and perhaps extended more toward and placed more emphasis on the idea of *agencement*. Given that we are talking about relational phenomena, of networks of causality and opportunity, it is not surprising that there should be some overlap and confusion in terminology. Equally, there is overlap and confusion between 'assemblage' and 'articulation'. But, particularly in terms of design cultures, it is useful to bring their specificities into focus.

Just as a generalized idea of design cultures involves the interactions and relationships of the activities of designers, producers, consumers and objects, images and spaces, so 'assemblages constitute the bringing together of human and non-human to form specific networks'. The development of thinking around assemblages, particularly by Latour (2005), Callon (2005) and Law (1994), derives in part from the work of Foucault and Deleuze and Guattari. They allow one to think beyond 'traditional' boundaries such as the nation-state, the family or class in the way that social practices are formed and enacted. Instead, the emphasis is on the practices themselves providing a starting point for analysis and understanding. Within this, therefore, things are seen to have agency just as people are. Humans and non-humans are actors within networks. From this thinking flows actor-network theory (ANT), which has figured prominently in the social sciences and, for them, brought the role of design increasingly into view.

Given the changing nature of people, things and, indeed, the relationships between these (i.e. their networks), so assemblages are always ephemeral. They are constituted and reconstituted just as fashions, technologies, political causes, financial interests and so on come to bear on them.

Thinking in terms of networks and relationships is productive. However, this approach does also carry some dangers. The first is that it runs the risk of 'flattening out' the network and its components so that all actors are viewed as equal with equal power. In reality, particular actors hold things up or back, speed interactions up or slow them down, or wield power over other actors in the network. Indeed, the examples of Apple's control of its software and its brand against its competitors reveal this. Second, when thinking of networks, it is tempting to see them as going on forever, that they don't have boundaries. Does, for instance, the network that constitutes smart-phones and their use finish when they tie up with so many other media?

ARTICULATION

Within assemblages, therefore, it is perhaps useful to think in terms of 'articulations', particularly when it comes to thinking about design and design cultures. An articulation occurs when two things work together. This coming together is dependent on spatial and temporal circumstances (Featherstone 2011) – being in the right place at the right time – and is therefore 'a linkage which is not necessary, determined, absolute and essential for all time' (Hall 1996: 141). Articulation is consequently seen as being dynamic in that it is subject to change and even ephemeral. It is also productive in that the coming together of elements makes for new understandings and practices. There is, therefore, a double meaning in this term 'articulation', for it expresses both linking and description.

My fellow passengers on the train with their iPhones constitute an articulation. The organization of commuting – its routine structured by the working day and week, mobility facilitated by the technology of the train, the norms of behaviour that are understood between commuters or regulated by the train company – meets the activity of using an iPhone en route. This produces a social practice that is tacitly understood and tolerated among the passengers which would not have existed before the era of smartphones. (Perhaps strangers might have conversed with each other instead?) But the social practice that these travellers are engaged in also extends beyond the carriage as they tweet, go on Facebook or text lovers. The articulation here is, first, in the precise practice of commuting meets smartphone usage. Second, it is in the understandings of what this is. After all, the emphasis in what smartphones facilitate is on access to information technology *on the move*.

The concept of articulation derives from the work of the French philosopher Louis Althusser (1969) and was subsequently developed in cultural studies by Stuart Hall (1980, 1985) but was also elaborated by Laclau and Mouffe (1985). Hall understood that Marx's notion of base and superstructure could be employed in an over-deterministic and crude manner. In brief, this approach would accept that there would be a full correspondence of political, legal and ideological practices with economic ones – base being the forces of production that determine the culture, politics, institutions, the state, religion and other elements of a society's superstructure. An alternative post-Marxist view, fashionable in the 1980s, would be that there was no correspondence at all, and that their constituent parts worked independent of each other. Hall sought a 'third way' where there was no necessary guarantee of correspondence, but neither was there any assurance that there wouldn't be (Hall 1985: 94).

From this, Hall was also interested in a notion of 'difference' and 'unity'. Of 'unity', Hall saw this as distinct from identity in that the latter expresses something all-encompassing and structured. Being of a certain nationality, for example, is structured by a range of institutions such as its laws, education system and military organization. These are relatively clear cut. By contrast, unity is more complex as it is formed by combination. It is 'a structure in which things are related, as much through their differences as through their similarities' (Hall 1980: 325). Thus, Hall was seeking a more flexible and ephemeral conception of social formation. To return to the 'iPhone in the rail carriage' example, the unity is in how a mobile information technology comes into usage on the train. But that unity is also forged by difference, for example, to the same people once they are sitting at their office desks where the iPhone and its use is of less importance. This unity is also different from when the passenger gets home.

As we have seen, the term 'assemblage' is used quite broadly and can even be interchanged with *agencement* and *dispositif*. Loosely, it can also be used instead of articulation. However, 'articulation' encourages more focus and precision. We might think in terms of an assemblage that involves mobile technologies or smartphones; but we could define an articulation through iPhones, the particularities of their use and the Apple-specific networks that they engage. Here we are required to pay greater attention to the details – including design features – that produce unity and difference. The particular language, definitions and other ways through which iPhones are discursively constructed also come into view in an analysis of how they function within an articulation.

Ultimately, ANT, and the terms that are used within it, are less of an intellectual construction for seeing the world as a methodology to help us move through and investigate it. Ours is an era where the traditional certainties of politics, nation-state, geographical belonging, religion or the family are often loosened. Different ontologies are produced. These are formed through complex and dynamic relationships of people, locations, politics, materiality and other considerations. It is telling that this way of entering into social analysis has emerged at the same time as the rise of the so-called information society, with its objects and networks such as computers and websites that also produce knowledge (Lash 2010). It is also significant that it coincides with the rise of design and design culture with its emphasis on change, relationality and the production of meanings and practices that are embedded in a routine engagement with things.

BOUNDARY OBJECTS AND SPACES

Prior to the launch of the iPhone there was considerable speculation as to its design and acceptance. Steve Jobs' confirmation on 9 January 2007 that Apple would be launching an iPhone that year that would integrate telecommunications, internet, email and mp3 capabilities was just one point in a lengthy treadmill of rumours regarding the brand. However, prior to its launch, according to an annual digital music survey of 3,000 British consumers carried out by Entertainment Media Research and the law firm Olswang, it was predicted that take-up of the idea of combining mp3 and telecommunications capabilities might be patchy, particularly among younger consumers (Allen 2006). Their research found that most teenagers were open to an integrated machine but only just over half would pick a phone with a music player over a phone-enabled mp3 or iPod.

This resistance may be explained by a number of factors such as, for teenagers, the relative high cost of such apparatus or the lack of music storage facility delivered by mp3-enabled mobile phones. For example, the Motorola ROKR launched in 2005 incorporated iTunes capability and stored just 100 tunes. But we might also speculate that mp3 usage and mobile phoning for teenagers occupy different, though related, domains of practice. The collection, exchange, archiving, display and performance of music files cluster a range of specific technologies that were distinct from teenagers' communication practices. Mobile phones, MSN, emailing and making announcements on social media platforms such as Facebook or MySpace belong, for them, either to the social bonding of 'chat' or, crucially, as instruments to coordinate other practices such as meeting up. It might be that resistance to the convergence of music and communication, at this moment, came from a perception of these two different activities being irreconcilable in their ordered and routine lives (Julier 2007).

The smartphone sits on the boundaries between social practices. For teenagers this might be between communication and music appreciation. For the rail commuters described at the beginning of this chapter, this might be between home and the office, leisure and work. Practices are unstable, though: they only come into being in their performance; they are shaped as the constellation of varying, ephemeral, material and immaterial factors. They also nest upon one another, are mutually dependent or, sometimes, are in conflict.

Modern life, it seems, is full of boundaries. This is to the extent that the crossing of boundaries – mobility, in other words – has increasingly become an object of study in the social sciences itself (Urry 2007). Mobility can be read openly. It is not just about spatial mobility, as in getting from one place to another; it is also about, for instance, mobility between social practices, everyday identities or domains of work and/or home. Objects can sit on these boundaries between different spatial, temporal, social, cultural and/or economic domains.

The concept of 'boundary objects' was originated by Star and Griesemer (1989). They described these as 'objects which both inhabit several intersecting worlds … and satisfy the informational requirements of each of them'. These have to be both robust and flexible enough to adapt to each context while maintaining 'a common identity across sites' (1989: 393). As such, artefacts fulfill a specific role in bridging intersecting practices (Akkerman and Bakker 2011). In terms of work domains, Hermans and Hermans-Konopka (2010) argue that labour in the post-industrial age has become so fragmented that many people search for ways to connect across social and cultural (and I would add, spatial and temporal) practices to avoid fragmentation. Social media such as Facebook, LinkedIn and Twitter provide tools both for assembling social groups (of networking) and transcending that isolation.

Soja (1996) and Bhabha (1994) look at the intersections of practices to produce so-called 'third spaces' where hybridity and the production of new cultural forms of dialogue take place. Spaces such as cafés that provide free wireless internet connect nested practices and boundary objects. The boundary objects are smartphones and laptop computers, but also the café furnishings that combine household and office functions. In the wi-fi environment of Starbucks, Costa or Caffè Nero, leather sofas, coffee tables and stools lined along countertops nestle with standard café seating and tables. The practices might be leisure (Skyping, Facebooking, Twittering) or work (writing a report, emailing clients, finalizing a course essay). Mobile technologies are thus combined with these third spaces to produce new practices.

CONCLUSION

Everything is happening at the same time in networks. Humans are actors in that networks come into being through their performance. Non-humans are also actors in that they are also active in these. Things are arrangements, the result of things coming together, but also equipment in the way they act on other things. They may be active in the constitution of assemblages. These are 'coming togethers' of humans, non-humans and activities that may not necessarily be formed through traditional social practices such as in the workplace, the family or the nation. More precise but ephemeral meetings of interests take place as articulations.

If the jargon of ANT seems obtuse and confusing, then this may be because it destabilizes long-established categories and understandings. Just as Donna Haraway, writing in the relatively early years of the post-industrial, information age, envisaged the blurring of human–animal, human–animal–machine and physical and non-physical distinctions, so ANT does away with dualisms such as the individual and society. Everything is taken to act on each other and comes into being through their interconnection. They exist only relationally. Going with the flow of ANT's thinking takes a leap of the imagination as it requires one to consider the 'things between' as much as the things themselves.

The Apple design culture is itself a network of contingencies, affordances, dynamic connections and the dense clustering of productive, distributive and mediating activities that are mutually co-dependent. The Apple corporation headquarters in Cupertino, California, appears to be at the centre of a global, commercial web of component manufacturers, suppliers and assemblers, distribution channels both of the hardware and software and consumer practices. It maintains sufficient dominion over these to ensure its monopoly of its products, a process that is reinforced, not least, through intellectual property, including a vigorous protection of design rights. It provides and manages the metadata so that media content design and facilitation – that includes apps, music files or video material – may be drawn from a vast resource of professionals and enthusiasts, entrepreneurs and amateurs.

A colleague of mine at the museum where I am based told me that he had acquired an iPad tablet for the museum's industrial design collection. He knew that displaying it in a gallery, switched off, would be pointless. It would be no different than being on display in an Apple store. In fact, it would be even more redundant. And if it was displayed switched on, it would probably be just as unnecessary if visitors couldn't use its interface. Even if they could touch it, its functions would not be *their* functions. The iPad only fully comes into being when it is in use, serving wishes and needs that are particular to its specific owner. This perhaps demonstrates how networks only really exist when they are enacted. It also demonstrates the difficulty of representing such things as mobile technologies purely through the hardware, either for the museum curator or the design critic.

Studying, writing about or representing an enquiry into networks and mobile technologies through other forms engages a creative process in itself. It is as well to remember that iPhones have weight, texture, colour, dimension and volume. They give off sound, vibration and light. They are affective within themselves, but they are also affective *without* themselves through the spaces and networks that they and their users engage with. Thus it is productive to think in terms of combinations of products, people and environments, both virtual and physical.

Much of the abstraction of ANT thinking runs the risk of viewing objects as mere on/off, algorithmic entities without character and registers of affect. So how do you include and represent the aesthetic dimensions of design alongside the generalizations that describe networks? In the next and final chapter we consider in more detail some of the methodological challenges and possibilities that are available to the study of design culture.

CHAPTER 12
STUDYING DESIGN CULTURE

Design cultures function in many different ways and through many different mediums. Equally, the study of design culture calls into action a myriad of academic disciplines and sensibilities. So, what specific qualities might we look out for in its study? How do we define design cultures and what should we look out for? Chapter 12 provides an opportunity to reprise on the central themes that have emerged through the book's chapters, to briefly expand on recurrent methodological challenges that come into view and to consider how approaches to studying design culture may be pursued further. Within all this we consider the possibility that a 'design culture turn' has taken place, specifically within the economic framework of neoliberalism. A series of challenges to defining and conceptualizing design cultures and their study are presented and discussed. We then make a final reconsideration of how we might approach the objects of design culture through a spirit of enquiry.

'Design culture' is well-established both as an academic discipline and a descriptive term. Since the first edition of this book was published in 2000, Design Culture has emerged as a postgraduate degree title in a few universities and is offered as a component to several undergraduate courses. Equally, since that date, the term 'design culture' has been used with increasing ubiquity. So where do we take things from here?

The development, writing and revisions of this book have constantly reinforced a notion of design culture as heterogeneous. Indeed, from this one might justly talk of 'design cultures' in the plural in order to acknowledge the different ways and contexts by and through which they function. If much of design is about differentiation, then it follows that its cultural processes and outcomes are going to be distinct from one another according to location, everyday practices, history and historicity and a range of other factors that this book has touched on. If we are to talk of design cultures in the plural, then this suggests that these exist in different locations and temporalities, in distinct formats, manifestations, systems of valorization, rhythms, meters and intensities. Numerous entry points and exit strategies for its study present themselves. Nonetheless, if we accept Design Culture as a field of academic enquiry that embraces this understanding, then putting the term into the singular comes, naturally, with the territory.

Just as the ways by which design cultures function are varied, so we are able to draw on a range of theoretical tools to understand them. The approaches to analysing and understanding various expressions of design culture that are presented through this book are broad. If they include the study of the production, mediation, circulation and regulation of design, its students must become neo-experts in psychology, management, technologies, politics, cultural

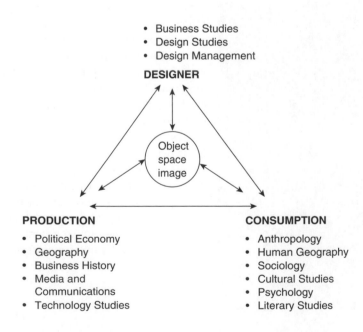

Figure 12.1   Domains of design culture and possible academic disciplinary sources

studies, economics, sociology, ethnography and human geography, notwithstanding design studies, design history and design management (see Figure 12.1). In addition to these, its students must be visually, materially and spatially literate. Design culture is about processes, people, relationships, flows, fluxes and vectors, but it is also about stuff. Knowing what this stuff is, being able to read it, handle it, experience it and think deeply and critically about it, provides us with its own starting point. If science and technology studies tell us that both people and things are actors, that they are affective in the processes through which we live and decisions are made, then all those parts should be fully understood. This means that not only people and institutions are studied but also that the patina of things should be closely observed.

It is therefore sensible, as I have demonstrated in the chapters of this book, to begin with the design object itself or, more likely, with a constellation of design objects (since we deal with suites of objects that can add up to a brand, a practice, a service or a value-chain). But whether we analyse the design of an individual product or the various manifestations that make up a product service, at least we have something that is more or less tangible. We can then move on to the design historian's most traditional question: 'Why does it look like it does?' Or we can otherwise go onto more interesting questions – that are more typical of this field of design cultures – such as: 'How is it functioning?', 'How is it performing a task in helping to produce meaning and value?', 'How is it circulating and communicating?'.

For these reasons, I'm not offering a set of 'how to do' Design Culture methods or advising on a key reading list before embarking on its study. Design cultures are flexible, mutant and mutable and should be investigated with equal flexibility. Likewise, I am coy about providing a 'reader' of key texts that the fledgling scholar should be acquainted with before embarking on its study. The breadth and depth at which they can be studied and the ways their understanding can be used are so diverse that it is more appropriate in this chapter to raise a series of questions that the student might be alert to. The study of design culture requires a particular sensibility that is attuned to it and, indeed, to appreciating the nuanced and significant role that it plays in contemporary life.

Before moving on to a series of challenges that are implicit in the study of design culture, it is productive to underline the notion of design culture as a particularly contemporary concept that springs from a set of geopolitical changes, economic movements and cultural expressions. By understanding design culture as an historical process we can get a feel for its sensibilities and significances.

A DESIGN CULTURE TURN

Several academic disciplines claim historical 'turns' that re-frame the ways by which they pursue their work. This is either where a component in society has taken up greater significance than previously, or within that subject area it has changed the way it is studied. Thus, for instance, we find a 'cultural turn' in social theory (Nash 2001) and in human geography (Barnett 2002). In Chapter 1 we saw that it has been argued that a 'visual turn' took place in Western society, coinciding with the growth of industrialization and mass markets in the 19th century. Here, with the advent of new visual technologies and forms of presentation, the visual is understood to take a more significant and, even, spectacular role. Alternatively, we saw that this 'visual turn' may instead be taken to mean where the visual becomes more ubiquitous but also accepted as commonplace in everyday life. Thus, one understanding is of quantities – as in, it is everywhere and normal; another is in qualities – as in, the visual forms a whole new way of perceiving the world.

In this section I want to argue for a 'design culture turn' that has taken place since the 1980s. This turn may be the result of a reaching of 'critical mass' and a 'coming of age' of design and how it functions in society. This is foremost an issue of quantity. As many of the statistics given in Chapter 2 testify, employment and education in design have risen exponentially throughout much of the world. Design, in addition to its growing variety of expression and application, has also achieved unprecedented visibility and institutional engagement. Furthermore, as we saw in Chapter 3, definitions and understandings of design have similarly accumulated to the point that it denotes both objects, spaces and images that are given designerly value through the intervention of specialist professionals, but also less tangible questions such as management or policy development are subject to design (as in 'design thinking'). Equally, Chapter 4 concludes by showing that the consumption of design is itself a practice that involves interrelationships of people and things within socially understood activities. In its 'coming of age', design, it seems, has taken on new qualities and functions.

Historically, the study of design (before we get to design culture) entails some relatively precise considerations. Leaving aside the basic, though not necessarily straightforward, question of learning how to do design and acquiring the discipline of being a designer, three meta-levels take place here. First, the study of design involves the observation and recording of how artefacts are – as in, what they look like, how they feel, what tasks are performed through them and so on. Second, it delves into how these artefacts are created, the design processes and the people that give rise to them. Third, it considers design as a profession by mapping and measuring it, qualifying its various sectors and understanding the various ways by which it performs its tasks. Each of these, for the most part, deals with clear and quantifiable challenges. For example, objects can be weighed; the processing of design projects can be tracked; designers can be counted. Indeed, through this the fields of design studies and design management have become redolent with close observations from which various principles have been derived. Despite, or perhaps because of, its lack of normative curricula and professional criteria, design is by no means short of broad, all-encompassing statements on what it is, how it is done and who does it (e.g. Lawson 1997, Cross 2006, Verganti 2009).

While design studies and design management focus primarily on design processes, often with a view to pinning down some objective viewpoint on what is an invariably subjective activity, the study of design culture could be said to be looser, more interpretative and flexible in its aims and sensibilities. This is about a 'coming of age' in which design culture signifies certain understandings, cognitive styles and imaginings. It is where design becomes established as commonplace not merely in terms of its 'attachment' to specific objects, but also via the workings of private and public life and the decision-making that mediates the two. Buying or renting an apartment can involve a calculation of the desirability of both its interior aspects and its location, each of which involves cultural as well as economic factors.

The growth of design studies and design management concurs with design's reaching a 'critical mass' – it has become pervasive enough to be able to support international design research conferences, be the object of statistical enquiries or fill the classrooms at business schools. Meanwhile, the emergence of a concept of design culture as an object of study and as a discursive term suggests a change of gear in the way that design functions in society and in economies. Questions in design studies or design management might be 'What is happening here?' or 'Is this typical?', 'How is does this provide a general model for practitioners?'. In Design Culture, more frequent questions might be 'What aspirations for and understandings of design are there?', 'How are these ideas of design circulated?' or 'How do these people live materially and socially?'. Further, these three questions may also be taken together so that the fit or disjunctures between them might be pursued. It is here that the relationship between design, production and consumption (or value, creation/circulation and practice) forms the conceptual framework for studying design culture.

This can be said to have been around or emergent as long as design has, in the modern sense of the word. While our understanding of design has been attached to industrial and economic systems of serial reproduction and the need for specialists in determining forms for this, so its public has been attenuated to its significance. Design and style have consistently been entangled with notions of cultural capital and conspicuous consumption.

However, just as there has been a take-off in quantity of design since the 1980s, so there has been a turn in its qualities. It is since the 1980s that design has been more intensely interlocked with questions of brand identity, with cultural political economy and policy, the structuring, ordering and dynamics of production systems, ways of being at work and a whole host of other components of life in the post-Fordist world of disorganized capitalism that was summarized in Chapter 2. Through the course of the various chapters in this book, I hope that I have shown that design has become more knowingly and thus strategically incorporated into these processes. This isn't just about an 'aestheticization of everyday life' (Featherstone 1991); it isn't just about making consumption more visually or materially spectacular. Design allocates resources, configures systems and prioritises interests, and its affective features in these are crucial, of course. This deeper, more complex state of design culture has risen through the era of neoliberalism.

In common usage, the term 'neoliberalism' has only circulated widely since about 2000 (Peck et al. 2009), yet its features have gained increasing traction in the capitalist world since the 1980s. This era of neoliberalism is typified by the deregulation of markets and the privileging of market forces, the gradual privatization of state-owned enterprises and its welfare systems, an emphasis on competitiveness and on individual, entrepreneurial practices and the foregrounding of financial interests over others such as communitarian, civic, social or environmental concerns (though where these render economic benefits, these too come into focus). In all these, design plays a significant and intensified role. Harvey (2005) points out that it is more accurate to see neoliberalism as 'a theory of political economic practices' rather than a complete political ideology. Neoliberalism is a way of organizing economy and society to the benefit of private enterprise, not an expressed political belief system. It has therefore been accommodated within various political frameworks, including the most rigid of right-wing dictatorships.

Neoliberalism is characterized by a constant transformation of economic practices. Its adherents, be they small-scale entrepreneurs, global corporations or governments, search for new forms and sources of value. These may, for instance, be undervalued resources, untapped consumer groups or practices that can be upscaled. Neoliberalism is constantly on the move, finding new territories and combinations. Likewise, designers 'dodge and weave' to find new marketplaces for their skills, create new needs and desires. Neoliberalism, like design, is a process of change more than an endpoint. Design takes advantage of and normalizes the transformations that neoliberalism provokes. It also conspires in neoliberalism's voracious championing of competitivity by supporting and showing differentiation. A full-blown account and analysis of design in the context of neoliberalism lies outside the scope of this book. I flag it up, though, as it helps us understand both the quantitative and qualitative advances of design culture in recent times.

WRITING DESIGN CULTURE

Throughout this book I have provided a number of case studies as a way into understanding how contemporary design culture functions. These have been arranged according to various discourses, contexts or practices – hence a chapter on high design, another on branded leisure and one on networks. In so doing, I have avoided organizing the book by design disciplines – such as by graphic, interior or industrial design. All of these carry nuanced ways of doing things according to their varying technologies and materials, points of reference in design history, educational traditions, relationships to other creative professions, speeds at which they operate, interactions with clients, conceptions of their end-users and so on. Hence each is a *discipline* in that it has normative elements through which its practitioners identify themselves and perform their work. And yet, much design work and training avoids overarching, rigid normative activities such as the foundation of national or regional educational attainment targets that are validated and run through professional organizations.

These disciplines maintain their own discourses and languages, technical descriptors and points of reference that have evolved and are in constant evolution rather than being fixed. Nonetheless, fragmentation, or deliberate differentiation, occurs within the professional practices of design. A contemporary design industry dedicated to disembedding itself from its own professional structures and, to a large extent, 'thinking through doing', will take considerable developments for a seamless integration of management, marketing, brand and design features to be reached in any widespread way. This notion may even be antithetical to many designers. I asked a senior consultant at a major branding consultancy what he thought of the role of planners in the design process. He took a dim view of their contribution, replying that: 'They are there to iron out the surprises.' Similarly, clients may aspire to greater consistency, but are aware of its pitfalls. As ownership of brands is diffused more extensively through the internal structure of a company or institution, so there is increased scope for the misinterpretation, modification or contestation of its values. Managers and designers alike know that in a dynamic economy a balance between corporativism and individualism must be struck. Overlaps, misapprehensions, compromises, misfits and deliberate interruptions of meaning are probably more likely in an era of disorganized capitalism.

This vignette draws out just one of the ways by which a design culture can be apprehended as a unity that is made up of differences. A design culture is a constellation of elements that may in themselves be in tension and contradiction. If studying and writing about design culture require a more elliptical, sometimes overarching view of practices and artefacts, we have to be sensitive to the various discursive features that exist within it. The culture of design can incorporate a babble of voices, representing various interests and motivations.

To give another example, we might take a national design culture such as that of Denmark. Historically, Danish design has been typified by its softened modernism, which retained natural finishes and exhibited a sculptural elegance that is seen through the works of luminaries such as Jacob Jensen, Hans Wegner and Arne Jacobsen. Yet, there is also a Danish design practice and

Danish design culture: various Danish creative industries and design reports

aesthetic that is quite apart from this. Denmark, or rather its capital, Copenhagen, is also home to Christiana, the alternative community that is based on collective self-governance and whose aesthetic is far from the sleek Nordic modernism that is extolled in design history books. Separately, but perhaps sharing a similar alternative spirit, the Danish city of Aarhus provides the base for KaosPilots, an independent business school that focuses on personal growth, creative enterprise and social innovation. Its aesthetic and ways of working are far from the cleaned-up image of traditional executive training. A third layer of Danish design culture is found in the central role it takes in broader, national creative industries policies. Several government-supported policy and mapping documents testify to an enthusiasm to embed design into wider industrial and public policies in a bid to establish Denmark and other Nordic countries at the leading of edge of competitive economies (Copenhagen Business School 2005; Danish Government 2007; Design2020 Committee 2011). Design is folded into a number of distinct features of the Danish creative industries – such as its film industries, high-end manufacture and fashion apparel – as part of an updating and rebranding of the country.

Thus we find three fields of design culture in Denmark working together. Needless to say, all three of them work relationally to other fields, including those outside it. The term 'Danish modern' overlaps with Scandinavian or Nordic modern and denotes a wider design sensibility; it also functions in opposition to other national or international movements as a way of differentiating or drawing in interest to a national design culture. The aesthetics and approaches expressed through Christiana or KaosPilots equally function to denote an alternative discourse that both resonates with international socially aware movements and contests the cleaner connotations of Danish modern. Finally, policy discourse in creative industries and design in Denmark runs in parallel with those at a more general Nordic (Fleming 2007) and European level (European Design Leadership Board 2012).

For the study of design culture, this discussion of Denmark exemplifies some of its challenges. How do you create a coherent account of a field where differentiation and fragmentation are so pervasive? Writing design culture is as much a methodological challenge as researching it is. It requires the author to think about voice and register, to consider the levels of academic formality or poetic expression to be employed. It necessitates the construction of multiple associations and the structuring of a narrative that reveals meaning while paying heed to the complex and possibly contradictory components that make up the culture of design.

We should be mindful that the culture of design is the product of specific historical processes. We can also accept that this gives rise to difference and contradiction even within the unity of its own processes. Design cultures may be defined through many scales and exhibit specific qualities in their various performances and functionings. They come in multifarious manifestations and work in diverse ways. Given this, there now follows an exposition of seven key challenges that are to be found in the study of Design Culture. They are summarized in Table 12.1.

SCOPE

We have to ascertain at what scale we wish to study design culture. In other words, how do we draw its map and fix its boundaries? What are we looking for in defining a design culture? Are we to view it as a national expression as we have just done above? Or are we to define it in other spatial terms, such as down to a household or an individual firm or up to some kind of macro level in terms of a kind of economy or society? We might even dispense with geographical categories and pursue design cultures that may be more defined through certain practices, such as fan groups, sports or leisure activities or the users of particular digital software usages. Even so, there is always the danger of boundaries becoming a bit arbitrary according to the researcher's whims.

Networks can go on forever unless we define some kind of organizing principle for them. A criticism of an ANT approach to design production that Bryson and Rusten (2011: 199–201) make is that firms and their assets have become less important than individuals and objects in networks. They go on to argue that much of the literature on creative industries that runs in parallel to this highlights knowledge, creativity and expertise but does not make reference to products. In this approach, companies are transformed into relational constructions of social networks and actors embedded in networks rather than structures or legal entities that have one primary purpose: that is, profit through the design, development and sale of products. Their concern is to ground the analysis of design in the constraints and possibilities that are afforded by real clients, markets, technologies, infrastructures and so on.

This is a useful reminder which can be extended to the issue of how to scope a study of design culture. By drawing on their critique, we might first ask what are the primary tasks, aims and reasons for the existence of a design culture? Second, how is it determined by the pragmatic features of resources and options? Third, how does it know and define itself ontologically? This last question is perhaps the trickiest as it requires an enquiry into self-understanding and the consideration of reflexivity with regard to how this knowledge in turn affects activity. The scope of study is therefore grounded evidentially in both practical and discursive questions.

CLOSED AND OPEN CONCEPTIONS OF DESIGN

Are we dealing with design that is defined as a professional activity or are we to take it as employing a wider constituency? Do we enclose design culture by limiting its study to designs as formed through the work of designers? Or do we open it up to all things that 'don't happen by accident'?

Behind this question of 'closed' or 'open' conceptions of design culture is the historically constructed varying understanding of the word 'culture' itself. Famously, Raymond Williams provided a dual definition in his 1976 text *Keywords*. Culture is either treated as a separate sphere from everyday life, existing as some thing or value that comes after an 'and', or it is routine, enacted and processual. The former idea of culture is taken to be something that is partaken of (e.g. I *go* to the opera, I *join* a book group, I *attend* design exhibitions). The latter is lived (e.g. this is my way of living, we have these shared understandings and ways of doing things, I am part of this local community).

The majority of this book has been concerned with the role of professionally produced design, yet, to re-cite Victor Papanek 'All men are designers ... design is basic to all human activity' (1972: 3). In editing *The Design Culture Reader* (2009), Ben Highmore takes the provocative step of not including any texts in this compilation that deal directly with the work of professional designers. Instead, his framing of design culture is in the ubiquitous and established things and places that layer up everyday life rather than, necessarily, the brand new. Similarly, Degen et al. (2008) explore how urban design and public art in a town centre are experienced within a wider cacophony of other visual data, such as shop fronts or advertising hoardings. This challenges the idea of there being any hierarchy of design objects for people. For Highmore, design culture is where cultural studies and social sciences converge around objects and their interrelationships with people, a view that is shared by this book. In this context, though while the objects are active on and in social relationships, actors appear not to be so active on the objects.

(Opposite) reproduction Arne Jacobsen designed 3107 chairs as seen in the cafeteria of the University of Southern Denmark; Arne Jacobsen designed ANT chairs as seen in the cafeteria of Kolding School of Design; Hans Wegner designed Round Chair as seen on former DFDS ferry Dana Anglia and built in Aalborg; funnel of Dana Anglia; (above) KaosPilots workshop in Bogotá, Colombia, 2012
Photos: Guy Julier

However, even in the most ordinary of lives, it may be that design becomes a deliberative act. For example, Bouchez (2012) argues that even if professional designers or the status of high design as mediated through magazines are taken out of this equation, in their process of home-making, consumers are actually engaged in making (through choosing, arranging or adapting) and meaning-making (through *thinking and talking about* choosing, arranging and adapting). This brings us on to thinking about design processes that invite consumers into the productive field, such as open source coding in computing or mass customization – both being examples of what has come to be called 'open design' (Van Abel et al. 2011). To push this further, one might take note of the ways that service design (discussed in Chapter 3), design anthropology (discussed in Chapter 6) or participatory design (discussed in Chapter 10) involve close analysis or the active involvement of end-users in the design process.

These are examples of the many ways by which the domains of design, production and consumption are brought into a closer orbit with one another. The density of actors within this and the dynamics of exchange between them intensifies the ways by which a design culture will function. Furthermore, in this process, value, that is intrinsic to the work of design, is imbricated into practice. The work of designers and producers is to develop artefacts and ways of being with them so that they become routine and lived. Equally, consumers engage with design in diverse ways at many different levels. Designs and design cultures are experienced knowingly. So, paradoxically, the idea of this intensification suggests that design becomes more spectacular and more obviously visible; in fact, design becomes more 'normal' and everyday.

This is not to say that, through this process, design begins to work more subtly in the background without our awareness. At times we will get duped; at others, we will learn more. It works on us and we work on it. Studying design culture includes, then, enquiry into the progressive 'normalization' of design itself. This would involve a sensitivity to the traffic flow between registers of culture and how design, culture and design culture itself are transformed in the process.

REFLEXIVITY AND HISTORICITY

Reflexivity exists within and for design cultures. Cultures are cumulative in that they are produced in part through an historical layering-up of occurrences. But we saw in Chapter 4 how historicity is employed to foreground certain aspects of tradition, heritage, experience or other knowledge about the past. History is used knowingly to produce particular narratives and justify certain positions. Further, a design culture is made up of a range of aspects, but its definition and articulation are a promotional tool. For example, the jacket blurb from the book accompanying a Victoria & Albert Museum 2012 exhibition on British design proclaimed it as a 'stunning record of Britain's rich design culture' (Breward and Wood 2012). Cultures may be represented as happenstance – that they come about through the influence of a set of uncontrolled forces. Conversely, we can think about a culture as having been self-consciously shaped to serve particular interests. Design culture has implicit in it a sense of it being a *designed* design culture. It probably sounds like a truism to say that the promotion of design itself through governmental policy or professional advocacy serves to consolidate and endorse a design culture. Design serves to push it in certain directions or highlight particular competitive strengths. Through this discourse, for example, Danish design culture becomes both a promotional trope and an organizing and legitimating force for policy decisions, or as one policy statement put it, 'In order to brand ourselves as *the* design society, we have to become *the* design society' (Design2020 Committee 2011: 48).

As a note of caution, though, it does not necessarily follow that if a design culture is reflexive that its constituent parts are also reflexive. For example, while designers purport to understand what users 'need', Kimbell (2011) suggests that by comparison with the social sciences, many are ill-equipped to challenge their own assumptions of the world by questioning the political or theoretical lens by which they see it. It is important to be critically aware of whether historicity is functioning self-consciously or not; and it is vital to assess the extent and limits of reflexivity.

MEDIATION

A further challenge is that in design culture *all things mediate* and *all mediations require things*. Danish design policy documents provide information about Danish design, quite obviously. But they form an integral part of Danish design culture, too. They report on its design culture, but they are also active in its formation. Just as a Jacobsen-designed chair or the KaosPilots logo tells us something about Danish design culture when interpreted as text, so, conversely, policy documents that are primarily textual are also, and nonetheless, active things in the networks that constitute it. They sit on shelves, are passed around or uploaded onto government or university websites.

An argument has been made to draw mediation out as a distinct 'moment' to be considered in addition to production and consumption (Lees-Maffei 2009). In Chapter 4, via the work of Johnson (1986) and Hebdige (1988), I identified mediation as a point of analysis within the study of design culture. I have also drawn attention to Bourdieu's (1984) notion of 'cultural intermediaries' where designers, among others, act to mediate trends, new styles, ideas or technologies. Equally, I have drawn from Fine and Leopold's (1993) proposition of 'systems of provision' for design culture. In these latter authors, there is a sense of sequentialism in that, broadly speaking, mediation is taken to be the activity that takes place at some time and place between production and consumption – that mediation filters and explains intentions for users. Thus, for instance, consumers see adverts, watch television shopping channels, visit design museums, read instruction manuals and so on, prior to purchasing or not purchasing. This consideration of mediation is, of course, important because it helps the observer of design move beyond the raw object of design and consider it as part of a set of series of manifestations – as, for example, we saw in the discussion of Starck's Juicy Salif lemon squeezer in Chapter 5.

However, mediation points in all directions; or, to make the point more challenging, everything mediates all the time. It is only a partial account that sees the process of mediation in design culture as being part of a linear sequence from production to consumption. We saw in Chapter 10 how design can be mustered as part of the internal branding process in inculcating corporate values among a workforce. Here, in this 'below the line' context, information moves within an organization either to reinforce its self-identity or as preparation for contact with clients or consumers. But mediation may be less deliberate. Just as there is a material culture of home dwellers, so, for example, a design studio has a material culture. Computers, sketch pads, workflow software, the arrangement of desks and chairs or the division of studio and meeting space all conspire to regulate and coordinate the ways by which design is undertaken. They mediate particular ways of doing design and form part of that 'project culture' that was discussed in Chapter 1. The 'circuit of culture' as expressed by Du Gay in Chapter 4 underlines this idea of mediation being multi-directional. Thus, within whatever scale a design culture is defined, mediation is embedded as an ongoing process in all its constituent parts.

DENSITY

A design culture can be tightly or loosely constituted. This means that there are close ties between its domains of design, production and consumption (and, possibly, in themselves) or that these are more distant from one another. Examples where these ties might be close is among distinctive locations or enthusiasms. In Chapter 7 we saw how the city of Barcelona produced a particular paradigm of how modern design has been used to work through its institutions, agencies and population in shaping urban identity. Through the design of its public spaces and amenities, publicity campaigns, the design and production of urban, bar, restaurant and domestic furniture, their frequent discussion through local media, its promotion by city authorities and the importance of particular retail outlets, a tight fit for the city's design production and consumption was achieved throughout the 1980s and 1990s (Julier 2005; Narotzky 2007). The number and close proximity of these elements provide a strong density and intensity within the design culture, and consequently a coherence between its domains and the objects that move through it. Conversely, a design culture which has a less dense constellation may provide more space for variation or counter expressions and practices.

The density of a design culture may not necessarily be spatial. This isn't just about, for example, the tight clustering of a design neighbourhood or creative quarter. In Chapter 11, I began by describing the density of smartphone users in a railway carriage. But I then moved on to discuss how corporations in this sector try to encourage a secondary sector of app designers not only by providing tools and systems for them, but also by building enthusiasms among them. Here the density is served mostly through digital platforms and is pulled together by a focus on the specific product type of the app. But other platforms such as enthusiast meet-ups or congresses such as MacWorld also function in bringing actors together. Studying design culture may involve identifying how such clusters are developed and maintained.

DYNAMICS

Following on from the issue of density, a consideration of dynamics may be fruitful. Here we have to take into account the speeds of movement between the constituent parts in design culture as well as how these provide impetus for a design culture's development and change. For instance, how fast are information, knowledge or artefacts themselves moved back and forth between producers and consumers? What are the temporal regimes between designers and clients (i.e. what expectations are placed in terms of the time taken to process design projects or its various parts)?

Picking up on social theory that is concerned with networks, and the flows of nodes within these (e.g. Castells 1996), I have attempted to highlight the relational qualities of design culture. This means that attention is drawn to how dependencies and meanings are created through the interrelationships between constituent parts in a design culture. These interrelationships require the movement of ideas or things. In itself, a design culture is always dynamic as these are prepared for and moved through its networks. The idea of 'flow' is perhaps useful to conceptualize this, but it must also be treated critically, for it makes movement sound as if it were constant, steady and uninterrupted without resistances, blockages or containments. The notion of an easy, continuous flow keys in with a neoliberal orthodoxy. Deregulation, new economy and financialization as described in Chapter 2 depend on the removal of national, legal and logistical barriers to the free movement of finance and goods. They also depend on the speeding-up of their the circulation. Several semi-academic texts support a vision of a globalized economy where location doesn't matter as much as the rapid filling-in of market opportunities (Coyle 1997; Cairncross 1997; Kelly 1998; Kasarda and Lindsay 2011). In their accounts, environmental disasters don't happen, economic policies do not constrain trade or protect consumers, powerful interests do not manipulate supply and demand. Contrastingly, it may be more accurate to talk in terms of 'flux' rather than 'flow', for this suggest that the dynamics are changeable (Lash 2010: 65). Investigating the ways that dynamics in design cultures are disrupted may be as productive as studying how they are facilitated.

To think about dynamics also addresses the challenges of historical analysis and consciousness. It is tempting to represent design cultures ahistorically, given that they involve, if you will, a strong focus on the horizontal interconnections of design, production and consumption. Any design culture research engages with historical processes as does design culture itself. Further, and as we saw in Chapter 11, the complexity of assemblages that make up a design culture conspires to propel it so that it is in a constant state of 'becoming'. Design's future orientation gives it a logic of continuous change that makes all objects, in a sense, unfinished.

MATERIALITY

The study of design culture begins and ends with materiality. All the case study chapters of this book begin with a description of my encounter with that key object. In this, I am viewing it as a problem that raises questions rather than describing it as a fact: my quest is to interrogate rather than draw conclusions. I am asking how it is situated and how I am situated in relation to it. How is it functioning, societally perhaps, and how is it functioning on me? This points toward Heidegger's notion of *dasein* (Heidegger 2005 [1927]) that denotes a state of being-in-the-world and its understanding. Through this, the individual is situated in relation to external phenomena. Investigating this state of being-in-the-world cannot lead to any fixed conclusions (Mulhall 2005); rather, it is a starting point for enquiry, of making sense of ourselves and the world around us. From *dasein*, Oosterling draws attention to how, in a similar way, design itself 'equates to making decisions about form in order to liberate ourselves from the arbitrariness of life' (2009: 120).

THE CULTURE OF DESIGN

It is rather late in the course of this book to unfold a discussion of Heidegger's phenomeno-logical philosophy. I use the briefest of references to his work to underline the importance of thinking of objects as *things* that are active on humans. In this, the way they help to construct and reinforce routines and outlooks is done by what they allow us to do and how they make us think about these. Things (and I use the word to denote not just products, but all design's mani-festations) are affective and thus we must pay attention to how they function in this respect. This isn't merely a case of how they denote and connote their significances. It isn't about sur-faces. Design things employ, in their materiality, or better still, their matter, bodily processes so that in use, they yield meaning. A useful way to think of this, which draws from ANT, is in terms of material semiotics (Law 2008). Encounters with objects, spaces and images involve engaging with them in a number of ways (looking, touching, smelling, hearing, moving through etc.). They also invariably involve shared discussion that also reinforces or generates meaning. Habitual encounters embed meaning. Significance takes place not just in terms of readings of 'objects as text' but also in routine use.

As students of design culture we must bring the same detached rigour to analysing and expe-riencing design artefacts as art historians do with fine art (e.g. see Acton 2004). Cognition itself is, of course, multilayered. We have considered domestic products, which are heavily elaborated with sign-value through their own form and the narrative systems around them, but which are also objects of intimate use. Likewise, elements of urban design may communicate to users on a direct visceral level – they may be touched, leant on, felt through your shoes – but they may com-municate the identity of a place on a global scale. Branded leisure spaces may offer spatially and temporally bounded experiences in which visitors immerse themselves while knowing that this is a temporary state of affairs. Users of computer gaming programs or informational documents engage at intuitive levels with them while keeping an eye on navigation bars and thinking about their overall configuration. We are knowing consumers and as such mobilize different forms and levels of engagement and interpretation in different scenarios.

While focused attention on a thing provides a productive way into studying design culture, it is important to think of this as just one of its possible iterations. Designing entails intensities that produce extensities (Lash 2010). Its input is in giving attention to the singular form (e.g. as a prototype, a brand manual or software coding) that results in multiple and, often, multifarious artefacts. The extensity may appear in several versions and formats that are encountered in a range of locations and moments. The design of an Olympic mascot, for example, becomes a logo, a toy or an animated figure (Busquet 1993). In studying design culture, we must be critical of any tendency to singularize the design object and be attentive to the multiple ways that it can be encountered and the relationship between each of these.

Finally, studying design culture opens up a potential to vigorously and thoughtfully reintro-duce questions of aesthetics into its related academic fields. Shove et al. argue that while ANT has opened up challenging approaches to the agency of things, it has also led to a 'potentially leaden view of stuff' (2012: 10). Further, they suggest that it has a tendency to divert away from what is actually going on in the relationship between people and things. They go on to argue for greater attention to be paid to materiality in understanding practice and its dynamics. Likewise, Tonkinwise (2011) maintains that in the rise of 'design thinking' amongst management, organi-zational and design studies, questions of style have dropped out of the equation. Aesthetics upset the 'algorithmic modes of operation' of managerialism where stylistic elements are 'too

Table 12.1   Summary of seven challenges in the study of Design Culture

Feature	Summary	Some issues to consider
Scope	• How we define a design culture	• territorial boundaries • cultural practices • technological affordances • political motivations • ideological processes
Closed or open conceptions of design	• How design is defined by expertise	• processes of distinction and cultural capital • professionalization and amateur practices • design and a wider field of visual and material culture • participatory, ethnographic or 'open' approaches to design
Reflexivity and historicity	• How a design culture is knowing of itself • How historical experience is appropriated and used	• 'design culture' as a promotional descriptor • positionality of actors – how they become aware of their own perspectives and actions are formed and how this knowledge is used • which histories become discursively important
Mediation	• How design information is defined and circulated	• objects through which mediation takes place • intended audience • multi-directionality of mediation
Density	• Clustering or dispersion of actors	• thickness of links between actors • spatial or temporal relationships • correspondence or not of material expressions and discursive understandings
Dynamics	• The speeds and intensities of interchange • Collective understandings or commercial aspirations	• facilitation and disruption • production/consumption cycles • material, information and technological resources • competition and differentiation • political and commercial orthodoxies
Materiality	• How things are active and affective	• the multifarious platforms and media through which design things are encountered • embodied experience • multiple and multi-level cognition • routine and repetition

incalculable' even if a trend away from these is discernible, he writes (2011: 536). It is ironic that a field such as design, which is so centred on the visual, material and spatial world – its very *thingness* – should become so abstracted in social science or management discourses. Both of the examples discussed show that a detailed re-focusing on the materiality of design, and its affect, might shift the debate.

CONCLUDING REMARKS

Much of this book has traced the threads, narratives, strategies or coincidences by which design values are moved through its audiences and its proponents. It has reviewed systems whereby designers, producers and consumers are brought closer together. As part of this culture of design, various activities conspire to break down the temporal, spatial and cultural separation between these domains. Therefore I have concentrated on their interaction and relationships. Conversely, when a wide separation between designer, producer and consumer does happen, it results in poor products or services, business failure and/or ignorance of user needs. In turn, this may lead us towards considering discourses of 'good design' and 'bad design' to be centred less on the form of the artefact and more on the relationships it engages with. This is manifest both in design management thinking for profit maximization and in enthusiasms for social and environmental agency. The flows of these exchanges are not always equal or coherent and so part of the work of the scholar of Design Culture is in looking at how power functions through the regulation of these.

The conditions of disorganized capitalism have led to a more aestheticized, sign economy, we are told. Certainly many of the individual features of design conspire towards this conclusion. Designer products achieve most widespread recognition through the pages of lifestyle publications. The use of plastics throws product values on to their outer surface. Places are arranged for visual consumption. Interaction in digital media takes place on a flat surface. As such, products and services are liable to a constant layering of their mediation as sign is applied on top of sign. The range of moments and locations at which they are produced and consumed has been ignored by historians and commentators who pursue an essentialist view of design which focuses on them as individualized, singular objects.

This is not to say, though, that design has become entirely a question of visual representation. While it is necessary to illustrate it through photographs in a book, it must be remembered that design is manifested in many ways. Its interdisciplinary practice means that it may amalgamate a range of sensory features – of sound, smell, touch, feel, weight, movement and sight. These are always referential, by assimilating and arranging data of the known world into new configurations, or more straightforwardly by simulating pasts and places. So while design may reproduce and refine pre-existing situations and habits, it may also aspire to the invention of new ones. It is the stuff of both illusion and allusion.

The study of design culture is also multi-layered. Beyond analysing design's capacity to do things such as delight, confuse, provide comfort or stimulation, we can also step back and enquire into its wider functions. This book began by asserting the rise of design in our times. More specifically, I drew attention to how parts of the world have pulled themselves into the ambit of design culture within capitalistic contexts. Within these, competition gives rise to the constant reworking and redesign of its corporations, products, services and institutions. This is both internal in terms of their inner workings and structures and external in terms of their interfaces with others. Design is involved in a constant leap-frogging and positioning, helping actors to 'get ahead', 'reposition its offer' or 'create efficiency gains'. Thus it is discussed at government policy level in a way that is almost exclusively guided by an economic 'growth model' (e.g. European Design Leadership Board 2012). It is framed in terms of its ability to shape goods and services, but also regions and nations, for competitive advantage.

Meanwhile, the post-2008 debt crises, the dramatic rise of commodity prices experienced since 2000, climate change progressing faster than predicted, massive migration piling pressure on urban infrastructures, the growth of international crime – these produce a sense of a world in turmoil. It seems that the dominance of a growth model to justify what design is for, limits the discussion and misses its significance. Design is and has undoubtedly been implicated in bringing these other challenges about. However, to repeat, if the work of designers is in creating value, then this may not be purely economic. Design also stimulates environmental, cultural, social or communitarian value.

Just as designers create new forms and ways of being, so they re-design the processes and roles of design itself. Design cultures are transformative in that they depend on a constant process of change in the locations that they alight on. They also act on themselves. Design cultures reflexively work to be in a constant state of self-modification.

By researching design cultures and finding compelling ways of communicating that research, new territories, objects, social practices, economic arrangements and connective tissues between them may be revealed. We can begin to comprehend how a culture of design operates to support dominant systems and interests, or how it may provide new dynamics and vectors that help to reconfigure our priorities. By understanding the culture of design we can remove the barriers to its own change or, at least, know its limits.

REFERENCES

Abbott, Howard and Tyler, Mark (1997) *Safer by Design: A Guide to the Management and Law of Designing for Product Safety*, 2nd edn. London: Design Council.

Abrahams, Charlotte (1998) 'Not Just a Pretty Place', *The Guardian* Weekend, 19 December.

Acton, Mary (2004) *Learning to Look at Modern Art*. Abingdon: Routledge.

Adorno, Theodor and Horkheimer, Max (1979 [1947]) *Dialectic of Enlightenment*. London: Verso.

Agence pour la Promotion de la Création Industrielle (2002) 'L'offre de design en France' (report). Paris: Ministère de l'Économie des Finances et de l'Industrie.

Aitch, Iain (2003) *A Fête Worse Than Death: A Journey Through an English Summer*. London: Review Books.

Akkerman, Sanne and Bakker, Arthur (2011) 'Boundary Crossing and Boundary Objects', *Review of Educational Research*, 81(2): 132–69.

Akrich, Madeleine (1995) 'The De-Scription of Technological Objects', in W.E. Bijker and J. Law (eds), *Shaping Technology/Building Society – Studies in Sociotechnical Change*. Cambridge, MA: MIT Press, pp. 205–24.

Aldersey-Williams, Hugh (1987) 'Starck and Stardom', *Industrial Design*, 34: 46–51.

Aldersey-Williams, Hugh (1993) 'Reponse to Myth', in S. Yelavich (ed.), *The Edge of the Millennium: An International Critique of Architecture, Urban Planning and Communication Design*. New York: Whitney Library of Design, pp. 139–44.

Alessi (1983) *Tea and Coffee Piazza: 11 Tea and Coffee Sets*. Milan: Alessi.

Alessi (1996) *L'Oggetto Dell'equilibrio*. Milan: Electra/Alessi.

Alexander, C., Ishiwaka, S. and Silverstein, M. (1977) *A Pattern Language: Towns, Buildings, Construction*. New York: Oxford University Press.

Allen, Katie (2006) 'iPod fails to ring bells with phone option', *The Guardian*, 4 September.

Allen, Tony (2000) Managing Director, Interbrand/Newell & Sorrell. Interview with the author, 11 November 2000.

Althusser, Louis (1969) *For Marx* (trans. B. Brewster). London: Penguin.

Andrews, Grant, Yeabsley, John and Higgs, Peter L. (2009) *The Creative Sector in New Zealand: Mapping and Economic Role: Report to New Zealand Trade and Enterprise*. Thorndon: New Zealand Institute of Economic Research.

Anholt, Simon (2002) 'Foreword', *Journal of Brand Management*, 9(4/5): 229–40.

Appadurai, Arjun (1990) 'Disjuncture and Difference in the Global Cultural Economy', *Theory, Culture & Society*, 7: 295–310.

Archer, Michael (1997) *Material Culture: The Object in British Art of the 1980s and 90s*. London: South Bank Centre.

Argent, Patrick (1998) 'Graphic Design is Engulfed in Self-disillusionment', *Design Week*, 13: 42.

Armstrong, Carol (1996) 'Questionnaire', *October*, 77: 26–8.

Artus, Mark (1999) 'That's Entertainment', *Fitch Flypaper: The 'E' Issue*. Columbus, OH: Fitch.

Arvidsson, Adam (2005) 'Brands: A Critical Perspective', *Journal of Consumer Culture*, 5(2): 235–58.

Ashworth, Gregory (1990) 'The Historic Cities of Groningen: Which Is Sold To Whom?', in G. Ashworth and B. Goodall (eds), *Marketing Tourism Places*. London: Routledge, pp. 138–55.

Ashworth, G. and Goodall, B. (eds) (1990) *Marketing Tourism Places*. London: Routledge, pp. 138–55.

Aspara, Jaakko (2010) 'How Do Institutional Actors in the Financial Market Assess Companies' Product Design? The Quasi-rational Evaluative Schemes', *Knowledge, Technology and Policy*, 22(4): 241–258.

Attfield, Judy (1989) 'FORM/female FOLLOWS FUNCTION/male: Feminist Critiques of Design', in J.A. Walker (ed.), *Design History and the History of Design*. London: Pluto, pp. 199–225.

Attfield, Judy (2000) *Wild Things: The Material Culture of Everyday Life*. Oxford: Berg.

Australian Bureau of Statistics (2011) 'Employment in Culture' (report). Available at www.abs.gov.au (accessed 5/1/13).

Baker, Nicholson (1988) *The Mezzanine*. London: Granta.

Baker, Steve (1989) 'Re-Reading *The Corporate Personality*', *Journal of Design History*, 2(4): 275–91.

Bal, Mieke (2002) 'Visual Essentialism and the Object of Visual Culture', *Journal of Visual Culture*, 2(1): 5–32.

Balcioglu, Tevfik (1994) 'On Transformations of the Term Design with Reference to Mass Produced Objects', in G. Hasdogan (ed.), *Design Industry and Turkey: Proceedings of International Product Design Symposium, Middle East Technical University, Department of Industrial Design, 1994*. Ankara: METU, pp. 253–63.

Balibrea, M. (2001) 'Urbanism, Culture and the Post-industrial City: Challenging the "Barcelona model"', *Journal of Spanish Cultural Studies*, 2(2): 187–209.

Balmond, Sarah (2006) 'Designers Could Benefit from New Product Explosion', *Design Week*, 23 March.

Banham, Reyner (1960) *Theory and Design in the First Machine Age*. London: Architectural Press.

Banham, Reyner (1981 [1965]) 'The Great Gizmo', in P. Sparke (ed.), *Design by Choice*. London: Academy Editions, pp. 108–14.

Banham, Reyner (1996 [1973]) 'Power Plank', in *A Critic Writes: Essays by Reyner Banham*. Berkeley, CA: University of California Press, pp. 184–7.

Barbacetto, Gianni (1987) *Design Interface: How Man and Machine Communicate. Olivetti Design Research by King and Miranda*. Milan: Arcadia Edizioni.

Barberis, Peter and May, Timothy (1993) *Government, Industry and Political Economy*. Buckingham: Open University Press.

Barlow, J.P. (1994) 'The Economy of Ideas', *Wired*, 2.03: 84–90, 126–9.

Barnard, Malcolm (2001) *Approaches to Understanding Visual Culture*. New York: Palgrave Macmillan.

Barnard, Matt (2000) 'Make Your Mark', *Design Week*, 24 January.

Barnett, Clive (2002) 'The Cultural Turn: Fashion or Progress in Human Geography?', *Antipode*, 30(4): 303–410.

Barreneche, Raul (2008) 'Star Power' at *Art Info*, 24 January 2011. Available at: www.artinfo.com/news/story/29479/star-power (accessed 12/12/12).

Barrick, A. and Thorp, D. (1989) 'Leeds: Awakening to the Possibilities', *Building Design*, 18 June: 24–5.

Barthes, Roland (1975 [1970]) *S/Z*. London: Jonathan Cape.

Barthes, Roland (1983 [1957]) *Mythologies*. London: Jonathan Cape.

Baudrillard, Jean (1988) *Jean Baudrillard: Selected Writings* (ed. Mark Poster). Cambridge: Polity Press.

Bauer, Robert and Eagan, Ward (2008) 'Design Thinking – Epistemic Plurality in Management and Organization', *Aesthesis: International Journal of Art and Aesthetics in Management and Organizational Life*, 2(3): 64–74.

Bayley, Stephen (1979) *In Good Shape: Style in Industrial Products 1900–1960*. London: Design Council.

Beard, Alison (2008) 'Tea for Two?' in *Financial Times*, 18 October.

Beck, Ulrich (1992 [1986]) *Risk Society: Towards a New Modernity* (trans. M. Ritter). London: Sage.

Beckett, Andy (2006) 'Going Cheap', *The Guardian*, 28 February.

Bell, M. and Jayne, M. (2003) '"Design-led" Urban Regeneration: A Critical Perspective', *Local Economy*, 18(2): 121–34.

Benjamin, Walter (1970 [1936]) 'The Work of Art in the Age of Mechanical Reproduction', in *Illuminations*. London: Fontana.

Benson, Richard (1999) 'Flexible Friends', *The Guardian* G2, 4 February.

Berger, John (1972) *Ways of Seeing*. London: Penguin.

Berger, Suzanne and Piore, Michael J. (1980) *Dualism and Discontinuity in Industrial Society*. Cambridge: Cambridge University Press.

Berman, Marshall (1983) *All That is Solid Melts into Air: The Experience of Modernity*. London: Verso.

Best, Michael H. (1990) *The New Competition: Institutions and Industrial Restructuring*. Oxford: Polity Press.

Betsky, Aaron (1999) 'Ontario Mills, California: Castle of Consumption in the Empire of Signs', in R. Moore (ed.), *Vertigo: The Strange New World of the Contemporary City*. London: Laurence King, pp. 192–203.

Betsky, Aaron (2000) 'All the World's a Store: The Spaces of Shopping', in J. Pavitt (ed.), *Brand New*. London: V&A Publications.

Bhaba, Homi (1990) 'Introduction', in H. Bhaba (ed.) *Nation and Narration*. London: Routledge, pp. 1–9.

Bhabha, Homi (1994) *The Location of Culture*. London: Routledge.

Bianchini, Franco (1995) 'Night Cultures, Night Economies', *Planning, Practice and Research*, 10(2): 121–6.

Bianchini, Franco and Parkinson, Michael (eds) (1993) *Cultural Policy and Urban Regeneration: The West European Experience*. Manchester: Manchester University Press.

Biddulph, Mike (2003) 'Towards Successful Home Zones in the UK', *Journal of Urban Design*, 8(3): 217–41.

Billig, Michael (1995) *Banal Nationalism*. London: Sage.

Blackwell, Lewis (1995) *The End of Print: Graphic Works of Dave Carson*. London: Laurence King.

Blackwell, Lewis (1997) *David Carson: 2nd Sight: Grafik Design after the End of Print*. London: Laurence King.

Blauvelt, Andrew (1994) 'An Opening: Graphic Design's Discursive Spaces', *Visible Language*, 28(3): 207–17.

Bloch, Peter (1995) 'Seeking the Ideal Form: Product Design and Consumer Response', *Journal of Marketing*, 59: 16–29.

Block, Fred (1990) *Postindustrial Possibilities: A Critique of Economic Discourse*. Berkeley, CA: University of California Press.

Bond, Julian (1998) 'Multibuy Now, Pay Later', *Atticus: The Journal of Original Thinking in Communications Services*, 4: 16–17.

Booth, Peter and Boyle, Robin (1993) 'See Glasgow, See Culture', in F. Bianchini and M. Parkinson (eds), *Cultural Policy and Urban Regeneration: The West European Experience*. Manchester: Manchester University Press, pp. 21–47.

Boradkar, Prasad (2003) 'Material Things, Immaterial Music', *Proceedings of the IDSA International Design Education Conference*. New York: Pratt Institute, pp. 23–31.

Bouchez, Hilde (2012) 'Pimp Your Home: Or Why Design Cannot Remain Exclusive From a Consumer Perspective', *Design Journal*, 15(4): 461–78.

Bourdieu, Pierre (1984) *Distinction: A Social Critique of the Judgement of Taste* (trans. R. Nice). Cambridge, MA: Harvard University Press.

Bourdieu, Pierre (1992) *The Logic of Practice*. Cambridge: Polity Press.

Boym, Constantin (1992) *New Russian Design*. New York: Rizzoli.

Branzi, Andrea (1984) *The Hot House: Italian New Wave Design*. London: Thames & Hudson.

Branzi, Andrea (1988) *Learning from Milan: Design and the Second Modernity*. Cambridge, MA: MIT Press.

Branzi, Andrea (1989) 'We are the Primitives', in V. Margolin (ed.), *Design Discourse: History, Theory, Criticism*. Chicago, IL: University of Chicago Press, pp. 37–42.

Branzi, Andrea (1993) 'Design and the Second Modernity: Theorems for an Ecology of the Artificial World', in S. Yelavich (ed.) *The Edge of the Millennium: An International Critique of Architecture, Urban Planning and Communication Design*. New York: Whitney Library of Design, pp. 125–7.

Breen, Brian (2005) 'The Business of Design', *Fast Company*, 93: 68.

Breward, Christopher and Wood, Ghislaine (2012) *British Design from 1948: Innovation in the Modern Age*. London: V&A Publications.

British Design Innovation (2007) 'The British Design Industry Valuation Survey – 2006 to 2007' (report). Brighton: BDI.

British Tourist Authority (1997) *Branding Britain*. London: British Tourist Authority.

Brown, Julian (1999) Studio Brown. Interview with the author, 5 August 1999.

Brown, Mark (2006) 'On Island of Dance, Rave Gives Way to Dance', *The Guardian*, 14 August.

Brown, Tim (2009) *Change by Design: How Design Thinking Transforms Organizations and Inspires Innovation*. New York: Harper Collins.

Bruce, Margaret and Daly, Lucy (2006) 'International Evidence on Design: Near Final Report for the Department of Trade and Industry' (report). Manchester: University of Manchester.

Bryson, John R. and Rusten, Grete (2011) *Design Economies and the Changing World Economy: Innovation, Production and Competitiveness*. Abingdon: Routledge.

Bryson, Norman (2002) 'Visual Culture and the Dearth of Images', *Journal of Visual Culture*, 2(2): 229–32.

Buchanan, Peter (1986) 'Spain: Poetics of Modernism', *Architectural Review*, CLXXIX: 1071. May: special edition.

Buchanan, Richard (1992) 'Wicked Problems in Design Thinking', *Design Issues*, 8(2): 5–21.

Buchanan, Richard (1998a) 'Branzi's Dilemma: Design in Contemporary Culture', *Design Issues*, 14(1): 3–20.

Buchanan, Richard (1998b) 'Review of J. Woodham (1997) *Twentieth-Century Design*', *Journal of Design History*, 11(3): 259–63.

Buckley, Cheryl (1998) 'On the Margins: Theorizing the History and Significance of Making and Designing Clothes at Home', *Journal of Design History*, 11(2): 157–71.

Buesa, M., Hidalgo, A., Conrado Llorens, C. and Zahera. M. (2001) 'El Diseño en España: Estudio Estratégico'. Madrid: Federación Española de Entidades de Promoción de Diseño Available at: www.idepa.es.

Bull, Michael (2005) 'No Dead Air! The iPod and the Culture of Mobile Listening', *Leisure Studies*, 24(4): 343–55.

Business Ratio Plus (1998) *Design Consultancies*. London: ICC Business Publications.

Busquet, Jordi (1993) *Cobi al Descobert*. Barcelona: Parisfal Ediciones.

Butler, Judith (1990) *Gender Trouble*. London: Routledge.

Cairncross, Francis (1997) *The Death of Distance: How the Communications Revolution Will Change Our Lives*. Boston, MA: Harvard Business School Press

Callon, Michel (2005) 'Why Virtualism Paves the Way to Political Impotence: A Reply to Daniel Miller's Critique of The Laws of the Markets', *Economic Sociology: European Electronic Newsletter*, 6(2): 3–20.

Callon, M., Méadel, C. and Rabeharisoa, V. (2002) 'The Economy of Qualities', *Economy and Society*, 31(2): 194–217.

Calvera, Anna (2000) 'Historia e historias del diseño: la emergencia de las historias regionales', Keynote paper given at La Habana, Cuba Conference, 'La Emergencia de las Historias Regionales'.

Cameron, Andy (1998a) 'The Medium is Messy', *Eye*, 30: 6–7.

Cameron, Andy (1998b) 'Dissimulations'. Available at: http://ma.hrc.wmin.ac.uk/kids/ma._theory. 3.2.db (accessed 13/02/99).

Campbell, Colin (1998) 'Consumption and the Rhetorics of Need and Want', *Journal of Design History*, 11(3): 235–46.

Campì, Isabel (2003) 'De la industria sin diseño al diseño sin industria', *La Vanguardia: Culturas* (Supplement), 8 October: 4–5.

Capella, Juli (1997) 'Rinuncio al design e mi metto a disposizione della società', *Domus*, 794: 52–6.

Carr, Raymond and Fusi, Juan Pablo (1981) *Spain: Dictatorship to Democracy*. London: Allen and Unwin.

Carrier, James G. (2003) 'Mind, Gaze and Engagement: Understanding the Environment', *Journal of Material Culture*, 8(1): 5–23.

Carrington, Noel (1976) *Industrial Design in Britain*. London: Allen and Unwin.

Castells, Manuel (1996) *The Rise of the Network Society*. Oxford: Blackwell.

Castells, Manuel (2001) *The Internet Galaxy: Reflections on the Internet, Business, and Society*. Oxford: Oxford University Press.

Caves, Richard (2000) *Creative Industries: Contracts Between Art and Commerce*. Cambridge: Harvard University Press.

Cawood, Gavin (1997) 'Design Innovation and Culture in SMEs', *Design Management Journal*, 8(4): 66–70.

Center Parcs (2012) 'Annual Review 2012' (report). Available at: www.centerparcs.co.uk (accessed 18/12/12).

Centre for International Economics (2009) 'Creative Industries Economic Analysis'. Available at: www.enterpriseconnect.gov.au.

Chan, Melanie (2006) 'Reality Kicks Back: A Study of the Discourses of Virtual Reality'. Unpublished PhD thesis, Leeds Metropolitan University.

Chaney, David (1996) *Lifestyles*. London: Routledge.

Chatterton, Paul and Hollands, Robert (2003) *Urban Nightscapes, Youth Cultures, Pleasure Spaces and Corporate Power*. London: Routledge.

Cheng, Jacqui (2012) 'Apple's Secret Garden: The Struggle Over Leaks and Security'. Available at http://arstechnica.com/apple/2012 (accessed 8/3/13).

CITF – Creative Industries Task Force (1998) *Creative Industries Mapping Document*. London: Department of Culture, Media and Sport.

CITF – Creative Industries Task Force (2001) *Creative Industries Mapping Document*. London: Department of Culture, Media and Sport.

Clegg, Sue and Mayfield, Wendy (1999) 'Gendered by Design: How Women's Place in Design is Still Defined by Gender', *Design Issues*, 15(3): 3–16.

Clynes, Manfred and Kline, Nathan (1960) 'Cyborgs and Space', *Astronautics*, September: 26–7, 74–5.

Coates, Nigel (1988) 'Street Signs', in J. Thackara (ed.), *Design after Modernism: Beyond the Object*. London: Thames & Hudson, pp. 95–114.

Cohen, G.A. (1978) *Karl Marx's Theory of History: A Defence*. Oxford: Clarendon Press.

Collier, David (1993) 'Visual Metaphors for Interactive Products'. Paper given at *Doors of Perception 1* conference, Netherlands Design Institute. Conference proceedings published at www.doorsofperception.com.

Cooley, Heidi Ray (2004) 'It's All About the Fit: The Hand, the Mobile Screenic Device and Tactile Vision', *Journal of Visual Culture*, 3(2): 133–55.

Copenhagen Business School (2005) 'The Danish Design Industry Annual Mapping' (report), Copenhagen: Imagine.

Copps, Alan (1996) 'This is a Sequence from an Action-packed Movie ... It is Selling a New Car as Drama', *The Times* Car, 3 February.

Corrigan, Peter (1997) *The Sociology of Consumption: An Introduction*. London: Sage.

Cousins, Mark (1994) 'Danger and Safety', *Art History*, 17(3): 418–23.

Coyle, Diane (1997) The Weightless World: Strategies for Managing the Digital Economy. Cambridge, MA: MIT Press.

Crace, John (1999) 'Whose Bright Idea is it Anyway?', *The Guardian* Education, 5 October.

Credit Suisse (2006) 'iPod: How Big Can It Get?' (report). Geneva: Credit Suisse.

Crilley, Darrel (1993) 'Architecture as Advertising: Constructing the Image of Redevelopment', in G. Kearns and C. Philo (eds), *Selling Places: The City as Cultural Capital, Past and Present*. Oxford: Pergamon, pp. 231–52.

Cross, Nigel (1982) 'Designerly Ways of Knowing', *Design Studies*, 3(4): 221–7.

Cross, Nigel (2006) *Designerly Ways of Knowing*. Berlin: Springer.

Crosthwaite, Andrew (1999) *How Advertising Affects Customer Loyalty* (pamphlet). London: Institute of Practitioners in Advertising.

Crowley, David Ernyey, G., Mrozek, J. and Ferkai, A. (1992) *Design and Culture in Poland and Hungary, 1890–1990*. Brighton: Brighton University.

Csikszentmihalyi, Mihaly (1975) *Beyond Boredom and Anxiety: The Experience of Play in Work and Games*. San Francisco, CA: Jossey-Bass.

Csikszentmihalyi, Mihaly (1991) 'Design and Order in Everyday Life', *Design Issues*, 8(1): 26–34.

Danish Government (2007) 'DesignDenmark' (report), Copenhagen: Schultz.

Davenport, Russ (1999) Project Leader, Leeds Landmark, FaulknerBrowns. Interview with the author, 22 November 1999.

Davidson, Martin (1992) *The Consumerist Manifesto: Advertising in Postmodern Times*. London: Routledge.

de Certeau, Michel (1984) *The Practice of Everyday Life*. Berkeley, CA: University of California Press.

Deal, T.E. and Kennedy, A.A. (1982) *Corporate Cultures: The Rites and Rituals of Corporate Life*. Reading, MA: Addison-Wesley.

Debord, Guy (1967) *The Society of the Spectacle*. Cambridge, MA: Zone Books.

Degen, Monica (2003) 'Fighting for the Global Catwalk: Formalizing Public Life in Castlefield (Manchester) and Diluting Public Life in el Raval (Barcelona)', *International Journal of Urban and Regional Research*, 27(4): 867–80.

Degen, M., DeSilvey, C. and Rose, G. (2008) 'Experiencing Visualities in Designed Urban Environments: Learning from Milton Keynes', *Environment and Planning A*, 40(6): 1901–20.

Deleuze, Gilles and Guattari, Felix (1988) *A Thousand Plateaus* (trans. B. Massumi). London: Continuum.

Derrida, Jacques (1976 [1967]) *Of Grammatology* (trans. G.C. Spivak). Baltimore, MD: Johns Hopkins University Press.

Design Continuum (1999) www.dcontinuum.com/do/capabilities.html#pl (accessed 12/05/99).

Design Council (1998) *Design in Britain 1998–9: Facts, Figures and Quotable Quotes*. London: Design Council.

Design Council (2003) *Design in Britain 2003–2004*. London: Design Council.

Design Council (2010) 'Design Industry Research'. Available at: www.designcouncil.org.uk.

Design Exchange (1995) *Design for a Strong Ontario: A Strategy for Ontario's Design Sector*. Toronto: Design Exchange.

Design Industry Voices (2009) 'Design Industry Voices 2009: How it feels to work in British digital and design agencies right now' (report). Available at www.designindustryvoices.com (accessed 27/08/12).

Design Industry Voices (2010) 'Design Industry Voices 2010: How it feels to work in British digital and design agencies right now' (report). Available at www.designindustryvoices.com (accessed 27/08/12).

Design Industry Voices (2011) 'Design Industry Voices 2011: How it feels to work in British digital and design agencies right now' (report). Available at www.designindustryvoices.com (accessed 27/08/12).

Design Week (1998) 'Consultancy Survey', *Design Week*, 26 March.

DESIGN|focus (2006) 'Milano Made in Design' (report). Milan: Viappiani.

Design2020 Committee (2011) 'The Vision of the Design2020 Committee' (report). Copenhagen: Danish Enterprise and Construction Authority.

Dew, Tom (1999) 'Developing a Critique of New Media'. Unpublished essay, Leeds Metropolitan University.

Dewey, John (1934) *Art as Experience*, reprinted in 1989, *John Dewey: The Later Works, 1925–1953*, vol. 10. J. Boydston (ed.), Carbondale, IL: Southern Illinois University Press.

Dilnot, Clive (1984) 'The State of Design History, Part II: Problems and Possibilities', *Design Issues*, 3(2): 3–20.

DiSalvo, Carl (2012) *Adversarial Design*. Cambridge, MA: MIT Press.

Dormer, Peter (1990) *The Meanings of Modern Design: Towards the Twenty-First Century*. London: Thames & Hudson.

Drakuliç, Slavenka (1988) *How We Survived Communism and Even Laughed*. London: Vintage.

Drivers Jonas, Regeneris Consulting and Taylor Young (2003) 'Northern Quarter Development Framework' (report). Manchester: Manchester City Council.

du Gay, Paul (1996) *Consumption and Identity at Work*. London: Sage.

du Gay, Paul (1997) 'Organizing Identity: Making Up People at Work', in P. du Gay (ed.), *Production of Culture/Cultures of Production*. London: Sage/The Open University, pp. 285–344.

du Gay, P., Hall, S., Janes, L., Mackay, H. and Negus, K. (2013) *Doing Cultural Studies: The Story of the Sony Walkman. 2nd Edition*. London: Sage/The Open University.

Dunne, Anthony (2005) *Hertzian Tales: Electronic Products, Aesthetic Experience, and Critical Design*. Cambridge, MA: MIT Press.

Dunne, Anthony and Raby, Fiona (2001) *Design Noir: The Secret Life of Electronic Objects*. London: Aubust/Birkhauser.

Dunne, Anthony and Raby, Fiona (2012) 'Critical Design FAQ'. Available at: www.dunneandraby.co.uk/content/bydandr/13/0 (accessed 6/12/12).

Dyer, Gillian (1982) *Advertising as Communication*. London: Methuen.

Dyson, James (1998) *Against the Odds: An Autobiography*. London: Orion Business.

Eco, Umberto (1986) *Faith in Fakes*. London: Bracken.

Edensor, Tim (2002) *National Identity, Popular Culture and Everyday Life*. Oxford: Berg.

Edwards, Barry (1999) Project Manager Dynamic Earth, Event Communications. Interview with the author, 8 October 1999.

Ellwood, Iain (1998) 'The Future of Retail Sites, a Paradigmatic Shift from the Retailing of Commodities to the Commodification and Consumption of Brand Experiences'. Paper given at 'Design Innovation: Conception to Consumption' 21st International Annual Conference of the Design History Society, University of Huddersfield.

Ericson, Magnus and Mazé, Rámia (eds) (2011) *DESIGN ACT – Socially and Politically Engaged Design*. Berlin: Sternberg.

Espada, Arcadi (1997) *Contra Catalunya: Una Crónica*. Barcelona: Flor del Viento.

European Design Innovation Initiative (2012) 'Design for Growth and Prosperity: Report and Recommendations of the European Design Leadership Board' (report). Helsinki: DG Enterprise and Industry of the European Commission. Available at: http://ec.europa.eu/enterprise (accessed 4/1/13).

European Design Leadership Board (2012) 'Design for Growth and Prosperity' (report). Brussels: DG Enterprise and Industry.

Evans, Jessica and Hall, Stuart (eds) (2002) *Visual Culture: The Reader*. Thousand Oaks, CA: Sage.

Fallan, Kjetil (2008) 'De-scibing Design: Appropriating Script Analysis to Design Hitory', *Design Issues*, 24(4): 61–75.

Fallan, Kjetil (2010) *Design History: Understanding Theory and Method*. Oxford: Berg.

Featherstone, David (2011) 'On assemblage and articulation', *Area* 43(2): 139–142.

Featherstone, Mike (1991) *Consumer Culture and Postmodernism*. London: Sage.

Feifer, Maxine (1985) *Going Places: The Ways of the Tourist from Imperial Rome to the Present Day*. London: Macmillan.

Fernández, Josep-Anton (1995) 'Becoming Normal: Cultural Production and Cultural Policy in Catalonia', in H. Graham and J. Labanyi (eds), *Spanish Cultural Studies: An Introduction. The Struggle for Modernity*. Oxford: Oxford University Press, pp. 342–5.

Fine, Ben (1995) 'From Political Economy to Consumption', in D. Miller (ed.), *Acknowledging Consumption: A Review of New Studies*. London: Routledge, pp. 127–57.

Fine, Ben and Leopold, Ellen (1993) *The World of Consumption*. London: Routledge.

FIRJAN (2011) 'Mapeamento Da Indústria Criativa No Brasil' (report). Rio de Janeiro. Available at: www.firjan.org.br/economia (accessed 22/11/12).

Fischer Fine Art (1991) *Pioneers of Modern Furniture*. London: Lund Humphries.

Fiske, John (1989a) *Understanding Popular Culture*. London: Routledge.

Fiske, John (1989b) *Reading the Popular*. London: Routledge.

Fitch (1999) 'Reality Bites', *Fitch Flypaper: The 'E' Issue*. Columbus, OH: Fitch.

Fleming, Dan (1996) *Powerplay: Toys as Popular Culture*. Manchester: Manchester University Press.

Fleming, Tom (2007) 'A Creative Economy Green Paper for the Nordic Region' (report). Oslo: Nordic Innovation Centre.

Florida, Richard (2002) *The Rise of the Creative Class: And How It's Transforming Work, Leisure, Community and Everyday*. New York: Basic Books.

Flusty, Steven (1997) 'Icons in the Stream: On Local Revisions of Global Stuff', in A. Betsky (ed.), *Icons: Magnets of Meaning*. San Francisco, CA: Museum of Modern Art and Chronicle Books, pp. 52–65.

Forty, Adrian (1986) *Objects of Desire: Design and Society Since 1750*. London: Thames & Hudson.

Foster, Hal (2002a) *Design and Crime (and Other Diatribes)*. London: Verso.

Foster, Hal (2002b) 'The ABCs of Contemporary Design', *October*, 100: 191–9.

Foster, J., McChesney, R. and Jonna, R. (2011) 'Monopoly and Competition in Twenty-first Century Capitalism', *Monthly Review*, 62(11): 1–39.

Foucault, Michel (1977) *Discipline and Punish* (trans. A. Sheridan). London: Allen Lane.

Foucault, Michel (2007) *Security, Territory, Population: Lectures at the Collège de France 1977–78*. Basingstoke: Palgrave Macmillan.

Frayling, Christopher (1999) 'Flight of the Phoenix', *RSA Journal*, 3/4: 48–57.

Friedel, Robert (1994) *Zipper: An Exploration in Novelty*. New York: Norton.

Frith, Simon and Horne, Howard (1987) *Art into Pop*. London: Routledge.

Froud, J., Haslam, C., Johal, S. and Williams, K. (2000) 'Shareholder Value and Financialization: Consultancy Promises, Management Moves', *Economy and Society*, 29(1): 80–110.

Fuad-Luke, Alastair (2009) *Design Activism: Beautiful Strangeness for a Sustainable World*. London: Earthscan.

Funk, J. L. (2001) *The Mobile Internet: How Japan Dialed Up and the West Disconnected*. Hong Kong: ISI.

Gabra-Liddell, Meret (ed.) (1994) *Alessi: The Design Factory*. London: Academy Editions.

Galbraith, J.K. (1958) *The Affluent Society*. London: Hamish Hamilton.

Galbraith, J.K. (1967) *The New Industrial State*. London: Hamish Hamilton.

Gardner, Carl and Sheppard, Julie (1989) *Consuming Passion: The Rise of Retail Culture*. London: Unwin Hyman.

Gibson, William (1994) *Virtual Light*. London: Viking.

Giddens, Anthony (1991) *Modernity and Self-Identity: Self and Society in the Late Modern Age*. London: Polity Press.

Gideon, Sigfried (1948) *Mechanization Takes Command: A Contribution to Anonymous History*. New York: Oxford University Press.

Goldman, Robert and Papson, Stephen (1998) *Nike Culture: The Sign of the Swoosh*. London: Sage.

Gottdiener, Mark (1997) *The Theming of America: Dreams, Visions and Commercial Spaces*. New York: HarperCollins.

Graham, Stephen and Marvin, Simon (1996) *Telecommunications and the City: Electronic Spaces, Urban Places*. London: Routledge.

Greenhalgh, Paul (1988) *Ephemeral Vistas: The Expositions Universelles, Great Exhibitions and World's Fairs, 1851–1939*. Manchester: Manchester University Press.

Grossman, Lev (2007) 'Invention of the Year: The iPhone', *Time Magazine*, 1 November.

Guterson, David (1995) *Snow Falling on Cedars*. London: Bloomsbury.

Hajer, Maarten A. (1993) 'Rotterdam: Re-designing the Pubic Domain', in F. Bianchini and M. Parkinson (eds), *Cultural Policy and Urban Regeneration: The West European Experience*. Manchester: Manchester University Press, pp. 48–72.

Hall, Peter (1996) 'Strange Fruit', *ID Magazine*, 43: 78–81.

Hall, Stuart (1980) 'Race, articulation and societies structured in dominance' UNESCO ed. *Sociological Theories: Race and Colonialism.* Paris: UNESCO, pp.305–45.

Hall, Stuart (1985) 'Signification, Representation, Ideology: Althusser and the Post-Structuralist Debates', *Critical Studies in Mass Communication*, 2(2): 91–114.

Hall, Stuart (1996) 'On postmodernism and articulation', in D. Morley and K-H. Chen (eds), *Stuart Hall: Critical Dialogues in Cultural Studies*. London: Routledge, pp. 131–50.

Hamilton, Doug and Kirby, Keith (1999) 'A New Brand for a New Category: Paint it Orange', *Design Management Journal*, 10(1): 41–5.

Hanna, Jeannette (1997) 'The Rise of Interactive Branding', *Design Management Journal*, 8(1): 34–9.

Haraway, Donna (2006 [1985]) 'A Cyborg Manifesto: Science, Technology, and Socialist-Feminism in the Late 20th Century', in J. Weiss, J. Nolan, J. Hunsinger and P. Trifonas (eds), *The International Handbook of Virtual Learning Environments*, pp. 117–158.

Harris, Nick (1999) Executive Producer, Acquisitions & Licensing, DK Interactive Learning. Correspondence with the author, 20 December 1999.

Harrison, Bennett (1994) *Lean and Mean: The Changing Landscape of Corporate Power in the Age of Flexibility*. New York: Basic Books.

Harvey, David (1989a) *The Condition of Postmodernity: An Enquiry into the Origins of Cultural Change*. Oxford: Basil Blackwell.

Harvey, David (1989b) *The Urban Experience*. Oxford: Blackwell.

Harvey, David (2005) *A Brief History of Neoliberalism*. Oxford: Oxford University Press.

Haug, W.F. (1986) *Critique of Commodity Aesthetics: Appearance, Sexuality and Advertising in Capitalist Society*. London: Polity Press.

Hayward, Stephen (1998) '"Good design is largely a matter of common sense": Questioning the Meaning and Ownership of a Twentieth-Century Orthodoxy', *Journal of Design History*, 11(3): 217–33.

Hebdige, Dick (1979) *Subculture: The Meaning of Style*. London: Comedia.

Hebdige, Dick (1988) *Hiding in the Light: On Images and Things*. London: Comedia.

Heidegger, Martin (2005 [1927]) *Being and Time* (trans. J. Macquarrie and E. Robinson). Oxford: Blackwell.

Helfand, Jessica (1997) 'Geometry is Never Wrong', *Eye*, 24: 6–7.

Helft, Miguel and Carter, Shan (2011) 'A Chief Executive's Attention to Detail, Noted in 313 Patents', *New York Times*, 25 August.

Hemisphere (2003) 'A Brand Strategy for Manchester: Stage 1 Summary: Brand Values & Positioning' (report). Manchester: Hemisphere.

Henwood, Doug (1995) 'Info fetishism', in J. Brook and I. Boal (eds), *Resisting the Virtual Life: The Culture and Politics of Information*. San Fransisco, CA: City Lights, pp. 161–71.

Hermans, H.J.M. and Hermans-Konopka, A. (2010). *Dialogical Self Theory: Positioning and Counter-Positioning an a Globalizing Society*. Cambridge: Cambridge University Press.

Heron, Steve (1999) Senior Designer, IDEO. Interview with the author, 2 November 1999.

Herrmann, M., Millard, A. and Royffe, C. (2000) 'Sustainable Landscape Design in Practice', in J. Benson and M. Roe (eds), *Landscape and Sustainability*. London: Spon.

Herz, J.C. (1998) 'Toggle your Joysticks with Pride'. Paper given at 'Doors of Perception 5: Play', Netherlands Design Institute. Conference proceedings, published on CD-ROM. Amsterdam: Netherlands Design Institute.

Heskett, John (1986) *German Design: 1870–1918*. New York: Taplinger.

Heskett, John (1989) *Philips: A Study of the Corporate Management of Design*. London: Trefoil.

Hesmondhalgh, David (2000) *The Cultural Industries*. London: Sage.

Hess, Allen (1993) *Viva Las Vegas: After-Hours Architecture*. San Francisco, CA: Chronicle.

Heward, Tony (1994) 'Retailing the Police: Corporate Identity and the Met', in R. Keat, N. Whiteley and N. Abercrombie (eds), *The Authority of the Consumer*. London: Routledge, pp. 240–52.

Hewison, Robert (1987) *The Heritage Industry: Britain in a Climate of Decline*. London: Methuen.

Hewison, Robert (1997) 'Fool Britannia', *Blueprint*, 144: 30–1.

Highmore, Ben (2009) *The Design Culture Reader*. Abingdon: Routledge.

Hochschild, Arlie Russell (2003 [1983]) *The Managed Heart: Commercialization of Human Feeling*. Berkeley, CA: University of California Press.

Hollington, Geoff (1998) 'The Usual Suspects', *Design*, Summer: 62–3.

Hollington, Geoff (1999a) Interview with the author, 25 June 1999.

Hollington, Geoff (1999b) Correspondence with the author, 5 November 1999.

Holtzman, Steven R. (1997) *Digital Mosaics: The Aesthetics of Cyberspace*. New York: Simon & Schuster.

Horsham, Michael (1994) 'The Great I AM', *Blueprint*, May: 25–6.

Howard, Elizabeth and Davies, Ross (1988) *Change in the Retail Environment*. Harlow: Longman.

Howells, Richard (2001) *Visual Culture: An Introduction*. Cambridge: Polity Press.

Howkins, John (2001) *The Creative Economy: How People Make Money from Ideas*. London: Allen Lane.

Hsiao, S. and Chen, C. (1997) 'A Semantic and Shape Grammar-based Approach for Product Design', *Design Studies*, 18(3): 275–96.

Huxor, Avon (1995) 'Virtual Worlds: Design as a New Frontier'. Paper given at 'Futures: Visions and Revisions', Design History Society 18th Annual Conference, Middlesex University.

Huygen, Frederique (1989) *British Design: Image and Identity*. London: Thames & Hudson.

Imagination (1998) 'Building Bridges: A Year in the Life of the Aurora Project' (unpaginated in-house publication). London: Imagination.

Intel (2012) 'Global Study: Women and the Web' (report). Available at www.intel.com/conten/dam/www/public/us/en/documents (accessed 31/08/13).

Jackson, Peter and Thrift, Nigel (1995) 'Geographies of Consumption', in D. Miller (ed.), *Acknowledging Consumption: A Review of New Studies*. London: Routledge, pp. 204–37.

Jacobs, Jane (1961) *The Death and Life of Great American Cities: The Failure of Town Planning*. New York: Random House and Vintage.

Janson-Smith, Deirdre (1999) Event Communications. Interview with the author, 8 October 1999.

Jay, Martin (1988) 'Scopic Regimes of Modernity' in H. Foster (ed.), *Vision and Visuality*. New York: Dia Art Foundation.

Jencks, Charles and Silver, Nathan (1972) *Adhocism: The Case for Improvisation*. New York: Doubleday and Company.

Jessop, Bob, Kastendiek, Hans, Nielsen, Klaus, Pedersen and Ove Kaj (eds) (1991) *The Politics of Flexibility: Restructuring State and Industry in Britain, Germany and Scandinavia*. Aldershot: Edward Elgar.

Joffe, Avril and Newton, Monica (2008) 'The Creative Industries in South Africa'. Available at: www.labour.gov.za.

Johnson, Richard (1986) 'The Story So Far: And Further Transformations', in D. Punter (ed.), *Introduction to Contemporary Cultural Studies*. London: Longman, pp. 277–313.

Jones, Amelia (ed.) (2003) *The Feminism and Visual Culture Reader*. New York: Routledge.

Jones, Helen (1999) 'The Write Stuff', *Design Week*, 17 September.

Jones, Mike (1991) 'Going Public, Going Bust', *Design*, January: 13–19.

Joseph, Claudia (2006) 'iPod City', *Daily Mail*, 11 June: 56–7.

Julier, Guy (1991) *New Spanish Design*. London: Thames & Hudson.

Julier, Guy (1993) *Thames & Hudson Encyclopedia of the 20th Century: Design and Designers*. London: Thames & Hudson.

Julier, Guy (1995) 'Design Institutions and the Transition to Democracy: A Comparative Case Study of Spain and Hungary'. Paper given at 'Design, Government Initiatives and Industry' International Conference, Brighton University, Brighton.

Julier, Guy (1996) 'Barcelona Design, Catalonia's Political Economy and the New Spain', *Journal of Design History*, 9(2): 117–28.

Julier, Guy (1998) *The Teapot: An Appreciation*. London: Aurum.

Julier, Guy (2005) 'Urban Designscapes and the Production of Aesthetic Consent', *Urban Studies*, 42(5–6): 869–88.

Julier, Guy (2007) 'Design Practice within a Theory of Practice', *Design Principles & Practices: An International Journal*, 1(2): 43–50.

Julier, Guy and Moor, Liz (eds) (2009) *Design and Creativity: Policy, Management and Practice*. Oxford: Berg.

Kasarda, John and Lindsay, Greg (2011) *Aerotropolis: The Way We'll Live Next*. New York: Farrar, Straus and Giroux.

Kearns, Gerry and Philo, Chris (eds) (1993) *Selling Places: The City as Cultural Capital, Past and Present*. Oxford: Pergamon.

Keat, Russell and Abercrombie, Nicholas (1991) 'Introduction', in *Enterprise Culture*, London: Routledge, pp. 1–20.

Keat, R., Whitely, N. and Abercrombie, N. (eds) (1994) *The Authority of the Consumer*. London: Routledge.

Kelly, Kevin (1998) *New Rules for the New Economy: 10 Radical Strategies for a Connected World*. London: Fourth Estate.

Kenan Institute Asia (2009) 'Economic Contributions Of Thailand's Creative Industries'. Available at: www.kiasia.org.

Key Note (1990) *Advertising Agencies: An Industry Sector Overview* (report). Hampton: Key Note Publications.

Key Note (1996) *Market Report: Design Consultancies* (report). Hampton: Key Note Publications.

Kimbell, Lucy (2009) 'The Turn to Service Design', in G. Julier and L. Moor (eds), *Design and Creativity: Policy, Management and Practice*. Oxford: Berg, pp. 157–73.

Kimbell, Lucy (2011) 'Rethinking Design Thinking: Part 1', *Design and Culture*, 3(3): 285–306.

Kimbell, Lucy (2012) 'Rethinking Design Thinking: Part 2', *Design and Culture*, 4(2):129–148.

King, Emily (1995) 'The End of Print?'. Paper given at 'Futures: Visions and Revisions', Design History Society 18th Annual Conference, Middlesex University, London.

Kinross, Robin (1992) *Modern Typography: An Essay in Critical History*. London: Hypen Press.

Kinross, Robin (1997) 'Where the Dear God Lives', in S. Heller and M. Finamore (eds), *Design Culture: An Anthology of Writing from the AIGA Journal of Graphic Design*. New York: Allworth, pp. 199–202.

Kitchen, Sarah (1990) 'Leeds: The Smotherer of Invention', *Building*, 23 February: 24–5.

Kitchin, Rob (1998) *Cyberspace: The World in the Wires*. Chichester: Wiley.

Knorr Cetina, Karin (2001) 'Objectual Practice', in T.R. Schatzki, K. Knorr Cetina and E. von Savigny (eds), *The Practice Turn in Contemporary Theory*. London and New York: Routledge.

Kochan, Nicholas (1996) *The World's Greatest Brands*. London: Macmillan Business.

Koh, Daniel (2004) Personal correspondence with the author, 21 January 2004.

Kopytoff, Igor (1986) 'The Cultural Biography of Things: Commoditization as Process', in A. Appadurai (ed.), *The Social Life of Things: Commodites in Cultural Perspective*. Cambridge: Cambridge University Press, pp. 64–94.

Koskinen, Ilpö (2005) 'Semiotic Neighborhoods', *Design Issues*, 21(2): 13–27.

Koskinen, Ilpö and Kurvinen, Esko (2005) 'Mobile Multimedia and Users: On the Domestication of Mobile Multimedia', *Telektronikk*, 3(4): 60–8.

Kotler, P., Haider, D. and Rein, I. (2002) *Marketing Places: Attracting Investment, Industry and Tourism to Cities, States and Nations*. New York: Free Press.

Kristensen, Juliette (2006) 'How I Bought an iPod and Fired My Therapist: An Exploration of Apple's Digital Sound Player and Its Role as a Mobile Technology in Social Experience'. Unpublished paper given at 'Design and Evolution', Annual Design History Society Conference, Technical University of Delft.

Laclau, Ernesto and Mouffe, Chantal (1985) *Hegemony and Socialist Strategy: Towards a Radical Democratic Politics*. London: Verso.

Lacroix, Marie-Josée (ed.) (2005) *New Design Cities*. Montreal: Les Editions Infopresse.

Landow, George P. (1992) *Hypertext: The Convergence of Contemporary Critical Theory and Technology*. Baltimore, MD: Johns Hopkins University Press.

Landry, Charles (2000) *The Creative City*. London: Demos.

Landscape Design Associates/Bioscan (UK) Ltd (1992) 'Center Parcs: An International Approach to Environmental Issues' (unpublished internal report).

Lanham, Richard (1993) *The Electronic Word: Democracy, Technology and the Arts*. Chicago, IL: University of Chicago Press.

Lash, Scott (2002) *Critique of Information*. London: Sage.

Lash, Scott (2010) *Intensive Culture: Social Theory, Religion and Contemporary Capitalism*. London: Sage.

Lash, Scott and Lury, Celia (2007) *Global Culture Industry*. Cambridge: Polity.

Lash, Scott and Urry, John (1987) *The End of Organized Capitalism*. London: Polity Press.

Lash, Scott and Urry, John (1994) *Economies of Signs and Spaces*. London: Sage.

Latour, Bruno (1987) *Science in Action: How to Follow Scientists and Engineers through Society*. Cambridge MA: Harvard University Press.

Latour, Bruno (2005) *Reassembling the Social: an Introduction to Actor-Network Theory*. Oxford: Oxford University Press.

Laurier, Eric (1993) 'Tackintosh: Glasgow's Supplementary Gloss', in G. Kearns and C. Philo (eds), *Selling Places: The City as Cultural Capital, Past and Present*. Oxford: Pergamon, pp. 267–90.

Law, Andy (1999) *Creative Company: How St Luke's Became the Ad Agency to End All Ad Agencies*. New York: Wiley.

Law, John (1994) *Organizing Modernity*. Oxford: Blackwell.

Law, John (2008) 'Actor-network theory and material semiotics', in B. Turner (ed.), *The New Blackwell Companion to Social Theory*, 3rd edn. Oxford: Blackwell, pp. 141–58.

Lawson, Bryan (1997) *How Designers Think: The Design Process Demystified*, 3rd edn. London: Architectural Press.

Layfield, R., Chinn, L. and Nicholls, D. (2003) 'Pilot Home Zone Schemes: Evaluation of The Methleys, Leeds. Prepared for Charging and Local Transport Division, Department for Transport' (report). Wokingham: TRL Ltd.

Leach, Neil (2002) 'Belonging: Towards a Theory of Identification with Space', in J. Hillier and E. Rooksby (eds), *Habitus: A Sense of Place*. Aldershot: Ashgate, pp. 281–98.

Leeds City Council (1998) *Leeds Economic Handbook*. Leeds: Leeds City Council.

Lees, Grace (1997) 'Balancing the Object: The Reinvention of Alessi', *Things*, 6: 74–91.

Lees-Maffei, Grace (2009) 'The Production–Consumption–Mediation Paradigm', *Journal of Design History*, 22(4): 351–76.

Lefebvre, Henri (1994 [1974]) *The Production of Space* (trans. D. Nicholson-Smith). Oxford: Blackwell.

Legg, Stephen (2011) 'Assemblage/Apparatus: Using Deleuze and Foucault', *Area*, 43(2): 128–33.

Leiss, W., Kline, S. and Jhally, S. (1990) *Social Communication in Advertising: Persons, Products and Images of Well-Being*, 2nd edn. London: Routledge.

Leonard, Mark (1997) *BritainTM: Renewing Our Identity*. London: Demos.

Lévi-Strauss, Claude (1969) *The Raw and the Cooked* (trans. by J. and D. Weightman). London: Cape.

Lloyd, Richard (2006) *Neo-Bohemia: Art and Commerce in the Post-Industrial City*. London: Routledge.

Lloyd Jones, Peter (1992) 'Time and the Perception of Everyday Things', in S. Vihma (ed.) *Objects and Images: Studies in Design and Advertising*. Helsinki: University of Industrial Arts, pp. 58–75.

Lloyd Morgan, Conway (1999) *Starck*. New York: Universe.

Loewy, Raymond (1951) *Never Leave Well Enough Alone*. New York: Simon & Schuster.

Lorenz, Christopher (1986) *The Design Dimension: Product Strategy and the Challenge of Global Marketing*. Oxford: Blackwell.

Lupton, Ellen (2005) Personal communication with the author, 8 January 2004.

Lupton, Ellen and Albrecht, Donald (2000) *Design Culture Now*. Princeton, NJ: Princeton Architecture Press.

Lury, Celia (1996) *Consumer Culture*. Cambridge: Polity Press.

Lury, Celia (2004) *Brands: The Logos of the Global Economy*. Abingdon: Routledge.

Lycett, Kevin (1999) Communication Design Solutions. Interview with the author, 2 December 1999.

Macdonald, Nico (1997) 'Not As Other Media', *Eye*, 26: 6–7.

Mackenzie, Donald (2009) *Material Markets: How Economic Agents are Constructed*. Oxford: Oxford University Press.

Maier-Aichen, Hansjerg (2004) *Idea Factory: un repte global en un marc de recessió mundial*. Barcelona: Eina Escola de Disseny i Art, PlecsEsparsos.

Malpass, Matthew (2012) 'Contextualising Critical Design: Towards a Taxonomy of Critical Practice in Product Design'. PhD thesis, Nottingham Trent University.

Mañà, Jordi (1983) *Diseño y la Exportación*. Barcelona: Centro de Estudios Internacional.

Manchester City Council (2003) 'Manchester: Knowledge Capital' (report). Manchester: Manchester City Council.

Manovich, Lev (1997) 'The Aesthetics of Virtual Worlds: Report from Los Angeles', in A. Kroker and M. Kroker (eds), *Digital Delirium*. Montréal: New World Perspectives, pp. 288–300.

Manuelli, Sara (2000) 'Searching for an Identity', *Design Week*, 14 January.

Manzini, Ezio (1986) *The Material of Invention*. Milan: Arcadia.

Manzini, Ezio (1992) *Artefactos: Hacia una Nueva Ecología del Ambiente Artificial* (trans. C. Ordóñez and P. Cattermole). Madrid: Ediciones Experimenta.

Manzini, Ezio (1998) 'Products in a Period of Transition: Products, Services and Interactions for a Sustainable Society', in T. Balcioglu (ed.), *The Role of Product Design in Post-Industrial Society*. Ankara: Middle East Technical University, pp. 43–58.

Margolin, Victor (1995a) 'The Product Milieu and Social Action', in R. Buchanan and V. Margolin (eds), *Discovering Design: Explorations in Design Studies*. Chicago, IL: University of Chicago Press.

Margolin, Victor (1995b) 'A Reply to Adrian Forty', *Design Issues*, 11(1): 19–21.

Markussen, Thomas (2013) 'The Disruptive Aesthetics of Design Activism: Enacting Design Between Art and Politics', *Design Issues*, 29(1): 38–50.

Marling, Karal Ann (1997) *Designing Disney's Theme Parks: The Architecture of Reassurance*. Paris: Flammarion.

Marres, Noortje (2012) *Material Participation: Technology, the Environment and Everyday Publics*. Basingstoke: Palgrave Macmillan.

Martín, Jesus (1992) 'De potencia industrial a economía de servicios', *Economics*, 55: 30–40.

Martin, Roger (2009) *The Design of Business: Why Design Thinking is the Next Competitive Advantage*. Cambridge, MA: Harvard Business Press.

Marx, Karl (1957 [1867]) *Capital: Volume One*. London: Everyman.

Marx, Karl (1964) *Karl Marx: Early Writings* (ed. T.B. Bottomore). New York: McGraw-Hill.

Marx, Karl and Engels, Friedrich (2004 [1848]) *The Communist Manifesto*. Peterborough: Broadview Press.

Mason, Bruce and Dicks, Bella (1999) 'The Digital Ethnographer', *CyberSociology*, 6, August. Available at: www.socio.demon.co.uk/magazine/6/issue6.html (accessed 21/11/99)

Massey, Simon (2000) 'There's More to a Good Brand Than Design', *Design Week*, 21 January.

Mau, Bruce (2004) *Massive Change: A Manifesto for the Future of Global Design Culture*. London: Phaidon.

Mazé, Rámia and Redström, Johan (2009) 'Difficult Forms: Critical practices of design and research', *Research Design Journal*, 1 (1): 28–39.

McAlhone, Beryl (1987) *British Design Consultancy*. London: Design Council.

McCarthy, John (2006) 'Regeneration of Cultural Quarters: Public Art for Place Image or Place Identity?', *Journal of Urban Design*, 11(2): 243–62.

McCoy, Michael (1993) 'Design and the New Mythology', in S. Yelavich (ed.), *The Edge of the Millennium: An International Critique of Architecture, Urban Planning and Communication Design*. New York: Whitney Library of Design, pp. 132–8.

McCracken, Grant (1990) *Culture and Consumption: New Approaches to the Symbolic Character of Consumer Goods and Activities*. Bloomington and Indianapolis, IN: Indiana University Press.

McCurdy, Howard E. (2001) *Faster, Better, Cheaper: Low Cost Innovation in the US Space Program*. Baltimore, MD: Johns Hopkins University Press.

McDonough, Michael (1993) 'Gods Too Ancient and Contradictory: In Response to Andrea Branzi', in S. Yelavich (ed.), *The Edge of the Millennium: An International Critique of Architecture, Urban Planning and Communication Design*. New York: Whitney Library of Design, pp. 128–31.

McGrane, Sally (1999) 'For a Seller of Innovation, a Bag of Technotricks', *New York Times* Circuit, 11 February.

McHoul, Alec and Roe, Phil (1996) 'Hypertext and Reading Cognition', in B.L. Gorayska and J.L. Mey (eds), *Cognitive Technology: In Search of a Human Interface* (Advances in Psychology 113). Amsterdam: Elsevier Science, pp. 347–59.

McRobbie, Angela (1998) *British Fashion Design: Rag Trade or Image Industry?* London: Routledge.

McRobbie, Angela (2002) 'Clubs to Companies: Notes on the Decline of Political Culture in Speeded Up Creative Worlds', *Cultural Studies*, 16(4): 516–31.

Meggs, Philip B. (1983) *A History of Graphic Design*. London: Allen Lane.

Meikle, Jeffrey (1998) 'Material Virtues: On the Ideal and the Real in Design History', *Journal of Design History*, 11(3): 191–9.

Metz, Christian (1974) *Language and Cinema* (trans. D.J. Umiker-Sebeok). The Hague: Mouton.

Miller, Daniel (1987) *Material Culture and Mass Consumption*. Oxford: Blackwell.

Miller, Daniel (1988) 'Appropriating the State on the Council Estate', *Man*, 23: 353–72.

Mirzoeff, Nicholas (1998) *The Visual Culture Reader*. New York: Routledge.

Mirzoeff, Nicholas (1999) *An Introduction to Visual Culture*. New York: Routledge.

Mitchell, C. Thomas (1988) 'The Product as Illusion', in J. Thackara (ed.), *Design After Modernism: Beyond the Object*. London: Thames & Hudson, pp. 208–15.

Mitchell, C. Thomas (1993) *Redefining Designing: From Form to Experience*. New York: Van Nostrand Reinhold.

Mitchell, W.J.T. (1994) *Picture Theory*. Chicago, IL: Chicago University Press.

Mitchell, W.J.T. (2002) 'Showing Seeing: A Critique of Visual Culture', *Journal of Visual Culture*, 1(2): 165–81.

Molotch, Harvey (1996) 'L.A. as Design Product: How Art Works in a Regional Economy', in A.J. Scott and E.W. Soja (eds), *The City: Los Angeles and Urban Theory at the End of the Twentieth Century*. Berkeley, CA: University of California Press, pp. 225–75.

Molotch, Harvey (2003) *Where Stuff Comes From: How Toasters, Toilets, Cars, Computers, and Many Other Things Come to Be as They Are*. London: Routledge.

Mommaas, Hans (2004) 'Cultural Clusters and the Post-Industrial City: Towards the Remapping of Urban Cultural Policy', *Urban Studies*, 41(3): 507–32.

Moon, Michael (1999) 'Branding in the Networked Economy', *Design Management Journal*, 10(2): 61–70.

Morelli, Nicola (2002) 'Designing product/service systems. A methodological exploration', *Design Issues*, 18(3): 3–17.

Morgan, N., Pritchard A. and Pride, R. (2002) *Destination Branding, Creating the Unique Destination Proposition*. Oxford: Butterworth-Heinemann.

Morris, Kenneth (1997) 'Shake Hands with the Brand: Crafting the Message for the Medium', *Design Management Journal*, 8(3): 27–32.

Morris, L., Rabinowitz, J. and Myerson, J. (1998) 'No More Heroes: From Controllers to Collaborators', *Design Management Journal*, 9(2): 22–5.

Mottram, Simon (2000) Consultant, Circus. Interview with the author, 11 January 2000.

Moulaert, F. and Swyngedouw, E.A. (1989) 'A Regulation Approach to the Geography of Flexible Production Systems', *Environment and Planning D: Society and Space*, 7: 327–45.

Mulhall, Stephen (2005) *Heidegger and Being and Time*, 2nd edn. London: Routledge.

Muller, W. and Pasman, G. (1996) 'Typology and the Organization of Design Knowledge', *Design Studies*, 17(2): 111–30.

Muñiz, A. and O'Guinn, T. (2001) 'Brand Community', *Journal of Consumer Research*, 27(4): 412–32.

Mureta, Chad (2012) *App Empire: Make Money, Have a Life, and Let Technology Work for You*. Hoboken, NJ: Wiley.

Murray, Richard (1998) 'Jumping on the Brand Wagon', *Design Week*, 27 March.

Myerson, Jeremy (1990) 'All's Fair in Love and War', *Design Week*, 27 April.

Myerson, Jeremy (1997) 'Tornadoes, T-squares and Technology: Can Computing Be a Craft?', in P. Dormer (ed.), *The Culture of Craft*. Manchester: Manchester University Press, pp. 176–85.

Myerson, Jeremy (1999) 'Class of the Century', *Design Week*, 17 December.

Napier, Christopher (1994) 'Brand Accounting in the United Kingdom', in G. Jones and N. Morgan (eds), *Adding Value: Brands and Marketing in Food and Drink*. London: Routledge, pp. 76–102.

Narotzky, Viviana (1998) 'Going Public: Design, Consumption and Urban Identity in Barcelona'. Paper given at 'Design Innovation: Conception to Consumption', 21st International Annual Conference of the Design History Society, University of Huddersfield.

Narotzky, Viviana (2000) '"A Different and New Refinement": Design in Barcelona 1960–1990', *Journal of Design History*, 13(3): 227–43.

Narotzky, Viviana (2007) *La Barcelona del diseño*. Barcelona: Santa & Cole.

Nash, Kate (2001) 'The "cultural turn" in Social Theory: Towards a Theory of Cultural Politics', *Sociology*, 35(1): 77–92.

NDI – Netherlands Design Institute (1994) *Design Across Europe: Patterns of Supply and Demand in the European Design Market*. Amsterdam: Vormgevingsinstituut.

Nederveen Pieterse, Jan (1991) 'Fictions of Europe', *Race and Class*, 32(3): 3–10.

Nederveen Pieterse, Jan (1995) 'Globalization as Hybridization', in M. Featherstone, S. Lash and R. Robertson (eds), *Global Modernities*. London: Sage, pp. 45–68.

Negus, Keith (2002) 'The Work of Cultural Intermediaries and the Enduring Distance Between Production and Consumption', *Cultural Studies*, 16(4): 501–15.

Nevett, T.R. (1987) *Advertising in Britain: A History*. London: Heinemann.

Nevins, James and Whitney, Daniel (eds) (1989) *Concurrent Design of Products and Processes*. New York: McGraw-Hill.

Nielsen (2012) 'State of the Media: The Social Media Report' (report). New York: Nielsen.

Nielsen, Jakob (1998) 'The Increasing Conservatism of Web Users', Alertbox for 22 March: www.useit.com/alertbox.

Nielsen, Jakob (1999) 'Stuck with Old Browsers until 2003', Alertbox for April: www.useit.com/alertbox.

Nixon, Helen (1998) 'Fun and Games Are Serious Business', in J. Sefton-Green (ed.), *Digital Diversions: Youth Culture in the Age of Multimedia*. London: UCL Press, pp. 21–42.

Nixon, Sean (2003) *Advertising Cultures: Gender, Commerce, Creativity*. London: Sage.

Nordic Innovation Centre (2004) 'The Future in Design: The Competitiveness and Industrial Dynamics of the Nordic Design Industry' (report). Available at: www. nordicdesign.org.

Nutley, Michael (1998) 'Health and Fitness', *Design Week: The Big Picture: Leisure*: 49.

Nuttgens, Patrick (1979) *Leeds: The Back to Front Inside Out Upside Down City*. Otley: Stile.

O'Connor, J. (2001) 'Cultural Industries and the City: Innovation, Creativity and Competitiveness', Report for Economic and Social Research Council. Available at: www.esrcsocietytoday.ac.uk (accessed 12/05/06).

OECD (2012) *OECD Factbook 2011–2012: Economic, Environmental and Social Statistics*. Paris: OECD Publishing.

Offe, Claus (1985) *Disorganized Capitalism*. Oxford: Polity Press.

Olins, Wally (1978) *The Corporate Personality: An Inquiry into the Nature of Corporate Identity*. London: Design Council.

Olins, Wally (1982) 'How Wolff Olins Learnt about Corporate Identity', *Penrose Annual*, 74: 221–9.

Olins, Wally (1988) *A Force for Change*. London: Metropolitan Police Force.

Olins, Wally (1999) *Trading Identities: Why Countries and Companies are Taking on Each Others' Roles*. London: The Foreign Policy Centre.

Oosterling, Henk (2009) 'Dasein as Design/Or: Must Design Save the World?', in L. Martz and Z. Sybrand (eds), *From Mad Dutch Disease to Born to Adorn: The Premsela Lectures 2004–2010*. Amsterdam: Premsela, pp. 115–140.

Øresund Committee (1999) *Hello* (pamphlet). Copenhagen: Øresund Committee.

Packard, Vance (1957) *The Hidden Persuaders: On Psychology and Advertising*. London: Longmans, Green.

Papadopoulos, N. and Heslop, L. (2002) 'Country Equity and Country Branding: Problems and Prospects', *Journal of Brand Management*, 9(4/5): 294–315.

Papanek, Victor (1972) *Design for the Real World*. London: Thames & Hudson.

Papanek, Victor and Hennessey, James (1974) *Nomadic Furniture: How to Build and Where to Buy Lightweight Furniture*. London: Studio Vista.

Pawley, Martin (1998) *Terminal Architecture*. London: Reaktion.

Peck, J., Theodore N. and Brenner N. (2009) 'Postneoliberalism and its malcontents', *Antipode: A Radical Journal of Geography*, 41(6) 1236–58.

Peters, Tom and Waterman, Robert (1982) *In Search of Excellence*. New York: Harper & Row.

Petroski, Henry (1996) *The Pencil: A History of Design and Circumstance*. New York: Knopf.

Pettinger, Lynne (2004) 'Brand Culture and Branded Workers: Service Work and Aesthetic Labour in Fashion Retail', *Consumption, Markets and Culture*, 7(2): 165–84.

Pevsner, Nikolaus (1936) *Pioneers of the Modern Movement: From William Morris to Walter Gropius*. London: Harmondsworth.

Phelan, Cel (1999) Marketing Director, Event Communications. Interview with the author, 8 October 1999.

Phillips, John (2006) 'Agencement/Assemblage', *Theory, Culture & Society*, 23(2–3): 108–109.

Pibernat, Oriol (ed.) (1999) *Dissenyadors a Ciutat Vella*. Barcelona: Ajuntament de Barcelona.

Pickering, John (1999) Copywriter, *Imagination*. Interview with the author, 7 October 1999.

Pilditch, James (1970) *Communication by Design: A Study in Corporate Identity*. New York: McGraw-Hill.

Pilditch, James and Scott, Douglas (1965) *The Business of Product Design*. London: Business Publications.

Pizzocaro, Silvia (2000) 'Research, Theory and Design Culture: A Knowledge Growing within Complexity', in S. Pizzocaro, A. Arruda and D. De Moraes (eds), *Design Plus Research*, Proceedings of the Politecnico di Milano Conference. Milan: Politecnico di Milano. Available at: http://pcsiwa12.rett.polimi.it/~phddi/uk/01/dpr00/intro.htm (accessed 15/01/05).

Plant, Sadie (1993) 'On the Matrix: Cyberfeminist Simulations', in R. Shields (ed.), *Cultures of Internet: Virtual Spaces, Real Histories, Living Bodies*. London: Sage, pp. 170–83.

Policy Research Institute (1996) *The Cultural Industries in Leeds* (report). Leeds: Leeds Metropolitan University/Leeds City Council.

Poster, Mark (1990) *The Mode of Information: Poststructuralism and Social Context*. Cambridge: Polity Press.

Powell, Kenneth (1989) 'The Offense of the Inoffensive', *Architects' Journal*, 8(189): 24–9.

Powell, Kenneth (1992) 'What Have We Done To Our Cities?', *Daily Telegraph*, 11 April.

Poynor, Rick (1991) 'The Designer as Author', *Blueprint*, May: 30–1.

Poynor, Rick (1999) 'Publishing by Numbers', *Eye*, 8(31): 6–7.

Project on Disney (1995) *Inside the Mouse: Work and Play at Disney World*. Durham, NC: Duke University Press.

Raban, Jonathan (1974) *Soft City*. London: Hamish Hamilton.

Rancière, Jacques (2004) *The Politics of Aesthetics*. London: Continuum.

Rancière, Jacques (2010) *Dissensus: On Politics and Aesthetics*. London & New York: Continuum.

Ray, Paul (2001) *The Cultural Creatives: How 50 Million People Are Changing the World*. New York: Random House.

Reavley, Gordon (1998) 'Inconspicuous Consumption'. Paper given at 'Design Innovation: Conception to Consumption', 21st International Annual Conference of the Design History Society, University of Huddersfield.

Reckwitz, Andreas (2002) 'Toward a Theory of Social Practices: A Development in Culturalist Theorizing', *European Journal of Social Theory*, 5(2): 243–63.

Rees, Emma (1998) 'Leisure Futures', *Design Week: The Big Picture: Leisure*, October: 24–5.

Relph-Knight, Linda (1998) 'Team Leaders', *Design Week*, 27 March.

Rheingold, Howard (1994) *The Virtual Community*. London: Secker and Warburg.

Richardson, Darren (1999) Director, Gardiner-Richardson. Interview with the author, 13 January 1999.

Rittel, Horst and Webber, Martin (1973) 'Dilemmas in a General Theory of Planning', *Policy Sciences*, 4(2): 155–169.

Ritzer, George (1996) *The McDonaldization of Society*. London: Sage.

Robertson, Keith (1994) 'On White Space/When Less is More', in M. Bierut, W. Drenttel, S. Heller and D.K. Holland (eds), *Looking Closer: Critical Writings on Graphic Design*. New York: Allworth, pp. 61–6.

Robins, Kevin (1997) 'What in the World's Going On?', in P. du Gay (ed.), *Production of Culture/Cultures of Production*. London: Sage/ Open University, pp. 11–47.

Rojek, Chris (1985) *Capitalism and Leisure Theory*. London: Tavistock.

Rojek, Chris (1993) *Ways of Escape: Modern Tranformations in Leisure and Travel*. London: Macmillan.

Rowan, David (2010) 'What's app? A look at the emerging apps economy' (report). London: NESTA.

Rudd, Nicholas (1999) 'Going Direct: Design and Digital Commerce', *Design Management Journal*, 10(1): 17–22.

Russell, Beverly (1996) 'Starck Raving Genius of Design', *Graphis*, 52: 30–41.

Sabel, Charles (1982) *Work and Politics: The Division of Labour in Industry*. Cambridge: Cambridge University Press.

Saco, Roberto and Gonsalves, Alexis (2008) 'Service Design: An Appraisal', *Design Management Review*, 19(1): 10–19.

Salaman, Graeme (1997) 'Culturing Production', in P. du Gay (ed.), *Production of Culture/Cultures of Production*. London: Sage/ Open University, pp. 235–84.

Salvador, Tony, Bell, Genevieve and Anderson, Ken (1999) 'Design Ethnography', *Design Management Journal*, 10(4): 35–41.

Sanders, Julian (2006) 'Royalties May Be the Answer', *Design Week*, 28 September.

Sassen, Saskia (1999) 'Digital Networks and Power', in M. Featherstone and S. Lash (eds), *Spaces of Culture: City, Nation, World*. London: Sage, pp. 49–63.

Sassen, Saskia (2003) 'Reading the City in a Global Digital Age: Between Topographic Representation and Spatialized Power', in L. Kraus and P. Petro (eds), *Global Cities: Cinema, Architecture and Urbanism in a Digital Age*. New Brunswick, NJ: Rutgers University Press, pp. 15–30.

Satué, Enric (1997) 'Lo "Stile Barcellona": un gioco da bambini', *Domus*, 794: 88–97.

Scase, Richard and Davis, Howard (2000) *Managing Creativity: The Dynamics of Work and Organization*. Milton Keynes: Open University Press.

Schatzki, Theodore (1996) *Social Practices: A Wittgensteinian Approach to Human Activity and the Social*. London: Routledge.

Schiller, H.I. (1995) 'The Global Information Highway: Project for an Ungovernable World', in J. Brook and I. Boal (eds), *Resisting the Virtual Life: The Culture and Politics of Information*. San Francisco, CA: City Lights, pp. 17–34.

Schmitt, Bernd and Simonson, Alex (1997) *Marketing Aesthetics: The Stategic Management of Brands, Identity, and Image*. New York: Free Press.

Schofield, Jack (1999) 'It's So Smart to Be Simple', *The Guardian* Online, 2 December.

Schofield, Jack (2000) 'Life with the Creature Feature', *The Guardian* Online, 13 January.

Schön, Donald A. (1991) *The Reflective Practitioner: How Professionals Think in Action*. London: Basic Books.

Schudson, Michael (1993 [1984]) *Advertising, the Uneasy Persuasion: Its Dubious Impact on American Society*. London: Routledge.

Scott, Allen (1998) *The Regions and the World Economy: The Coming Shape of Global Production, Competition, and Political Order*. Oxford: Oxford University Press.

Scott, Nigel (2005) 'Brand loyalty', *Yorkshire Evening Post: Marketing Leeds Special Supplement*, 27 September.

Seago, Alex and Dunne, Anthony (1999), 'New Methodologies in Art and Design Research: The Object as Discourse', *Design Studies*, 15 (2): 11–17.

Sennett, Richard (1976) *The Fall of Public Man*. New York: Vintage.

Shields, Rob (1991) *Places on the Margin: Alternative Geographies of Modernity*. London: Routledge.

Shove, E., Pantzar, M. and Watson, M. (2012) *The Dynamics of Social Practice: Everyday Life and How It Changes*. London: Sage.

Shove, E., Watson, M. and Ingram, J. (2005) 'The Value of Design and the Design of Value'. Paper presented at 'Joining Forces', Design Conference, Helsinki.

Shove, E., Watson, M., Hand, M. and Ingram, J. (2007) *The Design of Everyday Life*. Oxford: Berg.

Silverstone, R. and Haddon, L. (1996) 'Design and the Domestication of Information and Communication Technologies: Technical Change and Everyday Life', in R. Mansell and R. Silverstone (eds), *Communication By Design: The Politics of Information and Communication Technologies*. Oxford: Oxford University Press, Chapter 2.

Silverstone, R., Hirsch, E. and Morley, D. (1994) 'Information and Communication Technologies and the Moral Economy of the Household', in R. Silverstone and E. Hirsch (eds), *Consuming Technologies: Media and Information in Domestic Spaces*. London: Routledge, Chapter 1.

Sinclair, Adrian (2006) Director, Heads Together. Interview with the author 6 September 2006.

Slater, Don (1997) *Consumer Culture and Modernity*. London: Polity Press.

Slater, Don (2002) 'Markets, Materiality and the "New Economy"', in J. Stanley Metcalfe and A. Warde (eds), *Market Relations and the Competitive Process*. Manchester: Manchester University Press, pp. 95–113.

Smales, Lindsay (1994) 'Desperate Pragmatism or Shrewd Optimism? The Image and Selling of West Yorkshire', in G. Haughton and D. Whitney (eds), *Reinventing a Region: Restructuring in West Yorkshire*. Aldershot: Avebury, pp. 35–60.

Smales, Lindsay and Whitney, David (1996) 'Inventing a Better Place: Urban Design in Leeds in the Postwar Era', in G. Haughton and C.C. Williams (eds), *Corporate City: Partnership, Participation and Partition in Urban Development in Leeds*. Aldershot: Avebury, pp. 199–218.

Smith, Marquard (2005) 'Visual Studies, or the Ossification of Thought', *Journal of Visual Culture*, 4(2): 237–56.

Soja, Edward (1996) *Thirdspace: Journeys to Los Angeles and Other Real-and-Imagined Places*. Oxford: Blackwell.

Sontag, Susan (1978) *On Photography*. London: Allen Lane, Penguin.

Southerton, Dale (2003) '"Squeezing Time": Allocating Practices, Co-ordinating Networks and Scheduling Society', *Time & Society*, 12(1): 5–25.

Southgate, Paul (1994) *Total Branding by Design: How to Make Your Brand's Packaging More Effective*. London: Kogan Page.

Sparke, Penny (1988) *Italian Design: 1870 to the Present*. London: Thames & Hudson.

Sparke, Penny (1990) '"A Home for Everybody?": Design, Ideology, and the Culture of the Home in Italy, 1945–72', in P. Greenhalgh (ed.), *Modernism in Design*. London: Reaktion, pp. 185–202.

Sparke, Penny (1995) *As Long as It's Pink: The Sexual Politics of Taste*. London: Harper Collins.

Sparks, Leigh (1994) 'Delivering Quality: The Role of Logistics in the Postwar Transformation of British Retailing', in G. Jones and N. Morgan (eds), *Adding Value: Brands and Marketing in Food and Drink*. London: Routledge, pp. 310–35.

Spencer, Herbert (1969) *Pioneers of Modern Typography*. London: Lund Humphries.

Spivak, G.C. (1988) 'Can the Subaltern Speak?', in C. Nelson and L. Grossberg (eds), *Marxism and the Interpretation of Culture*. London: Macmillan, pp. 271–313.

Star, Susan Leigh and Griesemer, James R. (1989) 'Translations and Boundary Objects: Amateurs and Professionals in Berkeley's Museum of Vertebrate Zoology, 1907–39', *Social Studies of Science*, 19(3): 387–420.

Stevenson, Deborah (2004) '"Civic Gold" Rush: Cultural Planning and the Politics of the "Third Way"', *International Journal of Cultural Policy*, 10(1): 119–31.

Stewart, James and Williams, Robin (2005) 'The Wrong Trousers? Beyond the Design Fallacy: Social Learning and the User', in D. Howcroft and E. Trauth (eds), *Handbook of Critical Information Systems Research*. Cheltenham: Edward Elgar, Chapter 10.

Stickdorn, Marc and Schneider, Jakob (eds) (2010) *This is Service Design Thinking*. Amsterdam: BIS Publishers.

Sturken, Marita and Cartwright, Lisa (2001) *Practices of Looking: An Introduction to Visual Culture*. New York: Oxford University Press.

Sudjic, Deyan (1985) *Cult Objects: The Complete Guide to Having It All*. London: Paladin.

Sushi (1999) 'X Factor', *Sushi*, 3 (unpaginated).

Suskind, Patrick (1987) *Perfume*. London: Penguin.

Sutton, Damian (2009) 'Cinema by Design: Hollywood as Network Neighbourhood', in G. Julier and L. Moor (eds), *Design and Creativity: Policy, Management and Practice*. Oxford: Berg, pp. 174–190.

Sweet, Fay (1998) *Alessi: Art and Poetry*. London: Thames & Hudson.

Sweet, Fay (1999) *Philippe Starck: Subverchic Design*. London: Thames & Hudson.

Taylor, Damon (2011) 'Design Art Furniture and the Boundaries of Function: Communicative Objects, Performative Things'. PhD Thesis, University of the Arts London/University College Falmouth.

Taylor, P., Funk, C. and Craighill, P. (2006) 'Who's Feeling Rushed? (Hint: Ask a Working Mom)' (report). Available at: www.pewresearch.org (accessed 18/12/12).

TDR Capital (2012) 'Center Parcs Europe' (report). Available at: www.tdrcapital.com (accessed 18/12/12).

Terragni, Emilia (2006) *Phaidon Design Classics*. London: Phaidon.

Thackara, John (ed.) (1988) *Design after Modernism: Beyond the Object*. London: Thames & Hudson.

Thackara, John (1997) *Winners! How Today's Successful Companies Innovate by Design*. Aldershot: Gower.

Thackara, John (2005a) *In the Bubble: Designing in a Complex World*. Cambridge, MA: MIT Press.

Thackara, John (2005b) 'Creativity and the City', in M-J. Lacroix (ed.),*New Design Cities*. Montreal: Editions Infopresse, pp. 266–7.

Thackray, Rachelle (1999) 'Me and My Partner: Michael Wolff and Piers Schmidt', *The Independent* Business Review, 7 April.

Thompson, John (2010) *Merchants of Culture: The Publishing Business in the Twenty-First Century*. Cambridge: Polity.

Thornton, Sarah (2009) *Seven Days in the Art World*. London: Granta.

Thorpe, Ann (2008) 'Design as Activism: A Conceptual Tool'. Conference paper presented at 'Changing the Change', Turin.

Thorpe, Ann (2012) *Architecture & Design versus Consumerism: How Design Activism Confronts Growth*. London: Earthscan.

Thrift, Nigel (2005) *Knowing Capitalism*. London: Sage.

Toffler, Alvin (1980) *The Third Wave*. London: Collins.

Tomes, A., Oates, C. and Armstrong, P. (1998) 'Talking Design: Negotiating the Verbal–Visual Translation', *Design Studies*, 19(2): 127–42.

Tonkinwise, Cameron (2011) 'A Taste for Practices: Unrepressing Style in Design Thinking', *Design Studies*, 32(6): 533–545.

Toporowski, Jan (1989) 'The Financial System and Capital Accumulation in the 1980s', in F. Green (ed.), *The Restructuring of the UK Economy*. Hemel Hempstead: Harvester Wheatsheaf, pp. 242–62.

Touraine, Alain (1995) *Critique of Modernity* (trans. D. Macey). Oxford: Blackwell.

Trétiack, Philippe (1999) *Raymond Loewy and Streamlined Style*. Paris: Assouline.

Trias, Josep Maria (1988) 'El logotipo olímpico', *On*, 91: 15–20.

Tso, Judy (1999) 'Do You Dig Up Dinosaur Bones? Anthropology, Business, and Design', *Design Management Journal*, 10(4): 69–74.

Tuomi, Ilkka (2002) *Networks of Innovation: Change and Meaning in the Age of the Internet*. Oxford: Oxford University Press.

Turkle, Sherry (1997) *Life on the Screen: Identity in the Age of the Internet*. London: Phoenix.

Turner, Louis and Ash, John (1975) *The Golden Hordes: International Tourism and the Pleasure Periphery*. London: Constable.

UK Trade and Investment (2011) 'Creative Industries in China: Opportunities for business' (report). London: London Development Agency.

UNCTAD (2010) 'Creative Economy: A Feasible Development Option' (report). Geneva: UNCTAD.

United Nations (2010) 'Creative Economy Report'. Available at: http://unctad.org (accessed 28/08/12)

Urban Unlimited (2004) 'Shadow City' (report). Rotterdam: Urban Unlimited.

Urry, John (1990) *The Tourist Gaze: Leisure and Travel in Contemporary Societies*. London: Sage.

Urry, John (1995) *Consuming Places*. London: Routledge.

Urry, John (2007) *Mobilities*. Cambridge: Polity.

Valentine, Matthew (1998) 'Creative Mind Games', *Design Week*, 6 November.

Van Abel, B., Evers, L., Klaassen, R. and Troxler, P. (2011) *Open Design Now: Why Design Cannot Remain Exclusive*. Amsterdam: BIS Publishers.

van den Munckhof, Crissij and Dare, Lucy (2000) Vamp. Interview with the author, 11 January 2000.

van der Will, Wilfried (1990) 'The Body and the Body Politic as Symptom and Metaphor in the Transition of German Culture to National Socialism', in B. Taylor and W. van der Will (eds), *The Nazification of Art: Art, Design, Music, Architecture and Film in the Third Reich*. Winchester: Winchester Press, pp. 14–52.

Van Doren, Harold (1940) *Industrial Design: A Practical Guide*. New York: McGraw-Hill.

Van Hinte, E. (1990) 'The Limits of Flexibility', *Industrieel Ontwerpen*, 3: 45–6.

Vargo, S.L. and Lusch, R.F. (2004), 'The Four Service Marketing Myths: Remnants of a Goods-Based Manufacturing Model', *Journal of Service Research*, 6(4): 324–35.

Veblen, Thorstein (1970 [1899]) *The Theory of the Leisure Class*. London: Unwin.

Venturi, R., Scott-Brown, D. and Izenour, S. (1972) *Learning from Las Vegas: The Forgotten Symbolism of Architectural Form*. Cambridge, MA: MIT Press.

Verganti, Roberto (2009) Design Driven Innovation – Changing the Rules of Competition by Radically Innovating what Things Mean. Boston, MA: Harvard Business Press.

Vergo, Peter (ed.) (1989) *The New Museology*. London: Reaktion.

Vinodrai, Tara (2009) 'The Place of Design: Exploring Ontario's Design Economy'. Available at: http://martinprosperity.org.

Vinogradoff, Paul (1999) Consultant, Wolff Olins. Interview with the author, 2 November 1999.

Virilio, Paul (1997) *Open Sky* (trans. J. Rose). London: Verso.

Vogelstein, Fred (2008) 'The Untold Story: How the iPhone Blew Up the Wireless Industry', *Wired*, 16,02.

Walker, John A. (1983) *Art in the Age of Mass Media*. London: Pluto.

Walker, John A. (1989) *Design History and the History of Design*. London: Pluto.

Walker, John and Chaplin, Sarah (eds) (1997) *Visual Culture: An Introduction*. New York: Palgrave Macmillan.

Walsh, V., Roy, R., Bruce, M. and Potter, S. (1992) *Winning by Design: Technology, Product Design and International Competitiveness*. Oxford: Blackwell.

Walters, David (1981) 'The 1970s in retailing', *International Journal of Retail and Distribution Management* (March/April): 8–15.

Walters, David (1983) 'The 1980s in Retailing: A Prospective View, Part 2', *International Journal of Retail and Distribution Management* (January/February): 21–5.

Walton, Mark and Duncan, Ian (2002) *Creative Industries in New Zealand*. Thorndon: NZ Institute Of Economic Research. Available at: http://nzier.org.nz.

Wang, James (2012) 'Digitimes Research: Smartphone Sales in China to Grow 137% to 189 Million Units in 2012', 26 December. Available at: www.digitimes.com/news/a20121226PD209.html (accessed 30/1/13).

Wansborough, M. and Mageean, A. (2000) 'The Role of Urban Design in Cultural Regeneration', *Journal of Urban Design*, 5(2): 181–97.

Ward, Stephen (1998) *Selling Places: The Marketing and Promotion of Towns and Cities, 1850–2000*. London: Spon.

Warde, Alan (2004) 'Practice and Field: Revising Bourdieusian Concepts', Centre for Research on Innovation and Competition, Discussion Paper 65, Department of Sociology, University of Manchester.

Warde, Alan (2005) 'Consumption and Theories of Practice', *Journal of Consumer Culture*, 5(2): 131–53.

Waterfall, Simon (2000) Creative Director, Deepend. Interview with the author, 11 January 2000.

Weber, Max (1978 [1922]) Economy and Society*: An Outline of Interpretive Sociology*. Berkley, California: University of California Press.

Wei, X., Qu, H. and Ma, E. (2010) 'A Study of the Effects of Leisure Time on China's Economic Growth: A Neoclassic Growth Model', *Tourism Analysis*, 15(6): 663–72.

Weibull, J., Matthiessen, C.W., Nordstrom, L., Lauring, P. and Holmqvist, L. (1993) *Øresund: Past, Present and Future*. Malmö: Corona/Norden.

Weinbren, Grahame (1995) 'Mastery: Computer Games, Intuitive Interfaces and Interactive Multimedia', *Leonardo*, 28(5): 403–8.

Wells, John (1989) 'Uneven Development and De-industrialisation in the UK since 1979', in F. Green (ed.), *The Restructuring of the UK Economy*. Hemel Hempstead: Harvester Wheatsheaf, pp. 25–64.

Wernick, Andrew (1991) *Promotional Culture: Advertising, Ideology and Symbolic Expression*. London: Sage.

West, Joel and Mace, Michael (2010) 'Browsing as the killer app: Explaining the rapid success of Apple's iPhone', *Telecommunications Policy*, 34 (5–6): 270–286.

Whitely, Nigel (1991) 'Design in Enterprise Culture: Design for Whose Profit?', in R. Keat and N. Abercrombie (eds), *Enterprise Culture*. London: Routledge, pp. 106–205.

Whitely, Nigel (1993) *Design for Society*. London: Reaktion.

Whitely, Nigel (1994) 'High Art and the High Street: The "Commerce-and-Culture" Debate', in R. Keat, N. Whitely and N. Abercrombie (eds), *The Authority of the Consumer*. London: Routledge, pp. 119–37.

Whittaker, Mary (1990) 'Leeds: Has the Renaissance Started?', *Architecture Today*, 5: 15–16.

Williams, Raymond (1974) *Television, Technology and Cultural Form*. London: Fontana.

Williams, Raymond (1985 [1976]) *Keywords: A Vocabulary of Culture and Society*. Oxford: Oxford University Press.

Williamson, Judith (1988 [1978]) *Decoding Advertisements: Ideology and Meaning in Advertising*. London: Marion Boyars.

Wittgenstein, Ludwig (1968) *Philosophical Investigations* (trans. G.E.M. Anscombe). Oxford: Blackwell.

Witz, A., Warhurst, C. and Nickson, D. (2003) 'The Labour of Aesthetics and the Aesthetics of Organization', *Organization*, 10(1): 33–54.

Wolff Olins (1999a) *Britain: Bye Bye Bulldog* (pamphlet). London: Wolff Olins.

Wolff Olins (1999b) *Deutschland als globale marke/A global brand for Germany* (pamphlet). London: Wolff Olins.

Wollen, Chad (1998) 'The Hurricane of Innovation', *Atticus: The Journal of Original Thinking in Communications Services*, 4: 8–9.

Wood, Phil (1999) 'Cultural Industries and the City: Policy Issues for the Cultural Industries at the Local Level'. Keynote speech to the Cultural Industries and the City Conference, Manchester Metropolitan University, 13–14 December. Available at: www.comedia.org.uk/downloads-3.htm (accessed 24/04/06).

Wood, Phil (2001) 'A Piece of the Action: Regional Strategies for the Creative Industries'. Paper given at the 'Conference: Convergence, Creative Industries and Civil Society: The New Cultural Policy', Nottingham, 28 September. Available at: www.comedia.org.uk/ downloads-3.htm (accessed 24/04/06).

Wood, S.L. and Ullman, D.G. (1996) 'The Functions of Plastic Injection Moulding Features', *Design Studies*, 17(2): 201–13.

Woodham, Jonathan (1997) *Twentieth-Century Design*. Oxford: Oxford University Press.

Woudhuysen, James (1998) 'Beyond the Dogma of Globalisation', in T. Balcioglu (ed.), *The Role of Product Design in Post-Industrial Society*. Ankara: Middle East Technical University, pp. 93–112.

Wozencroft, Jon (1987) *The Graphic Language of Neville Brody*. London: Thames & Hudson.

Wren, Phil (1999) Director, Fitch. Interview with the author, 7 October 1999.

X-Leisure (2010) *Making the Case for Leisure: A Report on the Continuing Strength and Stability of the Leisure Industry*. London: X-Leisure.

York, Peter (1984) *Modern Times*. London: Heinemann.

York, Peter (1988) 'Culture as Commodity: Style Wars, Punk and Pageant', in J. Thackara (ed.), *Design after Modernism: Beyond the Object*. London: Thames & Hudson, pp. 160–8.

Zittrain, Jonathan (2008) *The Future of the Internet and How to Stop It*. Yale: Yale University Press.

Zukin, Sharon (1989) *Loft Living: Cultural and Capital in Urban Change*. New Brunswick: Rutgers University Press.

Zukin, Sharon (1991) *Landscapes of Power: From Detroit to Disney World*. Berkeley, CA: University of California Press.

Zukin, Sharon (1995) *The Cultures of Cities*. Cambridge, MA: Blackwell.

INDEX